Public-Private Partnerships

Success and Failure Factors for In-Transition Countries

Edited by
Paolo Urio

UNIVERSITY PRESS OF AMERICA, ® INC.
Lanham • Boulder • New York • Toronto • Plymouth, UK

Library of Congress Control Number: 2010920570
ISBN: 978-0-7618-5070-0 (paperback   )
eISBN: 978-0-7618-5071-7

The research project and this publication have been funded by the Geneva International Academic Network (GIAN), which has been replaced by the Swiss Network for International Studies (SNIS).

Contents

Illustrations

FIGURES

TABLES

BOXES

Preface and Acknowledgments

Paolo Urio

Public-private partnerships (PPPs) have experienced a considerable de-velopment in Western countries during the last 30 years or so, and many international organizations, private consultants, politicians, and university scholars have supported the development of these institutional arrange-ments not only for developed countries but also for in-transition ones. Their profound conviction is that PPPs are a powerful means for raising easily and rapidly the necessary funds, and for providing and/or upgrad-ing timely and efficiently the infrastructures needed by the countries con-cerned. Nevertheless some criticism has also been voiced, especially by research institutes and NGOs.

It is in this context that this research has put together the competencies of 3 partners, all of them interested in deepening their understanding of the functioning of PPPs and of their impact on economy, society and pol-ity: namely the "Laboratoire de recherches sociales et politiques appliqués" (RESOP—a research unit within the Faculty of Economics and Social Sci-ences of the University of Geneva—UNIGE), the United Nations Institute for Disarmament Research (UNIDIR) and the United Nations Economic Commission for Europe (UNECE).

This book is the result of this cooperation which began at the beginning of 2004 with the preparation of the research project that was submitted to the GIAN (Geneva International Academic Network) in September 2005; the research was conducted from March 2006 to June 2008.

So many persons and institutions have made possible the realization of this research, that it is almost impossible to mention them all, and for this I deeply apologize to those who are not mentioned hereafter. But let me at least mention those who have constantly provided their support, knowledge, and advice to the research team. And first of all the GIAN who financed the project: our thanks go first of all to its scientific committee and more especially to its president, Prof. Edouard Dommen, who has given us some invaluable insights on the nature and definition of PPPs.[1] Our thanks go also to Randal Harbour, the secretary general of the GIAN, who has constantly given his cheerful support throughout the entire duration of the project and has provided logistic and administrative facilities to the research team.

We extend our thanks to the institutions that have provided in-kind resources for this research for an amount equivalent to the GIAN grant, i.e. UNECE, UNIDIR, and UNIGE. Our thanks also go to the Europe China Management Improvement foundation (ECMI) which has covered the cost of the research coordinator's stay in China in October 2007 and October 2008, when he worked with the Chinese team on the development of PPPs in China. We thank the Swiss Agency for Development and Cooperation (SDC) for providing a grant that has been very useful to cover the overhead costs of UNIDIR.

Dr. Marco Giugni, played the role of deputy research coordinator, and hosted the administration of the project at the RESOP (of which he is the director) on the premises of the UNI-MAIL building of Geneva University, and has participated in all the meetings of the research team. We have benefited from his vast experience as a researcher and methodologist. His inputs have been invaluable not only for the design of the research project and of the 3 questionnaires we used to collect the data, but also for their analysis. The undersigned is also grateful for his numerous and clarifying remarks on the drafts of the second chapter defining the theoretical framework of the research; and this has enabled us to considerably improve the logic and coherence of the research process.

The research team benefited immensely from the vast knowledge of PPPs that Dr. Geoffrey Hamilton has put at our disposal, with the transmission of documents and the constructive participation in many of our research meetings, in spite of a very busy agenda. Dr. Hamilton is Chief of Cooperation and Partnerships Section at the United Nations Economic Commission for Europe (UNECE) and the major artisan of the Team of Specialists on PPPs, previously called PPP Alliance (until reform of the UNECE in 2004-5) for infrastructure development established within the Commission.

Our thanks also go to Dr. Patricia Lewis, the director of UNIDIR, who has supported this research from the beginning and has put office space and equipment at the disposal of our senior researcher, Dr. Olivier Brenninkmeijer, as well as to Thomas Zacharewicz, in charge of providing research on Poland and of the statistical data analysis, and has given administrative support on the premises of UNIDIR offices at the Geneva Building of the United Nations. Moreover, Dr. Olivier Brenninkmeijer has played the role of project manager, thus providing an invaluable support for the administrative tasks of the deputy project coordinator.

This research would not have been possible without the help of the research teams we have been able to set up in China, Poland, Russia and Ukraine. These teams were responsible for providing written and oral information about the respective situation of their countries. They not only helped our researchers to choose the persons to be interviewed, but also performed part of the interviews, translated a summary of these interviews into English, and contributed to the writing of the chapters on the 4 countries.

Thus, with regarding to the Chinese team, Prof. Hu Angang, Director of the China Research Centre at Tsinghua University in Beijing has supported our research by setting up a small but efficient research team headed by Prof. Yang Yongheng; Mr Zhang Wankuan, a PhD candidate at Tsinghua University in the framework of doing research on PPPs in China for his dissertation, has effected all the interviews in China. Moreover, the Chinese team provided an efficient support to the undersigned during his stay in Beijing in October 2007 and October 2008. Yang Yongheng and Mr Zhang Wankuan are co-authors of the chapter on China.

In Moscow we were most fortunate in being able to count on the vast experience of Prof. Vladimir Varnavsky, the lead professor and author of the first analytical work on PPPs in the country in 2005 entitled "Public-Private Partnerships in Russia." He and his assistants helped our researcher, Tatiana Chernyavskaya in charge of the research in Russia and Ukraine, to get acquainted with the Russian situation. He helped with the choice of persons to be interviewed, conducted himself several interviews and became a co-author of the Chapter on Russia.

For the Polish country study, we benefited from the deep knowledge of PPPs of Mrs Kozłowska. Being a lawyer and the director of the consulting company Investment Support, she has both a theoretical and practical experience of PPPs. She has been particularly helpful in selecting the interviewees and providing information on the last development of PPPs in Poland.

In Kiev we were provided with support for the Ukrainian study from a PhD researcher, Mr. Oleg Gurynenko, who is currently working on his thesis related to the PPPs in Ukraine. Coming from the private sector, Mr. Gurynenko was able to provide evaluation of the current situation of PPPs and understanding of their development. He conducted a number of interviews, contributed written material and provided pertinent policy recommendations for the Chapter on Ukraine.

Last but not least, I am very grateful to the members of the Geneva research team for their excellent contribution to the completion of this research, which, as the experienced reader will easily understand, had to cope with numerous difficulties. These were due mainly to the physical and cultural distance between Geneva and the four in-transition countries. The merit of having been able to overcome these difficulties is certainly to be attributed to the excellent atmosphere of cooperation that has prevailed for the duration of the research among the members of the research team. Moreover, it has been particularly beneficial to work with a multicultural team with different academic backgrounds. This has been clearly an advantage, given the interdisciplinary nature of this research.[2] Moreover, this excellent cooperation has made it possible to organize numerous and efficient research meetings during which opinions, remarks and even critiques were exchanged in a pleasant and constructive atmosphere during the entire duration of the research, from the definition of the research design to the writing of the several drafts of the chapters of this report. As a consequence, while we have decided to sign the chapters individually for which we have assumed the main responsibility, the final result is the outcome of a collective endeavour.

Thanks to the unfailing and efficient contribution of the people and institutions I have just mentioned, my task as the coordinator of this research has been quite an easy one. My constant concern has been to keep the research on the right track, i.e. in line with the research design and the deontological requirements that aim at discovering facts from rigorous in-field inquiry, interpreting them in the light of well established theoretical frameworks, and informing the reader of the possible departure from methodological rigour that can often occur in the research process, due to lack of reliable data and/or sufficient research means.

The major difficulties that have arisen are in fact the reverse of the disadvantages versus the advantages of working with a multicultural team, with different academic backgrounds. Theoretical frameworks defined within various disciplines can not only be different but sometimes also contradictory. As the members of the research team are also the authors of the chapters on Western countries and on the four in-transition countries, it is possible that the attentive reader may find some differences in interpreting the results of the research. Should these differences appear to be too important, I am the only one to be blamed.

Furthermore, I have not tried to harmonize differences in writing styles. While these may be perceptible because of linguistic backgrounds of the authors, I believe that these stylistic differences do not diminish the clarity and the rigour of the texts and, in addition, I wanted to respect the different cultural backgrounds of the researchers in the team. The only intrusion into this domain has been to ask Olivier Brenninkmeijer, Ms Madeleine Urio and Ms Ruxandra Mathia, to correct the English from a purely grammatical point of view. But here again, should the reader find that the differences in style make the reading too cumbersome, I am the only one to be blamed.

According to some experts who have been informed of our research, it seems that it is the first time that an enquiry of this type has been realized in in-transition countries. Our hope is that the results presented in this book will provide the reader with some useful empirical findings and theoretical insights that will help him/her to forge his/her own opinion about PPPs and (who knows?) maybe also to revise some pre-conceived ideas about them. If we can achieve this, our efforts will have not been in vain.

NOTES

1. Eduard Dommen, "La taxinomie de partenariats public-privé, une première approximation," Geneva, 2006, manuscript kindly supplied by the author.

2. Olivier Brenninkmeijer, our senior researcher, studies mediation, development, security and education in the context of public-private partnerships. He holds a PhD in international relations. Tatiana Chernyavskaya comes from Russia with deep family roots in Ukraine, and therefore speaks Russian and Ukrainian, but also English and French and has some knowledge of Chinese and Spanish, with university training in economics and international relations; Thomas Zacharewicz is a French national of Polish origin, an economist and political scientist who speaks French, Polish, English, Spanish, and has some knowledge of Russian. Marco Giugni, the deputy research coordinator, with university training in sociology and political science, speaks French, Italian, and English. Paolo Urio, the research coordinator, is a political scientist with a first degree in international relations and a PhD in economics and social sciences; he speaks French, Italian, and English.

I

INTRODUCTION

1

Origins, Objectives, and Methodology of the Research

Paolo Urio

BROAD AND SPECIFIC OBJECTIVES OF THE RESEARCH

The broad aim of this research is to ask how government and the private sector can deliver efficient, sustainable, peaceful and equitable development through constructive collaboration. The specific form of collaboration considered here is Public-Private Partnerships (PPPs), in which public and private entities engage to accomplish public projects and services.

While both the State and the private sector can create jobs, the greatest obstacles to their ability to do so are a lack of effective basic infrastructure and services combined with poverty and insecurity. The latter poses not only a risk factor for the affected population, but also for the private sector. Local businesses and international companies are less likely to invest in unstable or fragile regions where the government is unable to supply even basic infrastructure services. Such situations remain debilitating and limit the development of small and medium enterprises or the investments by multinational corporations. In addition, so long as access to resources through infrastructure and services is absent to an entire population or discriminatory towards a specific community, the chances are that both poverty and political instability will remain. Such circumstances are particularly prevalent in societies where there is extreme income differentiation between the poorest and wealthiest social groupings, or where large minority communities remain marginalized.

The specific aim of this research is to determine how, and under what circumstances and conditions the State and the private sector can collaborate through Public-Private Partnerships (PPPs) to achieve efficient, sustainable, peaceful, and equitable development.

Three partners joined their forces in order to realize these objectives by conducting a research in four in-transition countries: China, Poland, Russia and Ukraine:[1] The University of Geneva (UNIGE), the United Nations Institute for Disarmament Research (UNIDIR) and the United Nations Economic Commission for Europe (UNECE). Each of them has approached this research with its specific and legitimate interests. The "Laboratoire de recherches sociales et politiques appliquées" (RESOP) has the general objective of conducting applied research in the various domains of the social sciences that may produce interesting results useful for orienting the practice of both public and private institutions. This research is one of the many important applied researches in which the RESOP has been involved in the past, especially in the domain of public policy and public management.

UNIDIR is an autonomous institute within the framework of the United Nations. It was established in 1980 for the purpose of undertaking independent research on disarmament and related problems, particularly international security issues. Research projects are grouped under three headings: Global Security and Disarmament, Regional Security and Disarmament, and Human Security and Disarmament. From the research, UNIDIR produces and disseminates a range of publications. UNIDIR holds a number of meetings and conferences throughout the year on topics that range from disarmament to human security. In Geneva, the institute is one of the three co-organizers of the Geneva Forum. UNIDIR was interested in this research for testing the capability of PPPs to improve security for countries in a pre-PPP stage.

The United Nations Economic Commission for Europe (UNECE) is one of five UN regional economic commissions. UNECE strives to foster sustainable economic growth among its 55 member countries. To that end UNECE provides a forum for communication among States; brokers international legal instruments addressing trade, transport and the environment; and supplies statistics and economic and environmental analysis. Reflecting interest in PPPs as tools for development and the critical role of the private sector, in 1995 the UNECE agreed to establish an Alliance of public and private sectors for infrastructure development to increase the capacity of governments to promote successful PPPs for sustainable development. It consists of an informal association of professional experts coming from the public and the private sectors, whose willingness is to work with United Nations to promote the use of PPP structures in central and Eastern Europe and CIS. The Alliance is a business-and action-oriented body to engage governments interested in applying PPPs and to offer them advice and support. It works closely with other bodies such as the EBRD, OECD, UNIDO and UNCITRAL. This Alliance fundamentally would improve the environment for PPPs in the region with the following benefits accruing: Accelerated delivery of projects; Raised awareness of governments about the potential of PPPs; Saving of resources through the involvement and pooling of all groups' efforts in achieving clearly defined goals; Direct involvement of the private sector in delivery of advice and support with the benefit to the private sector of access of interested governments; Development of pilot projects and facilitating country's initial efforts to establish the appropriate institutions and training; Reach-out programmes to NGOs and domestic private sectors including local banks. UNECE was therefore expecting to obtain from this research some encouraging findings, in line with its policy agenda.

However, the reader should be aware of the fact that this research has not been conceived and conducted with the aim of promoting PPPs (which is clearly a policy option to which RESOP—as an academic institution—could not subscribe), but with the purpose of discovering under what conditions PPPs may contribute to the improvement of economic efficiency, sustainable development, equity and security in the countries concerned. All our four countries (i.e. China, Poland, Russia and Ukraine) have experienced command (or planned) economy under communist rule for at least 30 years; their governments have therefore organised and managed practically all the economic sectors, private property being reduced to a minimum. Only recently they have introduced market mechanisms. Consequently, the subsidiary, but important, research question is: to what extent can PPPs provide a viable alternative to the traditional (i.e. by the State) provision of public services and infrastructures. For the purpose of evaluating if PPPs constitute a viable alternative we have tried to evaluate their contribution to economic efficiency, sustainable development, equity and security. This is not an easy task. But if one cannot give a reasonable answer to these questions (and by reasonable we mean founded at least in part on scientific evidence) the only rationale left in favour of PPPs would be very heavily based upon purely political and/or ideological grounds.

SCOPE AND MEANING OF PPPS

PPPs have been used by industrialised countries for over 30 years,[2] in such different fields as utilities, transportation, environmental policy, technology policy, criminal justice, health care, education, welfare. This trend can be considered as the second wave of proposals for reforming (i.e. improving) the way of providing services to the population, after the first wave based upon privatisation. Although PPPs can not be confused with pure (and complete) privatisation, they are certainly to be placed somewhere on the continuum between complete provision by the State and complete provision by the private sector.[3] By organising the provision of services through a co-operation between the 2 sectors, it is hoped to combine the strength of both, while avoiding the failures of both. More explicitly, we can agree that: "Among advocates, partnerships represent the second generation of efforts to bring competitive market discipline to bear on government provision of goods and services. As distinct from the first generation of privatising efforts, partnering involves a sharing of both responsibility and financial risks."[4] The definition of PPPs is not an easy task, given the great variety of institutional arrangements that could be classified under this label.[5]

DISTINCTION BETWEEN "HARD" AND "SOFT" INFRASTRUCTURE

For a research on PPPs potential for countries in transition from planned to market economy, it is important to distinguish, in the list of types of infrastructure's domains mentioned above, those that imply the provision of services where the physical component is very important (like transportation and energy), and those aimed more specifically at improving human capital (like education and health). We can label the former "hard" infrastructure, and the latter "soft" infrastructure. The distinction makes sense for these countries, as the development of "soft" infrastructure is an important prerequisite for sustaining the development of the "hard" infrastructure, and for achieving sustainable development in the medium and long runs.

WHO ARE THE PARTNERS INVOLVED

While it is generally admitted that there are no serious problems in identifying the actual partners on the side of the public sector, there is no clear consensus on the side of the private one: should one include NGOs, and, more generally, non-profit organisations? Savas is quite clear in excluding the latter.[6] Nevertheless, some empirical evidence points in favour of the inclusion of non-profit organisations, as they seem to constitute a serious potential partner for PPPs aimed at providing services in education, health care, and more generally in welfare policies.[7] In fact, in these domains financial return for private companies is not at all certain. As we have seen before, investment in these services is particularly important for countries in transition from planned to market economy. Moreover, marginalized and vulnerable groups generally need services that they are not in a position to pay for. It is therefore difficult to encourage private companies to invest in these services, unless the State comes in with some subsidies.

EXPECTED BENEFITS FROM PPPS

In spite of a huge literature in favour of PPPs, scientific empirical evidence is generally mixed and balanced. Success or failure depends on many factors that need to be identified and analysed. To begin with, improved economic performance (as compared to the provision by the State alone) is difficult to assess. Moreover it may be altered by transaction costs, and capture phenomena. Finally, economic performance may be achieved at the expense of other evaluation criteria, which are essential for the present research, such as quality, equity, accessibility, public scrutiny and accountability. This could happen for example if savings are realised at the expense of reduced wages, and reduced job security; or in case of differential service provision according to the financial capacity of different target groups.

The considerations briefly presented above favour research aimed at identifying the circumstances and conditions in which the State and the private sector can collaborate through Public-Private Partnerships (PPPs) to achieve efficient, sustainable, peaceful, and equitable development.

IDENTIFICATION OF THE FACTORS
AFFECTING THE IMPLEMENTATION OF PPPS

Before we could choose our countries, we had to determine what are the favourable and unfavourable factors that might affect the adoption and the implementation of PPPs. In fact, PPPs must first exist before one can evaluate their contribution to economic efficiency, sustainable development, equity and security. In other words, satisfying the conditions facilitating the adoption and implementation of PPPs is not sufficient for realizing efficiency, sustainability, equity and security. As a long tradition of research on the implementation of public policies has demonstrated since the seminal work of Pressman and Wildavsky, implementation is not synonymous with the realization of policy objectives, not to speak of unintended (and maybe also unwanted) consequences.[8] But as countries at a pre-PPP stage have by definition (as well as in reality) a limited experience with PPPs, it was reasonable to first find out how Western countries had coped with PPPs (and similar institutional arrangements) during at least the last 25 years.[9] In doing this we took care not to assume from the beginning of our research that the so-called "good practices" with PPPs in the West could be transferred as they are to other countries. For this reason, once we had chosen our in-transition countries, we started to collect information about the present situation in those countries, taking into consideration the factors having an impact on the adoption and implementation of PPPs within the domains of politics and administration, the legal system, and the economy (especially the present stage of economic development). In accomplishing this task we have benefited from the knowledge of the in-country research teams we have established in the countries concerned. During this stage, we also tried to determine to what extent the implementation of PPPs in Western countries contributed to the improvement of efficiency, sustainability, equity and security.

THE CHOICE OF THE IN TRANSITION COUNTRIES

The choice of the countries has not been an easy task, first of all because (as is often the case for this type of research) resources were rather limited. It would have been better to cover all the Eastern European countries (including Russia). But as this has not been possible, we have been confronted with the task of making a "reasonable" choice, although not entirely "rational," at least from the point of view of statistically founded sampling procedures.[10] Briefly explained, our choice has been first oriented by the resources at our disposal that limited our choice to 4–5 countries. In choosing these countries our criterion has been that of diversity rather than of similarity. We are aware that this choice can be criticized, as some scholars prefer to work with similar cases in order to facilitate the discovery of general rules. We nevertheless have opted for diversity mainly because the proponents of PPPs (and more generally of a greater intervention of the private sector in the provision of infrastructures and public services) consider that this type of provision can be beneficial in all situations (i.e. in all countries) provided that some institutional arrangements are effected. These are well-known, and can be summarized as follows: in the economy, more space should be given to the private sector within a free market economy, as this institutional arrangement based upon competition has the result of making the private sector more efficient than the public one, which tends to work in a monopoly situation. Not only the private sector becomes more efficient under these circumstances, but is, for the same reason, more sensitive to introducing innovation and to improving quality. Moreover the private sector can very quickly mobilize the huge amounts of money necessary for the development of very expensive infrastructures and services.

To sustain this type of private (or semi-private) provision of infrastructure and services, several institutional conditions must be introduced in the polity that can be summarized under the label of "good governance," which is in fact based upon the Western model of organizing the State and its interface with the economy. Of course different arrangements are covered by this label, but the core of the model is very well-established: accountability, transparency, democracy, financial rigour and liberalization of the global economy. If the two sides of this model are correct (i.e. the one for the economy and the complementary one for the polity), it should be possible to implement it in any of the countries in a pre-PPP stage, no matter their present differences. Of course this is a normative proposal, based upon some (real or supposed) empirical evidence. But independently of whether this proposal is real or supposed, the reality is that this model has been proposed to developing and in-transition countries, and supported by international institutions such as the World Bank (WB), the International Monetary Fund (IMF), the World Trade Organization (WTO), the European Organization for Cooperation and Development (OECD), and also by the European Union (EU). The most radical form this model has taken is represented by the so called "Washington consensus," an informal, but very effective agreement between the US Treasury, the IMF and the WB.[11] The thesis of the proponents of this model is further supported by the thesis of the convergence, which postulates that the validity of the Western model, and its internationalization (thanks to the liberalisation of the global economy) will force all the countries to adopt a free market economy, and this will inevitably drive them to also adopt the political counterpart of the model. Therefore in order to test the validity of these theses, a research like ours would be in a better position by choosing countries in a pre-PPP stage with large differences, rather than with close similarities. Hence the choice of four countries with very different characteristics. Basic data on the four countries we have chosen, in terms of population, surface, GDP, etc. are given in the Table 1.1.

Here we would like to insist on the qualitative characteristics upon which we have based our choice. The first three countries are former communist regimes, having experienced communist party rule and planned economy for a long time. Only after the collapse of the Soviet Union and of its zone of influence, have these countries introduced a democratic political system and a market economy.[12] That they are now in the process of increasing the size of their private economy is not therefore surprising. Nevertheless, the question is: how far have they gone in the transition towards the Western model, and is this transition sufficient for the development of PPPs, which is one of the major questions our research has tried to answer. Among these three countries Poland is the only one to have become a new member of the European Union. As such it has already shown the proof of having adopted the essential characteristics of the Western model. Let us bear in mind that to join the EU an applicant country must meet the following criteria established by the European Council in 1993: (1) Stability of institutions guaranteeing democracy, the rule of law, human rights and respect for and protection of minorities; (2) The existence of a functioning market economy as well as the capacity to cope with competitive pressure and market forces within the Union; (3) The ability to take on the obligations of membership including adherence to the aims of political, economic and monetary

Table 1.1. Countries' Main Political and Economic Profile

		POLAND	UKRAINE	RUSSIA	CHINA
General information	Population (in million)	38.1	46.2	142.3	1,321
	Total area of the country (in km²)	312,679	603,628	17,075,400	9,596,960
Political structure	Official name	Republic of Poland	Ukraine	The Russian Federation	People's Republic of China
	Form of State	Semi-presidential Republic	Semi-presidential republic	Semi-presidential Republic	One-party rule by the CPC
	Electoral system	Universal direct suffrage	Universal direct suffrage	Universal direct suffrage	–
	Head of State	Lech Kaczynski	Victor Yushchenko	Dmitry Medvedev	Hu Jintao
	Prime Minister	Donald Tusk	Yuliya Tymoshenko	Vladimir Putin	Wen Jiabao
Key economic data	GDP (current US Dollar, in billion)	421.9	141.2	1,289.6	3,242
	Real GDP growth (in %, 2008/2007)	6.6	7.7	8.1	11.9
	GDP per head (current US Dollar)	16,291	7,008	14,661	5,478
	Inflation (annual percentage, national data, in %)	4.2	12.8	9	4.8
	Unemployment (in %)	12.8	2.3	6.2	9.2

Source: All the political information presented here for the four countries is dated July 2008. The economic data give however the information available for the year 2007, from the Country Reports of the Economist Intelligence Unit, July 2008.

union. Moreover, as a member of the EU, Poland can count on the "help" of the Union and of its individual members for improving its adequacy to this model, as it has to adopt the European legislation, and comply with the European policies. Now, some of these policies are very much in favour of the development of the private sector, especially for the provision of infrastructure and services. Finally, the country has already developed several PPPs. So, among these former communist countries, Poland seems to be the one with the highest probability of developing PPPs in the near future. In Chapter 5 Thomas Zacharewicz explains what the chances of Poland are for further developing PPPs.

A bit more distant from the EU (and the Western model) we have chosen Ukraine. This former communist country is a potential candidate to the EU, but for the moment (contrary to Poland) it has not yet shown the proof of being an "acceptable" candidate, in spite of the orange democratic revolution of 2004, and the 2005 motion voted by the European Parliament affirming its wish to establish closer ties with Ukraine in view of a possible EU membership. In fact, amongst the 3 former communist countries Ukraine seems to be the one that is less advanced on the road towards PPPs. If this country takes all the measures needed for starting negotiations in view of its accession to the EU, then it is likely that the development of PPPs will be basically supported by the same favourable factors as those just mentioned for Poland. In this context it is worthwhile to mention that the attribution to Poland and Ukraine of the 2012 European Football Championship has been considered by many as an incentive to the development of PPPs for the construction of the infrastructure necessary for the organization of this event.[13] Nevertheless, it seems that this possibility is more likely to occur for Poland than for Ukraine, if we pay credit to recent information by the media saying that Ukraine experiences some difficulties in facing the organization of this event, in particular because of the lack of adequate infrastructures.[14] But this could be the occasion for attracting private capital, more likely from abroad than locally. But is the country ready to attract foreign investments? This is what Tatiana Chernyavskaya and Oleg Gurynenko analyse in Chapter 7.

The third of the former communist countries chosen for this research is Russia. Choosing the former leader of the Eastern communist bloc has been almost unavoidable, as this country presents so many interesting features for our research. First, Russia has many characteristics that could be an advantage for the development of private initiatives: large surface and abundant natural resources, a population of about 140 million and a well-educated workforce, economic and military strength, and significant advances in research and technology. Second, after the chaotic years of the Eltsin era, when the shock therapy of rapid liberalization produced several negative consequences, such as the impoverishment of a large portion of its population, the appropriation of public assets by members of the former nomenklatura (several of them of a clearly mafia character), Putin's new era has given the country the stability it needs, and the population a renewed faith in its destiny. It is nevertheless worthwhile to mention here the sharp criticisms Putin's Russia has attracted from the West, as soon as he started to limit the inflow of foreign investment (especially in sectors considered as strategic), to fight against some of the former nomenklatura members, and to limit the freedom of the political parties of the opposition and the freedom of the press, as it is defined by western standards. In spite of this criticism, it appears that the new trend in Russian politics and the more rigorous policies implemented under Putin's leadership have given the country not only the stability mentioned above, but also the economic growth needed for the development of a more robust and healthy economic system, favourable to private initiatives. In spite of its relative greater distance from the Western model (at least compared to Poland), Russia seems to offer a favourable political, economic and social environment for the development of PPPs. Within this framework, Russia has already developed legislative, regulatory and institutional arrangements favourable to the implementation of PPPs. Moreover, the selling to foreign countries of its natural resources has given the government substantial financial means that could be invested in PPPs projects, thus granting to the government an additional advantage for attracting private investors, domestic and foreign, as this means that the government is in a position to share the financial risk with potential private investors.[15] Tatiana Chernyavskaya and Vladimir Varnavsky analyse these trends in Chapter 6.

Finally, China was introduced in our research for reasons similar to those that made us choose Russia. Of course, China is even more distant than Russia from the Western model, in spite of having introduced market mechanisms in its economy that have produced some spectacular results. Like Russia, and maybe even more so in the long term, China has several characteristics favourable to the development of its economy: size of country and of its population, natural resources, cheap but fairly well-educated manpower, a fast developing education system at all levels but especially at the university level, very fast developing competences in science and technology, and a stable economic and political system. As in the case of Russia, and even more so, Western observers are criticizing China on the account of democracy and human rights, and would like China to adopt measures to bring it closer to the Western model. The Chinese react by insisting on the peculiar characteristics of their civilization, opposing the "Beijing consensus" to the "Washington consensus," thus claiming its own path towards modernization.[16] Since the middle of the 90s China has experimented institutional arrangements of the PPPs type. This has been done, as often is the case in this country, on an experimental basis, using PPPs when the circumstances are favourable, but bailing out PPPs when changes in the situation make the re-collectivization (or more often the re-municipalization) possible and/or advisable. And that explains the relative limited experience in this field. But as for other innovations introduced into the Chinese economy after 1978, the Chinese leadership is learning very fast and should PPPs prove to be a good alternative to fully private or fully state provision of infrastructure and services, there is nothing that could prevent the Party-State to use more widely this type of institutional arrangements. The leadership has proved to be able to take its decision on the basis of practical evidence much more than on ideological considerations. Of course this will need some further adjustments of a political, legal and administrative nature, not to mention the problem of the relationships between central and local governments, which are even more important than in other countries given the considerable size of China in terms of surface and population.[17] These developments and opportunities are analysed by Yang Yongheng and Wang Wankuan in Chapter 8.

DATA AND METHODS

The next step in the research process consisted in a series of interviews conducted in the four countries with a choice of representatives of the public sector, the private sector, and of civil society (especially NGO and university researchers). It must be said from the beginning that, given our limited resources, it has not been possible to work with a statistically representative sample of these three categories. Bearing this in mind, the analysis of the answers to our questions we will provide in this report must be observed with some care: they cannot be interpreted as reflecting proportionally the distribution of values and beliefs, attitudes and opinions regarding PPPs in the four countries.[18] We are nevertheless confident that we have been able to identify the major positions of these actors, as they correspond (categorically) to those we know to exist in the West where a lot of research is already available in this respect.

In practice, we used 3 questionnaires. For the face-to-face interviews the choice of interviewees has been done with the purpose of having representatives of public and private sectors, and civil society. In principle preference has been given to people with at least some experience and knowledge of PPPs. A total of 79 people have been interviewed; the distribution by countries and by sectors is given in table 1.2. As we have already said, the analysis of these face-to-face interviews is presented in the second part of this report.

At the end of the interview we asked the respondents to fill in a standardized questionnaire. Unfortunately, the response rate has been rather disappointing. Luckily we had previously decided to send by e-mail or ordinary

Table 1.2. People Interviewed Face-to-Face by Semi-Directive Questionnaire. Distribution by Countries and Sectors

Countries	Public sector	Private sector	Civil society	TOTAL
China	10	6	4	20
Poland	5	4	5	14
Russia	10	6	9	25
Ukraine	9	6	5	20
TOTAL	34	22	23	79

post a standardized questionnaire to a choice of people representing public sector, private sector, and civil society. For this second questionnaire the criteria for choosing the interviewees was the same as for the face-to-face interviews, i.e. people with at least some experience and knowledge of PPP.[19] Moreover we also targeted some Western interviewees, in order to benefit from the opinion of people coming from countries having a well established experience in PPPs. In spite of several recalls, the combined return rate of these 2 standardized questionnaires is about 40%, which would be considered rather low in the West. But considering that this type of research methodology is not very often used in our four countries, we can be moderately satisfied with this outcome. As these two questionnaires were practically identical, we decided to merge them; the distribution by countries and by sectors is given in table 1.3.

In this way we obtained a total of 124 interviews, 22 for Western countries, 28 for Poland, 26 for Russia, 15 for Ukraine, and 33 for China. Knowing that there have been 8 cases for which it has not been possible to determine the sector (4 for China and 4 for Ukraine), the percentages cal-

Table 1.3. People Interviewed by Standardized Questionnaires by Countries and Sectors. (N and % Calculated on Valid Data)

Countries	Public sector N %	Private sector N %	Civil society N %	Valid data Total N %	Missing data N	TOTAL N
China	25 86.2%	3 10.3%	1 3.4%	29 100%	4	33
Poland	18 64.3%	7 25.0%	3 10.7%	28 100%	0	28
Russia	8 30.8%	5 19.2%	13 50.0%	26 100%	0	26
Ukraine	6 54,5%	5 45.5%	0 0.0%	11 100%	4	15
Western countries	4 18.2%	10 45.5%	8 36.4%	0 100%	0	22
TOTAL	61	30	25	116	8	124

*People representing Western countries: 8 USA, 4 Switzerland, 2 France, 2 United Kingdom, 2 Germany, 1 Spain, 1 Ireland, 1 Austria, 1 Belgium.

culated on the total of valid data, i.e. 116, gives the following distribution: 52.6% for the public sector, 25.9% for the private sector and 21.6% for civil society (i.e. for NGOs and Universities). There are great differences between the four countries, the public sector being more represented in Poland and China (and to a lesser extent in Ukraine), the private sector in the West and Ukraine, Universities and NGOs in Russia. But, as we said before, the aim of these questionnaires was not to obtain a proportional representation of the opinions of persons working in these 3 sectors, but to identify the main arguments, ideas, attitudes, and eventually proposals existing in the four countries. The analysis of these questionnaires, which gives a preliminary overview of the values and beliefs, attitudes and opinions, is presented by Thomas Zacharewicz in Chapter 4.

In this chapter we will limit our remarks to the distributions of the interviewees according to the level of knowledge on PPPs, as we can reasonably make the assumption that this will inevitably have an impact on the answers regarding the dimensions of our research, both for their appreciation of the conditions favourable or unfavourable to the adoption and implementation of PPPs, and for the impact of PPPs on efficiency, sustainability, equity and security. It must be noted that our questionnaire does not measure the actual level of knowledge, but simply the knowledge the respondents thought they had about PPPs, i.e. the subjective level of knowledge. The importance of this remark becomes plausible when we cross this variable with the country and the professional sector. If we use the subjective level of knowledge and we control for country, we obtain the data presented in table 1.4.

It is not surprising that Western people are more confident than people in in-transition countries about their knowledge of PPPs (77.3%), given the longer practice of PPPs in these countries and the great percentage of people from the private sector and especially from NGOs and Universities. More surprising is the difference between China and the other 3 in-transition countries. Only among the Chinese there are people who confess that they have no knowledge at all of PPPs (39.1%); and the rest (60.9%) say that they know only a little about them. In the other countries the level of knowledge is quite high. Apart from the hypothesis that the actual knowledge is carefully translated in the answers of our respondents (but which we cannot verify) the only alternative interpretation could be based upon a cultural difference, the Chinese being more modest than Russian, Polish and Ukrainians.

The data about the knowledge of our respondents are even more interesting, if we control the subjective knowledge with the sector of activity, as shown in table 1.5.

People working in the public sector are less confident about their knowledge of PPPs than the respondents of the private sector and of universities

Table 1.4. Our Respondents' Knowledge of PPPs by Country. (Only Takes Into Account Valid Answers, i.e. Does Not Take Into Account Missing Answers)

			country of respondent					Total
			western countries	Poland	Russia	Ukraine	China	
How acquainted are you with PPP?	Not at all	Count	0	0	0	0	9	9
		% within country of respondent	.0%	.0%	.0%	.0%	39.1%	9.2%
	A little	Count	5	14	13	0	14	46
		% within country of respondent	22.7%	50.0%	56.5%	.0%	60.9%	46.9%
	Quite a lot	Count	7	9	7	1	0	24
		% within country of respondent	31.8%	32.1%	30.4%	50.0%	.0%	24.5%
	Very much	Count	10	5	3	1	0	19
		% within country of respondent	45.5%	17.9%	13.0%	50.0%	.0%	19.4%
Total		Count	22	28	23	2	23	98
		% within country of respondent	100.0%	100.0%	100.0%	100.0%	100.0%	100.0%

Table 1.5. Our Respondents' Knowledge of PPPs by Professional Sector. (Only Takes Into Account Valid Answers, i.e. Does Not Take Into Account Missing Answers)

		Public sector	Private sector	NGOs, universities	Total
How acquainted are you with PPP?	Not at all				
	Count	8	1	0	9
	% within q64new	16.3%	4.0%	.0%	9.3%
A little	Count	27	6	12	45
	% within q64new	55.1%	24.0%	52.2%	46.4%
Quite a lot	Count	7	9	8	24
	% within q64new	14.3%	36.0%	34.8%	24.7%
Very much	Count	7	9	3	19
	% within q64new	14.3%	36.0%	13.0%	19.6%
Total	Count	49	25	23	97
	% within q64new	100.0%	100.0%	100.0%	100.0%

and NGOs: 16.3% confess to have no knowledge at all, 55.1% only a little knowledge and only 28.6% quite a lot or very much. This may explain their cautious attitude towards PPPs, especially in countries where the State, for which these people work, has been for a long time the exclusive provider of infrastructures and public services.[20] On the contrary, only 4% of people from the private sector confess to no knowledge, (which is quite plausible), 24% a little, and 72% quite a lot or very much. NGOs and universities are somewhat in the middle, with none with no knowledge at all, 52.2% with at least little knowledge (about the same as the pubic sector) but with 47.8% with quite a lot or very much. So it seems that among our respondents representatives of the private sector are more knowledgeable than the others, at least if we accept that there is no substantial difference between subjective and actual knowledge.

In spite of the limits of the conclusion that can be drawn from the analysis of the data provided by these questionnaires, we have used them as a first general overview of the opinions expressed by respondents representing the public and the private sector, as well as civil society. As we have said before, a comparison between these opinions and those currently expressed in the West, gives us the assurance that these data cover all the main opinions existing in our four countries. For this reason we have introduced the chapter analysing these data (i.e. Chapter 4) at the beginning of our report.

PLAN OF THE BOOK

Having described the rationale of our research design in this first chapter we can now briefly present the 2 parts and the 8 chapters of this report. In the first part (Theory and practice of PPPs: is the Western experience useful for in-transition countries?) we present the theoretical framework of the research, a preliminary analysis of the opinions of the major stakeholders, and the analysis of the contribution of PPPs in Western countries.

In Chapter 2 Paolo Urio, drawing from the available literature on theory and practice for the provision of public services in both Western and in-transition countries, has summarized our considerations about the definition of PPPs, our major concepts (namely economic efficiency, sustainable development, equity, and security), as well as the theoretical framework and the major hypothesis of the research. Finally, considering that the role of the State is one of the most important factors (if not the most important) for orienting the reforms in the transition process, PPPs have been replaced within the context of the development strategy of the governments concerned.

In Chapter 3 Olivier Brenninkmeijer provides an in depth analysis of the introduction of PPPs in Western countries, discussing the rationale in favour of PPPs, the actors' interest and strategy; the favourable conditions for adopting and implementing PPPs, namely the legal context and cultural contexts, democratic participation, accountability, transparency and oversight; the necessary mastery of the complexity and long-term duration of PPPs contracts; the necessity to define a clear and fair sharing of risks between the private and the public partners; the importance to assess the contribution of PPPs to security, and the evaluation of financial risks. The chapter also provides an assessment of the contribution of PPPs to efficiency, sustainability, equity and security in Western countries.

For the purpose of giving the reader an immediate and overall idea about the opinions on PPPs in our four countries, in Chapter 4 Thomas Zacharewicz presents the analysis of the standardized questionnaires thus giving a preliminary idea of the arguments presented by our respondents on the feasibility and impact (actual an/or potential) of PPPs in their countries.

In the second part of the report (PPPs in in-transition countries: favourable conditions and contributions to efficiency, sustainable development, equity and security) we present the analysis of the situation of PPPs in our four in-transition countries: Ch. 5 on Poland by Thomas Zacharewicz, Chapter 6 on Russia by Tatiana Chernyavskaya and Vladimir Varnarvski, Chapter 7 on Ukraine also by Tatiana Chernyavskaya and Oleg Gurynenko, and Chapter 8 on China by Yang Yongheng and Wang Wankuan. These chapters present the general political, administrative, legal and economic environment for the purpose of determining the favourable and unfavourable conditions for the adoption and implementation of PPPs. They also provide an evaluation of the contribution (actual and/or potential) of PPPs to efficiency, sustainability, equity and security in these countries. They end the analysis with some policy recommendation.[21]

In the Conclusion Paolo Urio summarizes the results of the research and the policy recommendation, by replacing them within the framework of the theoretical considerations developed in Chapter 2, and more specifically in the light of the development strategy of the countries concerned.

NOTES

1. We will explain later the choice of these countries.

2. As for other reforms put forward in the last quarter of the XX Century, many examples of PPPs during the XIX Century have been reported in the literature.

3. E. S. Savas, one of the most influential references in favour of privatisation, places PPPs within the privatizations institutional arrangements. It is interesting to note that Sava's book published in 2000 (in fact an updated and expanded edition of the 1987 book) is entitled: *Privatization and Public-Private Partnerships*, New York, Chatham House, 2000. PPPs are explicitly referred to on pages 105–106. Savas defines 10 different types of institutional arrangement for providing services to the

population concerned: Government service, Government vending, Intergovernmental agreements, Contracts, Franchises, Grants, Vouchers, Free market, Voluntary service, Self service. Only the first 3 are considered as non-private. See also H. V. Savitch, "The Ecology of Public-Private Partnership: Europe," in J. Pirre (ed.), *Partnership in Urban Governance*, London, Macmillan, 1998. See also: R. Batley, "Public-private relationships and performance in service provision," in *Urban Studies*, 33 (4-5), 1966, pp. 723-751, and *Public Private Partnership. A Guide for Local Government*, British Columbia, Ministry of Municipal Affairs, May 1999, p. 5.

4. United Nations Development Programme, 1998, quoted by Stephen H. Linder and Pauline Vaillancourt Rosenau, "Mapping the Terrain of Public-Private Partnership," in Pauline Vaillancourt Rosenau (ed.), *Public-Private Policy Partnership*, Cambridge, Mass, The MIT Press, 2000, p. 6.

5. We deal with this problem in general terms in Chapter 2 and with reference to the Western experience in Chapter 3.

6. Savas, op. cit., 2000, p. 106.

7. Vaillancourt Rosenau, op. cit.

8. Jeffrey L. Pressman, and Aaron Wildavsky, *Implementation, The Oakland Project*, Berkeley, Univ. of California Press, 1984 (third edition) (First edition: 1973)

9. In fact we also considered research done on PPPs (and more generally of privatizations) in developing countries. Many research institutes and international organizations have published some empirical evidence in this domain. We also benefited from some preliminary work done by the UNECE.

10. Of course it was not possible to make a random sample taking into consideration all the Eastern European countries, and even by taking all the developing and in-transition countries. But other techniques are available, e.g. factor analysis. The author of this chapter has used this technique for making a choice among the 26 Swiss cantons for a research on the political culture of Swiss high civil servants. For a methodological presentation see Horber Eugène, Joye Dominique, 'Typologie des cantons suisses', *Annuaire suisse de science politique*, 1979, pp. 215-232. This experience has shown that using a more simple procedure (called "reasoned sampling," that take into account the main characteristics of the countries to be chosen—in our case the Swiss cantons) one can arrive at a choice not dissimilar to that of a more sophisticated methodology, like factor analysis. For this reason, we have used for this research the more simple, but quite reliable, "reasoned" technique, as we explain hereafter.

11. "Washington Consensus," is the name that economist John Williamson gave in 1989 to a list of ten policy recommendations for countries willing to reform their economies. Williamson's ten prescriptions reflecting his interpretation of the Washington consensus in the early 1990s were: 1. Fiscal discipline, 2. Redirect public expenditure, 3. Tax reform, 4. Financial liberalization, 5. Adopt a single, competitive exchange rate, 6. Trade liberalization, 7. Eliminate barriers to foreign direct investment, 8. Privatize state owned enterprises, 9. Deregulate market entry and competition, and 10. Ensure secure property rights. See John Williamson, (ed.) *Latin American Adjustment: How much has Happened*, Washington DC; Institute for international Economics, 1990, and John Williamson "Democracy and the Washington Consensus," *World Development*, Vol. 21, No 8, 1993, page 1331.

12. We are not going to discuss here the relative adequacy of these countries to the Western model. What is important here is to stress their departure from the soviet model and their adoption of the Western political and economic model, even if, from the point of view of many observers, the transition is not yet completely satisfactory.

13. Not only PPPs seems to be a good solution for the construction of the stadiums and other sorts of sport infrastructure, but also for the infrastructures necessary for the success of this event, namely transportation (roads, railways, airports).

14. The President of the Ukrainian Football Federation, Grigori Sourkis, has recently declared that for the moment no Ukrainian airport satisfies the requirements of the European Football Union (UEFA) and he expressed fears that Ukraine could lose the organization of this event. As reported by the Geneva newspaper *Le Temps*, April 23, 2008.

15. For a brief, but excellent comment on Putin's Russia see the article by the Geneva professor of Russian language and literature Georges Nivat, "Russie: une transmission du pouvoir énigmatique," Geneva, *Le Temps*, March 4, 2008.

16. Yujiro Hayami, "From the Washington Consensus to the Post-Washington Consensus: Retrospect and Prospect," *Asian Development Bank*, Vol. 20, N. 2, 2003, pp. 40–65. Joshua Cooper Ramo, *The Beijing Consensus*, London, The Foreign Policy Centre, 2004.

17. For a brief but excellent comment on the present situation in China see the article by the Swiss sinologist Nicolas Zufferey, "Pour mieux comprendre le débat sur la Chine, le Tibet et les Jeux olympiques" Geneva, *Le Temps*, April 4, 2008.

18. This is not necessarily a problem, as decisions about what to do in the reform process are generally taken within the framework of the structure of power, and here the question of representation is not the most important, unless it is considered from the point of view of democratic proportional representation of the opinions of the stakeholders within the decision-making process.

19. We used a question for measuring the level of knowledge of our respondents.

20. People representing Western countries: 8 USA, 4 Switzerland, 2 France, 2 United Kingdom, 2 Germany, 1 Spain, 1 Ireland, 1 Austria, 1 Belgium.

21. These aspects will be dealt with in the 4 chapters of Part 2 that will present an analysis of the situation in the four countries.

II

THEORY AND PRACTICE OF PPPs: IS THE WESTERN EXPERIENCE USEFUL FOR IN-TRANSITION COUNTRIES?

2

Under What Conditions Can Public-Private Partnerships (PPPs) Improve Efficiency, Equity, Security and Sustainable Development?

Paolo Urio

In this chapter[1] we will place PPPs in the framework of some fundamental theoretical and practical considerations concerning the development of countries in transition. In the introduction we will begin by defining PPPs and the major fundamental values at stake in the public domain that PPPs may enhance or hamper, i.e. efficiency, equity, sustainability and security. We deliberately leave aside the definition of the content of transition in emerging economies (towards what type of economic, legal, political, and social system?) for reasons we will clarify in the following paragraphs.

As PPP is clearly one of the reform proposals of New Public Management, the rationale, advantages and difficulties of this institutional arrangement will be better understood by replacing it within the general context of the reforms proposal of the last part of the XX century (section 1.1). This will lead us to introduce, discuss, and justify the choice of the 4 values defined in the introduction, as the yardsticks against which the results of PPP should be evaluated. We will then be sufficiently armed to present and discuss (in section 1.2) our major research goals and hypotheses. As we will consider that domestic conditions and guidelines are of primary importance for viable PPPs, we will discuss them in section 1.3.

In the second part of this chapter, we will analyse the role of PPPs in the strategy of countries at a pre-PPP stage. The distinction between soft and hard infrastructures (section 2.1) will serve as an introduction to the analysis of the place of PPP within the development strategy (section 2.2). Then in section 2.3 we will take into consideration the potential private partners, and the domains in which they will be more likely to invest. And finally, we will develop some ideas towards a model for integrating PPPs into the development strategy of countries in a pre-PPP stage (section 2.4). In the conclusion we will raise the question about the direction of the transition process.[2]

INTRODUCTION

Definition of PPPs

Let us start with the definition of PPPs. The task is not easy as there is no definition generally accepted by practitioners or academia. Within the vast and diverse literature, let us take as our starting point the general definition given by a paper prepared by the Fiscal Affairs Department of the IMF that leaves space for a great variety of organisational arrangements: "Public-Private partnerships (PPPs) refer to arrangements where private sector supplies infrastructure assets and services that traditionally have been provided by the government."[3] It is true that the IMF recognizes that this definition does not help to come to an agreement on what does and what does not constitute a PPP. From its own perspective, the IMF further limits the scope of this definition by considering that "a typical PPP takes the form of a design-build-finance-operate (DBFO) scheme. Under such scheme, the government specifies the services it wants the private sector to deliver, and then the private partner designs and builds a dedicated asset for that purpose, finances its construction, and subsequently operates the asset and provides the services deriving from it. This contrasts with traditional public investment where the government contracts with the private sector to build an asset but the design and financing is provided by the government. In most cases, the government then operates the asset once it is built. The difference between the two approaches reflects a belief that giving the private sector combined responsibilities for designing, building, financing, and operating an asset is a source of the increased efficiency in service delivery that justifies PPPs."[4] But the IMF also recognizes that other forms of cooperation between the public and the private sector may come under the general category of PPP. The typology of such arrangements is presented in the Table 2.1.

David Hall, Director of the Public Services International Research Unit (PSIRU), proposes another approach that is interesting as it shows the different situations regarding operation, finance, construction and ownership for different types of PPPs, namely: outsourcing, the British Private Finance Initiative, concessions, lease, and BOT (see Table 2.2).[5] This approach considers that no matter what the situation is, in the end the public sector

Table 2.1.   Types of PPPs According to the International Monetary Fund

PPP Schemes and Modalities

Schemes	Modalities
Build-own-operate (BOO) Build-develop-operate (BDO) Design-construct-manage-finance (DCMF)	The private sector designs, builds, owns, develops, operates and manages an asset with no obligation to transfer ownership to the government. These are variants of design-build-finance-operate (DBFO) schemes
Buy-build-operate (BBO) Lease-develop-operate (LDO) Wrap-around addition (WAA	The private sector buys or leases an existing asset from the government, renovates, modernizes, and/or expands it, and then operates the asset, again with no obligation to transfer ownership back to the government.
Build-operate-transfer (BOT) Build-own-operate-transfer (BOOT) Build-rent-own-transfer (BROT) Build-lease-operate-transfer (BLOT) Build-transfer-operate (BTO)	The private sector designs and builds an asset, operates it, and then transfers it to the government when the operating contract ends, or at some other pre-specified time. The private partner may subsequently rent or lease the asset from the government

From: IMF, "Public-Private Partnerships", paper prepared by the Fiscal Affairs Department (in consultation with other departments, the World Bank, and the Inter-American Development Bank), March 12, 2004, p. 8.

Chapter 2

Table 2.2. Types of PPPs According to David Hall, Public Services International Research Unit

		Out-sourcing	PFI	Conces-sion	Lease	BOT
Operation	Operation of service	X	X	X	X	X
Finance	Capital investment financed by private operator		X	X		X
	Recouped by user charges			X	X	
	Recouped by contract from municipality	X	X			X
Construction	Construction of asset by private company		X	X		X
Ownership	public during and after contract	X	X	X	X	
	private during contract, public after			X		X
	Private indefinitely					

From David Hall, "PPPs: a critique of the Green Paper", available on the website of the Public Services International Research Unit (PSIRU), Univ. of Greenwich, London, 2006, p. 18, available on PSIRU's website: www.psiru.org.

retains or recuperates ownership on the infrastructure concerned by the PPP, and that the capital invested is recuperated either by user charges or by contract from the municipality.[6]

The Federal Highway Administration of the US Department of Transportation, which has a long experience in PPPs, defines 6 different types of PPPs[7]: Design Bid Build, Private Contract Fee Services, Design Build, Build Operate Transfer (BOT), Long Term Lease Agreements, Design Build Finance Operate (DBFO), and Build Own Operate (BOO). We remark that the American experience with PPPs is wider than the European one, and consequently the US interpretation is broader "and covers a variety of instruments through which government involves business and not-for-profits in the realization of public policy goals."[8]

Finally, the Oxford Handbook of Public Management further expands the concept by adding Public leverage to Contracting-out, Franchising, Joint ventures, and Strategic partnering.[9]

Confronted with such a diversity, we totally agree with E. Dommen, who rightly complains about the lack of coherence (both internal and external) of these various typologies and definitions, and points to the "catch word" status of the expression "PPP," whose objective is not to give the concept an analytical function, but to emotionally attract as many supporters as possible; if one tries to give the concept an analytical content, it will inevitably lose its emotional attraction power and will lose many friends.[10] And because this has been the case in recent years, Dommen can conclude that the life of the catch word "PPP" is coming to its terminal phase.[11]

Dommen's prophesy might be right, but we have to admit that many initiatives in favour of PPPs are still supported today by powerful actors both in the private sector and within the major international organizations and in most Western governments as well.[12] Instead of discussing the many definitions and typologies of PPP, our research will have the general purpose of discovering the very essence of PPPs, by testing the validity of the case in favour of PPPs. This will be done at 2 levels: first by taking into consideration *the conditions* which will favour the adoption and implementations of PPPs. These can be administrative, technical, legal, political, and cultural, and will be very much dependant on the national and local situation of the countries who will implement PPPs. Second, by evaluating *the results* of PPPs on the basis of several fundamental values we will define hereafter.

But before we deal with these definitions we propose to start with the following "reasonable" definition, which is sufficiently clear for the purpose of our research: under the term PPP we will take into consideration all arrangements between the public and the private sector (both domestic and foreign) based upon a contract that may improve all or some of the four basic operations: design, construction, finance and operation of public services, no matter the mix of them. We further consider PPP for both physical capital infrastructure (like power plants, roads, etc.) and human capital infrastructure (like health and education); and we will comprise within the private sector both private-for-profit and private-not-for-profit organisations, including all kinds of stakeholders (including community organisations).[13]

We will further consider that PPPs may have an impact on 4 fundamental values, that are at stake in the public domain, and that the contribution of PPPs should be evaluated against these values: efficiency, equity, sustainability, and security.

Definition of Efficiency, Equity, Sustainability, and Security[14]

We will define hereafter the fundamental values we have chosen for evaluating the impact of PPPs, and will justify their choice hereafter in section 1.1.

"Efficiency" is used in the sense of a relationship between resources and results, as it has been defined in the well-established mainstream of cost-effectiveness (or cost-benefits) analysis. It may assume two orientations: either one fixes the level of cost and then maximizes benefit, or fixes a level of benefit, and minimizes cost. Both are considered rational, and the choice will depend on considerations that can be political, financial, administrative, social, ideological, national or international.[15]

"Equity" is used here with reference to the fair distribution of goods and services, in particular access to vital resources and infrastructure. The word links the expression "human security" and "sustainable development" by referring to the needs of the recipients of goods or services to which a government can respond. The objective of equitable development is to reduce either economic marginalisation or political discrimination of vulnerable groups such as minorities or women, and to prevent future socio-political tensions or grievances expressed in communal or political conflict.

"Sustainability" *of economic development* refers to the human, social, political, economic and technological development that meets the needs of the present without compromising the ability of future generations to meet their own needs. Sustainable development is intimately linked to human security; without security, development is impossible. However, sustainability also includes another element, namely the fair distribution of economic and social development to all members of a community or country—hence the emphasis here on equitable access to resources and infrastructure. In addition, sustainable development can also be taken to mean the protection of existing assets as well as future assets still to be developed, such as infrastructure that is vital for economic and social development and for the preservation of the natural environment.[16]

"Security" is taken here as one of the most important values contributing to sustainable development. For the purpose of our research, the expression applies to all security considerations (community-level public safety, national security and international security) that are potentially influenced by, or can influence infrastructure and the preservation of vital assets for sustainable development.[17] So defined, security is clearly also linked to equity and efficiency as explained below, and has in fact a double face: on one side security refers to a safe institutional, political, social, and physical environment favourable to the development of PPP initiatives, with both domestic and international investors,[18] but on the other side, this concept also refers to the overall security of the neighbouring region, eventually of the whole international system. So defined, the realization of security appears to be a necessary condition for the implementation of a domestic environment favourable to the fulfilment of the other three values: efficiency, equity and sustainability. To further define the content of security, let us enumerate the requirements for both domestic authorities and private investors:

The responsibility of the domestic public authorities in matters of security can be briefly enumerated along the following components:[19]

- First, the countries concerned must be able to reduce to a minimum all sorts of criminal activities, and to keep the remaining ones under control.[20]
- Second, there should be no serious threats of conflict with neighbouring countries, and the government at all levels (central and local) should adopt measures to guarantee a sufficient level of prevention against possible threats of terrorist activities.
- Third, there should be a sufficient level of security for the implementation of laws and regulations, more particularly regarding economic activities, especially as far as property and intellectual rights are concerned; moreover, the government should not be able to change the existing legal rules without going through a well established and transparent procedure.[21]
- Fourth, there should be clear regulations favouring the development of sound economic and business activities, especially those defining the legal forms of private companies, their governance, competition, taxation, bookkeeping, and labour relations. The same should be done for financial markets and insurance companies.
- Fifth, there should be appropriate procedures for ensuring accountability, monitoring and transparency of both governmental and private activities, including PPPs.
- Sixth, the word security is also used with reference to "social security" that is linked to the existence of a fair (even if minimal) safety net and a fair policy of income (re)distribution, as these are the best guarantees against social and political unrest, that will inevitably jeopardize stability and security, and as a consequence increase social risks for private investors and will discourage private investment in general, and more especially for PPPs.

But security should also be a concern for the private investors who should in particular:

- First: contribute to economic development within the framework of the Government's development strategy
- Second: contribute to the improvement of the infrastructure
- Third: transfer to the public sector the technology and expertise for building & managing infrastructure
- Fourth: transfer to the recipient public authority knowledge for assuring security of infrastructure

- Fifth: transfer to the recipient public authority knowledge for protecting the environment
- Sixth: introduce and comply with legal practices according to international standards, especially in contract law, and promote the rule of law.

Having defined PPPs and the fundamental values at stake in the public domain, we are now in a position to discuss the status of PPP within the reform process of the last part of the XX century, and to justify the choice of the 4 fundamental values.

1. SOME BASIC ARGUMENTS:
PUBLIC-PRIVATE PARTNERSHIPS
AND DEVELOPMENT STRATEGY

1.1 PPPs, contracting out, New Public Management, and the "Washington Consensus"

Two remarks: first, PPP appears to be another expression for referring to the policy of contracting out State activities.[22] In this sense PPP corresponds to one of the major dimensions of New Public Management (NPM), and for some experts, even to the essence of NPM.[23] Seen in historical perspective, contracting out is not, and by far, something new. Examples of contracting out can be found in the XVIII and XIX century.[24] It is nevertheless true that, after the huge development of State intervention in economy and society (approximately between the end of the XIX century and the late 1970s) contracting out has become, since the beginning of the 1980s, part of the vast NPM programme and of its major explicit goal, i.e. the reform of the State and the improvement of its efficiency.[25] This would in turn improve the efficiency of market economy, thanks to the elimination of part of the State regulations, the privatisation or the contracting out of State activities, the decrease of the level of taxation, and the adoption by the State bureaucracy of the managerial tools of the private sector.[26] Although NPM is generally meant for reforming the States in developed countries, there is no doubt that it is part of a broader policy programme in which the so-called "Washington Consensus" constitutes its counterpart for developing and in transition countries.[27] Or, if you prefer, the general set of coherent policies aimed at improving the efficiency of the State has two ideological, theoretical and methodological similar components: one addressed to developed States (the NPM) and another meant for developing and in-transition countries (the "Washington Consensus").[28]

Second, and more interesting, we believe that contracting out, and the larger set of reforms under NPM, should be evaluated taking into consideration not only their advantages in strict economic terms (like saving on the public budget, sustaining the development of the market economy, increasing the GDP, etc.) but also in terms of its impact on society as a whole[29], and on the physical environment.[30] In other words, any institutional arrangement (including PPPs) aimed at improving the provision of resources and services to the population concerned should be evaluated taking into consideration three sets of interrelated phenomena linked to 3 basic structures: economy, society and environment.[31] Moreover we believe that PPPs should also be part of a general development strategy defined by the countries that benefit from PPPs. We will develop this last point in paragraph 2.2 below. Figure 2.1 summarizes these ideas.

The three structures of Figure 2.1 (Economy, Society, and Environment) are based upon some fundamental values that are not necessarily in harmony. Both theory and experience show that the underlying values cannot be maximized simultaneously.[32] Starting from the seminal work of Deborah Stone, and simplifying her approach, I have proposed to take into consideration four values that are at stake when a policy is set up and implemented: economic efficiency, equity, freedom and security.[33]

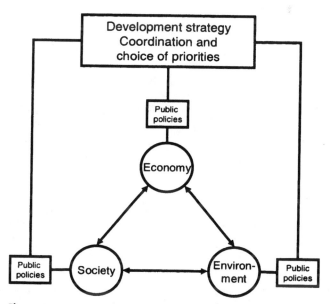

Figure 2.1.   General Model of a Sustainable and Equitable Economic Development 1.

By studying the process of adopting and implementing public policies, and by following the suggestions of D. Stone, I came to the following conclusions: first, as suggested by Stone, these values are coupled by pairs, and there are clearly several trade-offs between the 2 couples of these values, i.e. between efficiency and equity, and between security and freedom;[34] but second, we can consider that economic efficiency and freedom are better developed in the market, whereas security and equity are better safeguarded by the State; so the fundamental trade-off is between freedom and efficiency on one side, and equity and security on the other. Theoretically, one can then formulate the hypothesis that, if a society gives too much space to the State in order to maximize security and equity, it will lose in efficiency and freedom, and vice-versa if it leaves too much space to the market. Although quite interesting, stimulating and efficient in the research process on public policies, this approach presents nevertheless at least four difficulties which must be addressed before we proceed any further.

First, it is not easy to discover in practice what values are typical of each of the three structures of figure 2.1. And this is certainly even more difficult for in-transition countries that very likely have historical experiences and cultural patterns different from that of Western countries in the framework of which our approach has been developed. For example, efficiency and equity are certainly present in both economy and society; but which one is the dominant one, i.e. the typical one, in the 2 structures? Nevertheless, by examining the development of Western countries since the industrial revolution, and more recently the impact of globalization on both developed and developing countries, one can, with a sufficient amount of confidence, identify *efficiency* as the typical value (in the weberian sense of the word) of the economic structure.

The second difficulty is linked to the opposition between security and freedom and to the rather narrow definition of the concept of freedom, implicit in the typology of the 4 values, as it is clearly linked predominantly to the market.[35] Whereas it is true that access to the market gives people the money which allows them to be more or less free in society, money gained in the market is by no means the only factor giving freedom to individuals. Moreover, we are aware of the fact that the concept of freedom may have very different meanings in different cultures.[36]

Given these problems, we prefer to leave out freedom, as it is not a value directly at stake in this research. In fact the major goal of the proponents of PPPs is to provide services in a more efficient and timely way compared to the provision by the State. Of course freedom can be a by-product of this provision, but not its primary goal. This will not forbid us, at the end of this research, and if the information collected is adequate, from eventually trying to determine whether PPPs have in fact improved the freedom of the people concerned, thanks to the services provided.[37] In doing this, we will not forget, as we said before, that freedom can have different meanings in different cultures.

The third difficulty is linked to the fact that the approach based upon efficiency, equity, security and freedom leaves out the fundamental concept of sustainable development. We will introduce this concept in conjunction with equity. If one can consider that the major function of the State is to safeguard the cohesion of society as a whole, by integrating the human and the physical environments, and not only to set up and implement the legal and institutional environment favourable to the functioning of the economy, one can assume that *equity* (of the distribution of wealth) is the typical value linked to the social structure, and *sustainability* (of the economic development) the one linked to the environment and the durability of a country's societal values and public goods. The role of the State will be therefore to find a level of efficiency, equity and sustainability acceptable to all (or the majority) of stakeholders within a given society (see Figure 2.2).

The experience of NPM in developed countries is quite interesting in this respect. NPM proposals have been based upon the empirical evidence that

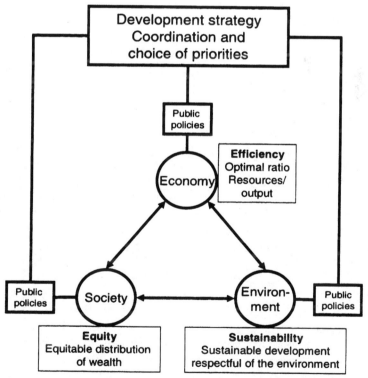

Figure 2.2. Typical Values of Economy, Society and Environment.

Western States who had intervened "too much" in economy and society, have considerably reduced the fundamental value of a market economy, i.e. efficiency both for market and State.[38] But on the other hand, in the NPM era that started around 1980, the implementation of the NPM policies, while it has improved efficiency of both enterprises and governments, has considerably reduced equity, i.e. a "fair" distribution of wealth. Not only income distribution has become more unequal, but, at its lower end the number of poor people has increased.[39] Needless to mention the negative consequences of the development of the Western economy on the environment that nowadays is being addressed with considerable difficulty by the international community.[40] Hence, the development of the concept of sustainable development, i.e. a strategy of economic development that preserves nature (especially non-renewable resources) and safeguards the interests of future generations. Another interesting consequence is that this situation has created a significative level of social unrest, or at least of opposition to the official policies of some of the Governments concerned, both nationally and internationally.[41]

In this respect China (one of the countries of our research) presents an interesting experience, that points in the same direction. Whereas during the Mao era, the planned economy maximised equity (the Gini index being around .22) efficiency was very low, with huge numbers of poor people. The development strategy that followed that era (based upon the introduction of some market mechanisms) eliminated almost completely extreme poverty, produced spectacular results with an increase of GDP around 10% for 2 consecutive decades, but resulted in a huge increase of inequality (Gini around .45), in new forms of poverty (as the traditional forms of solidarity were not replaced by a modern safety net) and in considerable damages to the environment and to the health of millions of people.[42]

The two examples briefly presented above show that society, economy and environment are closely interrelated, and that the management of the problems related to them necessitates the implementation of policies that will have to manage a complex set of interrelated trade-offs between Efficiency, Equity, and Environmental protection. An important effort of coordination will be necessary and, as resources are limited even in the event of private (foreign and domestic) investment, priorities will have to be established. It is our opinion that coordination will have to take place within the framework of a development strategy, in which the introduction of PPPs will take place and within which they should be evaluated. Of course, the relevant decisions will have a heavy political (and even ideological) character.[43] The examination of these phenomena is clearly outside the scope of our research. But we certainly cannot totally ignore that the feasibility of our practical proposals for PPPs will depend on these kinds of considerations.

The fourth and last difficulty concerns the concept of *security*, which even more than the other values, is not clearly and exclusively linked to any of the three structures, but is a typical trans-structural value, as it can be assured or hampered by the economy (for example if the market excludes some people), the environment (if pollution threatens the health of the population), and by society (if its structure is unfair for some people).[44] In the introduction to this chapter we have tried to overcome this difficulty by apprehending this value both in relation to the investors (domestic and foreigners) and in relation to the recipient country. We can now complete figure 2.2 by adding security to efficiency, equity and sustainability (see Figure 2.3).

The content of the public policies suggested by Figure 2.3, related to the four components of the development strategy, will be briefly described in section 2.4. We are now ready to discuss our major research goals and hypothesis.

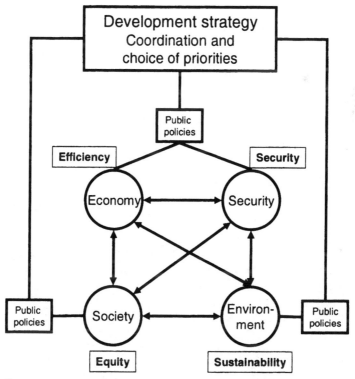

Figure 2.3. General Model of a Sustainable and Equitable Economic Development 2.

1.2 Our Major Research Goals and Hypotheses

Based upon the ideas discussed so far, our research project has given the following definition to our major hypothesis and goals:

"Public Private Partnerships (PPPs) enable governments to provide citizens with costly Infrastructure and public services that they might not otherwise have been able to afford. The international community has recognized this and now encourages the establishment of PPPs, but not of any kind. Rather, these partnerships need to take sustainable development, including the reduction of poverty, human security, social equality, and good governance into consideration.

However, there are currently no benchmarks, guidelines or selection criteria that governments and the private sector can use to measure the extent to which they contribute to peace, security and sustainable development.

The general aim of this project is therefore to bridge the gap between the current reality of PPPs and the vision of PPPs that contribute to sustainable development. The project's objective is, on the one hand, to analyse and evaluate the potential for public-private partnerships to contribute to sustainable development and human security, and, on the other hand, to establish guidelines and benchmarks to help such partnerships preserve existing assets and provide equitable access to resources for the communities affected."[45]

Our research is clearly based upon two fundamental hypotheses. The first one is that *PPPs may contribute to the economic development* of the countries concerned *by attracting* actors from the *private sector to finance*, or at least to provide their *expertise* on some activities considered to be of "public" importance. We will not discuss here the related problems of defining "public goods," private "goods" and the mixed category of "merit goods."[46] But this distinction should be kept in mind, as many PPPs will concern the controversial category of "merit goods": The latter possess a part of "public good" that cannot be entirely based upon scientific evidence, as is the case for purely public or private goods, and therefore must be approved through political decision-making procedures.

Second, if the partnership between public and private actors is to deliver interesting results, *PPPs should maximize the respective strengths of public and private sectors and minimize their weaknesses.* In the literature on PPPs it is further said that an effective and efficient PPP should be based upon some common goals, and that the private partner should acquire a sense of "social responsibility" and the public actor a sense of "managerial culture." This sounds quite reasonable, and we agree that these questions are at the heart of the design of PPPs. The problem is that the two partners (especially if the partner on the private side is a private company)[47] have quite specific and different operating strategies, philosophies, and institutional environments that monitor and control their activities, and give them the necessary legitimacy: the public actor will be more oriented by equity, security and effectiveness, the private partner by efficiency, especially if it is a private company, and for the proponents of PPPs they usually are.[48] It follows that one of the difficulties of our research will be to discover the conditions that will allow to balance and integrate the behaviour of the two partners.

Very often the rationale in favour of PPPs is based upon postulates, i.e. on self-evident truths not to be submitted to empirical tests. This is clearly not the perspective of our research, whose goal is to discover the conditions (which could vary from one domain and from one country to another) under which PPPs can deliver interesting results in practice and not only in theory.[49] By "interesting results" we mean results that enhance at least one of the 4 values (equity, efficiency, sustainability and security), without at the same time worsening the 3 others.

Given the difficulties mentioned above, a more realistic hypothesis could be that an efficient and equitable PPP, favourable to sustainable economic development and contributing to the country's security should be based not on common goals, but on fundamentally non-contradicting interests, bounded in a legal document that should contain the following necessary and minimal elements that will be further developed as one of the results of our research. This document should:

(a) specify the characteristics of the service or goods to be delivered in terms of quantity and quality, and the time framework,
(b) clearly identify the beneficiaries, and the condition of access,
(c) define the organisational setting, including the respective responsibilities and roles of both partners (financial, decisional), and the procedures for settling disputes and for assuring transparency, monitoring, and accountability for both partners.

The difficulties we have just mentioned have already been recognized by the academic literature,[50] and even the IMF recognizes that "Much of the case for PPPs rests on the relative efficiency of the private sector. While there is an extensive literature on this subject, the theory is ambiguous and the empirical evidence is mixed."[51] It further recognizes that "the case for PPPs is weaker where the government cannot write complete contracts because service quality is non-contractible."[52] Moreover, independently of the cases in which service quality is non-contractible, it has been widely recognized that PPP contracts are by nature incomplete.[53]

We are convinced that our hypothesis and goals, as well as the results of our research will make sense only if placed in the framework of the general model of Figure 2.3. It follows that the most difficult task of our research will be to define what conditions the implementation of PPPs in countries in a pre-PPP stage must comply with, in order to sustain economic development, equitable access to the services provided, and the preservation of the environment, while safeguarding security, both for local populations and foreigners who are considering to invest and work in these countries.

1.3 Conditions and Guidelines Favourable to Viable PPPs, and the Importance of Domestic Characteristics

The identification and definition of these conditions will depend upon three different sources of information:

1. the analysis of the already existing evidence from the experience of developed and in-transition countries with PPPs experience;
2. information collected in countries in a pre-PPP stage[54] through documentary sources, as well as interviews with the major stakeholders[55];
3. the analysis of the general conditions existing in the latter countries.

The difference between the second and the third source of information is the following: the second is based upon the analysis of opinions, attitudes, values, and strategies of the main actors (micro-analysis); the third on the analysis of structural characteristics, namely (1) the social and political culture, (2) the economic, legal, political, administrative and environmental structures, (3) the geo-political situation of the countries concerned (macro-analysis).

Evidence from previous research shows[56] that it would be foolish to simply transfer to countries at the pre-PPP stage the so-called "best practices" that have proved to deliver "satisfactory" results in developed countries, without considering whether the domestic conditions are favourable or not to such a transfer.[57] But it would also be foolish not to learn from the experience and knowledge acquired by developed and in-transition countries with PPP experience. It follows that the problem is: how to take advantage of this experience so that it will be useful for designing and implementing PPPs in the countries at a pre-PPP stage.

Therefore, for achieving this research goal, and in order to provide useful and practical guidelines, we should have a very clear idea about the impact that domestic characteristics may have on the success or failure of the implementation of PPPs in the countries concerned.[58] Clearly it is not enough to look only for technical conditions which should be implemented for a successful PPP.[59] Whereas the latter can be easily discovered from the experience of developed countries, it is very likely that their best practices will have to be adapted to the local situation, and this may turn out to be a more difficult task. Moreover, it may even be necessary to change some of the domestic conditions *before* PPPs can be introduced in these countries with a reasonable chance of producing the expected positive results.

The last remark should be qualified by the following: if we really wish PPPs in transition countries to become a means for finding their own way, or, in other words, if we wish PPPs to enable these countries (in conjunction with a variety of other organisational arrangements) to cease to be indefinitely dependent on the "support" of developed countries or of international organisations, and to become effective and equal partners in the global system, it is important not to impose on them institutional arrangements that (at least for the time-being) may not only be unfitted to their culture, but also not necessarily favourable to their medium and long term national interest.[60] And this leads us to the analysis of the relation between PPPs and the national development strategy.

2. THE ROLE OF PPPS IN THE STRATEGY OF THE COUNTRIES AT A PRE-PPP STAGE

2.1 Hard and soft infrastructure[61]

Before we go any further, it must be stressed that it is important to bear in mind, for the countries concerned, the distinction between soft and hard infrastructure, the two vast domains where PPPs may provide an alternative to services entirely produced and distributed by the State. The first one, "hard infrastructure," refers to physical resources and services (like roads, railways, energy, housing, etc.). Although hard infrastructure is not aimed at directly developing the human capital, it contributes nevertheless in a decisive manner to its improvement, provided people are in a position to have an equitable access to these resources. In order to enable people to take advantage of physical infrastructure it is necessary to develop the second type of infrastructure: "soft infrastructure," whose aim is not to develop anything physical, but to directly improve human capital, namely attitudes, knowledge, skills, as well as physical and mental health. It is the domain of education, science and technology (including the dissemination of innovation and best practices) health, and more generally, the development of safety nets.[62]

It is clear that this distinction, as in the case for almost all distinctions in the social domain, has its limits. For example, the provision of health care while clearly being in the category of soft infrastructure as it affords people the good health necessary to accede to the resources produced by other infrastructures both hard and soft, necessitates some kind of hard infrastructure in the form of hospitals, diagnostic centres, laboratories, etc. Nevertheless, the distinction maintains its validity insofar as it points to the different nature of the services provided: human capital resources vs. physical ones: human capital resources (especially education, health, and adequate lodgings) directly improve the capacities of the people to have access to the labour market, and this will in turn allow them to earn the money necessary to acquire the other resources vital for a (at least) decent way of living. If people are excluded from the market for one reason or another, or if work does not provide sufficient financial means (as is the case for the working poor) some sort of redistributive policies will be necessary to enable these people to have access to resources, either by subsidizing the production of these services, or by directly subsidizing the people concerned. In this perspective, safety nets are to be considered as soft infrastructure insofar as they are in fact a substitute for human capacities allowing people excluded from the market (because of illness, accidents, unemployment, or old age) to have access to resources, thanks to the insurances covering these situations. Figure 2.4 summarizes this discussion.

Of course, these two interrelated types of infrastructure are essential for the harmonious development of any society, including developed countries. But in countries in transition it would be useless to develop hard infrastructure (especially if it is wholly funded and provided by foreign organisations) without previously (or at least simultaneously) developing soft infrastructure. Moreover, hard infrastructure PPPs should be designed to favour the transfer of knowledge and technology to the local workforce and elites. Otherwise, they would simply provide services and yield returns to investors (foreign and domestic), without improving the human capital, thus perpetuating the dependence of the countries concerned not only on

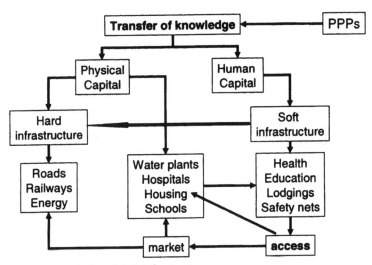

Figure 2.4. Hard and Soft Infrastructure.

foreign investment (which is not necessarily negative)[63], but also on foreign knowledge and technology. This transfer is fundamental for building an institutional system in all domains (polity, economy, and society) capable of developing and sustaining the (relative) independence of the countries concerned that will permit them to be integrated as equal and effective partners into the world system.

2.2 PPPs and the Development Strategy

The considerations developed so far are clearly in favour of a comprehensive approach in which PPPs are part of the strategy these countries have to set up (or have already set up) for managing their transition process.[64] The main purpose of this strategy is twofold (see Figures 2.1, 2.2 and 2.3). First, it has to coordinate, both synchronically and diachronically, the various policies driving the transition process. Second, as resources are limited, it also has to set up priorities. The analysis of these processes (given their highly sensitive political and ideological content) is clearly outside the scope of our research. But we certainly cannot ignore that the implementation of PPPs may not deliver the expected results, or may even produce an inefficient allocation of resources, unless they are part of a comprehensive strategy of development, integrating investment in hard and soft infrastructures.

The final, strategic decision in favour of PPPs needs to be preceded by 4 prior decisions: the "time decision," the "efficiency decision," the "management decision," and the "who will pay? decision." The "time decision" refers to the fact that providing a new service (or improving an existing one) will depend on the urgency of the matter. If there is no urgency, the government could first implement a set of policies aimed at improving the economy, which will eventually enhance its fiscal capacity. It will then be able to finance the provision of the service concerned by the State. The urgency will depend on several domestic factors, such as the demand from the citizens and their intermediate organizations. But one external factor will play a determinant role, and this is globalization. Not the globalization of the economy, but globalization of information, and above all the access, even for population living in remote areas, to the image of the living conditions of developed countries. This is very likely the most powerful factor determining the urgency of financing services permitting the population to adopt the way of life of developed countries, and, if public money is not sufficient, to resort to private money, either domestic or foreign, invested either in fully foreign-funded companies or in PPPs. Nevertheless, it should be noted that the choice in favour of PPPs based upon the urgency, is valid only if the government suffers a lack of liquidities. If this is not the case, the government should turn to the other prior decisions, and first of all to efficiency.

The second prior decision is the efficiency one. If the government comes to the conclusion that private provision of services is more efficient than State provision (and/or if quality is better) then it would favour private investment. But we have already seen that the evidence in favour of private efficiency is mixed. Moreover, financing through the market is generally more costly than through government borrowing, and management of important infrastructures like hospitals, prisons, and schools by private bodies may be more expensive.[65] Consequently, decision in favour of private provision might be heavily oriented by ideological considerations.

The "management decision" concerns some of the advantages for public management put forward by proponents of PPPs, deriving from sharing tasks between the public and private partners. In particular the government must evaluate what are the benefits of transferring to the private partner the construction and the management of the infrastructure or service concerned, as well as the advantages of postponing the payment to the future. Finally, do PPPs permit to transfer the risk to the private partner, or at least to sharing it? These decisions are not simple as the evidence in favour of PPP is at best ambiguous.[66]

Dealing with the fourth prior decision, the government must choose who in the end will pay the service provided. The previous discussion suggests a truism that is perhaps worth mentioning: money must come from somewhere. If private companies are the only investor in a PPP, money will have to come from consumers, and as this will have to cover production costs (including profits) this may pose some problems for equitable access. If on the contrary, the money comes from the government (either for PPPs totally or partially funded by public money)[67] this may pose problems of high taxation (that may be supported by companies and/or tax-payers), increasing public debt, reduced efficiency and quality of the service provided.

The final decision in favour of private provision will be based upon a delicate balance between the evaluations of the dilemmas posed by the 4 prior decisions, to which the government will certainly add some strategic considerations, which may exclude from private provision sectors considered of political and economic strategic importance. These considerations will certainly orient the government decisions in this domain.

Moreover, in case the government decides in favour of private capital it must be able to attract private investors.[68] In this context, a reasonable hypothesis is that investors, both local and foreigners, will be willing to enter PPPs in sectors where return is attractive and safe.[69] Most of the time, this will be the case for hard infrastructure and much less (or not at all) for soft infrastructure.[70] Three options are open to the government:

(a) the government decides to invest alone, because it considers that the sector concerned is very important from a social and/or political (i.e. strategic) point of view[71];

(b) the government is ready to invest in a PPP, either assuming alone, or sharing the financial responsibility with a private partner;

(c) the government is ready to set up a PPP, but is not willing to invest, and simply wants to set up rules for the private contracting partner.

Under these circumstances it is possible that the government may be inclined to heavily invest "its own" money in hard infrastructure, alone or in PPPs.[72] In this case there will be little public money left for investing simultaneously in soft infrastructure, both for entirely State-provided services and for PPPs. But we have already made the hypothesis that for soft infrastructure it will be difficult to attract private money, because returns are less attractive for private investors, especially from abroad. Therefore, in these sectors, the government will most of the time be left alone to bear the burden of investing.[73] Now, soft infrastructure constitutes one of the major pillars for sustaining the economic development; and it needs a huge amount of money, as it comprises education (at all levels), health, and safety nets. Without investment in these sectors a long-term strategy of development allowing these countries to become effective and equal partners in the global economy is likely to fail. This situation places the government before several dilemmas. If the government were to invest very heavily in hard infrastructure and leave soft infrastructure to private investors (domestic and/or foreign, either in PPPs in fully foreign-funded companies), private investors might be tempted to invest if there is a sufficiently large middle-upper class ready to cover the cost of providing the service concerned. But this will inevitably exclude from the service the lower income classes, unless the government comes in with a minimal service to satisfy at least their basic needs. But as it has invested heavily in hard infrastructure, will it have enough money left?

On the contrary, the government could (as it is often suggested in the West) leave hard infrastructure totally open to wholly foreign-funded companies and concentrate its meagre monies in soft infrastructures. The problem is that by making this choice, it will run the risk of making access to hard infrastructures difficult for marginal and disadvantaged groups. In order to avoid this consequence, the government may then consider investing in both hard and soft infrastructures through PPPs. In this case the problem is that the investment in soft infrastructure (for the purpose of reducing the selling price and thus safeguarding equity of access) will diminish the government's capacity of investing in hard infrastructure. And this dilemma poses again the question of urgency. What is more urgent: developing soft infrastructure that will improve human capital necessary for providing the citizens and the economy with the highly competent workforce it needs, or hard infrastructure necessary for boosting economic development? And is there an optimal mix of both? If yes, how could the government manage the inevitable trade-offs? And how can it gain support from (or at least control) the stakeholders who would prefer a different choice of priorities?

Of course the final decision will depend on the relative importance that the government will attribute to the different types of hard and soft infrastructure. But there is one problem that will remain open: in any case the financial burden will be very heavy and some trade-offs will have to be made. Figure 2.5 summarizes this discussion.

Moreover, even if private money is abundant for hard infrastructure, it is not at all certain that private investors will join PPPs in sectors that are in harmony with the priorities set by the development strategy; and they may even prefer to invest in fully foreign funded companies.[74] In both cases this may be another source of an inefficient allocation of resources.

Finally, the considerations developed so far suggest that the development strategy of the countries concerned cannot ignore the fundamental distinction between domestic and foreign private investors. Even if this is (once again) clearly outside the scope of our research, we cannot ignore this important element of the development strategy, as for many potential PPPs it would be a mistake to count only on foreign investors, especially on multinational companies. Domestic private investors may be interesting in sectors where foreign investment is not likely or in sectors that the government considers as strategic, and for this reason it does not want to open the market to foreign companies.[75] Moreover, PPPs with private local partners may be more suitable not only for providing resources and services, but

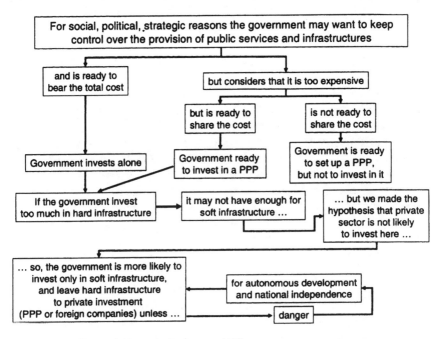

Figure 2.5.   The Government's Options and Dilemmas.

also for safeguarding the environment and guaranteeing an equitable access to them. Nevertheless, for this last situation to be true, several conditions must be met: (1) the central government has passed an effective legislation and is capable of monitoring its implementation at the local level; (2) there is not a "corruption propensity" among local officials, (3) there are clear rules for determining access to services, (4) the legal system is sufficiently developed and reliable at the local level for settling disputes. If these conditions are not fully met, a first step in the right direction could be to associate NGOs (Non Governmental Organizations) and/or NPOs (Non Profit Organisations) in the provision and monitoring of these services.[76] It goes without saying that these conditions are also valid for foreign investment.

2.3 Who Will Be the "Private Partners" and In What Sectors Are They More Likely to Invest, and To Realize at Least One of the 4 Values?

The last paragraphs bring us to consider what partners will be most likely to intervene on the side of the "private" term of the partnership. It is without doubt that all viable partnerships should be taken into consideration. That is, partnerships that improve simultaneously efficiency, security, equity and environmental protection, or at least, one of these without damaging the others. Nevertheless, it is reasonable to forecast, as we have already suggested, that there are domains for which some partners will be more likely and/or suitable than others.

All domains in which PPPs could be introduced may pose problems for at least one of the 4 fundamental values defined in Figure 2.3 (Efficiency, Equity, Security and Sustainability):

- from the point of view of *security* related to wars (both civil and international) or to terrorism, and to *sustainability* and environmental protection, the most sensitive ones are hard infrastructure like power plants and electricity transmission stations, IT and communications, chemical and pharmaceutical industries, roads, railways, and water;
- from the point of view of *equity* the most sensitive ones are clearly those in the category of soft infrastructure: education, health, safety nets, and *security*, to which we propose to add two hard infrastructures clearly more closely linked to soft infrastructure and human capital, i.e. water and housing;
- from the point of view of economic *efficiency*, all domains may be sensitive, especially when they need to draw from the economy resources which, if left there, would be used to further boost the economic development and the increase of GDP (instead of financing "bureaucratic" activities), or when the State passes regulations that increase the cost of production.[77]

The contradictions that appear in the enumeration above, once again point to the complexity of the development and transition process, and strongly suggest considering PPPs in the framework of an overall development strategy that will consider different types of private actors according to the needs of the policy concerned. The private sector is basically composed of 2 types of actors: private-for-profit and private-not-for-profit organisations. The first category comprises commercial enterprises (including for-profit private hospitals, schools and universities). The second category comprises all kinds of non-profit organisations, including hospitals, schools and universities, NGOs and NPOs, such as voluntary institutions, religious groups and community-based organisations.[78] As noted before, we will always quote simultaneously NGOs and NPOs to stress the non-profit character of these organisations. There is sufficient empirical evidence that these private actors are more likely to join PPPs in some domains than in others. And moreover their contribution will be more effective and efficient in some sectors than in others.

We will now briefly comment on some special cases, i.e. water, housing, education, health, and safety nets. This is necessary because implementation of PPPs in these domains may be more difficult and problematic than in others, especially regarding equitable access.

Water

The provision of clean water is generally considered as a hard infrastructure, but as it provides a resource for human survival more vital than electricity, gas or transportation (and is moreover a natural monopoly) its link with "soft infrastructure" is so close that it certainly needs special attention. PPPs in water provision should therefore comply with very strict requirements for making it accessible at a cost affordable for the entire population.[79] The difficulty for attracting private money is the following: apart from problems of security, the main obstacle will be the level of expected return. If this is rather low, the only possibility open to the government for attracting private investment would be to subsidise the provision of this service. Moreover, some strict measures should be taken for limiting the use of drinkable water, and for recycling used waters. Also it is essential to set up strict rules defining the quality of water and assuring the investment needed for the constant maintenance and update of the infrastructure. In this context, the British experience of privatisation of water supply strongly suggests the creation of an agency (the regulator) for supervising compliance with the above mentioned rules.[80] Last but not least, if compliance with such measures could not be reasonably assured by PPPs with private investment, the government should consider the possibility of managing this natural monopoly as a legal one, i.e. as a State monopoly, totally financed by public money. Here again, our mission is not to interfere with the government's choice and will. But, given the very special characteristic of this resource, we certainly cannot leave these considerations completely outside the scope of our research.

Housing

Housing is less problematic than water, but as it is also a basic resource, along with a decent income, access to clean water, education, health, and a decent safety net. Moreover, given its importance in transition countries for improving the living conditions of a large part of their population, it also needs special attention. Nevertheless, the difference with water provision is that housing allows more opportunities for private investments. The most important difference is that it is not a natural monopoly, and this has not pushed the governments to create a legal monopoly. Experience in Western countries allows to envisage many different possibilities for providing this resource: the most interesting one in the perspective of PPPs consists in segmenting the market into a "free market" where competition among private investors provides different types of lodgings at market prices for those who can afford them, and a regulated market where government intervenes for providing housing to those who cannot afford market prices. The possibilities go from the provision of lodgings by the government (generally local governments, eventually with the support of central government) financed totally with public money, to measures for encouraging private investments (e.g. preferential fiscal treatment, provision of public land at a preferential rate) or even the establishment of a PPP funded by a mix of public and private money.

It must be said, as we have already suggested, that as far as the "free market" is concerned, and depending on government's regulations, foreign private investment may even not need nor want to join a PPP. On the contrary, PPPs may be envisaged in the regulated part of the market, where we will find the same problems as for water: government subsidies would be necessary for providing sufficient return for private investors and equitable access for low income households, generally at prices lower than market prices). Here again, as for water, some strict rules are necessary: first, for deciding who is entitled to enter and exit the "regulated market," second for the construction of this type of lodgings. The latter concerns: type and quality of construction materials, sanitary and kitchen facilities, size of rooms, and last but not least construction standards for diminishing the use of energy (namely heating and air conditioning).

Education, Health, and Safety Nets

Each of the "soft infrastructure" sectors (education, health and safety nets) would require a long treatment. Here we will limit ourselves to the some fundamental considerations.[81]

First, these sectors are less likely to attract private (domestic and foreign) investments, for reasons similar to those already mentioned for water and low rent lodgings, unless the government comes in with enough money to attract private investors in PPPs, or if it leaves part or the entire sector to the market and if, in this case, at least part of the population is willing to purchase these services at market prices. And we run the risk of coming across the same problems mentioned above: (a) an overspending of public money not necessarily in tune with the development strategy, and/or (b) an inadequate government financing, that will result in a selling price high enough to prevent access for vulnerable groups of citizens (e.g. in the case of higher education)[82] or in a dual system (e.g. for health and safety nets) one for the lower incomes and another (more generous) for medium and upper bracket incomes.[83] In all these cases a satisfactory level of equity would not be attained, or at least it would be debatable.[84]

It is in these domains that on the side of the "private" end of the partnership it would be advisable to look not only for private companies, but also for NGOs and NPOs. Although these organisations are in principle more suitable for realising equitable access for vulnerable groups to the services concerned, they will have more difficulties in providing enough money for PPPs. Nevertheless, the government should consider (as in the case of housing mentioned above) the possibility of "segmenting the market," by setting up PPPs with private investors for the middle and upper classes of households (or leaving it to the free market), and try to cooperate with NGOs and NPOs for providing these services to the lower classes. In the latter case the government may also consider the possibility of providing these services through public agencies, and evaluate whether a hierarchical organisation is preferable or not to a contracting out strategy.

2.4 Towards a Model for the Integration of PPPs Into the Development Strategy of Countries in a pre-PPP Stage

Starting from the considerations developed so far, we propose to summarize them in a model presented in Figure 2.6. We have completed figure 2.2 and 2.3, that presents the 4 dimensions of our research (Economy, Security, Society and Environment) and we have added the major relevant policies that will realize the values we have discussed in the previous paragraphs, as being of fundamental importance for implementing PPPs in countries in a pre-PPP stage.

The coordinated and integrated goal of these policies (represented in Figure 2.6 in the middle of the quadrangle: Economy-Security-Society-Environment) is to build a society that improves the attainment of the 4 values (efficiency, equity, sustainability and security) and that should present the following characteristics:

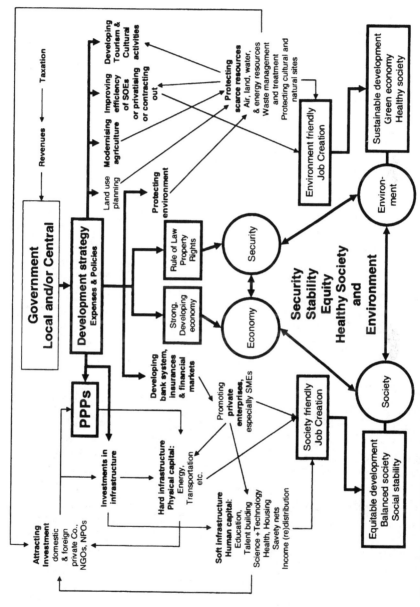

Figure 2.6. PPPs Within the Government's Development Strategy.

- an economy developing with a level of *efficiency* compatible with a *sustainable* pace,
- human activities (both private and public) organised and coordinated in a way that *preserves the environment,* and more particularly scarce and non-renewable natural resources,
- human activities (both private and public) organised in a way that realizes a balanced society with a reasonable, acceptable, and improving level of *equity,* and *security.*

It is moreover generally accepted that social, economic and political stability will favour the attainment of this integrated goal, which can be realized by different means, among which PPPs may be an interesting alternative. Valuable PPPs will have to satisfy this integrated goal at least on one of its values without harming the others. The main purpose of our research is to discover what are the conditions necessary for realizing this goal.

Let us now briefly comment on Figure 2.6. The figure is divided into 4 parts: in the upper middle part we have placed the government (central and/or local) with its development strategy, comprising the coordination of different types of public policies aimed at developing the economy, assuring security, safeguarding social cohesion, and protecting the environment. In the lower middle part, we have reproduced the quadrangle of our 4 basic components of figure 2.3: Economy, Security, Society, and Environment, to which these policies are addressed. In each of these domains, PPPs may provide an interesting alternative to infrastructures and services provided entirely by the government.

The left part of figure 2.6 presents the choice open to the government to organise alone or through PPPs the provision of hard and soft infrastructures; the policy of developing an efficient and reliable banking and insurance system, and financial markets; the related policy of sustaining and promoting the private sector (especially SMEs, as the major source of jobs creation). These policies should contribute to a *"society friendly job creation,"* i.e. a situation where the development of an efficient and competitive economy (source of jobs and revenues) is balanced by a set of policies aimed at the development and support of the human capital. This is done by developing education at all levels (including adult education) and providing a reasonable but efficient safety net, including health care and insurance, old age pensions schemes, and unemployment insurance that will result in equitable development, a balanced society, and social stability.

For practical reasons not all the policies aimed at the realisation of economic development, in which PPPs could be a possible choice, could be represented in the left part of figure 2.6. For this reason, in the right part of the figure we have added other policies that could benefit from a PPP strategy, and first of all land use planning (including urbanisation and urban regeneration). This is a transversal policy aimed primarily at defining what type of economic activities can be developed on what part of the national territory. Not only it provides the economic actors with the legal security they need when planning their activities, but it also sustains several policies, namely economic development and the modernization of agriculture. This is interesting not only for improving the efficiency of this sector (for satisfying national strategic goals of assuring a relative autonomy in food production, and for favouring the exportation of some agricultural products), but also, in the general framework of the strategy of economic development, for a policy of transfer of manpower to the other sectors. The reform of SOEs is another important domain, not only for improving the efficiency of these enterprises on both the domestic and the global market, but also for environmental protection. In some countries (and China is a good example, as the size of this sector is still quite big) SOEs are a domain where PPPs could be a viable alternative to governmental provision. Finally, we have introduced the development of tourism (especially eco-tourism) and cultural activities that can contribute to both environmental protection and job creation. These policies will contribute to an *"environment friendly job creation"* that will result in a sustainable economic development, a "green" economy, and a healthy society.

Society friendly job creation and environment friendly job creation are the result of a set of measures taken by the government (alone or in co-operation with the private sector) that converge towards the creation of a safe and secure society, where the gains in GDP are equitably distributed among its members. And this is the best guarantee against social and political instability, which in turn is favourable for the development of economic activities, be it by the State or by the private sector (domestic and foreign) or through PPP-like institutional arrangements.

Let us now summarize the dynamic suggested by Figure 2.6: the government collects its revenues from taxation,[85] and invests this money in policies that should be coordinated so that they realize the integrated goal defined above. This can be achieved in many ways:

- by investing in the 2 types of *infrastructure,* alone or in partnership with private enterprises (local, national or foreign) or with NGOs and NPOs; the choice will be based upon the motives and considerations explained above, and the competitive advantage of the country in the short, medium and the long term;[86]
- it must set up an efficient *banking and insurance system,* and a robust *financial market;*
- this will help sustain the development of *enterprises* (both public, private and mixed) especially *SMEs,* as they are the main source of job creation;

- it must modernise *SOEs*, or privatise them in different ways[87]: by fully privatising them (with or without a regulator) or by contracting out their activities (with or without a competitive tendering procedure); and in the case of a shareholder company the government should decide whether it wants to keep part of the shares, a golden share, or none);
- it must define a clear and reliable land use planning (including urbanization);
- it must set up a policy of *environmental protection*, including waste management;
- it must modernise the *agriculture* in order to increase productivity; this will enable the transfer of rural manpower to the second and third sectors. At the same time modernisation will introduce production techniques respectful to the environment;
- it must develop *tourism*, and more particularly eco-tourism (this being linked to the modernisation of agriculture), source of jobs and revenues;
- it must develop *cultural activities*, source of jobs and revenues;
- linked to the 2 previous items, it should *protect cultural and natural sites*;
- it should develop several strategies for assuring *security*, according to the general scheme described in the introduction;
- in order to reinforce the above-mentioned policies,
  o it should set up a modern (even if limited) *safety net*, that will help to provide equitable access to resources and services, will help to sustain internal demand, and will avoid the appearance of social and political unrest, and
  o a *legal and regulatory framework* in the perspective of introducing practices assuring transparency, evaluation, accountability and *good governance*.

The model suggests *several virtuous circles* that will sustain the strategy of economic development, and more specifically thanks to the attraction of domestic and foreign investments towards both fully privately funded companies and PPPs:

(a) the development of soft infrastructure will put at the disposal of private companies a well-trained local manpower, and this will further increase their willingness to join PPPs, joint ventures, or to set up entirely privately funded companies;
(b) the same is true for hard infrastructure: a good communication network (roads, railways, telecommunications) and housing will attract investment, especially from abroad and these activities will attract new investors;

(c) the development of an efficient banking system, of insurances, and robust financial markets will favour the development of both domestic and foreign companies, including SMEs; moreover, an effective regulatory framework implemented by competent supervisory bodies in these domains, will encourage foreign investors to join domestic companies in joint ventures, public bodies in PPPs, or even to create private companies;

(d) the policies of environmental protection, land use planning, and modernization of agriculture will contribute to the creation of an attractive environment for both domestic and foreign investment;

(e) similarly, a policy of protecting scarce resources will not only help SOEs to achieve their reforms by adopting production processes respectful of the environment, but will also help develop tourism and cultural activities, which in turn will contribute to the development of a pleasant environment capable of further attracting private investment.

The coordination and harmonisation of these policies pursue the integrated goal of sustaining the process of change,[88] leading to a balanced, secure and stable society, giving equitable access to resources and services to all citizens of the present and future generations, thanks to the organisation of a sustainable economic development, whose production processes will create wealth and jobs in a manner that is friendly to both society and environment.

The inter-dependence between soft and hard infrastructure is at the heart of the development strategy we have briefly described. Both are necessary for developing the country. A well-educated workforce, in good health, and having the assurance to be able to count upon reasonable safety nets in case of problems, is a prerequisite for the development of all the economic sectors. It is also a powerful factor for promoting a more open and dynamic society, and to realize economic, social, and political stability, as well as a reasonable level of security, provided that wealth is distributed equitably amongst the different components of society. Education in advanced technologies (both technical and managerial) will help the country to develop those sectors that will free it from dependence upon outside countries, at least in the strategic sectors defined by the government. Fundamental research and R&D within both public and private institutions will further improve the innovation capacity of the country, necessary to compete in the local and global markets. So the development of soft infrastructure will be a powerful driver for managing, maintaining, and improving hard infrastructure. But infrastructures (both soft and hard) must first be built. And we have made the hypothesis that this may not be always possible for in-transition countries, as competences may not be locally available, and investments may exceed the fiscal capacity of the State. If this is the case, and if the development of infrastructures is considered urgent, then PPPs might be a good choice. Nevertheless, we have pointed out the difficulties that may face in-transition countries on the road to PPPs. Trade-offs will be necessary between infrastructures and especially between hard and soft infrastructures. These decisions will depend on political, technical, local and international conditions. This chapter has tried to build upon both theory and empirical evidence already available to suggest a research framework for discovering these conditions and propose a first evaluation of the actual and potential contribution of PPPs in four in-transition countries. But there remains an unanswered question which is of fundamental importance to these countries: what does transition mean? Towards what reality, towards what type of economy, of polity and society? We would like to conclude this chapter by briefly suggesting some ideas about the possible outcome of the integration of these countries into the international system.

CONCLUSION: TRANSITION TOWARDS WHAT?

We would like to conclude this chapter by discussing a hypothesis (for some a postulate) that is often presented in the discussion about countries in transition. Most of the time, it is assumed that the countries concerned "will inevitably" (or "should necessarily") evolve towards forms of political, legal, administrative, and management organisation similar to those of Western countries. This is in particular the case when these countries begin to introduce into their society some of the features of Western culture, like market mechanisms, legal arrangements especially in the form of contract law, etc.[89] The hypothesis (or the postulate) is that these innovations will inevitably lead to a mechanical transposition of the whole set of institutions, values, and rules of behaviour typical of Western countries. If the in-transition countries fail to do so, the inevitable judgment is that they have not yet attained the high standard of development established by Western countries. PPPs are just a special case of this context. The problem is that this attitude does not take into consideration the characteristics of the countries concerned at their present stage of development. This is certainly one of the reasons why many in-transition countries have found themselves worse off after having implemented some of the prescriptions of Western countries and/or of Western dominated international organisations.[90] The same may be true for PPPs. We should therefore be very careful when defining the guidelines for a successful PPP. Three fundamental concepts should be treated with great care in this context.[91]

First, the market economy and its laws and practices are too often presented today in a simplified form that ignores the long historical process, and different forms that a market economy can present at different stages of its development. Imposing on the rest of the world the present organisation of the market economy as it exists in the West (i.e. in the US and EU) would not be of much help neither for the development strategy nor for the implementation of PPPs in the countries concerned by our research.[92] Second, the legal system upon which liberal States are founded may also present substantial differences, and third, the same is true for the related concept of democracy.

It would be unfair, and unrealistic, to expect that in-transition countries immediately and simultaneously adopt the same organisation and rules of behaviour as Western countries.[93] And it is not at all certain that they will evolve towards the same type of organisation. And even if they do, this will take at least several years or decades before they attain the same level of formal rules, practical experience, and maybe more fundamentally, the same cultural values, and the personality necessary for the functioning of an economic system "Western style." Therefore, it seems to me more realistic, at least at the beginning of the introduction of PPPs, to look for "functional equivalents" to the organisational arrangements that we consider in the West as more suitable to the development of a healthy society, i.e. arrangements suitable for developing the economy, assuring security, equitable access to the wealth so created, and respectful of natural and not-renewable resources.[94]

This does not mean that we do not believe in the existence of universal values, but these must be fundamental values of the human species, and not the values of a parochial, even if successful, culture.[95] The content of these universal values may be better discovered and understood if we place them under the general value of freedom from any physical and psychological manifestation of violence.[96] The realization of this fundamental value implies that individuals be empowered, i.e. be entrusted with the resources that will enable them to take part in the common activities of producing and distributing resources (i.e. wealth) within society, and to receive in return an equitable access to these same resources. These can be briefly defined as any kind of assets capable of empowering the individual, and making him capable of freeing him from physical and psychological violence. These resources cannot be limited to the economic and financial ones, but belong to a wider category: social and legal rules, goods and services, information, knowledge, skills, ideas, and values.[97] Only if the linkage between the participation in the creation of wealth and the return from it is realised, everyone will benefit from an equitable access to basic resources.

The realisation of this goal may take some time, a few decades for countries that have already developed some of the conditions favourable to development, but some other countries may need much more time. It may also need an incremental approach and process, through which factors of physical and psychological violence are removed one after the other, rather than through a sudden, comprehensive "revolutionary" change. In the West we have too often forgotten how long it has taken for us to set up an open, participatory society,[98] where the values of efficiency and solidarity are equally considered as important.[99] We know how difficult it is to maintain an acceptable equilibrium between these two values, and that the equilibrium we have arrived at today (both within national states and internationally) is considered by many as basically unsatisfactory.[100]

The conclusion is that we should favour all kinds of institutional arrangements (including PPPs) that allow the countries concerned to manage their transition process towards more freedom from any physical and psychological manifestation of violence. Freedom here is taken as a consequence not only of better formal rules protecting individual rights, but also as a more equitable distribution of resources, and a better preservation of the environment for both present and future generations. This may not correspond "at once" to our idea of an open and participatory society as we know it in the West today. But it would help the countries concerned to start the journey we have started more than 2 thousand years ago with a reasonable chance of succeeding.[101] And we cannot exclude that they will choose to follow another way, which at the end of the journey may improve their society to such an extent that it will become the standard for the rest of the world.

NOTES

1. This chapter is a revised and enlarged version of an internal paper prepared to orient the research at its beginning. It develops theoretical as well as practical considerations based on the research project document, and is limited to the research experience and to the references to the literature known to the author in the field of public management and New Public Management—NPM (including contracting out and PPP).

2. When we were about to write the final version of this report, OECD published a very interesting book about PPPs: OECD, *Public-Private Partnerships. In Pursuit of Risk Sharing and value for Money*, Paris, 2008. We will take advantage of the insights provided by this book in the final chapter of this report.

3. IMF, "Public-Private Partnerships," prepared by the Fiscal Affairs Department (in consultation with other departments, the World Bank, and the Inter-American Development Bank), March 12, 2004, p. 4.

4. Ibidem, p. 7.

5. David Hall, "PPPs: a critique of the Green Paper," Public Services International Research Unit (PSIRU), Univ. of Greenwich, London, 2006, available on its website www.psiru.org.

6. We remark that in some cases the capital is recuperated by both means; this happens when the municipality subsidizes the service concerned with the purpose of reducing the selling price to the customers-citizens.

7. For the definition see their site http://www.fhwa.dot.gov/PPP/options.htm, consulted 28.03.07. They even add a general category "Other Innovative PPPs."

8. Chris Skelcher, "Public-Private Partnerships and Hybridity," in Ewan Ferlie et al., The Oxford Handbook of Public Management, Oxford, Oxford Univ. Press, 2005, p. 348.

9. Ibidem.

10. Edouard Dommen, " La taxinomie des partenariats public-privé, une première approximation," manuscript kindly provided by the author, pp. 1–3: "Le PPP relève du mot déclic. Ces mots ne sont pas censés exprimer de concept analytique; le leur reprocher, c'est se méprendre sur leur fonction, qui est d'éveiller une réaction et d'orienter une attitude. Ils sont censés rassembler et mobiliser. (…) Les associations émotionnelles et culturelles des mots déclic sont ainsi plus importantes que leur contenu sémantique. (…) les spécialistes ressentent le besoin de donner un sens technique précis au mot déclic afin d'en faire un outils de travail. (…) Or, plus on dompte le concep0t de la sorte, moins il titille l'imagination et plus il perd de son attrait émotionnel. (…) plus on précise le contenu du mot moins il compte d'amis."

11. Ibidem, loc. cit, p. 3: "Le cycle de vie du mot partenariat public-privé semble s'annoncer courte: répandue à partir du début des années 1990, elle semble déjà s'approcher de sa phase terminale."

12. See more particularly the websites of the United Nations, The World Bank, The International Monetary Fund, The Asian Development Bank, The European Bank for Reconstruction and Development, The European Union.

13. The inclusion of non-for-profit organizations is today generally accepted, as they may contribute to the realization of public goals. In this sense: Chris Skelcher, "Public-Private Partnerships and Hybridity," in Ewan Ferlie et al., The Oxford Handbook of Public Management, op. cit., p. 347.

14. It is necessary to remark once and for all that the definition of the concepts of efficiency, security, equity, and sustainability is an extremely complex and difficult task, as there is not a sufficient level of consensus among academics, politicians, and more generally, all the major stakeholders. Moreover this diversity is certainly due to differences in historical experience and culture. We will come back to this problem in paragraph 2.2 below.

15. The theoretical rational foundations of cost-benefit analysis have been established for example by Anthony Downs, *Inside Bureaucracy*, Boston, Little, Brown & Co., 1967, Herbert A. Simon, *Administrative Behavior. A Study of Decision-Making Processes in Administration Organization*, New York, The Free Press, 1997 (4th ed.), and Aaron Wildavsky. "The Political Economy of Efficiency: Cost-Benefit Analysis, Systems Analysis and Program Budgeting," *Public Administration Review*, December 1966, pp. 292–310. Tevfik F. Nas, *Cost-Benefit Analysis. Theory and Application*, London, Sage, 1996. A bibliography referring to practical application can be found in Gilles Gauthier and François Huppé, *Cost-Benefit Analysis, An Extensive Bibliography*, Boucheville (Québec, Canada), Morin, 1991.

16. The basis for this definition is taken from: World Commission on Environment and Development, *Our Common Future*, Oxford University Press, 1987, p. 43.

17. Questions of critical infrastructure built specifically for military/national defence purposes are not considered in this study.

18. This of course is necessary for attracting private investment both for PPPs and fully foreign funded enterprises.

19. Several of these dimensions are clearly linked to the Rule of Law (or to the "Etat de droit"). For the importance of this dimension, and to the related concept of accountability for soft infrastructure: World Bank, *Making Services Work for Poor People*, Washington, D.C., 2003. Let us remark that all the concepts of the enumeration (their definition and exact practical content) are subject to debate, and more particularly the protection of property right, and even more the protection of intellectual property, that can be used (and is often used) by Western countries to maintain a dominant position in the market of certain goods. In this sense: Joseph Stiglitz and Andrew Charlton, *Fair Trade for All. How Trade Can promote Development*, New York, Oxford University Press, 2005, especially pp. 141–149 and 162–163, and Ha-Joon Chang, *The Myth of Free Trade. And the Secret History of Capitalism*, New York, Bloomsbury Press, 2008, especially pp. 122–144.

20. We refer here to all sorts of crimes, including economic criminality and of course terrorists' activities.

21. The exact content of the protection of property right is of course one that is open to discussion. Even more so for the concept of intellectual property that can be used (and is often used) by Western countries to maintain a dominant position on the market of certain goods. In this sense: Stiglitz and Charlton, *Fair Trade for All*, op. cit., Chapters 3 and 4, especially pp. 32, 51, 61–62, and 73; Richard Waters, "Intellectual Property. Invention shop or troll factory?, *Financial Times*, April 26, 2006, p. 7, and Chang, loc. cit.

22. In this sense: Edouard Dommen, loc. cit.

23. In this sense see Jan-Erik Lane, *New Public Management*, London Routledge, 2000.

24. See for ex. Simon Domberger, *The Contracting Organization. A Strategic Guide to Outsourcing*, Oxford, Oxford Univ. Press, 1998, pp. 8–9. "Contracting was commonplace (...) in eighteenth- and nineteenth-century England. Services provided by the private sector under contract included prison management, road maintenance, the collection of public revenue, and refuse collection. (...) Similarly in nineteenth-century France, the rights to build and operate railways and water storage and distribution facilities were auctioned by competitive tender."

25. In the first phase of NPM priority has been put on privatising State's activities; but since the second part of the '90s contracting out has become the preferred device, either because in some countries there was not much left to be privatised or because privatisations had lost their initial appeal to decision-makers.

26. See our articles on NPM and contracting out: Paolo Urio, "La gestion publique au service du marché," in Marc Hufty (sous la direction de), *La pensée comptable. Etat, néolibéralisme, nouvelle gestion publique*, Paris, Presses Universitaires de France, Cahier de l'IUED, Genève, pp. 91–124, and "L'avenir des contrats de prestations," in Bellanger, François, and Tanquerel, Thierry (eds.), *Les contrats de prestation*, Genève et Bâle, Helbing & Lichtenhahn, 2002, pp. 109–130.

27. For the definition of the "Washington Consensus" see John Williamson, *Latin American Adjustment: How Much Has Happened*, Washington D.C, Institute for International Economics, 1990, and "Democracy and the Washington Consensus," *World Development*, 1993, Vol. 21, No 8, p. 1331; for a critique see Joseph E., Sti-

glitz, "Post Washington Consensus," published on the Website of the Initiative for Policy Dialogue, Columbia University, and Yujiro Hayami, "From the Washington Consensus to the Post-Washington Consensus: Retrospect and prospect," *Asian Development Review*, 2003, Vol. 20, No. 2, pp. 40–65.

28. In this framework the State is conceived as an institution whose main goal is to serve the market, and as a consequence, the economic development and the improvement of the well-being of the entire society. In this sense, see for ex., World Bank, *China 2020*, Washington D.C, 1997, 7 vol.: Vol. 1: *Development Challenges in the New Century*, p. ix. According to this view, and in the perspective of NPM and the "Washington Consensus," economic development will necessarily improve the well-being of the populations concerned, eliminate extreme poverty, substantially reduce poverty, and drive the countries towards liberal democracy. For the thesis of a causal link between freedom in the market economy and freedom in the political arena see Friedman, Milton, *Capitalism and Freedom*, Chicago, Univ. of Chicago Press, 1962 (1982 with a new Preface by the author), Ch 1: "The relation between economic freedom and political freedom," pp. 7–21, et Ch. 2 "The role of government in a free society," pp. 22–36.

29. See for ex. P. Urio, "La gestion publique au service du marché," loc. cit.

30. We use this qualifying adjective to make the distinction between human and physical environments.

31. See for ex. Beat Bürgenmeier, *Economie du développement durable*, De Boeck, 2005; OECD, *Réconcilier l'économique et le social. Vers une économie plurielle*, Paris, OECD, 1996, and Gabrielle Antille, Beat Bürgenmeier, Yves Flückiger, *L'économie suisse au futur : une réforme en trois piliers*, Lausanne, Réalités sociales, 1997. It is significant that the World Bank has published its world development report of 2006 with the title: *Equity and Development*, The World Bank and Oxford Univ. Press, 2005. The World Bank has presented its new orientations towards development in its 2004 world development report, *Making Services Work for Poor People*, World Bank and Oxford Univ. Press, 2003.

32. Deborah Stone, *Policy Paradox. The Art of Political Decision Making*, New York, Norton, 1997 (2nd edition),

33. Paolo Urio, "La gestion publique au service du marché," loc.cit.

34. Whereas there is a large consensus on the first trade-off, the second is rather controversial, as the concept of freedom is not universally defined in the same way.

35. For a stimulating treatment of the concept of freedom see Christian Bay, *The Structure of Freedom*, New York, Atheneum, 1965 (second ed., with a new preface).

36. In this context it suffices to mention the statement of former Chinese Premier Li Peng, who in August 1997 attacked 'the Western world order', supported a call from Indonesia for a review of the UN Human Rights Charter to place less stress on individual rights ...," quoted by Colin Mason, *A Short History of Asia*, New York, Palgrave, 2000, p. 2

37. In this context it is interesting to note that Milton Friedman, in *Capitalism and Freedom*, op. cit., considers that free of charge services provided by the government in fact limit (or even destroy) the freedom of people, making them totally dependent on the State.

38. The general pattern is the following: generous welfare policies, too numerous regulations of all kinds (including those protecting the environment), relatively

non-efficient heavy investments in hard and soft infrastructure, and consequently heavy taxation, and high compulsory contributions by the private sector to the safety nets set up by governments. The perception that the State has intervened "too much" is even –and obviously—more accurate in at least 3 of the countries of our research (Poland, Ukraine and Russia). The fall of the communist regimes has indeed opened the door to a massive campaign of privatisation at the beginning of the 1990's and to a general adoption of the NPM's main principles. Similarly, a process of privatisation, although not of the same importance and in different institutional settings, was initiated by China at the beginning of the1980'.

39. Not to mention the appearance of the social category of the working poor. Among the vast literature in this domain, the working papers available on the Website of the *Luxemburg Income Study* are worth reading.

40. Needless to say, these problems have arisen well before the NPM. But NPM has not reversed the trend.

41. It is enough to mention the negative vote of the French and Dutch citizens on the European Constitution, and the social protest movements in France, Italy, Germany, etc., and the opposition to the WTO negotiations.

42. It is true that since the mid nineties the Government has adopted several policies to fight against these negative consequences. The eleventh 5–year plan has clearly defined the policies to be adopted to further address these problems. I have analyzed China's strategy in Paolo Urio, *Reconciling State, market, and Society in China. The Long March towards Prosperity*, London and New York, Routledge, 2009.

43. For example the policies towards capital liberalisation, property rights, privatisation, etc.

44. We are very well aware that efficiency, equity, and sustainability are linked not only to a single structure. But this is the inevitable problem of every approach that analytically separates in theory what is not separated in reality. See on this point the stimulating work of the French anthropologist Maurice Godelier, *Rationalité et irrationalité en économie*, Paris, Maspero 1974, 2 tomes, tome 2, especially pp. 134–140. Godelier considers two strategies for apprehending social phenomena: on the one hand, that of the open system consists in regarding a social phenomenon as a particular aspect of all the human activities, and on the other hand, the strategy of the closed system, which consists in regarding this same phenomenon as a particular field of activity linked predominantly (or even exclusively) to a single structure, which is generally the strategy used by analytical approaches. Nevertheless we are confident that the privileged (i.e. predominant) link of efficiency with economy, equity with society, and sustainability with environment corresponds to reality. More ubiquitous is the value of security, which is not predominantly linked to any structure. Moreover, it is also connected, but in our opinion not predominantly, with the legal structure. Finally, we may say that in doing so, we have proceeded according to the strategy used by Max Weber for building his typologies, trying to identify the "typical value" of the three structures, attributing equity to society, efficiency to economy, and sustainability to the environment.

45. From our research project document: *Creating a New Dynamic for Public-Private-Partnership for Peaceful, and Sustainable Development: Human Security and Equitable Access to Resources in Countries at the Pre-PPP Stage*, Geneva, p. vii.

46. Nor will we discuss the theory of market and government failures. The concept of "merit goods" has been developed by Richard A. Musgrave.

47. We will discuss later the different types of partners that can intervene on the private side. For the moment let us remind the reader that we will consider both for-profit and not-for-profit private partners.

48. Yidan Wang defines these roles in the following manner (for health and education): "Generally, the public sector or the government attempts to provide health and education services to all at a minimum cost or free. The government develops policies to try to provide equity of access to such services. Non-profit institutions and local communities in many cases have special concerns for reaching the poor and the disadvantaged that are often neglected by the government. These differences in service areas provide a basis for complementing the roles of each other. Business corporations, on the other hand, are concerned with making profit. Unlike the government, for-profit organisations are less concerned with issues such as equal access. They have a tendency to maximize profit in their activities.,"Yidan Wang (ed.), *Public-Private Partnerships in the Social Sector. Issues and Country Experiences in Asia and the Pacific*, Asian Development Bank Institute, 2000 (available on their Website), pp. 5–6.

49. For example the statement that provision of public services through PPPs will inevitably be more efficient than the provision by public authorities. Even the first sentence on our goals and hypothesis mentioned above, as stated in our research project document, did not avoid this bias: "*Public Private Partnerships (PPPs) enable governments to provide citizens with costly Infrastructure and public services that they might not otherwise have been able to afford. The international community has recognized this and now encourages the establishment of PPPs, but not of any kind.,*" (underlined by me). The use of the present tense ("*PPPs enable*") may suggest that PPPs actually enable governments, etc. But this is clearly not the perspective of our research, even if we further say that "*the international community has recognized this,*" which, from a scientific point of view, is certainly not a proof of the validity of the assertion. And moreover immediately after we add "*but not of any kind.*"

50. See: Pauline Vaillancourt Rosenau (ed.), *Public-Private Policy Partnership*, Cambridge, mass, The MIT Press, 2000. For a positive assessment of PPPs within the UN structure see Sandrine Tesner, *The United Nations and Business. A Partnership Recovered*, New York, St. Martin's Press, 2000, and for a critical assessment: Ann Zammit, *Rethinking UN-Business Partnerships*, Geneva, South Centre & UNRISD (United Nations Research Institute for Social Development), 2003. For a general, critical, and documented approach to PPPs, contracting out, and privatization, see the working papers of the PSIRU, Business School, University of Greenwich (www.psiru.org).

51. IMF, "Public-Private Partnerships," prepared by the Fiscal Affairs Department (in consultation with other departments, the World Bank, and the Inter-American Development Bank), March 12, 2004, p. 14.

52. Ibidem, p. 11.

53. See among others O. Williamson, *The Economic institutions of capitalism*, The Free Press, New York, 1985, and O. Hart, Incomplete contracts and public ownership: remarks and an application to Public-Private Partnerships, in *The Economic Journal* (113), 2003, p. 69–76.

54. The countries chosen are: Russia, Ukraine, Poland, and China. As we explained in Chapter 1, we have also chosen several Western countries for the purpose of discovering under what conditions PPPs have worked well or had difficulties in these countries.

55. According to the project document, the major stakeholders are: *On the governmental side*: Ministries and agencies responsible for finance, transportation, communication, economic development, labour and energy, as well as government offices that concern themselves with public security. *On the private business side*: International and domestic companies that are either already engaged in PPPs or are likely to engage in such partnerships when governments make them available. These companies may be active in the following sectors: Construction and civil engineering, Resource extraction, Shipping and distribution, Communications and information technology, Utility operation and maintenance, etc. *On the civil society side*: Non-governmental organisations, Non-profit organisations, and local community leaders concerned with access to vital infrastructure, education and health services, as well as the preservation of the natural environment.

56. See for ex. Joseph E. Stiglitz, *Globalization and its Discontent*, New York, W.W. Norton, 2002; Stiglitz, Joseph E. and Charlton, Andrew, op. cit.; Ha-Joon Chang (ed.), *Rethinking Development Economics*, London, Antrhem Press, 2003; Ha-Joon Chang, *Globalization, Economic Development and the Role of the State*, New York, Zed Books, 2003; Ha-Joon Chang and Ilene Grabel, *Reclaiming Development. An Alternative Economic Policy Manual*, New York, Zed Books, 2004, Ha-Joon Chang (ed.) *Institutional Change and Economic Development*, Tokyo, United National University Press, 2007, Ha-Joon Chang, *Bad Samaritans*, New York, Bloombury, 2008.

57. We use on purpose the rather vague concept of "satisfactory", because the definition of what is "satisfactory" depends on the theoretical concepts and on the empirical indicators used to define it (it could be economic efficiency, equity, sustainability, security; or more likely, in the perspective of our research, a combination of all of these indicators).

58. These may be ideological, social, cultural, economic, financial, geographical, environmental, political, as well as legal.

59. Technical conditions may be based upon economic, legal, managerial, financial theory and practice of Western countries.

60. Of course PPP cannot alone solve this problem, but it will be necessary to fundamentally revise the rules of the game of the global economy. See for ex. Stiglitz and Charlton, op. cit., and Joseph E. Stiglitz, *Making Globalization Work. The Next Steps to Global Justice*, London, Penguin, 2006.

61. The importance of this distinction for developing and in-transition countries has been suggested to us during several discussions with Prof. Hu Angang of Tsinghua University, Beijing. The World Bank has recognised the importance of soft infrastructure in its 2004 world development report, *Making Services Work for Poor People*, World Bank and Oxford Univ. Press, 2003. Sometimes, the distinction between "core" and "non-core" services is used (see, for example A.Riess, *Is the PPP model applicable across sectors?* EIB papers, vol.10, No 2 (2005), p. 13): for example, the construction of a hospital fits in the category of "non-core services," while the delivery of medical services is a "core service." Of course, the distinction between hard and soft infrastructures is not absolutely clear-cut, as some "soft infrastructures" need some "hard structures" to function like hospital, schools, etc., as is shown in Figure 2.4 below. But the distinc-

tion is better than that between core and non-core services, as it is based upon the target of the infrastructure, i.e. the distinction between human capital and physical capital. Clearly hospital, school, etc. are directed towards the improvement of the human capital. Roads and railways, also, of course, but not so directly. As I show in the Figure 2.4, it is access to human capital infrastructure (mainly education and health) that allows people of having access to the labour market, and through this to hard infrastructures; and in case they are excluded from the labour market, "safety nets," as a special case of soft infrastructure, can provide these people with the resources necessary to buy essential goods and services. The distinction between core and non-core activities (as used by companies, and more recently by public administrations) does not cover the same goal, as you can outsource both hard and soft activities, the criteria for outsourcing being the "centrality" of the activity compared with the general and fundamental function of the organization. It is much easier for companies, as they have generally some very coherent set of objectives, which is not generally the case for the State that has to reconcile the objectives of often contradictory policies.

62. Safety nets are necessary for helping people experiencing financial difficulties, that would otherwise exclude them from the social and economic systems: during childhood, when living in poor families, for acquiring the knowledge and skills necessary for entering the economic system; during active life for helping them to recover from illness or unemployment and for re-entering the economy; when retired, for helping them to have a decent life when not working any more in the economy.

63. Foreign investment can help create jobs and wealth, and accelerate the rate of GDP increase. Nevertheless, its potential for developing a mature economy is limited, unless 2 conditions are met: (1) foreign capital is not the only source of investment in sectors requiring high technology and knowledge, or, if in case of joint ventures, the transfer of technology and knowledge should be possible and encouraged; and (2) foreign investments are not mainly concentrated in low added-value production processes, whose products are exported abroad. In this case foreign capital will simply take advantage of cheap labour and will not contribute (at least in a significant way) to human capital development.

64. The importance of the role of the State for the development of in-transition countries has been recognised by authors like J.E. Stiglitz and H.-J. Chang: see Stiglitz, Joseph E. and Charlton, Andrew, op. cit..; and Ha-Joon Chang, *Globalization, Economic Development and the Role of the State*, op. cit.

65. See for health care the case of the results of the British Private Finance Initiative: Allyson Pollock, *NHS plc. The Privatisation of our Health Care*, London Verso, 2004. Of course the evaluation of the performance of PFI is not an easy task, and evidence in favour or against it is subject to debate. For a general evaluation of PFI see Norman Flynn, *Public Sector Management*, London, Sage, 2007 (5th edition)

66. Ibidem, pp. 252–269. For the argument in favour of postponing payment, Flynn says that: "The advantage to the Treasury was that they would not have to borrow the money and that the capital spending would not appear as public expenditure, thus keeping borrowing and spending low in the year in which the deal was done. (…) What PFI does to the public accounts is to accumulate future liabilities: once long term contracts are entered, there is no cheap way of exiting," pp. 252 and 254.

67. This is because we cannot exclude intermediate situations where the government subsidizes a service (that could be provided either by a SOE or by a private company) in order to reduce its selling price.

68. This discussion also suggests once again that decisions about the opportunity and the organisational form of PPPs should be considered within the framework of the government's development strategy.

69. We are not considering here situations of serious and violent instability, e.g. permanent threats of civil war and/or terrorism, which will in any case prevent investment (especially from abroad), but cases of "relative" instability which often characterize the situation of the countries concerned. Instability may have different dimensions, not necessarily exclusive of one another: political (both national and international), social, economical, and legal.

70. Nevertheless, there is a tendency to envisage PPPs in practically all domains of State activity. For example, this has been the case of the international Conference organized in Israel at the beginning of June 2007 by the UN Economic Commission for Europe (UNECE). The objectives and scope of the conference are defined as follows: "PPPs refer to contractual agreement formed between a public sector agency and a private sector entity that allows for greater private sector participation in the delivery of pubic services. PPPs are becoming increasingly commonplace for building new and upgrading existing facilities such as *schools, hospitals, roads, waste and water treatment,* as well as power plants and *telecommunication networks.* They can be a useful tool as part of *regional policy,* for *urban regeneration and sustainable development.* (...) ... the conference provides an opportunity for government and business to meet and discuss project ideas in sectors as: *transport, water, energy, and social services,*" in International Conference "knowledge sharing and capacity building on promoting successful public-private partnerships in the UNECE region," UNECE document ECE/CECI/PPP/2007/INF.1, 19 March 2007, p. 2. The parenthood with one of the more radical versions of NPM is therefore evident.

71. This might be a utility (like water), or sectors that are considered as strategic like armament industries.

72. In addition to the unquestionable utility of hard infrastructure, there are other reasons that may push the government to invest too heavily in hard infrastructure to the detriment of soft infrastructure: the most evident, and documented, is that it gives, at least in the short run, more visibility to the government's policies, and it can boost national pride.

73. Unless of course if it finds private partners who are willing to share the financial burden; this means that the government is ready to subsidise these PPPs with the purpose of reducing the selling price to customers.

74. This is also outside the scope of our research, but once again, we cannot ignore it, as it will depend on the level of openness of the domestic market to foreign investments.

75. It suffices to mention the recent decision of the Chinese government concerning the strategic domains: in December 2006 the State Assets Supervision and Administration Commission (SASAC) published a list of seven sectors critical to the national economy and in which public ownership is considered essential: armaments, electrical power and distribution, oil and chemicals, telecommunications, coal, aviation, shipping (Xinhua, Updated: 2006-12-18 21:00).

76. We will always quote simultaneously NGOs and NPOs to stress the non-profit character of these organisations.

77. Numerous regulations have this effect, e.g. regulations for environmental protection related to the process of production and to the management of industrial or agricultural waste; the regulations in the domain of industrial relations, of public health; safety nets, etc.

78. Adapted from Yidan Wang (ed.), op. cit., p. 5.

79. We mention *in passim* the possibility of making this resource accessible to people at a different price, depending on their financial situation. This could also apply to other resources, especially soft infrastructure (education, health, safety nets), but also transportation.

80. In fact there are 3 bodies regulating the provision of water: one for the price level, one for the quality of water, and one for environmental protection.

81. An interesting analysis of contracting out in Health Systems has been presented by Jean Perrot, "Le rôle de la contractualisation dans l'amélioration de la performance des systèmes de santé," Discussion paper n. 1, 2004, Department "Health System Financing, Expenditure and Resource Allocation," World Health Organisation, Geneva, 2004.

82. This may also be true for all levels of the education system if families are required to pay tuition fees at all levels.

83. For insurances the result would be that the lower income households will benefit from the State's insurance (that may not have a sufficient coverage from the point of view of equity), and medium and upper income families will widen the coverage by subscribing private insurances.

84. The danger of harming equity would be even greater if the government were ready to leave the provision of these services entirely to private companies.

85. Local authorities collect money from taxation (if they are allowed to do so by central government) and through transfers from central government. The management of fiscal policy is an important part of the government task: a too heavy taxation (on enterprises and/or on households) may harm the development by increasing the cost of production for enterprises and depressing the internal demand.

86. On the importance of evaluating the comparative advantage in the long term see Joseph Stiglitz, *Fair Trade for All*, op. cit, Ch. 2.

87. The choice will depend on considerations based upon economics, as well as on social and political considerations. Needless to say, the legal forms of the organisational arrangements may be very different and numerous.

88. In a prior version of this paper we used the term "modernization." We are grateful to Marco Giugni for having pointed to the ambiguous character of this concept. Change seems to be a more neutral term. Of course it points to the rejection of existing practices, rules, habits, and institutional arrangements. But this is what is actually going on in the countries concerned by this research. And we have already taken the position that this change may not drive these countries towards ways of organizing their society similar in all aspects to the Western model. We will further develop this point in the conclusion.

89. The list of innovations introduced first by the West is generally over-estimated. For example, Colin Mason, *A Short History of Asia*, New York, Palgrave, 2000, p. 5, reminds us that "eleventh century Sung society used credit banking and cheques, and could inoculate against smallpox." For an evaluation of Chinese contribution to

science and technology see the monumental work of Joseph Needham, *Science and Civilisation in China*, 7 volumes, Cambridge, Cambridge Univ. Press, different dates; for a shorter but complete account: Robert Temple, *The Genius of China. 3'000 Years of Science, Discovery and Invention*, London, Prion, 1998 (Introduced by Joseph Needham); for a general evaluation of the Eastern innovation transposed into Western countries see John M. Hobson, *The Eastern Origins of Western Civilisation*, Cambridge, Cambridge Univ. Press, 2004.

90. Here we refer again to the references of note 56 above.

91. It goes without saying that the following consideration would need a much wider development. Nevertheless I have opted for presenting them, even under a very short and therefore incomplete form, as they are, in my opinion, essential for a successful implementation of PPPs in the countries concerned. For a more complete discussion (focusing mainly on the case of China, but considering more generally the case of post-communist countries) see the special issue of Modern China, Vol 34, N. 1, January 2008, and more particularly the articles by Ivan Szelenyi, "A Theory of Transitions," pp. 165–175, and Sun Liping, "New Issues in the Field of the Sociology of Development," pp. 88–113.

92. See the fundamental works of Fernand Braudel, *La dynamique du capitalisme*, Paris, Flammarion, 1985; *Civilisation matérielle, économie et capitalisme* (XVe—XVIIIe siècle), Paris, A Colin, 1979, Vol 1: Les structures du quotidien; Vol 2: Les jeux du l'échange; Vol 3: Le temps du monde. For a brief analysis of different ways of analysing capitalism: Tom Bottomore, *Theories of Modern Capitalism*, London, Allen & Unwin, 1985. For the analysis of the variation of the institutions of capitalism: Peter A. Hall and David Soskice (eds.), *Varieties of Capitalism. The Institutional Foundations of Comparative Advantage*, Oxford, Oxford Univ. Press, 2001. For different types of welfare systems within capitalist societies: Gosta Esping-Andersen, *The Three Worlds of Welfare Capitalism*, Princeton, Princeton Univ. Press, 1990.

93. The case for the conditions necessary for becoming member of the European Community is of course very different from the perspective of our research. For countries wanting to join as full members the EC, it is not only a question of adopting measures necessary for attracting foreign investment "from outside"; it is a question of working "inside the Community" by necessarily respecting the same principles, rules and values upon which the EU is founded, i.e. those of a Western democracy and of a market (capitalist) economy "European style." Let's remark that countries in a pre-PPP stage may be in a quite different economic, political, legal, and social situation. This is the case for the countries chosen for our research where we have two countries that are clearly not candidates to the EU (Russia and China, and there are huge differences between them), Ukraine (that could become a candidate), and Poland who has recently become a member.

94. An interesting, even if not entirely convincing, analysis in this direction has been done for the Peoples Republic of China by Yi-min Lin, *Between Politics and Markets, Firms, Competition, and Institutional Change in Post-Mao China*, Cambridge, Cambridge Univ. Press, 2001

95. For the impact of Western culture on PPPs see Glen Paoletto, "Public-Private Sector Partnership: An Overview of Cause and Effect," in Yidan Wang, op. cit. pp. 30–47. Furthermore, we are convinced that the successful transposition of institutional arrangements (like PPP) to other cultures will also depend to the "good be-

haviour" of the actors concerned. In this respect it is evident that corporate scandals (of which the Enron one, though not an isolated case, is considered by many as the most representative) have done considerable harm to the image of market economy in developing countries.

96. We exclude in this context the use of "legitimate violence," We are aware that the definition of this concept is open to debate, although a good starting point may be the typology of legitimate domination developed by Max Weber. Of course, the level of socially "accepted" or "legitimate" violence can vary from one culture to another. The question is: shall we (Westerners) accept different levels of tolerance in other cultures, or are we going to intervene (directly or indirectly) to put an end to these situations? If yes, upon what grounds are we going to justify our intervention?

97. We have developed elsewhere the analysis of the role of resources within the context of power relations and structure: Paolo Urio, *Le role politique de l'administration publique*, Lausanne, L.E.P. 1984, Chapter 5. The resources are produced and distributed through several interactive processes, namely, decision-making by State authorities, socialization, information, social control, organisation, production, distribution, and legitimation.

98. In this context, I use this concept as an alternative to "democratic society" (I should add "as we know it in the West"), as it contains the 2 basic prerequisites for a democratic society: openness (including transparency) and participation. Without which it would be impossible to build a democratic society.

99. Among Western countries there is a considerable variation as to the mix of economic efficiency and social solidarity, some of them being more close to the "equal treatment" than others. But it is indisputable that all of them have taken into consideration both of them through democratic decision-making, thus allowing the majority of their citizens to approve the existing mix of efficiency and solidarity.

100. World Bank, *World Development Report 2006. Equity and Development*, Washington, World Bank and Oxford Univ. Press, 2005

101. We can trace back to ancient Greece and Rome the first intellectual and institutional dimensions of present-time Western countries. And we know all the regressions we had to go through, the last one being the dreadful period going roughly from 1914 to 1945.

3

Questions, Risks and Challenges: Public-Private Partnerships in Western European Countries

Olivier A.J. Brenninkmeijer

INTRODUCTION

This chapter provides an overview of public-private partnerships (PPPs) mostly in Western Europe that operate public services and public infrastructures. The aim is to identify recommendable practices and point towards difficulties or challenges that are specific to PPPs. These may be of interest for emerging economies and countries that currently undergo economic reforms and that are in a pre-PPP stage. While practices in the operation of PPPs can hardly be transposed from country to country, the experiences in Western countries provide useful insight for the evaluation of local or national political, administrative, economic and legal conditions, as well as the general development strategy of the countries concerned. This analysis will be done in the chapters of Part 2 of this study.[1]

Public-Private Partnerships are often likened to a form of partial or temporary privatisation Privatization can be seen as a process of handing over the management or the ownership of public assets to the private sector as on a continuum where, on the one side, the Government alone builds and provides all services to the public, and on the other side, the private sector has full control over and/or complete ownership of the same public services and infrastructures. In between there are many degrees of private involvement where the private sector becomes more or less involved. For example, the government may sell off some shares in a public corporation or it may hand over managerial control to a private provider for a limited period of time. This latter option is what a PPP usually represents on this continuum scale of privatisation

The PPP is an arrangement that allows the private sector to operate a public service or public infrastructure for a long period of time. Because this contractual period may last for many decades, PPPs are often seen as being closer on the side of full private control on the continuum scale of privatisation. In fact, for the duration of the PPP contract, the private sector partner can exercise almost as much control over the infrastructure or public asset as if this asset where its own private possession. This makes PPPs a different kind of government procurement method from traditional procurement because public authorities do not buy merely a building, a hospital or a road. Rather, the government buys the desired service that these infrastructures provide to the public; i.e. office buildings that are serviced, medical care in a new and fully functioning hospital, or complete roads with maintenance and security services included. This is often called a life-cycle project where the private provider designs, finances, builds and then operates or manages the final output for the public. Most PPP contracts end with a so-called "transfer" where the public sector takes over the finished and operational infrastructures from the private provider, sometimes for a fee providing that the public asset is in good operating condition.

In this procurement process, the government will not have to re-build or change anything that the private provider had already built and put into operation—or so is the ideal expected procedure. The reality, of course, may or may not work out according to this ideal. It is not uncommon that risks, unforeseen expenses or operational and institutional challenges bring such agreements to a halt or require that the parties re-negotiate their collaboration. But PPPs may also produce unforeseen benefits when they are not only well developed, but also based on real partnerships among people who have a shared interest to work together and who collaborate to overcome operational and institutional challenges. Such examples exist and point towards opportunities for innovation and healthy competition. This is often the argument used in favour of greater private sector involvement in public services and public infrastructure; namely that traditional state monopolies or State-owned enterprises (SOEs) need to be dismantled to allow for greater competition in bidding for projects and in a greater variety of services to the public.

As can be deduced from the above, public-private partnerships are a special kind of delivery of public services and public infrastructure based on long-term contracts. They are special because governments can thereby maximise the involvement of the private sector in the development and delivery of public services and public infrastructure without actually selling these public assets or public goods to private companies. What distinguishes PPPs from traditional government procurement of public services and public infrastructure is the interdependence that PPPs create between private involvement in the operation of public infrastructure and services on the one hand, and the risks associated with privately raised capital on the other hand. Public-private partnerships are binding contractual agreements through which a government buys a final product or service from a private provider. The latter carries out all the work for the government that can include initial design of an infrastructure, its construction, operation or the management of the service system, as well as delivery to the public. This may include refurbishing transportation networks, supplying water and sanitation systems, building and operating prisons, sea ports or airports, or constructing and managing schools, hospitals and social housing, and then delivering the service to the patients or students.

Traditionally, public services and the construction and maintenance of public infrastructure were usually looked after by national and regional or local government authorities. However, the private sector has always been intimately involved in the building and management these public assets such as infrastructures and services in all European countries. Governments often outsourced work on infrastructure construction and maintenance to private companies, but they retained control of the ongoing work or operational management of the public service. This included all infrastructures from transportation and communication systems, health services and education, to the management of water and other resources.

Today, while governments are still fully engaged in developing public infrastructure and providing public services, they are increasingly changing the way they do this. The reasons are manifold and include budget constraints, adaptation to new economic and social trends, environmental considerations and security. Underlying these are changes in government policy—parliaments and ministries make decisions on the basis of economic necessity and ideological trends. One such trend is the reduction of government involvement in delivering public services and the increasing space they offer to the private sector to enter this activity instead.

While the trend of government disengagement in the development and delivery of public services and public infrastructure is evident in many Western countries, this chapter accepts the assumption that all national governments are concerned about the quality of their public services and infrastructures. It is assumed here that governments continuously wish to improve public services to respond to the demands of their populations and to adapt the services and infrastructures to new and ever-changing social, economic and industrial needs. Functioning public infrastructures and services are also considered here as contributing directly to the intrinsic value of social goods or the societal value that provides quality of life to a population and that attracts industrial investment and economic development.

A new development in the domain of public services and infrastructure is that these have come to represent a new market for the private sector. With the creation of PPP-type procurement contracts, the private sector is becoming a major actor in public services and public infrastructure in Western countries. This is not without the commercial interest of businesses and international investment firms that see new opportunities in this new market. Multinational companies specialising in services such as water and waste management, public transportation or construction enter this market as soon as governments modify their policies and laws to accommodate PPP-type contracts. This change is supported by pressures coming from major national economies that favour international open competitive procurement, and international or regional actors such as the World Bank and the European Union.[2] They favour open international markets where international finance is expected to bring forth added values of economic competition into innovation and cost efficiency.

According to some estimates by global actors such as the European Bank for Reconstruction and Development or consultancies such as McKinsey, countries benefit economically as soon as their national infrastructure undergoes development or modernisation.[3] In Western countries, where public services and public infrastructure are already well developed, major changes requiring greater investment are nevertheless needed to adapt them to economic changes and the needs of ageing populations. At the same time, in emerging markets public infrastructure and services are being built sometimes with amazing rapidity to open up new economic zones and attract investment towards all other sectors of the local economy. In both Western and emerging markets, the private sector plays an important role not merely for construction and operation of public infrastructure, but as financier and service provider directly to the public. It seems almost a given today that greater involvement of the private sector is expected by many to bring more vital services to the public in all countries. It was with an eye towards poverty reduction through economic growth that the United Nations declared some years ago that infrastructure projects around the world are increasingly being managed and financed by the private sector in partnership with national or local governments.[4] Greater synergy is hoped for where private companies begin to collaborate with governments to improve basic services and help national economies out of vicious cycles of poverty, conflict and instability. The expectation that an improvement of infrastructure will help economies emerge from stagnation is not a new.

The private sector is bound to have an increasing role in the provision of public services. A research study by the international consultancy Deloitte finds that there is a global demand for infrastructure that reaches in the hundreds of billions if it were to be paid at today's cost.[5]

The International Project Finance Association and the World Bank estimate that project financing around the world for public services and public infrastructure will grow in relation to the need that countries adapt their regulations to facilitate public-private collaboration.[6] Their ability to attract investment in industry sectors is strongly dependent on their capacity to involve and regulate the private sector's participation in the development of public infrastructures. This is equally true for highly industrialised countries as it is for emerging economies and developing countries.

With the opening of the public sector to private involvement, a potentially enormous market for business is opening at the rate at which national governments modify their policies and laws to allow for this to happen. New industrial consortia are created especially to bid for large PPP contracts, and they receive the active participation from international financial institutions and consulting companies. Private industry is thus moving into a commercialisation of public infrastructure and public services for the long-term and for the life-cycle of projects. This involvement includes financing, design, construction, operation and service to the end-user and the public. This implies important changes away from traditional forms of government procurement. While the potential benefits are often enumerated by proponents of public-private partnerships, real problems challenge governments and private sector partners about the lack of transparency of contracts and public spending and raise expectations for greater accountability to civil society and stakeholders. This is the vision of PPPs that was outlined in the Johannesburg Declaration on Sustainable Development of 2002.[7] However to date, this vision remains more an aspiration than a reality. In fact, PPPs introduce new kinds of trade-off that may favour, for example, economic efficiency over social equity, or security over economic efficiency, etc. While the ideal of so-called "win-win" situations is appealing and which proponents of public-private partnership often mention, it is difficult to envisage how costs for greater security or long-term sustainability can be accounted for in projects that also must be socially equitable and financially more efficient than other forms of government procurement.

To highlight some of the challenges that PPPs introduce into the debates about efficiency, sustainable development, equity and security, this chapter provides an overview of public-private partnerships (PPPs) mostly in Western Europe that are in operation in the public services and public infrastructure context. The examples of PPPs also serve to highlight that procurement agreements can come in many shapes and involve various types of partners, including non-profit agencies. This overview includes a look at favourable and unfavourable conditions in which PPPs operate in order to establish a particular approach to new developments, namely efficiency, sustainable development, social equity and security.

PUBLIC-PRIVATE PARTNERSHIPS

Public-private partnerships (PPPs) are procurement models that offer the greatest possible involvement for the private sector in the delivery of public services and public infrastructure.[8] Most definitions consider PPPs to be long-term contractual agreements between public and private actors for the improvement of the public infrastructure and public services that, in addition to traditional outsourcing, include a life-cycle approach and privately generated financial investments. Typically, the private sector partner is involved in project planning, financing, building, operating and supplying the final services to the public.

In some countries, such as the United Kingdom, Ireland, Australia and New Zealand, the term "Public Finance Initiative" (PFI) is also used.[9] As opposed to the latter term, the word "partnership" confers the notion of loose friendship-like collaboration; however, a PPP is generally understood to be a binding type of procurement agreement that provides for an extended form of contracting out.[10] As with any procurement, a government agrees to buy assets or services from a private business provider, and the private company supplies the desired output.[11] There are numerous explanations and definitions of what PPPs or PFIs are, and some are discussed here to clarify the principal types that this chapter refers to.

Why Public-Private Partnerships?

Public-Private Partnerships are today one method among many for a government to obtain both a reduction of involvement in the development or operation of public infrastructure and services, and a postponement of public payments for the same service. Both these objectives answer to the current liberal trend for the State to reduce its involvement in domestic matters that can be provided by non-governmental actors, either private sector companies or non-profit associations.

For the private sector, PPPs offer a new entry into a market and access to a customer base that was hitherto closed or only open for a select number of small companies. Traditionally, European governments outsourced public infrastructure construction or the delivery of public services through procurements to companies they had established relations with or that were in the vicinity of the needed construction. At times, governments also used procurement of public services and construction as an addition to policies of local employment creation. With the advent of increasing liberal market principles, government procurement has become not only more competitive, but is opening up to competing companies at the national level and even from other countries. Indeed, many very large PPPs that demand expertise in construction, engineering and technical operations rely on private sector partners that are international companies with commercial interests in public infrastructures around the world.

Governments in Western countries open up their public services and infrastructure to international industry through competitive procurement and tendering to achieve a reduction of their own involvement in the detail management or operation of the given public infrastructure and service. It is a "hands-off" approach that allows governments to procure a complete service from the private partner. The latter coordinates the workflow from initial design to final delivery. By contracting work out to one single large operator—be it an international company or a local business—the government hopes to realise a rationalisation of the individual steps needed from initial design to final delivery and save itself from having to oversee these steps. This is the "life-cycle" approach to outsourcing to a single agent outside of the government. Sometimes, this outside agent is a non-profit association when the public service is local and needs local stakeholder input to operate effectively. In most large construction and technical operations projects, however, the outside partner is a large business firm or a consortium composed of a number of international or national companies. The development of a PPP may even include the special creation of an autonomous office, often called a "special purpose vehicle," that takes over the managerial responsibility of the entire project and is controlled by both the government and the private sector partners.

Through PPPs, governments aim at an advantage for themselves by purchasing an entire cycle of public infrastructures and public services from conception to completion that often includes long-term operations and service to the public, the end-user or the customer. This relieves the government from having to look after all the steps in the public infrastructure and services and frees it from the task of contracting individual private companies for each of these steps. This stands in contrast to traditional procurement methods were the government issues tenders and signs contracts with private suppliers for every step in an infrastructure or public service project.

Cost Efficiency

Next to the debate about the merits or disadvantages of privatisation or private control of public infrastructure and services, there is another controversial aspect that concerns cost efficiency. Market-type mechanisms, as the OECD calls them, are being adopted by Western governments by more and more ministries and departments. While there are great differences in how national and local governments adopt new measures that involve the private sector in public services and public infrastructure, one reason is that governments seek to reduce the immediate cost that capital-intensive public works require. Put differently, governments want to increase the "value for money" (VFM) of their public operations and seek out commercial or market-type methods to achieve this.

While some PPPs may prove to reduce the price tag for a public infrastructure in comparison to the price a government expects to pay for a similar traditionally-procured project, the evidence remains elusive. The "decision to use market-type mechanisms needs to be made on a case-by-case basis."[12] The reason why the cost efficiency debate is important is because it is very difficult to know the exact cost of a project that has been set up as a PPP. For example, before a PPP project is launched, its costs can only be estimated; they cannot be known in advance as when a single product or service is purchased "off the shelf." Once a PPP project contract has expired, it remains difficult if not impossible to calculate the total cost of the project from beginning to end.[13] One reason is that PPP projects are not financed through a single stream, but through combinations of sources. This can be seen when comparing with traditional procurement or outsourcing where the government knew from the start how much a given service or infrastructure will cost. Nevertheless there are some studies that prove that in some circumstances PPPs can be more expensive than the traditional way of providing public services. This is the case for the British form of PPP (called Private Finance Initiative—PFI) within the health sector in the UK and Scotland.[14]

Policy Priorities

Many if not all Western governments continuously undertake structural reforms driven either by economic demands or by ideological convictions. The globalisation of trade and information has internationalized markets for upstream production and downstream distribution. Competition for highly skilled employees and low-paid workforces has become as global as local and national competition to attract investment through lower taxation and better infrastructure services.

Policy responses to both global economic changes and ideologies about the role of government affect every country. This is all the more so in countries that have a strong tradition of centralised control over public services and public infrastructure. All countries together are also subject to another need for continuous reform and improvement, this is public approval. Citizens judge their political leaders on the basis of how they deliver effective public services over the long-term. Such judgements are obviously subjective to the extent that the public evaluates the quality and quantity of public services and infrastructure on the basis of culture, history and personal individual and collective experience. Governments are accountable to their populations in most political systems, and they are subject to ideologies and policy trends that promote improvements in the delivery of public services. As the global context changes within which governments act and react vis-à-vis their populations and the economy, so their views of their own role in society also changes.

With the liberalisation of markets during the past decades, the role of the state is also undergoing a re-evaluation. Many governments that follow the liberalisation of their economies also abide by the notion that the government's core function is to govern and leave industrial or technical industries over to the private sector. This leads to questions such as whether a government should manage hospitals, fire fighting services, airports or water and sanitation. Must these services be operated by a government, or can private operators look after such tasks? How members of governments, ministries or municipalities respond to these questions will define whether public services are outsourced or kept within a government's internal administration. Ultimately, this question is one of policy priorities; for example, should a government employ civil servants to carry out all basic services necessary to ensure quality of life for all citizens, or should a government concern itself with regulating and controlling their delivery instead and leave the business of the delivery operations to non-governmental actors?

This brings the discussion to the fundamental question of policy choice for any government, national regional or municipal. Depending on how its financial situation is, a government must either chose to spend only what it can afford at the time, or borrow from financial institutions or private partners and pay later.[15]

The importance is not only the question whether PPPs are more efficient in term of financial cost or "Value for Money" (VFM). Rather, the question whether governments should use PPPs at all must be asked. PPPs or PFIs must be seen as a "credit card" tool for public authorities to develop infrastructure services—to acquire them now and pay for them later. This is primarily a policy priority question that touches on the reasons for why a government would want to consider engaging in PPPs. The decision whether to engage in PPPs may depend on two principal factors:

First: The desire on the part of the government to boost local economic development by improving infrastructure services quickly. This facilitates other economic and industrial activities in the same region that can benefit from the infrastructure. This is especially an argument in emerging markets where a reinforcing relationship between infrastructure and market size yields gains in productivity. Infrastructure investments are also a form of jump-starting a local economy in regions where development is at a standstill or where high insecurity, violent conflict or war undercut all growth-oriented economic activity. In each case, a mutually reinforcing dynamic is sought where enhanced infrastructure and public services strengthen economic growth, which in turn, increases wealth creation for additional infrastructure and public services.

Second: The need on the part of the government to reduce government expenses and/or lower public deficits and still develop infrastructure and services. This consideration can be important either where a government already has high public deficits (USA, some European countries), but where infrastructure must be improved or else poor maintenance becomes a public hazard, or where upper limits on public debt are imposed as is the case in the EURO zone countries.

Another consideration is whether the government should prefer to opt for a public deficit to acquire capital intensive infrastructure services or use the "credit card" procurement method and pay later for the same service. In case of public borrowing to build infrastructure, it may seem acceptable that this expense be covered by taxpayers over several decades or even generations. As infrastructures are expected to last very long and benefit a local economy, a public deficit can be considered acceptable, even if the repayment takes many decades.

In this consideration of policy priorities, it may be advisable for a government not to engage the private sector in long-term PPP concessions when the factors mentioned above are not among its priority considerations. To engage in PPPs for financial aims only, such as obtaining better value for money or greater cost efficiency, may prove less beneficial for the public sector in the end, once the contract has expired after 10, 30 or more years.

FAVOURABLE AND UNFAVOURABLE CONDITIONS

There are many issues that PPPs bring to the foreground that may be considered as either positive or negative pre-conditions, as well as effects and consequences from the development of PPPs. Some examples of what to do and what problems to avoid are included in the discussion below. It follows, however, that this is by no means a complete list of do's and don'ts. Many more can and will be added as PPPs evolve in new environments and new markets on the threshold between public and private. First, a number of positive conditions are given below, followed by a number of consequences that present some of the most difficult issues and challenges to be considered by proponents of PPPs and governments contemplating them.

Culture, Equity and Economic Globalisation

There are historical and cultural differences among Europeans in their reaction to greater private involvement in public services and infrastructure. In various historical cases, people have collectively gone to the streets in protest over poor governance of public services. Individually, people may also decide to choose private services and buy their own solutions at private hospitals, private schools or private security services for their homes and businesses. Private companies see in the delivery of services a lucrative market, especially when its customer base and financial revenue steam are guaranteed by a government.

It is usually taken for granted that governments are obliged to procure services at the lowest possible cost as finances are public. While this has not always been the case depending on policy or ideology where administrations chose to promote employment or subsidise specific industry sectors (export subsidies, for example), the trend today favours open and liberal markets. This holds true for government procurements as well as for international companies that wish to capitalise on public infrastructure and public services.

An advantage of this liberal market approach is that it does favour open competitive tendering for government contracts. The private bidder who offers the desired service for the lowest price wins the deal. Competition is also expected to stimulate innovation by bidders. They are obliged to think of better ways to provide a service and maintain the expected quality or quantity. Innovation may come through changing methods of pricing, design, the composition of materials, finding less costly upstream suppliers, or changing managerial techniques and improving on operational processes.

To improve on cost effectiveness, governments have always outsourced public services to private businesses and to specialised non-profit agencies. What is new, however, is the intensity of the discussion and the integration of new contractual models for this collaboration. The intensity emanates from concerns that the sale of public assets through privatisation schemes has negative consequences especially with regard to quality and equity. In Germany, a characteristically strong public debate has emerged about PPPs that follows virulent criticism of privatisation.[16] This debate in the mainstream media, publications by labour unions and some political parties, focuses on the reduction of quality and coverage, and the increase of costs to the public. Special concern is in areas where the public service is meant to provide consistent equitable service even in areas that may be commercially unviable, as for example public transportation in remote areas, or the postal service.[17]

The debate is about social equity of services and the allocation of public goods that are intended to improve or at least maintain the societal value of a community and country. Equity implies a fair distribution of access to resources and services for all people within a country. National and local governments are expected to provide public infrastructure and services in an equitable manner without discrimination vis-à-vis remote communities that live far away from urban centres, or specific ethnic groups or people with few economic means. The principal element of the debate on equity and privatisation concerns the question whether a commercially-driven public service company will deliver the service for a fair price to all residents in a country, even those who live in remote places or who are not considered to be "financially interesting customers." With the introduction of PPPs, that is, long-term dedicated or life-cycle concession agreements, the debate also takes on another controversial element. This is the financial interdependence that arises through long-term PPP contracts when they are financed through international financial institutions that may have no cultural or other relation with the population and country in which the public service is to be provided. There is usually little to worry when a government out-sources a public service or the construction of public infrastructure to a foreign company through traditional procurement methods. This is mainly because as soon as the contract ends, the government regains full control over the public asset or service. However, with the extension of concession contracts over many decades, as is the case with PPP contracts, the foreign company's influence over the public service it delivers may not be to the liking of the end-user population. This can become particularly worrying to a local population in one country when a large financial service provider gains influence through a long-term PPP over the local public service in that same country to which, however, the foreign service provider has no cultural, political or social connection.

A multinational provider or water, for example, that has financial obligations to investment banks and asset management companies around the world can, through a long-term PPP contract, gain influence over the distribution of water in a local town or city in any one country. A new tension is created here that can only be defined as globalized interdependence; the foreign private provider has an influence in the local public services, but the local government remains ultimately accountable to the end-users of that privately-provided public service. The citizens and consumers will still hold their local or national government accountable for equitable access, for example, to the drinking water that is provided by a foreign company. This raises numerous other questions about legitimacy, democracy and the extent to which private commercial influence should be permitted. This is because through a PPP agreement, the local government may have entered into contractual obligations with a private provider, who in turn, may have financed its contribution into the local water system on the basis of international financial obligations that are completely detached from the local economy and from the local population of end-users. What all this means, is that through long-term "globalised" PPPs, local public infrastructure and public services can become intimately tied to global financial markets—something that was not as readily possible before the innovation of long-term PPP contractual models (this is discussed further below under the sub-heading "Security and Financial Risk").

Legal Context

The importance of clear and reliable judicial protection within a well developed legal context cannot be underestimated. The legal framework in any country forms the primary enabling environment for the collaboration between state and private industry. It implies "high standards of public and corporate governance, transparency and the rule of law, including protection of property and contractual rights."[18] Successful cooperation between the public and private sectors depends on a well developed body of legislation that govern private industry, financial flows, subcontracting rights and logistics, as well as all the aspects of industry that involve employees, upstream suppliers, customers and other stakeholders.

Regarding the stakeholders—the public and end-users in this case—the importance of an independent legal framework cannot be underestimated. The example of the private water management by a subsidiary of the French Suez in the city of Grenoble is of interest here.[19] The legal structure must be independent from political influence, for without such independence, the citizen and political groups that accused the water company of corruption could never have stood up against the more powerful politician's collusion with the water company. The French legal system was able to prosecute the guilty individuals and provide the necessary framework for a partial re-nationalisation of the water infrastructure before the concession contract had even come to its end.

Corruption is sometimes considered as an aspect of security, but also of transparent project operation. Germany's waste disposal privatisation also came under public scrutiny because of financial corruption and unacceptable policy influence lobbying. The "downside of competition for waste management markets" have become apparent in the form of collusion, corruption and fraud among companies and the public sector. The city of Cologne and other German cities have been faced with corruption where a few incineration companies influenced public decisions to benefit their private interests, undermining competition and political credibility."[20] A situation that also suffers from corruption in the waste disposal industry is in the Italian city of Naples.[21] This raises the question whether local or national governments should contract out work to businesses that are dubiously managed or involved in unsavoury dealings where transparency is lacking.

This also begs the question of who sets governance standards that can be incorporated into PPPs and other procurement contracts. One answer must come from international agencies such as the World Bank, the United Nations, the EU or the OECD. But also non-governmental organisations have an influence on the promotion and evaluation of governance practices. As example, a couple of specialised agencies evaluate governance methods and the prevalence of corruption. Most famous are, on the one hand, the

World Bank's *Worldwide Governance Indicators*, and on the other hand, the investigations carried out by Transparency International.[22]

The legal context is important where long-term PPP contracts are considered. Private companies will not invest where legal guarantees are not in place, or where the government does not offer financial compensation if legal guarantees are insufficient. Investors will not risk their investments unless they have assurances that their rights and responsibilities are legally established, protected and enforced by independent judicial bodies. This is particularly the case for long-term commitments which are high-risk by the fact that unforeseen events cannot be excluded. At the legal level, impartial and independent forums for dispute resolution, based on legal protection of private property and contractual obligations is necessary. These pre-conditions must be stipulated in the original contract between the parties.

In European countries, the rule of law is supported by an impartial judiciary. Within it the laws that govern industrial activity, commerce and financial investment, create confidence by the existence of independent arbitrational tribunals or commercial and civil courts. Within Europe, international investors also have legal protection and recourse to investor-state dispute settlement mechanisms that stand under international investment agreements and ratified by the host country. Without theses, PPPs would hardly be possible.

With regard to PPPs, most West European countries are introducing legal amendments to privatisation and concession laws to facilitate long-term contracts in which the private sector takes over management of public services and infrastructure. Legal modifications at times have to allow for private finances to be admitted into public services, or for PPPS to provide financial benefits to the private provider. An example of where legal amendments would imply changes in how government policy is designed can be found in Switzerland. The population has a right to initiate referenda to influence policy at the local or national government. As laws need to be adapted to allow for PPPs to invest in and earn a profit from public services, the public's right to stop such deals cannot be done away with. In the city of Zürich, this is currently one of the city authorities' concerns as a referendum gave the okay to the city to spend public funds to refurbish the police and justice centre. The city is considering creating a PPP contract to provide a less expensive alternative and which could be provide a finished public construction along with follow-up maintenance services without time delays. However, amendments to the legal framework must be evaluated first in light of how the public can continue to hold referenda in the future should it disagree with the terms in a long-term PPP contract. No satisfactory answer has yet been found.

The development of infrastructure, utilities and public services through long-term concession-type contracts with the private sector is still in its infancy in Switzerland.[23] Very few PPPs have been approved and special PPP acceleration and concessions laws are being debated that would optimise available taxation exemptions for public infrastructure and services, allow for concessions that last a project life-cycle, and prevent a diminution of the democratic referendum that allows citizens to vote for or against public projects. Other changes in the legal context that are being actively pursued can be found in Austria and France.

In Austria, various construction PPPs are being established, such as the building and maintenance of government offices. The first PPPs were in road construction and maintenance. To facilitate the financial management of both public and private funds, a special State agency was created. It is the *"Autobahnen- und Schnellstrassen-Finanzierungs-Aktiengesellschaft"* (ASFiNAG). It operates similarly to a "special purpose vehicle" and could be called a "structural" or "institutional" PPP as the EU refers to them. This offers the PPP the ability to manage the construction and improvement of national roads in an autonomous manner, and is intended to enhance oversight of public accounting. It also facilitates the initial private capital investments that are later and gradually paid back by the government through yearly instalments. Similar construction PPPs are also planned in the Austrian rail transport sector.

In France, PPPs are now being facilitated through various legal reforms. The PPP concessions as described in this chapter were not possible in France until recently. Under the traditional French procurement system, there were three procurement methods available that private providers could choose.[24] These were the traditional procurement where a private entity competes for a contract as in any outsourcing for specific jobs or services. Then, the restrictive concession (described below), but finally the public-private joint ventures (*sociétés d'économie mixte*). The concession, or "afermage" in France, has been used for many decades. In contrast to the more flexible concession agreement that the Anglo-Saxon legal system in the UK and in North America, the French government has traditionally applied a tightly restricted type of concession. This meant that a public service undertaken by a private provider (often specially created for the purpose) had to supply not only an entire life-cycle service (as many PPPs are elsewhere in Europe), and this service had to be entirely self-financed. The concessionaire could not to be paid by the government, except under exceptional circumstances, and had to obtain all its revenues from the end-user. This meant that only income-earning projects could fall under this traditional form of concession agreements and the most famous French concessions in this sense are the toll highways.

Legal changes in France have already been introduced to facilitate PPP concessions that allow for mixed financing and shared risk-taking and benefits. New laws provide for DBFM contractual models at both local and national government levels and are commonly referred to as partnership contracts. The legal amendments introduced allow for international competition of government tenders (to adapt also to EU requirements), to permit co-financing between public and private entities, to allow for private financing from a variety of sources including foreign asset management companies, and finally, to make deferred payments possible by the government to the private partner over the entire concession period.

A now famous example of a recently completed and highly publicised public-private partnership is the new freeway bridge of Millau.[25] It is a traditional concession where the private partner must earn the entire revenue though the toll fees charged to end-users. However, the government also accepts the risk of adding public funds if the number of road users is lower than the initially estimated number. However, so far, this has not been the case and the private partner is earning the expected revenue from toll-paying drivers.

The Millau bridge was opened to the public on 16 December 2004, six months before the expected date. Although the project was still agreed to under the concession model from before 2004, it represents an example of a public infrastructure project that was entirely designed and built by a private company. This company was Effiage, and it invested approximately 400 million Euros to build this bridge. In return, all vehicle drivers that wish to cross the bridge must pay a toll, and the private operator obtained a concession of 75 years to continue levying this fee and obtain a return on its investment. The construction of this bridge and the partnership has allowed the government to transfer the cost of construction to the private sector. The private partner, finally, will transfer control of the bridge to the French government, at the latest in the year 2124, and it is expected that the bridge will be in the condition that is comparable to other similar bridge constructions at that same age.

Given that contracts can last up to 90 years, it is important to consider the extent to which a government must tie itself to the terms of a contract. A government should always be able to keep its right to modify regulations or laws for the public interest, including changing legislation that has a direct impact on existing PPP agreements.[26] This protection for a government creates a link between a contractual agreement for public services to democratic rights by the public to oppose the contract. A government must be able to keep the right to modify "the rules of the game" when these become unacceptable in new circumstances or a changed policy environment. The example of water mismanagement in the French city of Grenoble suggests that governments should always maintain a supreme legal right to re-nationalise a public service or utility before the end of a contract if criminal offences and/or collusion and political lobbying can be proven.

Democratic Participation, Accountability & Oversight

Accountability is created through various sources or policies and regulations. It is developed when open competitive tendering procedures place the responsibility for public or parliamentary reporting on the shoulders of both parties. Accountability also arises where public or stakeholder participation is accepted and observed. This is particularly influential when reporting obligations are combined with public or parliamentary supervision. An example to illustrate the importance of democratic oversight and accountability is the case of the private water management of the city of Grenoble in France.[27] Another example is of the London Thames Water utility that was exposed to regulatory efforts by the government to respond to popular demands for better services. These cases indicate that public and political pressure can have a positive effect on the services supplied by a private company. In the French case of Grenoble, public pressure led to improvements of water management is discussed below. It holds lessons for the development of favourable conditions for PPPs that addresses at once public involvement through political parties, the importance of legal independence, and the need for security in terms fighting corruption and preventing governance crises.

The water scandal in Grenoble would not have come to light had it not been for a vocal civil society that could express its frustration through representatives in the city council. The democratic effect played a part in that politicians from left-leaning and environmental parties took on the public grievance as an election theme and won the council election in 1995. It began upon the news that a political leader had been involved in financial manipulations in favour of the private water company, public pressure groups and political parties with a strong environmental agenda protested against the rise of water prices and launched legal investigations into the financial records of the water company. They found that contract kickbacks, fictitious accounting and fraud had taken place between the politicians that had supported the privatisation of the water service and the water company Suez. Upon local government elections in 1995, the residents of Grenoble elected a new city council that had a stronger political focus on environmental and social policy. The city council decided then to reduce the amount of control that COGESE had over the water and sanitation infrastructure and "re-municipalised" 51% of the concession that was then controlled by a new publicly owned service, and the remaining 49% of control remained with Suez.

A very different approach, based on lessons learned in other countries, is the Dutch attempt to obtain broad political approval for its engagements in PPP contracts. The Dutch have begun to develop their own brand of PPPs that set the Dutch experience apart from the British experience, even though they officially consider the UK PFI as a model. In the Netherlands, however, broad political consent for PPP projects has helped offset potential anti-privatisation criticism. It also helped prevent lobbying from members of parliament or labour unions affiliated to the political parties to oppose the initiatives. The Netherlands government promotes PPPs via political programmes instead of individual projects. Thus, for example, a promotional program for public-private partnerships for the development of urban areas, or for water sanitation, first has to be approved either by the National or the provincial political authorities and parliaments.[28] The purpose is to ensure that modifications in public services obtain support from the democratically-elected parliament.

A way of encouraging greater public accountability and parliamentary trust in large PPP projects is through the creation of an autonomous Special Purpose Vehicle or SPV. In the agreement, such an SPV should allow for independent verifications and audits, as well as performance monitoring. The Dutch water treatment PPP project called Delfluent can be regarded as a good example of the creation of an independent consortium that allows for democratic (parliamentary oversight) and independence from specific commercial interests.[29] The local Delft government launched an international tender in 1999 and offered private companies an opportunity to propose the creation of a consortium in which the private and public sectors would share control, risks and responsibility. The tender included provisions for the design, finance, construction and operations of the site under a so-called DBFO procurement concession. The Delfluent company was incorporated in August 2003 and it signed the DBFO contract with the Delftland Water Board on 5 December 2003. The local government of Delft maintains ultimate responsibility for the quality of the output from the waste water treatment in both The Hague and Delft regions.

Finally, accountability can also be introduced through the inclusion of traditional community and new commercial stakeholders in PPPs for public services as can be found in Germany, for example. The development of PPPs has followed a bottom-up process where local municipal government offices initiated tenders and concessions with private companies.[30] PPPs were and still are mostly created for the construction or restoration of public buildings such as government administrative offices, police stations, prisons, schools, or public sports facilities. At the level of the German states (*Länder*) and at the national federal level, PPPs have been developed in the construction of highways, bridges, tunnels and other transportation facilities. Initially, the creation of public-private partnerships was only at the local municipality ("*Gemeinde*") level. Here, mostly municipalities or city governments engaged the private sector into binding partnerships for the delivery of mostly construction and the maintenance of physical public infrastructure. Thus, local administration initiated PPPs for schools and administrative buildings, as well as sports centres and local transportation infrastructure or security institutions such as prisons.

Competition and Long-Term Contracts

Competition is said to enhance economic efficiency. Within the liberal market, the logic of competition is broadly accepted as encouraging greater entrepreneurial dynamic and innovation. Actors are continuously obliged to find better and more cost effective ways of delivering a service or a commodity in order to maintain or enhance their position in the market or undercut the competition. This logic works in most industry sectors and services wherever competition remains open and ongoing. However, this is not so where industries can protect themselves from competition such as in a concession, nor does it always translate easily into services where the output is a value as much as it is a service. There are several reasons for this.

First, a personalised or person-to-person service is difficult to translate into a commodity when the expected result of the service is subjective. "To put it differently: the PPP model can be applied to all sectors if services can indeed be clearly specified, measured, and guaranteed—the trouble is that they cannot and [...] the extent to which they can differs across sectors."[31] What is more, the difficulty of measuring the quality of public services that can be considered as "soft infrastructures" is accentuated when the end output is as much a physical one as a value and dependent on the end-user's individual perception. Values are attached, for example, to services that provide individual satisfaction, a sense of security, or enjoyment. No contract, no matter how detailed it is, can prescribe how such personal values are to be created. What can be defined in a contract are ways of delivering a service. However, that may lead the provider to deliver what is expected in terms of physical output, but not what is expected in the form of added value. The dilemma is that an output cannot be defined in a contract unless it can be measured according to definable criteria. Without such definitions, a price cannot be assigned to the service and it cannot become a commodity for which a party is remunerated. The difficulty is that while the outcome of a service may be described very clearly, how the value is to be provided cannot be defined. Even in detailed descriptions of a delivery method, the person-to-person service remains in the realm of subjective human behaviour and perception. This includes things such as the way a teacher speaks to his or her pupils, or the way a nurse makes the patient feel better in a hospital. Good interpersonal relations increase effectiveness. Good teachers improve student performance and happy nurses can motivate patients to feel better sooner. However, this aspect of a service can hardly be defined in a commercial contract.

A key through which solutions are sought to circumvent this dilemma is by defining specific payment criteria that are incentive and result oriented. But the difficulty of defining a value-laden service is not eliminated thereby. For example, a private partner in a PPP can receive payments according to the number of students in school class or the number of beds filled in a hospital. But is this sufficient? If the private provider is paid for the number of beds filled, then the output of the service may be skewed in favour of the private company's profits; i.e., keep patients in the hospital for as long as possible without healing them. The issue here is twofold: First, that not every service can be commoditised because some depend on human care and attention, rather than on measurable results. Second, the payment method that is defined in a contract will inevitably influence how the private provider carries out the service. The latter must recover its investment and earn a profit, and it will interpret the contract as allowing it to do so. The payment method must therefore be based on performance criteria that can be measured, checked and evaluated in order to prevent that the end-user, or the hospital patient in this example, suffers a loss of quality service.

Not every public service or infrastructure can be subjected to open competition. Some public infrastructure and services constitute a natural monopoly. Only one actor, the government or a private agency, can hold such a monopoly. This is because competing actors cannot build parallel airports, water supply lines, sewage treatment plants or railroad and road networks in the same city or country. Some national infrastructures can be broken down into local geographic elements or systems, however, in an attempt to introduce a competitive element. This has been done in the communication sector, for example. Not only do many communication companies compete within individual countries, but they have also improved the service and reduced prices at the same time. However, the privatisation of communication was possible because its service to the customer could be quantified and its electronic technology allowed it to be broken down into system sections. This may not be possible with other large infrastructure systems such as electricity or water services. This is because these cannot be broken down into systemic sections with the help of technology. Electrical transmission networks remain large and expensive, and parallel systems managed by competing firms can hardly be introduced.[32] The same is the case with water delivery or waste water treatment, as well as for other infrastructures where parallel competition is difficult to introduce, such as with highways, railways, sea ports or airports. Breaking some of these systems down may merely create regional or local private monopolies instead of leaving a national State-operated monopoly— an option that is not necessarily more desirable. It is often better that within national and public natural monopolies, contracts with private providers allow for competition through more transparent bidding procedures and short-term contracts that allow for the entry of new private actors among providers that bring along more innovation.

Long-term contractual arrangements can be counter-productive if they eliminate the business logic of entrepreneurial competition and innovation. Most PPPs are set up on the basis of long-term contracts that give the private company a number of years or even decades to carry out the given task. The length of this period is to allow for a recovery of the private company's investment costs and earn a profit, and to provide stability and security for the provider vis-à-vis the competition. Commercial long-term and life-cycle PPPs are most often concession-type contracts that give the private company an exclusive right to build and operate a public infrastructure and/or public service. The longer such contracts last, the less opportunity there is for competitive pressures to bring prices down and innovation up. When agreements last for decades—usually 30 or more—it becomes difficult to see how a business logic of competition can still be considered advantageous. Within a safe timeframe and protected from competitive bids, the private provider can become inefficient and unwilling to adapt to changing needs. However, flexibility and adaptability are the hallmarks of successful companies that excel in today's rapidly changing globalised economy. Long-term concession contracts appear like a modern version of pre-liberal market protectionism where private infrastructure and service providers can find refuge. From a liberal-market perspective that favours economic efficiency, short-term outsourcing of public infrastructure and services through frequent competitive bidding may be far more cost effective than long-term concessions. This issue can also be questioned as follows: do governments favour a quick turn-over of short-term contracts in order to maximise competitive bidding among a larger number of potential private providers, or do they need to leverage large capital investments from the private sector and are therefore willing to give long-term concession exclusivity to only one private provider?

It is unlikely that these two aspects can ever be reconciled—competitive tendering and long-lasting concessions. This is also mentioned in recommendations on public procurements by international agencies such as the OECD.[33] Once a tendering process is finished and the government has selected the winning bidder to receive the concession contract, the competition that provided for innovative proposals vanishes. This is primarily because once the chosen private provider signs the contract, it has exclusive rights to provide the service for the duration of the contract period. No other external competitor can enter the project with competing offers until the contract comes to its agreed end. This is the particular characteristic of concession agreements. As many if not most PPPs are set up on the basis of some form of concession agreement, even if these include various forms of revenue streams or re-payment methods such as lease or end-user fees, the exclusivity that concessions give the concessionaire remains. This can be a problem when the concessionaire is not motivated to reduce operation costs on the basis of the payment incentives built into a concession revenue stream.

To compensate for the loss of open market competition during long-term concession contracts, other methods are sought to ensure efficiency and innovation. The principal means to ensure continued high performance on the part of the private provider is to make the payment method contingent on desired outputs. Payment methods can often be designed in such a way as to incentivise the private provider to deliver the kind of output that is desired. But all this hinges on the capacity to define the output clearly in a contract. To highlight the importance of the payment method, one need only ask whether a private provider, that operates a hospital for example, is paid by the public partner for the number of days that patients stay in a hospital, for the type of illnesses treated, or for the number of patients healed and released. Whichever method is used, it will result in different operational performances. For example, the company may try to keep patients as long as possible in the hospital, or try to send them home as quickly as possible to maximise its profits; and each extreme can lead to disastrous results for the patient.

Furthermore, where payment methods allow the private provider to earn extra income from offering additional (private) services, the general public may find itself marginalised in favour of those "customers" that can pay additional fees. In the United Kingdom, for example, the number of private beds in some public hospitals has risen because the private provider could "sell" a better and more expensive service to patients who are willing to pay the price. In this way, hospitals have sought to increase the number of private beds to raise their revenue.[34] But the example of private beds in public hospitals is not so different from other paid end-user services within public infrastructures. Toll roads, private security or school fees are a similar example, social equity is at risk where public services are offered to those who can pay for them. Put differently, open competition may be fine for those customers who can pay for a service or for the use of an infrastructure, but it will marginalise the general public who expect equitable access to public services paid for by their taxes. The structure of the payment method within a PPP contract is therefore most important and needs to be designed in such a way that the general public does not need to compete to obtain the services or have access to the public infrastructure.

Complexity of Contracts

It would not be an understatement to say that a contract with simple and clear output criteria will have a greater chance of being successful. The OECD concedes that there is "an emerging consensus" that the simpler the criteria for output rewards are in the tendering procedures, the more likely that contracts will result in fruitful PPPs.[35] In contrast, the more complex a contract becomes because of the diversity of financial sources, the types of risks and responsibilities allocated to the parties, and the payment methods included, the less likely it will be that a PPP contract will be put into operation smoothly until the end of the contract period. Complexity may introduce other risks. For example, reduce the number of potential bidding companies or consortia during the competitive tendering process because only a very small number of private providers can actually fulfil the criteria. This inevitably reduces the competitive element that is meant to introduce cost efficiency into the procurement process. Another consequence from very complex criteria in a proposed contract is that it becomes very difficult for the government that issued the tender to decide which private provider to select.

One might conclude, then, that complexity increases to the degree that sources of investment increase that are from a diversity of sources. At the same time, the longer a contract will last for, the more difficult it becomes to include provisions for change in the future. The length of a contract is intended to allow the private provider the necessary time to recover its investments and earn a profit, it also will make the contract more complex. This means that highly complex financial deals may create the risk of higher transaction costs.

A good example of such costs, first in finding the right commercial partners able to fulfil a highly complex tendered proposal, and then executing it can be seen in London city's metro PPP.[36] It is one of the largest PPPs in the world with one of the most complex concession agreements ever designed. Two main private partners and a large number of smaller concessions and subcontracts going to minor private firms are included. The London Underground Limited (LUL) is the public sector partner today responsible for overseeing the operations and maintenance of the entire public transportation metro network in London. Upon the recommendations of a large consulting company in 1997, the government and the LUL were separated into one operation company and three privately operated infrastructure companies, the so-called "infracos." The Underground became an example of the difficulty to provide very complicated public services through the involvement of two principal and many subsidiary companies and concessionaires.

Truly open competition for commercial partners never existed in the London underground PPP structure. First, the original infracos were created to accommodate at once the city authority's needs and the interests of various private companies that agreed to be involved in the PPP deal to maintain the underground system. These principal private companies are large and well-known construction and engineering firms, namely WS-Atkins, Balfour Beatty, Bombardier, EDF Energy and Thames Water. The infracos have been unable to keep costs down as was expected by the public authorities and one of them, Metronet, stands accused of spending more money than necessary to its concessionaires, which are also its shareholder construction and engineering firms. It is commonly acknowledged that this led to a lack of price competition as other outside and independent private companies could not enter the market to bid for contracts with Metronet.[37]

Governments may commit themselves into contractual "straightjackets" if they do not negotiate for a degree of regulatory flexibility. The more complex, or the longer a concession contract is to last, the more likely that aspects of the deal must be re-negotiated. This may arise for various reasons. For example, on the side of the private partner, it may undergo internal structural changes following a business merger, a new acquisition, or because it goes on or comes off the stock market. Another reason may be social where the private provider suffers because of problematic employee-employer relations. On the side of the public partner, a long-lasting contract may need to be re-negotiated because the government decides to introduce new regulations or legal amendments that modify the context of the agreement or the way the private provider is to deliver the output.

To reduce the number of costly re-negotiations and transaction costs, flexibility must be built into it from the start. The contractual agreement should clearly indicate when modification must be discussed and who will carry the burden of financial costs if any should arise. There is an almost unavoidable tension in every contract between flexibility and strong regulation and control. Oversight over the performance of a provider (whether public or private) is only possible where clear criteria and performance benchmarks have been established and agreed to by the partners beforehand. This requires that contracts have a durability and stability that both partners can trust and base their investment and operational decisions on. At the same time, there is a great difficulty in defining a balance between this necessary clarity in the contract and (for quality and quantity of the output) and the need for flexibility and adaptability. Without the latter, a government may find itself caught in a contractual agreement that may not respond to changing political, social or economic needs. While most contracts contain phrases that oblige the private partner to adapt its work according to government regulations and laws, this is similar to the obligation any business has to remain within the legal and regulatory obligations of the country it wishes to operate in. However, in long-term contractual arrangements, such as PPPs, "a case can be made for relying on formal agreements leaving little scope for regulatory discretion," and for which the OECD concedes that more flexibility in contracts is preferred in order to accommodate a changing environment.[38]

Another way to provide for some flexibility or resolve this dilemma of finding a balance between contractual stability and change is to incorporate regular reviews of the deal in the contract from the start. One example here is the London Underground PPP where a guarantee for financial flexibility is incorporated in the contract. It can be re-negotiated every 7.5 years following a review process. When there are disputes between the parties an agreed arbitration procedure that was included in the original agreement can be engaged in. Governments can build into a contract a provision for regular cooperative evaluations, or evaluations carried out by external independent agencies. In the tendering process and contract negotiation period, safeguards for flexibility can be included by the involvement from the start of external experts from specialised regulatory bodies. The example of Partnerships UK is one way for governments to obtain external support to build in flexibility and regulatory strength in a contract. The latter is operated by both private and public partners and provides advisory and regulatory support in the developmental process of a PPP.[39] The involvement of external verification and regulatory agencies that are acceptable to all negotiators in a PPP deal is one way to assure better future adaptability of a contract to the changing environment.[40]

Flexibility is also necessary for a political or policy-related aspect. It can never be excluded that a government administration may decide to modify policies on specific types of public infrastructure or services that then alter the context in which a PPP contract was agreed to. This then entails re-negotiations with the private partners which inevitable new transaction costs. It is, however, normally accepted that a state government has a sovereign right to modify any legislation or regulation if it sees such changes to be in the public or national interest. This leads to a problem of policy sovereignty verses contractual obligation. In any commercial sector where private companies work, regulatory changes or legal amendments must be incorporated into the company's work if it wishes to remain legally operational on the country's territory. However, where public services and public infrastructure are tied to a long-term contract, it becomes more difficult for a government to impose new regulations onto a private partner, unless the public partner accepts to pay for the added costs or compensation to a PPP deal that such changes will incur. This possible additional cost to a PPP is explained further under risk allocation below.

Finally, notwithstanding the best contract design, disputes can and do arise among the parties and some agreed methods to resolve them can be included in the contract. The contracts can include arbitrational instances to which the parties agree in advance and which can be engaged when they find themselves faced with serious problems for which an independent external mediator or arbitrator is needed. A sustainable contractual agreement or "sustainable arrangements" is supposed to be written in such a way that all stakeholders will have confidence that they will obtain treatment in case of disputes.[41]

There is a great need for better information and training in the development of PPPs, the negotiation of contracts, and the verification of an agreement's output. Many local governmental agencies are gradually familiarising themselves with PPP contracts, negotiation methods, preparation of standards, criteria and evaluation methods, etc. However, as the procurement process with PPPs is more complex than traditional procurement methods, more training and knowledge sharing is important.[42]

In the private water management example of the city of Grenoble in France, it also had become clear following the financial scandals that, during the years the Suez water company operated the city's water infrastructure, it invested far less to update and improve the service than had been expected.[43] This was a great disappointment because the Suez company had earned high profits during its full control over the city's water service.

What does this mean for this study? Public sector authorities must be very well informed and skilled in negotiating with the private sector. This is all the more important where the private firm or consortium is a powerful and experienced national or international company that can pay for experienced consultants and negotiating teams to bargain for a contract that will be in their favour. The public sector must prepare a call for tenders through a well-regulated procurement process. From the tender onwards, output criteria must be clearly defined and included in all procurement steps through to the end of the contract negotiations. Public services, whether operated by public enterprises or by private businesses need to be regulated and followed-up with by independent government appointed auditors and quality controllers. This is to ensure that once the contract is negotiated, that the public service provider will meet the required criteria.

Risk Allocation

A reason often given for why PPPs offer a potentially more cost-effective option for governments to procure large infrastructure and services is that they can shift risks onto the private partner. Risk allocation is determined by the model of agreement and the payment mechanism that is chosen. One of the most commonly accepted argument for why PPPs are thought to be more cost efficient for a government is because the latter can transfer risks and associated costs to the private partner. The principle generally accepted is that a risk is allocated to the party that is best able to absorb and control it. However, risk-allocation is not a straightforward affair and usually very difficult to carry out on the basis of expected outcomes and costs. Furthermore, it behoves to remember that each partner only accepts the risk it is willing to pay for should an unexpected event happen.[44] This means that the risk which can be mitigated by the private partner, for example, such as operational efficiency, should be borne by this partner. In contrast, the risk of a public-interest nature, such as public attitudes or modifications in the regulatory framework can be borne by the public partner.

In essence, risk analysis or the assessment of probabilities is a calculation of what is possible in the future based on what happened in the past; i.e., it is based on the assumption that the past determines the future. It is also assumed that it is possible to analyse what happened in the past and discover patterns. The basis of risk assessment is the systematic use of analytical and probability-based methods that have been developed over decades to better comprehend the cause and effect relationship.

In detail, risk assessment is the generation of knowledge linking specific risk agents with uncertain but possible consequences. The outcome of risk assessment is an estimation of risk in terms of probability distribution on the basis of consequences that have been identified and quantified. Core components to risk assessment are, first, an identification and an estimation of hazards; and second, an assessment of exposure and/or vulnerability. The estimation of risk for any given activity, such as the creation of a PPP, is through an evaluation of the strength of the relationship among: (a) the likelihood of an undesirable event, (b) the severity of this event, (c) the known hazardous characteristics and (d) the activity's vulnerability or exposure to this undesirable event.

The most common types of risks as discussed and that are included in the assessment of a PPP's financial viability are construction risk, availability risk, demand risk, transfer risk and regulatory risk. Besides these, there are forms of risk that are beyond the normal assessment capacity and for which insurance companies may provide some protection guarantees. The latter, together with most financial institutions and banks, specialise in risk evaluation. However, none can estimate the likelihood of an event that has never happened in the past, nor evaluate the vulnerability of a public service or infrastructure to hazards that have not yet manifested themselves. This is why contract renegotiation and related transaction costs are unavoidable. In addition, no financial institution or insurance can envisage the likelihood of drastic policy changes in government administrations or the effect that insecurity or environmental problems may have on the consumption of public services and thus on the revenue stream these are expected to provide. Another type of risk that cannot be assessed in advance is public opinion. Public and media pressures may focus on specific public sector activities and "serve to override specific commercial terms in a contract, generally resulting in a renegotiation of the contract at higher cost. Such risks need to be taken into account."[45]

Long-term contractual arrangements between financial institutions and builders of infrastructure always contain risk and careful assessments are most often made before contracts are signed and capital is invested. However, PPP contracts are not ordinary long-term construction contracts. What distinguishes them is the interdependence they create between private involvement in public services and public infrastructure operation and the risks associated with privately raised capital. This interdependence constitutes a risk that is not only linked to financial contracts with lenders and suppliers around the world, but also to the regional economic and political environments that affect them. A number of non-financial events can alter the contractual agreement considerably as soon as they impact on the financial health of any of the partners in the PPP deal. Such events can be changes in global economic conditions, as well as natural or man-made accidents or catastrophes for which insurance companies may provide some financial protection and compensation, but which due to their severity go beyond the risk or compensation that insurance packages and financial partners could estimate in advance.

For example, the French toll highways ("autoroutes") are probably the best-known privatised or semi-privatised transportation infrastructures in Europe. These were beset with financial problems not because of poor risk assessment or planning, but because the private partners could not earn a return on their investments through the road toll once Europe's economy suffered severely from the oil embargo in the 1970s. The result was that the national government had to bail out the private providers with tax-payers' money in order to keep the highways open. In contrast, a very recently completed PPP project is the Millau bridge which, so far, appears to prove a success in both, execution and financial management.

The London Underground offers another kind of example of the difficulty to provide very complicated public services through the involvement of several private companies that each have different PPP contracts with the public sector authority.[46] The two the principal private partners of the London Underground are Metronet and Tube Lines. Each is responsible for different metro lines, but obviously these cross each other not only at tube stations, but also throughout the city's operations infrastructure, from underground water and communications networks to above-ground managerial and public interfaces.

While risks can be broken down and covered for by the most capable partners, it remains nevertheless that when economic crises or large problems occur, the government is ultimately responsible to ensure that the public service remains operational. Government is accountable to its public and must in one way or another pay for or guarantee necessary services (inevitably with public funds and tax-payers' money). In contrast, the private partner usually negotiates for financial guarantees from the government within a PPP contract to cover for unforeseen events and high-risk conditions. The private partner will usually also contract adequate insurance to cover for unexpected costs and to reduce its risk. This implies that when risk-sharing can be defined and agreed to, a PPPs may offer the government a project with reduced risk-related cost, so long as unexpected costs do not arise and operational conditions remain unproblematic. It is obvious, however, that the longer a project is to last, the greater the risk of unexpected problems and events grows and needs to be covered and accounted for—a cost for which someone must be ready to pay.

Security and Financial Risk

As was pointed out earlier, PPPs introduce an extension of concession agreements with private companies for the delivery of public services. Rather than maintain full control over these services or infrastructures, governments leave it to the private providers exclusive rights to service a given market or population. With this contractual change of public procurement, there comes another change of global proportions, namely the globalisation of trade and financial markets. This introduces another type of risks into the picture of PPPs and public services. These risks are due to and associated with the financial conditions under which the private provider raises its finances for the PPP. If the money is raised on global financial markets, then the company may inadvertently render the delivery of public services contingent on the health of global finance.

As the "subprime" mortgage debt crisis shows, financial markets are not permanently stable and crises cannot be eliminated, not even in the most sophisticated economic sectors. In addition, the rapid growth of mergers and acquisitions during the past ten years, financial assets, liabilities and debt financing schemes have become globally interdependent. This raises the difficult question whether public services, in particular vital ones such as healthcare, water distribution, or transportation, should be made dependent on the financial health of private providers in PPP-type concession contracts that are, in turn, dependent on the financial credit they leverage out of global markets.

Public services operated and financed through large PPPs are often a direct product of this globalisation trend. In most large PPP or PFI deals, the private partners are not traditional firms with a simple hierarchy of business management – "traditional" corporate management by a CEO who shares the same culture with his or her regional managers. Rather, the business partners in PPPs are more often very large conglomerates of companies from different countries and business cultures that join forces to better compete for government tenders. Their motive is primarily profit sharing and increasing their investment capacity. The quality public services offered at the most reasonable price to end-users is hardly within the interest of asset managers. Nor is their intention one of earning less profit and spend more to ensure better environmental protection. Private companies are also not concerned about delivering public services to a public that cannot pay for them at market price. This is the responsibility of government; it must ensure that low-income earners within a population benefit from the public services infrastructure to the same degree as high-income customers. Therefore, agreements between public authorities and private providers must often include provisions for government subsidy to the private company so that it will supply the necessary equity in access and distribution.

In addition, the take-overs or even sometimes hostile buy-out of shares of firms of any size and culture changes management structures and ownership. Asset management companies and their CEOs focus on short-term profit-oriented strategies, often in disregard of the long-term stability of the companies they buy in to, or for the re-packaged debt / equity portfolios they invest in. Their investment and disinvestment strategies are purely financial transactions on a globalised financial market, but they do also affect real people tied to interdependent economic production chains. As the mortgage debt crisis in the USA shows, the ordinary end-user and customer of public services and commodities eventually feels the effect.

What does this mean for PPPs/PFIs? Public services and infrastructure, when financed through private funds that are leveraged out of asset management and debt financing schemes become less resilient to risks. PPPs become dependent on and susceptible to global economic and finance markets which are themselves linked to the way major players such as multinational banks package their debts or their assets. In addition, as the cost of borrowing is dependent on lending rates established by central banks, which in turn react to global and national political and economic pressures when to lower or increase their rates, public services in one locality can, through a PPP deal, become linked to financial operations in far-away banks, asset management companies or governments. In other words, globalised interdependency ties public services to financial markets in ways that never existed before; or to put it differently, the operation of public transport in a city can come to a grinding halt for millions of commuters because a private provider is in financial trouble and declares bankruptcy. The example of the London underground serves as a poignant example.

The fear of foreign influence in domestic public services is not a new concern for national governments and many governments have set ceiling limits as to how much percentage of a public infrastructure can be owned by non-national companies. On occasion, national governments wake up to this fact and try to protect "strategic" infrastructure from foreign influence. Thus, the Japanese government recently blocked the purchase of 20% of a national electricity company J-Power to a UK company called The Children's Investment Fund (TCI). For the first time, the blockage was justified by the Japanese government on the basis of "national security." The government declared that the British investment creates serious concerns for the security of nuclear energy production and the recycling of used nuclear fuel.[47]

Another element that places public services at an increasing risk in the wake of globalised PPP / PFI deals is public safety and security. All the large PPP contracts are complex and legally-binding concession agreements that tie public and private partners into long-lasting contractual obligations. The intervening variables that challenge public services in every case are crises. These may be natural catastrophes, accidents or terrorist attacks, or economic crises. They are crises in every instance and their prevention or the post-crisis recovery that is needed is inevitably a complicated affair. Rapid action for humanitarian relief or prevention inevitably requires clear and well coordinated management. However, proactive planning for costly prevention or for expensive post-crisis recovery is rarely a part of financial planning among public and private actors tied to contractual commitments. But not only the cost calculation is a risk factor, also the complexity of rapid decision-making following crises poses a serious challenge. This is for the simple reason that the more actors have a financial stake in decision-making, the slower decisions are taken. In situations of crisis, however, there may not be time for deliberation and the unexpected high costs of recovery may lead private providers to opt for their internal financial priorities. In many cases, crisis recovery is left to the government to deal with and to the ordinary citizen to pay for. While insurance contracts may offset unexpected expenses for the private providers, the end-user will not benefit from such protection when the metro or the trains stops operating or when drinking water is polluted due to industrial accidents or mismanagement.

EFFICIENCY, SUSTAINABILITY, EQUITY AND SECURITY

Cost and Value for Money

The debate about privatization and private control over public assets is most often linked to the argument that the best value for public money is the priority. This approach to the question of for or against PPPs hinges on how the cost of public services can be evaluated, and this is precisely the most difficult aspect of PPPs. Besides reports on the positive evolution of PPPs in Europe and the benefits of lessons learned in the UK regarding the PFI model, there are numerous critical evaluations and studies that contradict the positive appraisals. They question the method of Value for Money (VFM) calculation and the government's policy that underlies the maximisation of private sector involvement in public services and public infrastructure.[48] The criticism is strongest against those PFI or PPP contracts in which public service to end-users in the form of person-to-person care, as in a hospital, is the expected output in contrast to the mere construction or operation of a public facility.[49]

The question of how cost efficiency is evaluated is highly dependent on the political and ideological culture and history of a country. This is not merely a question of technical accounting procedures, although it is that as well. Rather, cost efficiency is a concept defined by national and individual values and policy priorities. While it is not possible here to define cost accounting procedures, nor provide technical and financial efficiency comparisons, it is possible to point towards the challenges that arise when speaking about PPPs. This is particularly important in light of the many proponents of PPPs who claim that such projects are more cost efficient than traditional procurement methods. In some countries, especially those with a tradition of financial redistribution, the price for the users of public infrastructure and services can be adjusted according to the financial capacity of the public to pay for them. In other political cultures, the cost to the end-user may be set artificially low for all citizens and then subsidized by the government (tax revenues). These are policy priority questions, and in any format of delivery and payment for them, there are possible models of public and private involvement and partnership.

A first reason for why it is very difficult to know the exact figure of finances invested in a PPP is because the private partner rarely divulges its internal financial arrangements with banks and financial institutions such as debt equity and asset management firms. There is therefore a lack of transparency from the private sector's side of the deal, in particular where private finances are sources from different types of financial institutions in different locations around the world.

In the public sector, however, it is normally expected in Western countries that governments can provide clear and transparent accounts of their annual expenses. In the traditional procurement of public infrastructure or services, financial management remained within the sole responsibility of the government. With the involvement of private providers who are given responsibilities that include financing, the roles of the buyer and the provider of the public service are not only separated, but also blended in various ways. This becomes especially the case when both partners provide finances and when the revenue stream is not a straightforward payment from government to private partner, but also a blend of revenue streams. For example a PPP project may include lease payments by the government inside a concession agreement through which the private provider collects user-fees and external revenues. Next to the revenue stream, the input of investment may also be a blend of different methods. Thus, a PPP can be financed by money that is brought in by the government as well as by the private partner(s), and that is leveraged out of capital funds, borrowed assets or equity funds. Each source of financing will have different cost structures attached that are linked to interest rates, grants or other external cost-determining factors.

To evaluate fully how much public services cost either through traditional procurement or through a PPP, and to know how much they contribute to human wellbeing and economic development is difficult if not impossible. The simple adding up of expenses for a government over the time period of a procurement contract is insufficient because it excludes externalities that can reduce or increase the total cost-benefit assessment. Each individual infrastructure or public service will have different costs and benefits depending on geographic, demographic and market characteristics, as well as on the capacity for the public sector to manage a complex tendering process for a PPP. For example, if a project is estimated to cost less in the form of a PPP than through a traditional procurement, this cost saving may be cancelled out through additional transaction costs, for example, if the public office in charge of the tendering and negotiation process needs far more time to negotiate the agreement with the private provider.

A difficulty in assessing the cost efficiency of PPPs is that governments often enter into such contractual agreements in order leverage the initial financial investment from the private sector. They do this either because they cannot raise the necessary finances alone, or because they want to avoid recording the capital-intensive expense that would have been necessary at the initial stage of the procurement in their financial records (as in off-the-record procurement). This allows the government to keep this initial capital cost off the government record. It is only at a later agreed stage during the contract period that the government pays the private partner back in regular instalments for the investment and expenses. Such payment instalments, however, may work out to cost the government more over the long-term than if the public sector had from the start built and operated the same infrastructure alone. This has been shown in appraisals of the costs within the British health service, for example.[50]

Another example to show how difficult it can be to estimate the total cost of a PPP project concerns the private provider's possible operational efficiency. This concerns its cost savings due to the external consequential value that it may bring into the deal. Here, the private sector may have more flexibility in sub-contracting work to other firms, or in purchasing what is needed than a government office. The private provider may also be able to obtain approvals for new capital financing more quickly than a government ministry as its work cycle is not dependent on public budgetary cycles or parliamentary approval. At the same time, however, the private sector may not be able to borrow money for the low rate at which public authorities can obtain loans, and they may be unwilling to subcontract work to other private firms according to open competitive bidding procedures—both factors that can again counter the expected cost efficiency enumerated above. All this is to say that differentials in cost comparison between public and private capacities and between the total costs of a public service procured in the traditional manner and another procured through a PPP is far more difficult and complicated than proponents of PPPs often argue.

Cost efficiency may also be considered in another light, namely the extent to which a government must record the expenses in cash or in-kind in its financial records. The European Union has tried to design recommendations on how this off-the-record option can be realised.[51] The Eurostat recommends that assets involved in long-term concession contracts such as in public-private partnerships can be classified as non-governmental assets and off the balance sheet in the public budget or financial expenses. This provides for how EU member countries can use a PPP model to keep expenses out of their fiscal reports by letting a private provider pay for a public infrastructure or service first. Repayments for the government are then a liability to be re-paid to the private provider over a number of years. For this to be possible, Eurostat requires that a PPP project can transfer two of the three principal risk categories to the private partner. These are that "the private partner bears the construction risk, and the private partner bears one of either availability or demand risk." This implies that for a government to be able to record a PPP off its annual balance sheet, the private partner must bear most of the risk. There is no doubt, however, that risk cannot always be classified so clearly. For example, is a change in consumer behaviour always a mere demand risk external to a PPP project, or could the government partner actually influence demand to the detriment of the private partner? This was the case with the PPP toll road and tunnel in Rostock, Germany, where the city government did not undertake timely road transformations on the old road to encourage drivers to take the new toll road instead.[52]

Next to this option of keeping the initial capital expense by the PPP's private provider off the government record, a government can also realise a cost efficiency in another way. It can design a PPP contract in which it provides public assets as an in-kind contribution to a private partner for a specified time. The latter then operates the public infrastructure and service to recover its investment and earn a profit, and then returns the public asset back to the government at the end of the contact period.[53]

What is more, some PPPs may actually provide revenue to the government. This is in the case of projects where the end-users pay a fee which over the entire contract period reaches over the cost recovery and profit that the private partner obtains. This occurs in two situations. One is the PPP such as toll highways, for example, where over the long-term, the government can record a revenue stream from the project.[54] The other case occurs where the contract provides that if the private partner earns unexpected "windfall" earnings, it is obliged to share these with the government partner.

The assessment of efficiency will have to depend on some dominant factors, namely the type of public infrastructure and/or service, the existence of comparable finished public infrastructures services that have been procured in the traditionally fashion and are operated by the government alone, and the type of revenue stream provided for in the contract. Studies abound that argue for and against PPPs and PFIs on the basis of how they evaluate the cost-benefit equation.[55] A very general conclusion that can be made as a footnote here is that hard infrastructure projects are generally more easily evaluated for their cost efficiency than soft public services. Some analysts, government offices and private companies involved in PPPs argue in favour of PPPs for their cost advantages while other analysts argue against PPPs, or at a minimum, recommend great caution. Although some analysts assert that PPPs offer better cost efficiency and value for money over traditional public procurement methods, the evidence from this research points towards an ambiguous result. Aspects of this cost efficiency question are discusses below within the context of project finances and risks the partners assume in PPP projects; however, the issue will remain a contentious one.

An example of how the advantages of PPPs are hailed can be found in the justification provided by one of the world's largest private contractors, the German firm Hochtief. It bases its argument on a study by the UK National Audit Office that on average some 17 percent of public infrastructure projects that have been realised in the UK are more efficient than non-PPP projects that were traditionally procured. The reasons for the cost savings are lower investment costs because the private partner looks at the project within a PPP the entire life-cycle. In this manner, whole costs can be optimised through contract periods of 20 to 30 years. In addition, there are shortened planning and construction times, as well as better business practices and maintenance of the projects.

Another advantage that is often mentioned to underline the cost benefit of PPPs is "economy of scale." Indeed, economies of scale play an important role in effective competition and lower costs. The term economies of scale refers to the situation in which the unit cost of production is lower in a factory, plant or other business of larger size than in a smaller one, even where the input material prices remain unchanged over a given period. The larger company may obtain inputs, including finance for investment, at a lower price than smaller companies. For example, economies of scale can be obtained regarding material input prices where producers of steel or concrete, for example, offer larger quantities at lower unit prices, a practice which favours large plants. Economies of scale can more often be obtained in both unit capital costs and unit labour costs. For example, in unit capital costs, an increase in the scale of output may not require a proportionate increase in the initial investment. This is mostly because many material assets of a company can produce higher output without needing a proportionate increase in size, strength or capital investment. Concerning the unit labour costs, here again an increase in the scale of a plant or business will not require a proportionate increase in the number of employees. For example, wither a construction company is small or large, it may operate with one engineer among its employees. Also, a larger business can more easily rationalise the work output of each employee and thus make labour more productive for the company's own profit. This implies that companies of larger size tend to have a price and profitability advantage over smaller companies and in this sense, economies of scale play a crucial role in the cost effectiveness sought for in public services and infrastructure.

What is more, economies of scale may also play a "non economic role." This is in government policy-making where large industrial groups may try to influence decision-making. The larger companies are and the more influence they can bring to bear on the labour and capital markets, the more they may manage to organise lobbying campaigns to influence government policy and secure government contracts. The economy of scale calculation is the principal reason for mergers and acquisitions among all sorts of companies. At the local and the international levels, the drive towards greater competitiveness and market share plays an important role in the formation of conglomerates that compete for government PPP contracts. Within the context of government procurements, PPPs offer large companies the advantage to compete when they make use of their internal economies of scale to propose a fully bundled service from beginning to end of a public infrastructure and service.

Cost efficiency may be obtained in PPPs in which an end-user fee contributes to cost recovery may also have a better chance of being financially sound for the public sector. Here, the government is not alone in repaying the private sector partner during the contract period. In contrast, when PPPs bundle construction and long-term services in one contract and, for example, include hospital health care, then the risk of reduced public control over the expenses may be higher.[56]

Within public procurements, to aim for the lowest cost at all times may be misleading. It can lead to problems in both private and public services. A focus on price and cost alone will, like in the open market of cheap consumerism, lead to a continuous reduction of quality. Where the market allows for the entry of competing providers, customers can re-orient their buying habits and opt for a quality-price calculation instead of a quantity-price ratio. However, where public services and infrastructure are a natural monopoly of one traditional provider (usually the government) because, for example, competing companies cannot build parallel water mains, electricity grids, airports or railroad tracks, unsatisfactory delivery of public services will lead to public call for a change in government policy where this is possible or to individual solutions.[57]

In conclusion, the efficiency of PPPs can be evaluated only where sources of finances and the flows of funds is transparent; and this is not a simple imperative. This is, because finances may include sources from various private lenders and investors, from public sources and from private borrowing by public authorities, as well as from end-user fees. How these various financial flows are assessed is not only a factor of accounting. It is also a factor dependent on the culture and method by which accounting procedures are recorded and audited by government or independent authorities. What all this may amount to, as suggested earlier, is cost-related appraisals become increasingly difficult as the interdependence between private and often multinational involvement in the operation of public infrastructure and services is tied to capital assets that have been raised through private firms around the world. Through the involvement of private finance in public assets, PPPs are a very different from of contract than traditional government procurement models.

Sustainable Development

Besides the aspects of PPPs mentioned above that include procurement, social equity, cost-effectiveness and risk allocation, some new considerations are gaining in importance. These are sustainable development and security. Within Western countries where information and debate is open, sustainable development and security have attracted much debate over recent years. This is in the context of the societal value that is given to public goods, public services and national infrastructure, its development and its perception in public awareness, in the media and popular dialogue, and in policy trends. Today, the importance given to sustainable development and security is on a rapid upswing, not least because globally well-known individuals have lobbied for their incorporation in the national policy of every country.[58]

The term sustainable development means that nothing should be done today that will reduce the health and welfare of future generations. Rephrased, maximising our human well-being today should be in a way that also permits equally good well-being in the future. This includes all aspects of human life, not merely the preservation of nature. Sustainability is equally important in industry, financial markets, international trade, social policy, international relations, research and development or human security for all. Sustainable development not only implies that the way industry and day-to-day human activities have to change, but also that our conception of human life must change. Human existence is not somehow separate from its environment. Rather, it is interdependent with the environment. The way human activity affects the health of the planet directly influences the health of each individual person. Sustainable development is therefore not merely an attempt to improve the way industry innovates cleaner production systems that pollute less and are more energy efficient. Sustainability is just as much a part of day-to-day decision-making at all levels, from the individual person to the collective policy-making in national governments.

Government procurement of public services and public infrastructure is an integral part of the way human decisions affect the sustainability of the quality of life for future generations. How governments purchase services, how they design procurement policies and agree to the delivery of public services has a direct effect on the long-term sustainability of economic development and human well-being. One reason for why it is so important that governments take measures to incorporate sustainable development in their activities is because they are among the most important buyers of goods and services within their national markets. Whether it is new government office buildings and office furniture, or highways and hospitals, in all development and usage of public services and infrastructure, the cost incurred on the natural environment and the importance given to sustainable development have a direct influence on how other industries in a country operate. But governments are not only buyers of services and infrastructure for which they set sustainability criteria and oblige private providers to put these into practice. State and regional governments often own and control State-owned enterprises (SOEs). In these cases, the government produces public assets and must then set the example through its development of public services and infrastructure according to regulations and laws that incorporate sustainable development principles. In doing so, public-sector enterprises, as well as government outsourcing according to sustainable development standards will incentivises private industry to incorporate the same standards.

SUSTAINABLE PROCUREMENT AND OPERATION

All Western European governments do recognise the importance of environmental protection and most political leaders and political parties have taken "green" policy proposals on board. Through their procurement, governments can create an important impact on a national economy and set an example to industry. This is one strong argument in support of sustainable procurement policies.

The OECD Environmental Outlook to 2030 outlines the criticality of global pollution and damage done to the nature by industry and modern life styles.[59] The report synthesises the greatest challenges that threaten our natural environment and eventually our globalised industrial economy. The study outlines policy measures that all industrialised countries and emerging economies should undertake to avoid a global environmental bankruptcy. The warnings signs of reduced biodiversity and increased pollution are taken seriously and the risk to national economies is real according to this study. Its recommendations follow on the heels of earlier reports and international conventions, such as the Stern Report (2006), the *Global Environmental Outlook* by the United Nations Environment Programme (UNEP), United Nations Framework Convention on Climate Change, the work of the World Business Council for Sustainable Development (WBCSD), and the first global report on the sustainability of modern society, the Brundtland Commission that published *Our Common Future* upon the first UN environment summit in 1992.[60]

With regard to sustainable development, the greatest challenges, however, are twofold: First, the elaboration of sustainable procurement regulations, and second, follow-up verification that the private partners abide by existing legislation and regulations. The principal reason why PPP or PFI contracts are of special concern when sustainable criteria or security are considered is because of their usually long-lasting concession contracts. The risk is that with long contracts, the partners are unwilling to introduce changes such as adapting to new security needs or new environmental protection standards.

In essence, contract-bound partners should remain capable to adapt to new needs as these come to the forefront either through new scientific research on issues such as global warming, or because of unexpected new security and public safety needs. For both of these considerations, there are plenty of examples in recent years that show how public infrastructure needs to adapt. For example, airports must incorporate new security measures to prevent airline high-jacking, and public transportation systems must prevent suicide bombing. Regarding sustainable development, new scientific evidence has already lead many countries to reconsider their regulations on reducing green-house gas emissions, impose recycling or demand that polluting industries clean up.

The longer a contract lasts, the more difficult it may be during the contract period to introduce modifications or new performance criteria that change the contractual obligations. For this reason, most contracts include phrases that oblige the parties to abide by government legislation and adapt their activities to new legislation when these become effective. This concerns environmental protection or security criteria just as much as it will concern construction regulations that builders must observe for any construction they engage in. The main purpose for including a clause on the need to observe current legislation is to avoid the need by the partners to re-open a contract in order to re-negotiate the implementation of new government legislation or benchmarks in matters.

National governments adapt their national legislation and benchmarks according to new needs, but also in their effort to adapt to regional or international standards. Concerning the member countries of the European Union and those that adapt their national legislation accordingly, such as European non-EU countries, new regulations and Directives coming from Brussels also introduce the need for public-private partnerships to adopt changes.

An interesting difference between Anglo-Saxon concession contracts and French ones is that the latter offer re-evaluations of the contract at regular intervals. This is the case, for example, with French highway concessions, in which a re-evaluation of the terms of reference are required every five years. One result of this is that French contracts are much shorter than Anglo-Saxon contracts which can be well over a hundred pages.[61] In these, all possible changes and needs for adaptation are included in the contract with provisions for re-negotiation of specific aspects when necessary. The Anglo-Saxon type of contract is not open to regular verification or adaptation and it is usually expected that a contract will not need to be reopened for negotiation. If any unexpected points of dispute or disagreement among the parties need to be resolved, they can either be taken up within a format of an ad-hoc settlement when the contract does not need to be amended, or re-negotiation is required to amend the contract. Either way, additional costs will arise for the project as a whole where differences need to be negotiated and new agreements arrived at.

The difficulty is that major changes in public awareness of environmental and sustainability needs demand adaptation and amelioration of public services infrastructure. Such changes touch in particular the need to improve continuously the criteria for sustainability, social equity and security in the procurement, development and provision of public services. Two principal reasons stand out: First, criteria for sustainable development for social equity and security may not be included in the original procurement process and contract and their application later may be difficult throughout the contract period. Second, another difficulty arises once criteria have to be added to a contract. These may be technical and/or financial.

When a procurement process is still ongoing and the contract has not reached its financial close, that is, the partners have signed the agreement, it is possible to Including new criteria that arises out of new needs for sustainable development, security or equity. This is where most Western governments are currently improving their procurement regulations and methods to include an increasing number of provisions in favour of sustainable development. This is sometimes referred to as sustainable or green procurement. However, once the contract has been negotiated, it becomes

difficult to add modifications. This will remain so for the entire duration
of the contact period unless provisions have been agreed upon in advance
that allow for modifications to be incorporated into an ongoing contract.

With the rapidly growing awareness of new needs for sustainable development, security or equity, governments must increasingly modify the way
they deliver public services or build public and maintain infrastructure.
When the government is alone responsible and carries out its public infrastructure and services on short-term outsourced contracts, such changes can
be added as they are adopted by political leaders or parliament. However,
when a government has locked a public work into a long-term contract
with private providers, then the modifications in a contract and the changes
demanded in how these providers operate must be adopted.

Any addition of new measures or criteria implies a cost. However, there
is also another reasons that not all future needs can be known at the time
of procurement. For example, during the long period of the PPP contract,
the environmental, social or security context may change and render some
of the original contractual obligations incomplete. The political and economic climate may change over time, as well as government policy and
international norms. Political parties that hold power may change during
the time of a contract period in national or municipal governments, or
security and social events external to a government's control may affect
public infrastructure and services and thus long-term contractual obligations between state authorities and private providers. For example, the
terrorist bombings in the London underground or on trains and train
stations in Madrid is changing the security context in which public and
private actors must work together. Less dramatic, but equally important is
the influence from growing public awareness about global warming and
pollution. Government must react and modify the way public services and
infrastructures are developed or operated (reducing water waste, improving recycling). Public buildings and infrastructure of all kinds now need
to be more energy efficient and "eco-friendly." It is therefore important
that changes in priorities can be re-negotiated into already existing PPP
contracts, even if these were established many years or decades ago when
awareness of the environment or of terrorist threats was absent. However,
modifying contracts to adapt them to new needs can become expensive in
terms of transaction costs—expenses that must be borne either by the State
or the private party or by both.

With the increasing awareness that economic development must not
threaten the continued health and welfare of future generations through
environmental degradation, the issue of sustainability has come to the forefront of political and social concerns. How governments procure services
and develop infrastructure is no exception. Construction, development,
and operation of public services and infrastructure are increasingly subject

to environmental impact assessments, internal reviews, and external evaluation and criticism from NGOs. Most Western governments have either established their own benchmark criteria or legally binding requirements for procurement and tendering processes, or they follow international recommendations and regulations.[62] The aim each time is to ensure that new construction projects conform to sustainability (and also security) needs and expectations. In the same way as any other procurement process, PPPs must be subject to sustainability criteria. This is especially important where public services industries, such as waste-water treatment, garbage and industry waste disposal or road and rail construction, all have a direct effect on the environment or on natural resources.

Next to the recommendations on sustainable development that individual countries establish for government procurements, some supra-national organisations have also developed international norms and standards which they promote. Thus, the Council of the Organisation for Economic Cooperation and Development (OECD) recommends that its member governments place environmental considerations within their procurement methods.[63] This is in parallel to the global awareness-raising efforts made by the United Nations and its specialised agencies to bring industry into its purview of international security and obtain the commitment from the business community to include environmental considerations in all forms of industry.[64] At the global level of the negotiation of trade standards, the World Trade Organisation has also issued a Government Purchasing Agreement that contains a relevant article.[65] The WTO here provides the right to national governments to demand that services it procures correspond to criteria it establishes, and that it is not obliged to modify national criteria in favour of international ones.

Another global agency that has influence through financial means rather than international law is the World Bank. It has become involved in analysing the environmental impact from industrial development and addresses questions of awareness-raising, control, and monitoring for governments when they procure services or privatise public assets. In its checklist for assessing environmental impact, the World Bank recommends numerous steps that governments should take to ensure that the delivery of public infrastructure and services are in conformity with broad sustainable development principles. Thus, it asks governments to ensure that responsibilities for environmental protection are clearly defined among the partners in a contract, how pollution clean-up, for example, should be paid for, how compliance with contractual obligations and environmental protection is to be monitored, whether public consultation with stakeholders are foreseen, for example, and whether dispute resolution methods are part of the agreement in case of disagreements on the observance of sustainability measures. In addition, the World Bank asks governments to ensure they maintain the capacity to enforce environmental regulations and implementing environmental management plans in case abuse, pollution or non-compliance is reported.[66]

The European Union also develops its own set of standards and recommendations for construction and environmental protection. Member countries must bring their legislation into compliance with the EU environmental body of laws and Directives and create the necessary agencies that look after and monitor their implementation. While the EU Sustainable Development Strategy does not make a direct connection between PPPs and sustainable development, it does lay importance on the sustainability that must be built into government procurement. For example, one of these EU directives is the Integrated Pollution Prevention and Control provision.[67] In addition, the European Union's Environmental Bureau declares that "sustainable development requires respect for nature and the preservation of our society's natural resource base."[68] The EU's Commission proposal for the Sixth Environmental Action Programme for the years 2001–2010 provides that public procurement should use environmental performance as one of the purchasing criteria.[69] The EU countries are also obliged to align their environmental criteria for impact assessments in accordance with the Strategic Environmental Assessment (SEA) directive. Thus, all government-private collaboration and procurement must encompass the principles set out in this EU directive regarding environmental impact assessments.[70] This is designed to ensure that environmental assessment are carried out before large infrastructure projects are built or transformed and to examine where or how the planned work impacts on the immediate natural environment. The purpose is to prevent negative consequences for the environment by including environmental and sustainability criteria into the project plan.

How environmental criteria are designed, used for impact assessments, added to procurement processes or used as criteria in the selection of tenders, remains within the domain of national authorities. The operation of sustainability, or, in other words, making sustainability a part of every procurement as well as of the on-going management of public infrastructure and services, requires several things. First, the process must meet the needs for services and utilities for the public or the consumers. Second, efficiency (value for tax-payers' money) must be realised through the entire life-cycle of the contract and generate benefits for the general public, the government and the economy at the same time as it minimises negative environment consequences. Some consequences are unavoidable, such as the use of non-renewable materials in construction, the emission of CO_2 in the atmosphere, etc. This implies that procurement processes and tenders could incorporate requirements for the most eco-friendly manufacture and production methods, and for reuse and recycling options.[71]

An operational obstacle to overcome in procurement regulations that governments design is the policy on the extent to which sustainability is to be a part of every aspect of the process. This is not an easy task and is bound to remain in constant flux as new information on the state of the global environment affects public opinion and policy trends. Finding a realistic balance, for example, between the following extremes will remain a constant challenge for any national or local government authority as it defines its procurement policy. On the one hand, there is the traditional economic approach that only considers cost efficiency as has been done so far in most Western countries that adapted their legislation in favour of open international competitive procurement. At the other extreme, a government authority may decide that it will cancel out the principle of open international competitive procurement and give priority to clean, green and sustainable procurement. It may even go so far as to insist on locally-purchased services and to contract out to local industry rather than open a procurement to international competition, in order to reduce the pollution that transportation of materials and people inevitably introduces to a project.

To procure products for which natural resources and services must fulfil environmental sustainability criteria will most likely cost more money for the government authority. This is often because sustainability considerations must encompass every step of a production chain both upstream and downstream, and suppliers, transport, installation, operation or usage must also follow environmental "green" criteria. Thus, public procurement can include requirements for products and services that are produced according to environmental criteria and include such items as office furniture and wood for construction provided from managed forests, as well as the use of recycled paper, biodegradable cleaning products, non-toxic paints, energy efficient office equipment, green electricity, etc.[72] In addition to environmental criteria, social requirements for so-called "social procurement" can and are also added. Thus, some governments insist on local employment, local SME support, fair trade and non-discriminatory employment practices.[73]

In other words, every aspect of a construction, refurbishment or development needs to undergo environmental impact assessments and follow-up verification that ground water, air, soil and other elements are not polluted and that unavoidable damage is reduced to a minimum or cleaned up. What is more, sustainability criteria are not only important for the development and construction of a project, they are equally important. The task for governments is therefore to develop standards for procurement that are at once environmentally friendly and retain value for money. The importance given during procurements to the lower possible cost (primacy for efficiency gains) must be weighed against the perception that "sustainable procurement" may cost more initially, but will prove less costly over the long-run.

Sustainable procurement may actually offer better value for money when whole-life costs and quality prove to be more environmentally friendly and diminish pollution clean-up and recycling costs, or reduce other damage to the natural environment at a later stage.[74] However, it can be envisaged that a failure to consider sustainability issues when developing a PPP may imply that a life-cycle project of 20, 30 or more years looses the opportunity to reduce the whole life costs.

Oddly, if initial costs increase because of the incorporation of stricter environmental protection criteria, then a compensated for them through longer term savings on life-cycle PPPs may prove to be a new form of assessing value for money.[75] Indeed, several recent reports emphasise that it is wrong to focus entirely on the lowest possible costs in procurement processes, and that government at all levels should consider "value for money" not necessarily as equating the lowest possible cost for procured services.[76] Some examples of PPPs have been developed to showcase aspects of sustainable development such as energy efficiency in the UK with special energy efficient medical surgery clinics. Others are social and environmental responsibility programmes similar to business CSR programmes where a PPP is claimed to provide better environmental protection.[77] A non-European example of environmentally friendly waste management through a profit-making PPP is the solid waste landfill is the Canadian City of Vancouver landfill PPP.[78] This is a project that provides waste disposal and produces clean energy. The private sector was brought into an agreement to transform a landfill site producing gases (including methane, a greenhouse gas that contributes to global climate change) for beneficial commercial uses. The private partner designed, financed, and constructed a so-called cogeneration plant that uses the landfill gas as fuel to generate electricity. This is sold to a local utility and provides one form of revenue. Another form of revenue comes from waste heat that is used to heat water which is sold to an agricultural greenhouse for heating purposes. The private partner and the City shares the revenues from the sale of electricity and thermal energy.

While this example offers valid ideas for the other sustainable PPPs, it is in many cases very difficult to reconcile commercial economic interests with the need for sustainability. The least expensive approach to waste management, for example, can lead to unsound environmental activities, such as the "waste tourism" that several European countries engage in. For example, the privatisation of waste management was considered an economically sound way to address a terrible pollution problem in Germany. New legal regulations were enacted to promote waste avoidance and recycling in 1996 (Kreislaufwirtschafts-/Abfall-Gesetz). This had become necessary because of the shortage of open land-fill disposal sites, groundwater pollution, and reports about waste exports to developing countries where pollution controls are lax or even inexistent. This information created sufficient political interest in a privatisation of the industry to find adequate solutions in waste management on German soil. The design of long-term concessions contracts for private providers, however, led to poorly estimated costs and risks of the investment cycles. This can be found in examples from Geneva and in German waste management installations. They were designed with an incineration over-capacity, in the expectation that with economic growth the tonnage of waste would also grow. However, with increased recycling, their over-capacity has led them to attract waste imported from other countries such as Italy in order to remain financially viable.[79] This means that public money in Germany or Switzerland is used to treat waste from other countries in order to keep the treatment plants financially profitable—an economic logic—but without considering that the international transportation of solid waste is hardly an environmentally-friendly strategy. The situation is similar with the incineration capacity that Geneva built and which is larger than currently necessary for local waste management needs.[80]

The erroneous estimation of the capacity of incineration plants was in part because contact time-frames were tied to the expected investment cycle of incineration facilities. However, this has proved problematic as the cycle of waste management is far longer and its cost externalities far more open to change (demographic change, reduction of waste, etc.) as waste products change or more are recycled instead. This type of side-effect from the liberalisation of the waste market, on the one hand, and the different time horizons on the basis of which public and private parties operate on the other hand, can only be reduced and controlled to benefit a country's population and natural environment if PPP contracts and government policies are "embedded in a sensible framework of regulations."[81] This implies, however, that absolute commercial efficiency must be weighed against environmental and sustainable criteria. This may well imply that in the future government procurement will need to limit its purchase of services to its local area instead of opening a market to national and international competition.

Creating a framework of regulation is a matter for policy-makers and thus for politicians and their ministries. The more complex a PPP is and the larger the number of stakeholders, the more important regulation and control by public authorities becomes. The London city authorities learned this in the 1980s and early 1990s following the privatisation of the water and waste water treatment of the city of London.[82] Private control over a public utility creates a much greater need for regulation and control by the public authorities and independent auditors. Three regulatory authorities were created to oversee water utilities and services in the UK. One office to regulate and control prices, investments and profits, another to control the quality of drinking water, and a third to verify the waste water treatment and oversee environmental protection. This added to the complexity of the water and sanitation work that Thames Water had to look after and caused some problems with regard to political and commercial agendas.

The regulatory structure of the London city water management became a system of diverging interests. The independence of the regulatory authorities—a policy usually recommended to prevent political or commercial influence—also introduced some complications. The interest of the regulators is two-fold, to ensure that the criteria they have to control for is kept up (water purity or environmental protection), and that new and more stringent criteria are developed and integrated (improved quality, better transparency, etc.). However, when different regulators share the same public service sector, each regulator may pursue an agenda that is not coordinated with the other regulators. In the case of the UK, the Drinking Water Inspectorate pushed up the requirements for water purity regardless of the costs and risks of diminishing returns for the water provider, while the Environment Agency demanded ever better environmental safeguards regardless of the cost to the provider, and finally, the Office for Water that is responsible for overseeing prices, tried to maintain low water prices for individual customers (households or industries) in London. While each regulatory agency may have its merits and fulfils important tasks, their individual mandates conflicted with each other leaving the private water provider caught in the middle. What is more, the diverging aims by regulatory authorities can also create a counter-productive effect on a public service. A private provider cannot at once obey different "masters" that all have their own mandates—lower prices, improved quality, better environmental protection, greater investment, etc. These examples indicate that sustainability in procurement processes and in the operation of public infrastructure and services is not merely a question of getting new environmental protection criteria to be adopted by the operators and providers, but also an issue of managerial coordination—a task that does not come easily to any complex project, let alone when new and ever-changing needs for greater sustainability must become a part of already complex PPPs

Equity and PPPs

The debate about privatization of public assets and the private control over public services is most often linked to the argument that financial efficiency for public money should be given priority. Closely linked to this concern for efficient spending of public funds is the question of equity. As in any privatisation effort by governments to reduce public spending and involve the private sector in public services, PPPs can pose new challenges to the principle of equity or universal access, just as PPPs can challenge the expectations with regard to cost efficiency. The most prominent example where equity becomes a concern is where there exists a risk of reducing access to persons who live in remote and commercially unprofitable areas. Another equity-related potential problem is an increase in the cost of a service to the population in general. Finally, a third objective often raised when public services take on commercial characteristics is where an end-product or service is sold to those end-users who are willing to pay for them. In each of these potential challenges to equity within PPPs, one of the most crucial elements required for governments to assure equity to their public is how equity is provided for in the PPP contracts. The public sector is accountable to the public for public services or end-users and is therefore responsible to ensure that PPP contracts will not lead to higher costs or end-user fees which not all members of the public can pay for.

Equity implies a fair distribution of access to resources and services for all people within a country. National and local governments are expected to provide public infrastructure and services in an equitable manner without discrimination vis-à-vis remote communities that live far away from urban centres, or specific ethnic groups or people with few economic means. The principal element of the debate on equity and privatisation concerns the question whether a commercially-driven public service company will deliver the service for a fair price to all residents in a country, even those who live in remote places or who are not considered to be financially interesting customers.

In the debate about equity, the heart of the matter is that all residents in a country ought to have equal access to a public services or public infrastructure, and that the cost of use for each resident is as low as possible. To achieve this, some governments subsidise public services or access to infrastructure for an entire population or for specifically members of the same society who live on reduced financial means.[83] When commercially-oriented practices and private business interests enter into public services and infrastructures, the first risk that must be prevented is that access to persons who live in remote and "commercially unprofitable" areas is not sacrificed in the name of cost efficiency. This issue is not uncommon in debates about the extent to which the postal service or national and regional trains should be operated by private companies instead of public civil servants.

The privatisation of postal services in Europe raises special concerns for areas where the delivery of mail would be commercially "unprofitable" if low postage rates are to be maintained through a country. This concern is due to the expectation that a public service, such as the delivery of mail, should provide low-cost and equitable service to all residents in a country, even those in areas that would be commercially unviable if the service were provided by a for-profit business. Options exist for a government when handing over responsibility of the operation of public services to business and still ensure equity. These are either to increase the price according to new criteria such as distance travelled as is already the case with train tickets and could also become the norm with postal services, or to negotiate for government subsidies where the cost of delivery for the private actor becomes unprofitable. The second alternative is being debated in Germany and has also raised some voices in Switzerland, for example.[84] The German government is studying the creation of a compensation fund and the conditions under which it can be used to guarantee equity. This fund could provide financial backing for postal services where costs of delivery cannot be recovered by postage income.[85]

The second equity-related challenge is when the general cost of a service to the population increases because a private provider is unable to operate at the same low cost to end-users as the public sector. The example often used to show that prices go down under privatisation is in the telecommunications industry where telephone costs have been cut many times during the past fifteen years. Competition has not only led to lower prices, but also to enormous innovation in technology. This has proven beneficial to all users. However, other public services and infrastructures cannot as easily be transformed into commercially viable enterprises. A telling example is the high costs incurred by a number of hospitals in the UK that have been contracted out to private providers under PPP or PFI concessions.[86]

The third concern over rising prices occurs where public services take on commercial characteristics as end-users are asked to pay for the use of a public service or public infrastructure. As already mentioned, the most common are user fees for water and electricity or tolls charged to drivers over roads, on bridges and through tunnels.[87] The principle of "pay for what you use" is usually considered fair; people who never drive, for example, or who use only little water in their household should not be asked to pay for those who water their gardens or drive long distances. At the same time, governments find themselves in a dilemma where equity is not in harmony with the "user-pays" principle, as for example, in situations where low-income commuters are obliged to travel long distances to go to work in inner cities because they cannot afford to live near to their places of employment. They pay higher ticket prices to travel on public transport over longer distances. Examples of price increases and fears of higher costs to users are common as soon as a privatisation of public service is mentioned. Besides higher costs for commuters due to rises in ticket prices or the introduction of tolls on roads, concerns are also raised with regard to rising road tolls for trucks and lorries, or a two-class public medical service with one side for the general public and another with extra services for those who can pay for them privately. In all private involvement in public services, the elaboration of the public-private partnership contract is key to ensuring that equity is safeguarded at a reasonable cost the public purse and the general public.

Human Security and Infrastructure Security

Little needs to be said about the importance of infrastructure and the services delivered through them by governments, by private companies and by public-private partnerships. The more advanced an industrialised economy, the greater its reliance on infrastructure that is shared with other people in the community, the country and the world. There is little that needs to be said as well of the complex interdependence that today's infrastructure is subject to for its normal daily operation. The supply chain of both commodities and information services is intimately tied to the infrastructure it relies on and provides, and for most people in Western countries, the infrastructure they use relies on a network of interdependent human-made systems and processes. All these are subject to security challenges that have their origin in common internal and external factors, as well as factors that are specific to who builds, manages, operates and owns the infrastructure.[88]

The common internal factor refers to problems that appear due to the usage, lack of correct maintenance or modernisation, poor management, etc. of infrastructure, as well as the risks associated with complex financial and operational conditions that can increase the risk of human-induced error or oversight. The common external factors are climatic and natural hazards (hurricanes, floods, earthquakes, etc.), or human-induced damage through malicious or violent activities (terrorism). These are all common factors because regardless of the type of infrastructure, they are all subject to these internal and external risks. The security-related factors that are specific to who operates a public service or public infrastructure project concern the influence that different actors have. For example, the more persons, agencies or companies share financial costs, operational risks and managerial responsibilities for a project, the greater the possibility that in times of security-related crisis, the coordination of maintaining public services or of humanitarian relief become difficult. The reason for considering security in relation to PPPs, then, is because of the increased risk that the complexity of a project represents an additional risk to security.

What is mean by security for this study? It is security of infrastructure managed or developed by PPPs in light of the following:

The prevention of calamitous consequences from natural disasters (earthquakes, avalanches and mud slides, forest fires, floods, hurricanes or violent storms, etc.), or from devastating human error that cause accidents and disasters (airplane or railway accidents, chemical, petroleum or radioactive pollution, explosions in industry, etc.).

The protection of vital infrastructure (critical centres of control or distribution)

Security of important trade and transportation infrastructure (shipping ports, border crossings, industrial areas, airports, etc.)

Emergency and life-support services that people need to survive during a crisis.

Transparent financial accounting to prevent corruption and financial fraud.

Dispute resolution when the PPP parties disagree on how to interpret their contract or share responsibilities.

Some recent or well-publicised examples of public infrastructure-related security problems are: *Security and Politically-motivated violence,* such as the terrorist attacks on 7 July 2005 on the London metro brought home the responsibility that a public transportation system has for the security of its users. Another example are the Madrid train bombings 11 March 2004. In the context of *Security and natural disasters*: it is possible to consider various floods in Europe and the USA, such as the flooding of the city of New Orleans in 2005; various floods in Germany in 2002, 2005, and 2008. *Security and human-made disasters*: for example, the highway bridge collapse in Connecticut, USA, in 2007. Finally, *security and Private security providers* offers another look at the private involvement of business interests in security. Here, instances in which PPPs provide the contractual basis exist with regard to private emergency services; private prison guards; private service providers for national defence forces.

The greatest challenge with regard to security and PPPs is the difficulty to reconcile long-term and stable contracts with the necessary flexibility to adapt to ever-changing security needs. Another reason for considering security in this study on PPPs is the extent to which security can become a commodity that is provided to the public by private providers during the very long life of a PPP contract. As with questions of regulations for sustainability in infrastructure and services, security can be regulated to some extent. However, its existence is not as easily measured as, say, pollution in ground water or the origin of natural resources that go into the production of concrete or steel. In this sense, security is more akin to a service that is evaluated along scales of individual values or expectations similarly to the way health services or old-age care in a home are evaluated. As with "soft" services, security is difficult to describe or define in a contract and requires that the desired output in the project contract is continuously ameliorated and adapted to incorporate new demands or expectations. This points towards the dilemma of engaging in commercially and financially viable contracts in public services and the need for constant adaptation to new and emerging security needs. PPPs that are of the dedicated and commercial type introduce the new dimension into this security-verses-flexibility dilemma. This is because such agreements are most often long-term concession contracts in which the private partner has the potential to influence security conditions that affect the public's real immediate security or how it perceives its security.

All causes of insecurity that affect not just individuals alone, but a community or country will affect in one way or another public infrastructure and services. For this reason, security issues that immediately affected public services and public infrastructure are of primary interest here. But this is not to exclude what if often called "human security"—and important concept that has come into general public discourse on security policy since it was first defined in the 1994 UNDP Human Development Report.[89] People need to feel safe and live in a secure environment where dikes hold water outside of cities, highway bridges do not collapse, airports remain safe against terrorism, etc.[90] In this sense, the expression "human security" is often used as a complement to State-centred security.[91] It adds to the security of the State the need for security that affects the individual within his or her context. Some definitions of human security also include the security from natural disasters or pandemics, as well as from the spread of viral diseases.[92] The reason for adopting this broader approach to security here is to bring attention to the influence that security-related issues have on public services and public infrastructure and how these are perceived by the public.

The context in which PPPs provide public services and infrastructures inevitably has an influence on the security of both the users and the infrastructure itself. Some types of infrastructure will be at a greater risk to security problems than others, as for example in the difference between a rural road that requires little maintenance and is not a target for terrorists and an important airport. Public services and infrastructure are therefore vulnerable to different degrees. Thus, information, transportation, education, health and other provisions can be brought to a standstill through major catastrophes or war-like conflicts. The number of natural catastrophes and security crises has risen over the recent past, this is due to both political tensions and natural (environmental) changes.[93] The industry most immediately affected by catastrophes of every kind is insurance. Insurance companies are at once concerned about preventing high costs from catastrophes and crises, and interested in lucrative contracts with both governments and private companies that develop or operate public infrastructure.

The London Underground security following the terrorism attacks of 7 July 2005 is an example of preparedness for collaboration in times of crisis. Security for all commuters is a principal concern for the London underground. The terrorism attacks caused an immediate halt to a large portion of the London transportation network with chaotic consequences in the streets and underground for commuters. In this moment of crisis, all parties in the complex London metro PPP had to cope, on the one hand, with the forced halt to operations of the lines that had been affected by the bombings, and on the other hand, the service had to ensure not only continued public transportation where possible, but also a rapid return to normal through the entire system. Because more than one private partner worked to provide the metro services, crisis management and a return to normal was a complicated and difficult process. However, after the event, the London city authorities praised the private partners for their effective "return to normal" following the terrorist attacks. In particular, once the terrorism bombings had occurred, the Infracos, that is the Tube Lines and Metronet private consortia, collaborated immediately with the police and to restore services for commuting customers.[94]

In order to ensure that services remain of high quality, procurement contracts have become longer, more complex, and include increasingly detailed descriptions of what is expected from the private sector partner and how security is to be provided or delivered. There is, in other words, a greater focus on regulatory principles in PPPs where previously more traditional government procurement often relied on inter-personal trust and cooperation. In the security sector, where trust and building confidence between the provider and the client is crucial, one would think, complex and regulatory contracts may prove counter-productive to actually delivery security. While it is still too early to come to conclusive evidence on the link between the capacity for PPPs to manage security crises, some indications are available on private provision of security in times of crisis. There are only few studies on security and public-private partnerships. One can safely assume, based on studies of critical infrastructure protection however, that service providers—whether they are government or private agents—must prepare to deal with crises and emergencies and assure the general public of their preparedness.

The first element needed in contractual arrangements to deal with problematic situations and crises is a provision for internal dispute resolution among the parties to the contract. Disputes can arise under normal conditions following the signature of contractual arrangements of any kind. Long-term concession and PPP contracts usually provide for amicable negotiation, or mediation and arbitration by an accepted neutral entity. However, when the conditions are not normal, that is, when crises have upset normal expectations, such as during a security crisis or following serious accidents, the criteria in the contract that was written for operations during normal times may have become invalid.

To avoid disagreements on important issues among the parties, dispute resolution methods must be agreed to in the original contract by all parties. This is particularly critical when the context in which an original contract was written, or when the criteria for its evaluation have changed. For example, some PPP contracts have a payment method on the basis of a quantitative output such as the number of passengers who travel through an airport or a city transportation system. However, with the security risk of terrorist attacks, accidents or other catastrophe, a simple payment method based on quantitative appraisals will leave the private sector partner possibly with misleading incentives. Instead, the quality of security should be the important criteria; the payment method would have to be adapted so that the private partner will work on the basis of a new incentive structure focussed on quality. How such quality is to be defined varies, but will inevitably include mediation mechanism in case disagreements arise among the parties in a contract, especially where these affect the sense of personal safety or the security of the public infrastructure system. To arrive at an amicable re-negotiation or the resolution of a dispute due to a changed security environment, both public authorities and private partners must envisage acceptable conflict resolution methods in the contract from the start.[95]

One can deduce from this, that complex public-private partnership agreements may negatively affect the way members of the public perceive their security as end-users of the public service. On the one hand, a PPP contract becomes complex when the division of responsibilities, risks and output criteria are difficult to define or remain unclear. On the other hand, a lack of clarity becomes apparent where decision-making power and control remain shared among actors from different sectors who joined the PPP for divergent interests. This can pose a serious challenge to the public's trust and security in case something goes wrong and it is unclear who takes over which responsibilities to look after the needs of the end-users. Put differently, this problem can also be stated as follows: can the drive for profit by the private partner in a PPP be reconciled with the public need to ensure that public services are supplied to the end-user even in times of crises or emergencies when "doing business as usual" is not possible?

One aspect of security preparedness that is common to all systems is clarity in preventive measures or in collaboration agreements should crises occur. Trust and a sense of security on the part of public infrastructure users depends on this clarity. At the opposite side of this equation, the more complexity, unclear and un-accountable structures are, the greater public doubts and a sense of insecurity are prevalent. Put differently, clarity equals confidence and lack of clarity invites distrust or fear. This brings the discussion to the clarity with which output criteria, evaluation criteria and payment methods are defined in a contract between the public and private partners.

However, when security is one of the output criteria that the private provider has to deliver in order to receive payments, a difficult challenge must be addressed. This is agreement among the parties on how to define security as an output criterion. Like other quality and value-laden output expectations, security related not only to safe and sound infrastructure design, or the presence of police or security officers in public spaces, but it must also respond to the simple human sense of "feeling safe"—not least a difficult task to accomplish in any contract.

All contracts, whether for "soft" services or "hard" infrastructure, contain criteria and descriptions of what kind of result is expected. The private provider takes on the responsibility to develop the project and the service that was agreed to in the contract. However, defining security and detailing criteria for it as output of a contract is not an easy matter. Providing security can be considered as a "soft" service. It is similar to providing social services as described in the examples of public-private partnerships in health or education. The difficulty to define security ears, like customer satisfaction or service quality, a major problem in procurement contracts. While it may be simple to define that the specific number of security officers have to control the doors and windows of a factory for a certain number of times at night, it is far more difficult to define how security is to be provided to the public, or to specific clients. This problem becomes even more critical in times of crises when, for example, a terrorist attack has occurred or a natural catastrophe has thrown normal day-to-day operations upside down.

In the past, security was ordinarily provided by government services, whether by the police in the street, public officers in jails and law courts, guards at the National border, or soldiers in the defence forces. But the drive towards privatisation has also brought the security sector on to the marketplace. In some way, security has become a commodity. Private actors have entered the security market and government policies on the legitimate use of violence are not merely laid out for civil servants and armed forces any longer. Rather, they must now be legally defined and recognised by the private sector. As with any industry, the more actors become involved in developing a given service, the more important it becomes for government authorities to define the contours and limits of the service. As pointed at in the above example of multiple environmental protection and safety authorities for the administration of water in the city of London, so the administration of security is also bound to become a complex issue of regulatory oversight. The need for coordination between public agents, the judiciary and the private companies involved therefore becomes ever greater.

The lack of coordination in the security field is most visible in times of crisis. Following many natural catastrophes, terrorist attacks, violent demonstrations or a large criminal acts, local or national governments are quickly criticised for not having sufficiently prepared in advance (prevention, risk mitigation), or for having insufficiently coordinated the response (emergency, recovery, rehabilitation). When many actors are involved in emergency response or crisis management, coordination becomes ever more complicated and difficult. It is in this setting where the privatisation of security becomes most critical, and it is in this context that PPPs pose a considerable challenge given their long-term hand-over of responsibility and risk to the private sector partner.

If in a financial crisis a private partner may declare bankruptcy, as the London Underground has recently experienced with Metronet, what about private partners simply giving up their part of a concession deal in cases of war, disaster or crisis? The fear of unmanageable public services in times of crises is one reason for why some countries block the sale of projects or national assets to foreign bidders or buyers, as the example of the Japanese Government's refusal to sell a portion of national electricity infrastructure to a UK firm on the grounds that this might increase the risk to national security. In times of crisis, the complexity of coordination becomes acute when actors are not only interdependent on each other through the production chain, but each has different national origins and invested financial capital into the project or infrastructure. Security threats or crises require that all partners co-operated to improve safety and security. However, the contribution of private finance in PPPs implies that the industry partner will also have control over management processes. How will this square with security for which the government is ultimately responsible?

An example of another disaster in the London Underground is the large fire at the Kings Cross and Pancras tube station. It devastated the station, burnt out the top level with all entrances and ticket halls, and caused the death of 31 people. This was in 1987 and blocked traffic on the connecting line platforms on the Victoria, Piccadilly, Northern, Circle, Hammersmith and City, and the Metropolitan trains.

According to an investigation carried out afterwards, the fire started underneath a wooden escalator where grease, garbage and probably a discarded match or cigarette combined to make the ideal environment for a fire. Smoking had been banned on the London Underground since February 1985 in consequence of a fire at the Oxford Circus station; however, smokers often lighted a cigarette when on their way out. The investigation that followed into the cause of the fire led to new fire precautions regulations.[96] These required a rapid replacement of all wooden escalators with steel ones and the installation of automatic sprinklers and heat detectors. Furthermore, mandatory biannual fire safety training for all station staff was introduced. While at the time, the London Underground was operated by the government, the precautions and fire safety training introduced new costs to operations that cannot be reduced. Prevention training and security monitoring remains a costly addition to any public infrastructure project and should be factored into any cost estimation of construction and operation, and improved upon as dangers and risks change over time as the terrorist attacks proved in 2005.

Among private-public cooperation in the recovery from disasters and major industrial accidents, there are many forms of collaboration that either develops in an ad hoc fashion at the moment of need, or is pre-planned and agreed to in contracts. In the case of PPP agreements, crisis management, emergency cooperation and recovery are rarely included. Exceptions exist, such as in PPPs that are contracted with business that specialise in emergency and security services. The Danish Falck company is such an example. Falck provides security, ambulance and fire fighting services in Denmark mostly in agreements with local governments. The company was established as a small family firm in 1906 and has since then grown into a global corporation with activities in more than 100 countries.[97] In the early 1990s, the company expanded further through takeovers and entered foreign markets across Scandinavia, Poland, the Baltic states, the Netherlands, and managed to acquire an American security corporation as well as a security company in Israel. In the year 2004 the company merged with a British security services firm called Securicor and changed its name to become Group4Securicor. Through this strategy, the company became the world's second-largest security firm, the largest being the Swedish based company Securitas.

However, the company changed so drastically at the international level that its image amongst the Danish public changed as well. The company benefited from its near monopolistic position in Denmark to acquire other companies and expand its business. This has brought about strong criticism within Denmark. Initially, it was considered to be a semi-public rescue company in Denmark, but then became to be seen as a private firm that used its privileged position in order to gain private wealth. Through its security services in partnership with the Israeli agencies, as well as in collaboration with American interests, Falck's international corporation was strongly criticised and especially where the Danish public suspected questionable ethical activities or business practices in the Middle East that did not match Danish political views. What is more, its American subsidiary was blacklisted by investment groups as not sufficiently ethical to stand up to stringent standards.[98] Still, Falck expanded its business in order to face up to global competition. At the same time, it encouraged just the kind of international competition that now reduces its own position within Denmark as other competitors enter the Danish market. "The implication of the new global competition is that it puts the national and local partnership strategy between the Danish public sector and Falck Denmark at risk."[99] The Danish government has begun to encourage more competitive bidding for future emergency services contracts and to move away from the privileged position that Falck maintained for so many years. At the same time, the European Union is putting pressure on all its members, including Denmark, to open up public services markets to greater international competition.

Difficult questions remain that touch on the seeming contradiction between local small-scale operations and global competition among very large MNCs and their consortia that bid for government tenders. Another difficult question that remains and that concerns social services in particular is the instability that international and global competition may bring to local communities that relied on locally-operated public services. Thus: First, can a company at once serve local communities with relatively small services such as emergency ambulance and fire-fighting when at the same time it wants to be a global player in other countries? Second, partnerships take time to develop, but can be destroyed a very quickly. Elements that can lead to the destruction of partnerships are global economic changes, globalised competition, political changes that demand changes in policy, and social changes (pressure from stakeholders) such as negative press.

Partnerships function best in stable environments, and this is the case for local emergency services where a municipality and the private provider agree on the terms and conditions of their collaboration, as well as in co-operative partnerships and in long-term concessions such as the PFI model in the United Kingdom. The example of the Danish Falck company seems to show that a private service provider can, on the one hand, deliver a locally adapted service, and on the other hand, compete on the global market for public-private partnerships. What this implies is that community services at the level of municipalities may become marketing battlefields for multinational service providers in the same way that very large and capital intensive infrastructure construction and development projects (airports, high-speed rail links, etc) are within the purview of globally active private service providers.

In the same way as public utilities such as water services become interdependent on international finance through PPPs, local security provision can follow the same commercial trend. The question at the heart of this tension between open markets and local or national control over public services and public infrastructure hinges on the responsibility and accountability for these services that governments take vis-à-vis their populations. In Western European countries, perhaps the greatest public good is the democratic political system. In all countries, public debate influences policy decisions where individuals, communities and interest groups voice their views to their political leaders. Politicians know they are to a great degree approved or disapproved by their constituencies on the basis of their management of public services. The best way to evaluate whether a service is fulfilling its intended function is to study feedback: ask the end-users what they need.[100] This is the way through which business has developed its marketing techniques to know what it can sell and how.

There are different methods by which PPPs can be evaluated and that include both subjective and objective considerations. These may include public satisfaction surveys (subjective); the actual physical state of infrastructure systems (objective); the ability of governments to pay the price of the construction or maintenance of public infrastructure and public services (Value for Money estimate, which is a quantitative assessment based on past experience of cost efficiency); and finally, the sustainability, security and long-term reliability of the same systems and services, which is a qualitative assessment. As any evaluation of performance must rely on established and agreed principles or criteria, and a regulatory and legal framework must underpin this. At the heart of this set of principles for the evaluation of PPPs, is the policy context within which political leaders and government ministries make their decisions. This brings the discussion back to the trends that characterise the policy-related decisions that governments make either in favour of greater private sector involvement in the public domain or not.

CONCLUSION

Public-private partnerships in Western Europe and other industrialised countries have arisen within a context of economic, legal, institutional and ideological traditions and trends that favoured their development. In the introduction to this chapter, it was suggested that PPPs are special kinds of procurement methods through which governments maximise the involvement of the private sector in the development and delivery of public services and public infrastructure. PPPs are different from any other kind of public procurement because they create a new kind of interdependence between public infrastructure and services and the risks associated with privately raised capital and private business interests.

Whether a government aims to involve the private sector to reduce its own size and budget, or whether it engages in PPPs as a way to postpone payment for capital-intensive public infrastructure construction, every government is held accountable by its citizens who judge their political leaders on the basis of how they manage public services. The less efficient and reliable public services become, the more a population becomes cynical about its political leaders and disenchanted with their performance. It behoves each government administration, therefore, to continuously update and improve public services, and adapt them to the current and future needs amongst the public. As economic and social circumstances change, the public changes in how it uses public services. Consumption habits and economic trade patterns form the greatest influence on how public services and infrastructure are used. For example, the increase of automobiles per household, the fashion of green garden lawns, or the rise in the number of mobile phones per capita all have an enormous impact on public services. New trends and new needs arise all the time. Thus, new awareness about environmental pollution and its consequences on health, food quality and life styles, as well as climate change and changing weather patterns, influence how the public evaluates public services and the political leaders that are expected to look after these services. The growing demand for better or more equitable access to services, for economic and cost efficiency, as well as for more sustainable approaches to everything, from driving automobiles or watering garden lawns to the resources that go into recycling old electronic cellular telephones, is continuously affecting public services and the development and maintenance of public infrastructure. These must adapt to ever-changing demands and needs, and the contracts under which both public and private actors engage in their development or maintenance must not be counterproductive to necessary change. This is not unlike the flexibility that businesses need to maintain to adapt to market demands, or that political leaders need to show they adapt to voters' expectations.

As consumption patterns and economic trade have changed greatly over the past decades, the context in which Western countries develop public services and infrastructure must adapt. The opening of public services and public infrastructure to a greater involvement of private sector finance and control through PPPs is one aspect of this change. However, the creation of PPPs opens many new questions and poses some serious challenges that concern their ability to adapt to ever-changing needs and expectations. These concern project costs for the public sector (and the tax-payer), the importance of social equity that public services are expected to guarantee, the increased importance of and possible additional cost associated with sustainability criteria in light of climate change and pollution, as well as the need to assure security of the same infrastructures and their users.

What makes is more challenging to ensure economic efficiency, equity, sustainability and security is the fact that PPP-type of procurement processes are mostly long-term concessions where the government surrenders an important aspect of its direct involvement with its public and its control over the public service for the duration of the contract. Put differently, the government's freedom to introduce and enforce new regulations is reduced by its contractual commitments within the long-term PPPs. Broken down, this means that long-term contracts limit a government's ability to quickly adapt a public service or the operation of a public infrastructure when social, economic, security, equity or sustainability conditions change. This is particularly important in situations where unexpected events alter the conditions in which the original PPP contract was negotiated and where re-negotiations and transfer costs place an additional burden on the public purse.

With the fast pace of economic, social and political change in modern industrialised societies, inflexible long-term contracts seem like a contradiction vis-à-vis today's society. The government takes on a new form of risk when it agrees to contracts that are inflexible and impose transaction costs whenever revisions of output criteria should be necessary. An important aspect of a contractual arrangement is therefore its robustness vis-à-vis conflicting interests among the parties. This is not achieved through inflexible contractual agreements, but through increased flexibility. For example, it is impossible to predict whether security threats or crises will require that the partners co-operated to improve safety and security and modify their contract. Any modifications become most difficult were each party has individual or diverging interests and also invested financial capital into their realisation. Each contract should therefore contain pre-agreed dispute resolution options and methods.

The debate is by far not over regarding the usefulness, the efficiency and the effectiveness of PPPs. This debate will last as long as governments continue to facilitate private business and private finance into public services and public infrastructure. This debate will primarily remain alive with regard to the cost to the consumers or tax-payers and the fair access to these services for all members of a society. The evaluation of the efficiency and effectiveness of PPPs can only be carried out on a case-by-case basis. The broad indications spelled out in this chapter with regard to cost efficiency are the following:[101]

First, cost efficiency can be gained through PPPs in which the payment method is based on simple and easily measurable output criteria.

Second, hard infrastructure projects are more likely to have easily measurable output criteria on the basis of which the financial revenue stream and payment method can be based.

Third, the more difficult it becomes to define the output criteria clearly along with the basis upon which the payment methods is structured in a PPP contract, the greater the risk that cost will rise. This may be because of the longer time it takes to negotiate an initial agreement, or through new transaction costs once the project is underway when re-negotiation or dispute resolution are necessary.

Fourth, the longer the PPP contract lasts, the more the risk of unexpected events or policy changes increases and the more likely it becomes that compensation-related indemnities will raise the total cost of the project. Additional payments may be made either through insurance compensations, higher discount rates or compensations directly from the public sector to the provider. In every case, their cost will be added onto the initially calculated value for money of the project either through compensation payments, or higher insurance fees.

In addition to assessing the efficiency and effectiveness in terms of social equity of PPPs, new elements of importance have entered this discussion. These concern criteria for sustainability and security. Long-term sustainability and security are becoming increasingly important next to social equity and cost efficiency. This brings the fundamental question of this chapter to its conclusion by asking: why would a government want to engage in long-term PPP concession agreements? When considering its answer, a government must ask what it wants to achieve. If one or more of the following possible objectives can be achieved through a PPP, then its interest in such contracts may be justified. These objectives for making this difficult decision are:

- To reduce government spending and save public money at all costs.
- To defer payment for public infrastructure and services to a future date, but without incurring additional costs over and above the expected cost for the same infrastructure or service under other (traditional) procurement conditions over the long term.
- To improve the quality, the equitable distribution and the sustainability of public infrastructure and services.

All three of these objectives can hardly be achieved at once, even though ardent promoters of PPPs and PFIs sometimes claim they can. As with most complex decisions, short-cuts may look appealing, but rarely prove their worth. The first of these options probably leads to reduced quality, reduced coverage (lack of equity) or reduced sustainability for the long-term. The second option is often integrated in discussions about PPPs as governments find they can defer payment (as with a credit card) to later instalments. The difficulty here, however, is whether they can then also avoid the added cost that a credit card scheme imposes on the buyer (the government). Finally, the third option is the most desirable, but will in most instances incur higher costs. The question, then, is whether the government can better continue to offer the public infrastructure and service on its own and deliver improved quality, equity, security and sustainability, or whether this can be done equally well or even better through a PPP with a private partner.

In conclusion, the government must decide whether to engage private firms in the delivery of public services and infrastructure. In addition, the government must decide to what extent it wants to allow private finance and private control to enter into public services. This inevitably includes the question whether any and all public services can be opened up to private involvement, or whether some vital public services should remain under total control of the public sector.

In addition to the above considerations, the government remains ultimately accountable to the public for the public services and public infrastructure, regardless of who delivers the service to the end-user. The public partner is therefore responsible to ensure that procurement processes and PPP agreements are in accord with public needs and expectations, especially as concerns cost effectiveness, equity, sustainability and security. To ensure that the dilemma of flexibility verses stability can be bridged, PPP contracts with private partners must contain clauses that allow for the addition of or the improvement of regulations that concern these four criteria. Government must continuously adapt their policies to public needs, as well as to new scientific findings or technological improvements that impact on public infrastructure and services. Policy adaptations must also be reflected in long-term PPP contracts to maintain the efficiency and effectiveness of public services. To ensure these through PPPs (and other procurement methods), governments must, first, give priority to the needs of the public and continuously adapt public policies and services; second, the governmental regulatory framework for social equity, security and sustainability must be clear and transparent so that the private partner can implement them; and third, these regulations must be continuously adapted without upsetting long-term PPP agreements. This is to incorporate the best standards at all times in the interest of long-term sustainability of public well-being, the natural environment and economic and financial stability.

NOTES

1. For a theoretical explanation, see Chapter 2 of this study.

2. For example: "The basic foundation of the European Community consists of the four freedoms of the Single Market, the free movement of goods, services, capital and persons (e.g. Europarl, 2000). In line with this idea are the principles of transparency, competition and the prohibition of e.g. nationally discriminating public procurement." From: Jakob Elder, Sascha Ruhland and Sabine Hafner, et al., Innovation and Public Procurement: Review of Issues at Stake, Study for the European Commission (No ENTR/03/24), Fraunhofer Institute for Systems and Innovation Research, Germany, December, 2005, p. 9.

3. European Bank for Reconstruction and Development, Public Private Partnerships, Background paper prepared by EBRD Infrastructure Banking team for the Second Regional Conference for South-Eastern Europe, Bucharest, October 25–26, 2001; Michael Barber, "Meeting the Demand for Improved Public Services: Governments face a productivity imperative because the public wants better services but not higher taxes," Commentary—McKinsey on public sector, The McKinsey Quarterly, October 2006.

4. United Nations. 2002. 'Partnerships for Sustainable Development'. Johannesburg World Summit. Commission on Sustainable Development. See further: http://www.un.org.esa.sustdev; and also: http://www.johannsburgsummit.org

5. Closing the Infrastructure Gap: The Role of Public-Private Partnerships, Deloitte Touche Tohmatsu, Deloitte Development LLC, 2006.

6. World Bank, Mobilizing Private Finance for Local Infrastructure in Europe and Central Asia, by Michael Noël Micheal and W. Jan Brzeski, Washington, D.C., 2005; and The International Project Finance Association. 'Private Finance'. See further: http://www.ipfa.org.

7. See further: <http://www.un.org/esa/sustdev/documents/WSSD_POI_PD/English/POI_PD.htm>

8. When referring to public services and public infrastructure, this chapter uses one expression which is "public infrastructure and services." This will include all services that are or were publicly operated by the government and that include both built infrastructure (roads, rail, water pipelines, etc.), as well as inter-personal services such as in hospital medical care, school teaching or the management of pensioners' homes.

9. The PFI is sometimes distinguished from PPPs in the sense that the public sector party is considered as the purchaser of public services, and that instead of owning the infrastructure (which the private party may have built), the two partners agree to create a special purpose agency that owns the built assets and receives regular payments from the government. Through an agreed transfer of funds, the private partner can thus recover its costs and earn a profit.

10. David Corner, "The United Kingdom Private Finance Initiative: the challenge of allocating risk," in Graeme A. Hodge and Carsten Greve, eds., The Challenge of Public-Private Partnerships: Learning from International Experience, Edward Elgar publisher, Cheltenham, UK, 2005, p. 46.

11. When mention is made of public services and infrastructure or their design, development, construction, management and/or operation, it implies government-initiated works. Such public infrastructure and services may be developed and operated by the private sector, but it is always the public sector that initiates them through a procurement process. For the purpose of this study, this includes "hard" infrastructure, such as construction of public buildings, transportation systems or water distribution, and "soft" infrastructure, such as healthcare and education or social care. See Chapter 2 of this report for a discussion of this "soft"—"hard" distinction.

12. Organisation for Economic Co-Operation and Development (OECD), Modernising Government: The Way Forward, Paris, 2005, p. 130.

13. Studies that appraise the cost effectiveness in a critical light include, among other, the following some examples: British Medical Association, BMJ journal, critical articles on the UK's hospital PFIs (PPPs) available at www.bmj.com; David Hall, "Privatising other people's water: the contradictory policies of Netherlands, Norway and Sweden," Public Services International Research Unit, University of Greenwich, London, July 2004; Mark Hellowell and Allyson Pollock, "Private Finance, Public Deficits: A report on the cost of PFI and its impact on health services in England," Centre for International Public Health Policy, University of Edinburgh, 12 September 2007; David Rowland, Allyson Pollock, Declan Gaffney and David Price, "Understanding the Private Finance Initiative: The School of Governor's Essential Guide to PFI," London, Unison, January 2002, 37p.

14. Mark Hellowell and Allyson Pollock, op. cit. and "The impact of PFI on Scotland's NHS: a briefing," ibidem, 8 December 2006. In her book on the reforms of the National Health Service, Pollock complains about the lack of statistical data allowing the comparison of the efficiency before and after the reforms, and that in many cases it has been difficult to obtain from the administration the data that were nevertheless available: Allyson Pollock, NHS plc. The Privatisation of Our Health Care, London, Verso, 2004.

15. This discussion on cost and policy priorities concerns only PPPs that require large capital investments at the start and are long-term commercial life-cycle projects

in which design, finance, development, operation and service are all bundled together and looked after by single private partner. Policy priorities will be different for public-private partnerships that are of different formats, as is the case in some social services, or where non-profit agencies, international organisations or international development agencies are a part of the cooperative agreement.

16. See for example: Alfred Luggenhösscher, "Kritische Thesen: PPP Pleiten, Pech und Pannen, oder strategisch geplante Schuldenfallen zum Nutzen der Berater, Betreiber und Banken?," Conference paper Podiumsdiskussion PPP, Essen, 4 May 2006; Robert Kösling, "PPP—Eine kritische Würdigung," UrbaneInfrastruktur, (article was also published in an annual for labour unions: Werden 2007—Jahrbuch für die Gewerkschaften), Berlin, Urbane Infrastruktur (robert.koesling@berlin.de), 2007, 6p.; Christoph Strawe, "Public Public Partnership: Die Neustrukturierung des öffentlichen Sektors zwischen Kommerzialisierung und Bürokratisierung," Rundbrief Dreigliederung, Öffentlicher Sektor, No.3, November, 2004, pp. 15–18. (Also awailable at: www.sozialimpulse.de/pdf-Dateien).

17. In contrast to critical assessments, the German government offers its appraisals, such as: "Möglichkeiten und Grenzen des Einsatzes von Public Private Partnership Modellen im kommunalen Hoch- und Teifbau" (PPP Schulstudie), Leitfaden V: PPP-Mustervertrag—Mitemodell mit Erbbaurecht, Bundesministerium für Verkehr, Bau und Stadtentwicklung (PPP Task Force / NL 11), Berlin, May 2007. Also: the SPD political party sees PPPs as a possible advantage for the development of urban areas and argues strongly against the critics in "Die neue Stadtentwicklungs und Wohnungspolitik," July 2005, See further: www.spdfraktion.de.

18. Organisation for Economic Co-Operation and Development (OECD), OECD Principles for Private Sector Participation in Infrastructure, Paris, 2007, p. 15–16.

19. Ernst Ulrich Von Weizsäcker, Oran R. Young, and Matthias Finger, eds., Limits to Privatization: How to avoid too much of a Good Thing, A report to the Club of Rome, London, Earthscan, 2005, pp. 21–24.

20. Raimund Bleischwitz and Akira Proske, "Waste Disposal—No time to waste: How to avoid too much of a bad thing," in Von Weizsäcker, Young, and Finger, op. cit., p. 110.

21. Giannakopoulos, N., "L'ingérence du crime organise dans la filière des déchets," in *Le Temps*, 5 March 2008, pp. 11 & 19.

22. World Bank, Worldwide Governance Indicators, 2007. See: www.govindicators.org; and for Transparency International, see: www.transparency.org.

23. Andreas Lienhard, "Public Private Partnerships (PPPs) in Switzerland: Experinces—Risks—Potentials," International Review of Administrative Sciences, Vol.72, No.547, pp. 552–553.

24. Maurice Button, ed., A Practical Guide to PPP in Europe, London, City and Financial Publishing, 2007, pp. 81–89.

25. Information on the Millau Bridge PPP taken from: Price Waterhouse Coopers, Delivering the PPP promise: A Review of PPP issues and activity, PricewaterhouseCoopers International Ltd., 2005, p. 24; and the website: http://viaduc.midilibre.com

26. Organisation for Economic Co-Operation and Development (OECD), OECD Principles for Private Sector Participation in Infrastructure, Paris, 2007, p. 15–16.

27. Von Weizsäcker, Young, and Finger, op. cit., pp. 21–24.

28. Wim Moerman and Toon Srijbosch, "PPP: the Dutch Approach," European Public Finance, Vol.1, 2003, article published through the Ministry of Finance website at: www.pps.minfin.nl.

29. Deloitte, Closing the Infrastructure Gap: The Role of Public-Private Partnerships, A Deloitte Research Study, Deloitte Touche Tohmatsu, 2006, p. 22; and the following websites: http://www.veoliawater.com/presence/Europe/Netherlands.htm; and: www.delfluent.nl

30. Examples of German PPPs are provided in: Urs Bolz, ed., Public Private Partnerships in der Schweiz, Schulthess Juristische Medien AG, Zürich, 2005; Christoph Strawe, "Public Public Partnership: Die Neustrukturierung des öffentlichen Sektors zwischen Kommerzialisierung und Bürokratisierung," Rundbrief Dreigliederung, Öffentlicher Sektor, No.3, November, 2004.

31. Armin Riess, "Is the PPP model applicable across sectors?" European Investment Bank, EIB Papers, Vol.10, No.2, 2005, p. 12.

32. To divide up large infrastructure may not be entirely possible. For example, electricity networks can be broken down into four segments. However, only the two segments can be made competitive on an open market, which are electricity generation and retail to final consumers. The other two segments cannot be divided and provided by competing firms. These are national transmission grids that take high voltage from the points of production to centres of demand, and the distribution of low-voltage electricity to final consumers.

33. Organisation for Economic Co-Operation and Development (OECD), OECD Principles for Private Sector Participation in Infrastructure, Paris, 2007, pp. 17 & 23. Also: Elder, Ruhland and Hafner, et al., op. cit., p. 9; H. Cox., "Questions about the initiative of the European commission concerning the awarding and compulsory competitive tendering of public service concessions," Annals of Public and Cooperative Economics, Vol.74, No.1, 2003.

34. Allyson Pollock, M., Matthew G. Dunnigan, et al., "The Private Finance Initiative: Planning the 'new' NHS: Downsizing for the 21st century," BMJ journal, British Medical Association, 1999, No.319, pp. 179–184. (See: www.bmj.com).

35. Organisation for Economic Co-Operation and Development (OECD), OECD Principles for Private Sector Participation in Infrastructure, Paris, 2007, p. 23.

36. Information on the London Underground PPP taken from: The Daily Telegraph, London, 19 July 2007, p. 4; The Economist, 28 April 2007, Vol. 383, No. 8526, p. 36; London Underground Limited, London Underground and the PPP: the third year 2005/06, Report for financial year ending 31 March 2006; Price Waterhouse Coopers, Delivering the PPP promise: A Review of PPP issues and activity, PricewaterhouseCoopers International Ltd., 2005, p. 24; Abby Ghobadian, David Gallear, Nicholas O'Regan and Howard Viney, eds., Public-Private Partnerships: Policy and Experience, Houndmills and New York, Palgrave Macmillan, 2004, pp. 21–23 & Chapter 18.

37. London Underground Limited, London Underground and the PPP: the third year 2005/06, Report for financial year ending 31 March 2006, p. 5. See also: The Daily Telegraph, London, 19 July 2007, p. 4.

38. Organisation for Economic Co-Operation and Development (OECD), OECD Principles for Private Sector Participation in Infrastructure, Paris, 2007, p. 24.

39. See further: www.partnerships.org.uk

40. Organisation for Economic Co-Operation and Development (OECD), OECD Principles for Private Sector Participation in Infrastructure, Paris, 2007, p. 24.

41. Organisation for Economic Co-Operation and Development (OECD), OECD Principles for Private Sector Participation in Infrastructure, Paris, 2007, p. 25.

42. This is one of the findings that underlies this writing and that was found in almost all the responses provided for this research.

43. Von Weizsäcker, Young, and Finger, op. cit. pp. 21–24.

44. Organisation for Economic Co-Operation and Development (OECD), OECD Principles for Private Sector Participation in Infrastructure, Paris, 2007, p. 14.

45. Organisation for Economic Co-Operation and Development (OECD), Modernising Government: The Way Forward, Paris, 2005, p. 136.

46. Information on the London Underground PPP taken from: The Daily Telegraph, London, 19 July 2007, p. 4; The Economist, 28 April 2007, Vol. 383, No. 8526, p. 36; London Underground Limited, London Underground and the PPP: the third year 2005/06, Report for financial year ending 31 March 2006; Price Waterhouse Coopers, Delivering the PPP promise: A Review of PPP issues and activity, PricewaterhouseCoopers International Ltd., 2005, p. 24; Ghobadian, Gallear, O'Regan Viney, eds., op. cit., pp. 21–23 & Chapter 18.

47. See further: "Tokyo bloque la montée de TCI dans J-Power," in Le Temps, 17 April 2008, p. 27.

48. See for example: Paul Grout, "Is the Private Finance Initiative a Good Deal?," CMPO Leverhulme Centre for Market and Public Organisation, University of Bristol, Issue No.6, December 2001, pp. 1–4; and Armin Riess, loc. cit.

49. See further for critical appraisals of the costs to the British public from PFI projects, particularly in the medical and hospital sector: British Medical Association, BMJ journal, available at www.bmj.com; Hellowell and Pollock, op. cit.

50. See further Ibidem.

51. European Union, European Commission and Eurostat, "Long term contracts between government units and non-government partners (Public-private-partnerships)," Luxembourg, Office for Official Publications of the European Communities, 2004; and, Eurostat, "Treatment of public-private partnerships," Eurostat news release, No.18, 11 February 2004.

52. See also: www.warnowquerung.de

53. European Union, European Commission and Eurostat, "Long term contracts between government units and non-government partners (Public-private partnerships)," Methods and Nomenclatures, Luxembourg, Office for official publications of the European Communities, August 2004, p. 5, Footnote 4.

54. European Union, European Commission and Eurostat, "Long term contracts between government units and non-government partners (Public-private partnerships)," Methods and Nomenclatures, Luxembourg, Office for official publications of the European Communities, August 2004, p. 5.

55. As an example, some influential texts consider the development of PPPs in a positive light, such as: British Columbia, Government of the Province of, Ministry of Municipal Affairs, Public Private Partnership: A Guide for Local Government, Victoria, British Columbia, Canada, May 1999; Deloitte, Closing the Infrastructure Gap: The Role of Public-Private Partnerships, A Deloitte Research Study, Deloitte Touche Tohmatsu, 2006; Hochtief, "Hochtief: Public-Private-Partnership (PPP)

Positionspapier," Unternehmens-Kommunikation, August 2006; Robert N. Palter, Jay Walder and Stian Westlake, "How investors can get more out of infrastructure," McKinsey Quarterly, McKinsey Company, February 2008; United Kingdom, Government-private office Partnerships UK (PUK); see further: www.partnerships.org. uk; United Kingdom, National Audit Office (NAO), "Helping the nation spend wisely," Annual Report 2005.

56. British Medical Association, BMJ journal, articles outline the lack of effective cost accounting in UK's hospitals that are operated through PFIs (PPPs). See further: www.bmj.com; Also, British Broadcasting Corporation (BBC), "PFI will cost jobs and beds," 6 July 1998.

57. Such solutions are sought by individuals in many Western countries. People who can afford private services chose private hospitals, private security or private schools.

58. Among such high-profile individuals are the American President W. Bush with regard to global insecurity vis-à-vis the "war against terror," and the former Vice-President Al Gore regarding global warming and environmental damage.

59. Organisation for Economic Co-Operation and Development (OECD), OECD Environmental Outlook to 2030, Paris, 2008.

60. United Nations Environment Programme (UNEP), GEO-4—Global Environment Outlook—Environment for Development, United Nations, 2007; World Business Council for Sustainable Development, see: www.wbcsd.org.

61. Information obtained from Ms Caroline Visser, former expert with the Netherlands PPP Unit and currently at the International Road Federation (www.irfnet. org), Geneva, January 2008. The Netherlands follows the English and North American formats for its PPP concession contracts.

62. National sustainability criteria continuously developed and adapted to conform to perceived national environmental protection needs as well as international standards and laws. For example, the UK is developing sustainable procurement regulations in consultation with a large number of stakeholders. See further: "PFI: Meeting the sustainability challenge," by Julie Hill and Joanna Collins, Published by Green Alliance, July 2004; and "Draft Strategy for Sustainable Construction: A consultation paper, July 2007, by Dept. for Business, Dept. for Environment, Food and Rural Affairs (DEFRA), Dept. for Culture, Media and Sport, Communities and Local Government. Also, most Western countries abide by internationally negotiated regulations, such as the Aarhus Convention, (http://ec.europa.eu/environment/aarhus/index.htm) or the Basel Convention (http://www.basel.int), etc. Governments also observe the influence that large NGOs have in the same area and that recommend various kinds of eco-labels or certifications in which a growing number of private companies take part. See, for example: "Environment and public procurement," a paper by the European Environmental Bureau, Greenpeace Europe, World Wildlife Fund, and Climate Action Network, Nov.2001.

63. Organisation for Economic Cooperation and Development (OECD), "Recommendation of the Council on Improving the Environmental Performance of Public Procurement," 23 January 2002.

64. The largest declaration in this direction was proclaimed at the global summit of the United Nations. See further the "Millennium Development Goals" (www. developmentgoals.org) and the UN's "Partnerships for Sustainable Development"

declaration from the Johannesburg World Summit, Commission on Sustainable Development, 2002. See also: http://www.johannsburgsummit.org or http://www.un.org.esa.sustdev

65. The WTO regulation provides that: "Nothing in this agreement shall be construed to prevent any contracting authority from imposing or enforcing measures necessary to protect order or safety, human, animal or plant life or health in particular with a view to sustainable development." World Trade Organisation (WTO), "Government Purchasing Agreement," 1996. See: http://www.wto.org

66. World Bank, The Environmental Implications of Privatization: Lessons for Developing Countries, Magda LOVEI and Bradford S. GENTRY, World Bank Discussion Paper No.426, Washington D.C., 2002, pp. 41–42.

67. European Union, European Commission's Interpretative Communication on the Community law applicable to public procurement and the possibilities for integrating environmental considerations into public procurement, COM(2001).

68. European Environmental Bureau (EEB), *EU Sustainable Development Strategy: From Theory to Delivery*, by John HONTELEZ and Maria BUITENKAMP, Brussels, EEB publication no.008, 2006, p. 3.

69. European Commission, Commission of the European Communities, "Commission Interpretative Communication on the Community law applicable to public procurement and the possibilities for integrating environmental considerations into public procurement," Brussels, July, 2001. See also: EurActiv, the European Coalition for Green and Social Procurement, 2002, http://www.euractiv.com.

70. European Union, Environmental Assessment Directive, Directive 2001/42/EC of the European Parliament and the Council, 2001.

71. J. C. Powell, R. Tinch, O. White and M. Peters, *Successful Approaches to Sustainable Procurement*, A report to the Department for Environment, Food and Rural Affairs, London, Defra, Environmental Futures Ltd., 2006, p. 12.

72. An area that has not yet been explored much, but which is rapidly gaining popular support is "buy locally" when possible and "fair trade" when purchasing goods or services from developing countries. Government procurements are not (yet) at this stage of socially and environmentally "responsible citizenship," but as private companies and consumers are modifying their behaviour, it will be a matter of time before public authorities adapt as well. Slower to adapt will inevitably be transnational regulations such as those of the EU and the WTO that currently demand open and free competition without preferential treatment for "local" or "fair-trade" providers.

73. Interestingly, this focus by a growing number of municipalities on local production can be interpreted as protectionism that goes against the principles of free trade and open international competition in procurement processes as promoted by many national governments, the EU, the OECD, the WTO and other regional financial institutions.

74. In part from: Powell, Tinch, White and Peters, op. cit., p. 209.

75. In the UK, the Office of Government Commerce (OGC) explains that "value for money" should include the added value of sustainable and environmentally acceptable procurement. See further: http://www.ogc.gov.uk/index.asp?id=377

76. Office of Government Commerce (OGC), London, "Managing Public Sector Procurement" Leaflet; and National Audit Office (NAO), Improving procurement:

progress by the Office of Government Commerce in improving departments' capability to procure cost-effectively, HC 361-I, 2003-2004, London, 12 March 2004; and, National Audit Office (NAO), Sustainable Procurement In Central Government, 2005.

77. For energy efficiency in PPPs constructions, see the samples provided by UK organisation Demonstrating Excellence at: www.constructingexellence.org.uk. For the Netherlands water management, see: www.delfluent.nl

78. This example taken from: UNECE "Governance in Public Private Partnerships for Infrastructure Development" Draft, TRADE/WP. 5/2005/2, 2 Nov.2005, and the 2007 draft paper on PPPs and Good Governance. Further data for this example was also taken from the Vancouver city internet site.

79. Bleischwitz and Proske, loc. cit., p. 110.

80. Another consideration with regard to the trade in solid waste is its potential security-related aspect linked to organised crime. Much of the collection and elimination of household waste in the Italian region of Naples is controlled by the local Camorra organised crime group and the agreement to have waste from that city incinerated in Geneva leaves open questions of transparency and who the financial deals where made with. ("Déchets napolitains: le risqué zero n'existe pas," and N. Giannakopoulos, "L'ingérence du crime organise dans la filière des déchets," in *Le Temps*, 5 March 2008, pp. 11 & 19.

81. Bleischwitz and Proske, loc. cit., p. 111.

82. Von Weizsäcker, Young, and Finger, op. cit., pp. 27-31.

83. Selective subsidies can be found in transportation tickets for students or the elderly, or in social housing. Broad State subsidies exist for an entire population also exist in most West European countries in the construction or maintenance of roads and railways.

84. Bernard Wuthrich, "La Poste perdra son monopole d'ici à 2012," *Le Temps*, jeudi 28 février 2008, p. 6.

85. Bundestags-Drucksache 14/1696 of 30 September 1999, page 9; as noted in Ludwig Gramlich, "Daseinsvorsorge und Liberalisierung: Briefmonopol und Universaldienst—wie lange klingelt der 'Postmann' noch?" in Politische Studien, Vol.58, No.414, July/August 2007, p. 101.

86. See for example: Hellowell and Pollock, op. cit.

87. The question of tolls on road is not only common for freeways or ferries, but is gradually being adopted for bridges and tunnels. Similarly, the operation of London city's user fees for driving inside the inner city perimeter is now debated in numerous other cities as well, either to replenish city finances or to reduce congestion and pollution. See for example: "Péages routiers: le coup d'éclat de la Ville de Genève," in Le Temps, jeudi 28 février 2008, p. 10.

88. In part from: Jan Metzger, "The concept of critical infrastructure protection," in Bailes and Isabel Frommelt, eds., op. cit., pp. 201-202.

89. United Nations, Human Development Report / *Rapport Mondial sur le Développement Humain 1994*, "Les nouvelles dimensions de la sécurité humaine," pp. 23-41, UNDP, New York, and the French edition aluded to here: PNUD, Editions Economica, Paris, 1994.

90. In the English language, the word "safety" is often used to mean the same as "security." However, "safety," or "being safe" is usually mentioned in relation to

the individual person's perception and condition, while the word "security" refers to a collective or system, such as a community, a country, an environment or an infrastructure.

91. Human Security Centre, *Human Security Report 2005: War and Peace in the 21st Century*, University of British Columbia, Canada, Oxford University Press, 2005, p.viii.

92. *Human Security Report 2005*, The University of British Columbia, Canada, Human Security Centre, Oxford University Press, 2005, p.viii.

93. Not counting crises due to violent conflict or accidents, some 950 natural catastrophes have hit human and natural environments in 2007. According to the Munich Re Insurance company, this is one hundred more incidents than the year before and represents the highest figure ever since the company began collecting data in 1974. Natural catastrophes were the most costly for insurers with costs reaching more than USD 75 billion for 2007, against USD 50 billion in 2006. The greatest financial costs were caused by an earthquake in Japan in July 2007, and quickly followed by hurricanes and strong storms that cause severe flooding. The human cost world-wide remains at an average of 15'000 to 20'000 per year from natural catastrophes alone, and populations in the least industrialised countries suffer the most due to their lack of infrastructure resilience. Information taken from "Le coût des catastrophes naturelles s'envole," in *Le Temps*, 28 December 2007, p. 17.

94. London Underground Limited, *London Underground and the PPP: the third year 2005/06*, Report for financial year ending 31 March 2006, p. 3.

95. Kevin Rosner, "Critical energy system infrastructure protection in Europe and the legitimate economy," Bailes and Frommelt, op. cit., pp. 215.; and also: Organisation for Economic Co-Operation and Development (OECD), *OECD Principles for Private Sector Participation in Infrastructure*, Paris, 2007, p. 25.

96. This so-called "Fennell Investigation" of 1989 resulted in the Fire Precautions Regulation of 1989 placed under section 12 of the1971 Fire Precautions Act.

97. Information for this discussion taken from Castern Greve and Niels Ejersbo, "Public-private partnership for infrastructure in Denmark: from local to global partnering?" in Hodge and GREVE, eds., op. cit., pp. 257–268; as well as from the following websites: www.group4securicor.com, and www.falck.com.

98. The Banco Investment Group blacklisted Falck's American subsidiary security company Wackenhut. From: Greve and Ejersbo, loc. cit., p. 264.

99. Ibidem, p. 265.

100. Dietrich Fischer, *Nonmilitary Aspects of Security: A Systems Approach*, Geneva, United Nations Institute for Disarmament Research and Aldershot, Dartmouth Publishing Company, 1993, p. 182.

101. These conclusions are confirmed in the following study done at the European Investment Bank which supports PPPs with finances and financial advice: Riess, Armin, loc. cit.

4

Public-Private Partnerships:
A Quantitative Analysis

Thomas Zacharewicz

One of the main goals of this research is to compare on one side, the international theoretical framework of public-private partnerships (PPPs) and the influence these structures have had on the development of public infrastructure and services and on the other side, the way PPPs are perceived by citizens and stakeholders. This section aims at presenting this last aspect as a complement to the other chapters of this report.

Between April and November 2007, research questionnaires were sent out and interviews conducted within five geographical areas. These include the four countries Poland, Ukraine, Russia and China, as well as Western countries (i.e. Western European countries and North America). The respondents were active in three different sectors: public administration, private companies and finally, Non-Governmental Organisations (NGOs) and research think tanks and universities. The questions asked dealt with the ability of PPPs to promote social and economic development while fulfilling the fundamental criteria of equity, security and sustainability; they sought to identify the necessary conditions in order to achieve these goals within the development of PPPs. Questions also addressed the obstacles that slow down or hinder the development of PPPs. Finally, the respondents were asked how they think the problems and challenges they identified could be overcome.

It must be pointed out that the countries in which this study was conducted have a rather short experience of PPPs, and the number of knowledgeable people on this topic remains quite limited. Therefore, this quantitative study does not aim at being representative of the general opinion.

Rather, it provides indicative tendencies that can be used as a comparative starting approach, together with recent theory and data available on operating PPPs.

The answers given by the sample respondents were interpreted according to three different variables used in this study. The first one, which will be the most often used, is the nationality of respondents. This variable allows a comparison of opinions between countries in which PPPs are underdeveloped, and countries where such partnerships have run for many years now.

The second variable used in this analysis is the professional sector of the respondents. Indeed, representatives from State administrations and private companies express different priorities with regard to PPPs; the former focus on increasing the allocative efficiency of projects (i.e. the quality and security of the services, their affordability for public sector and the population), while the latter express the objective of improving productive efficiency, often through a trade-off between production costs and benefits. Because of these reasons, these two sectors may have slightly different opinions about PPPs.

The third variable, much like the first, allows for a cross-country analysis. It is based on the level of knowledge respondents say they have about PPPs. The main advantage of this variable lies in its ability to reveal the differences between common opinions and more elaborate or educated views, especially regarding complex or polemical issues.

The results from this study are presented in the following order: Part I will provide general information on the identity of the sample respondents and on their degree of satisfaction with the delivery of current public services. Part II will focus on respondents' opinions of PPPs, their intrinsic efficiency, and the obstacles that hinder or delay their development. Part III will present ideas about PPPs and their ability to promote the three criteria that are equity, sustainable development and security. Finally, the last part (IV) proposes recommendations drawn from the responses, aiming to improve the implementation of PPPs and, more generally the quality of public services.

PART I. GENERAL INFORMATION

Across the geographical area where this survey was carried out, 124 respondents replied to the questionnaire and/or discussed their responses in one-on-one interviews. While this number does not seem large at first, it is important to remember that most of the respondents identified for this research were not easily found—they are mostly individuals known for their involvement with PPPs or for their independent expertise of these types of partnerships.

In the next paragraphs, the three variables are applied to the respondents in the following order: we start with their national origin, followed by their professional sector, and lastly their degree of knowledge of PPPs. Furthermore, this section will also provide some information on the respondents' general level of personal satisfaction about the delivery of public services.

Classification of the Respondents

The National Distribution

The 124 respondents to the questionnaire are divided up as follows: 22 of them come from Western countries, 28 from Poland, 26 from Russia, 15 from Ukraine, and 33 from China. As we previously said, these numbers are quite small, and should therefore not be understood as being representative of public or broad expert opinions about PPPs. Rather, these data offer an indicative and empirical perspective which will be compared and evaluated in the following chapters within more precise theoretical frameworks.

The Sectoral Distribution

The distinction of respondents according to the sector in which they work (public or private) allows to underline the different perceptions of PPPs, especially regarding the partners' individual priorities: the fulfilment of public interest for public administration, or achieving a good trade-off between costs and benefits (efficiency) for private companies.

As Table 4.1 shows, half of our respondents work in public institutions, while the other half work in private companies or NGOs:

Degree of Knowledge on PPPs

A general overview of the respondents' degree of knowledge shows that 45% of them assert being "a little" acquainted with PPPs, while 22% and

Table 4.1. Distribution of the Respondents Per Professional Sector

	Frequency	Percent
Public sector	61	52.6
Private sector	30	25.9
NGO, university	25	21.6
Total	116	100.0

23% respectively recognize that they are acquainted "quite a lot" and "very much." A cross-country analysis reveals significant differences that coincide with the country's general experience in developing PPPs. Predictably, the highest percentage of people with a strong level of knowledge is found in Western countries (77.3%). In the other countries, the average is around 20% (0% for China, 50% for Poland and 43.4% for Russia).[1]

Degree of Satisfaction with the Quality of Public Services and Infrastructure

Independently of the respondents' nationality, professional sector or level of knowledge of PPPs, some general tendencies appear from the questionnaires, such as a high dissatisfaction with the existing infrastructure and services. For example, to the question: "Are you satisfied with the current delivery of infrastructure services in your country," almost 80% of the respondents answered that they are "not at all satisfied" or "little satisfied." It is quite interesting to compare here the answers to this question with the answers given to question 6, which asked: "Have there been improvements or degradations in infrastructure services?" The data obtained shows the following:

- Water: 56.9% of the respondents think that there have been improvements (80% in Poland, but only 34% in Russia).
- Transport: 50% (62% in Poland and China, 39% for Russia and Western countries).
- Housing: 42% (75% in Poland, 54% in China, 26% in Russia, 10% in Western countries).
- Health: 38% (10% in Western countries, 33% in Poland, 56% in Russia, 50% in China).
- Energy innovation: 56% (100% in Western countries, 54% in Poland, 21% in Russia, 58% in China).

One can see that the difference between the percentages of the two questions indicates high expectations for the improvement of public services.

To the question "Which Sector Delivers Public Infrastructure and Services?," the answers give another dimension to the general understanding of the current delivery of infrastructure and services.

In our closed questionnaire, question 11 aims at identifying the sector providing public services, by asking: "In the sector you know best, is the private sector already engaged in operating some public services?." Generally, 87% of the respondents asserted that the private sector owns and provides less that 50% of the public infrastructure and services. Table 4.2 provides the summarised answers to this question: "In the sector you know the best does the public sector already operate some public services?"

Table 4.2. Respondents' Opinion About the Participation of the Private Sector in the Delivery of Public Infrastructure and Services

In the sector you know the best does the public sector already operate some public services?		Country of respondents					Total
		Western countries	Poland	Russia	Ukraine	China	
Not at all	Frequency	2	5	2	2	4	15
	Percent	9.1%	22.7%	10.0%	13.3%	15.4%	14.3%
Less than 20% of private operation and ownership	Frequency	9	9	14	11	14	57
	Percent	40.9%	40.9%	70.0%	73.3%	53.8%	54.3%
More than 20% of private operation and ownership	Frequency	9	5	3	2	8	27
	Percent	40.9%	22.7%	15.0%	13.3%	30.8%	25.7%
More than 50% of private operation and ownership	Frequency	2	3	1	0	0	6
	Percent	9.1%	13.6%	5.0%	.0%	.0%	5.7%
	Frequency	22	22	20	15	26	105
	Percent	100.0%	100.0%	100.0%	100.0%	100.0%	100.0%

One should keep in mind that this quantitative analysis is not based upon a statistical sample and therefore there may be a gap between the opinions expressed by our respondents and the actual distribution of opinions within each of the four countries. The answers to this question may not reflect reality; that is, the participation of the private sector in the delivery of public infrastructure and services could be higher or lower than what is expressed here through the respondents' opinions. What can be deduced however, is the fact that the public sector is perceived to be the main responsible for the low quality of infrastructure. This is shown by 80% of respondents unsatisfied with the quality of infrastructure and services. As the private sector is seen to have little influence on the delivery of these public services (see Table 4.2), the criticism expressed by the respondents is mainly directed to the performance of public institutions.

On the contrary, most people we have interviewed believe that the private sector is often more efficient that the public sector. This will be shown in Part II of this study.

PART II. PPPS EFFICIENCY AND BARRIERS TO THEIR DEVELOPMENT

The common belief that the private sector is able to provide public infrastructure and services more efficiently is not new. Since the 1980's and the appearance of the "new" public management ideas, the concept of more efficient private business management has spread around the world and found a wide echo among policy makers.

The respondents to our questionnaire generally expressed opinions that were in line with this ideological trend. However, some slight differences appear among countries and sectors. Nevertheless, two features were widely agreed upon: first, the overall superiority given to PPPs over traditional public procurement; and second, the existence and persistence of legal obstacles or psychological barriers which have hindered their development.

So, how confident are our respondents with regard to the private sector as a public service provider? In Question 13 (see Table 4.3), we asked whether people thought that "the introduction of private capital in the

Table 4.3. Respondents' Opinion About the Introduction of Private Capital in Public Services. Answers to the Questions: "Do you think that the Introduction of Private Capital in the Traditional Public Sphere Could Favour an Improvement of the Quality of Public Services?"

	Frequency	Percent
Not at all	4	4.1
A little	14	14.3
Quite a lot	38	38.8
Very much	42	42.9
Total	98	100.0

traditional public sphere could favour an improvement of the quality of public services." The answers are overwhelmingly positive, independently of the selection criteria of our respondents (that is their knowledge about PPPs, academic diploma or country).

These general results are confirmed by the fact that 94% of the respondents most acquainted with PPPs think that the introduction of private capital would increase the quality of public services "quite a lot" or "very much."

The same tendencies appear when asking respondents to which degree should private companies be involved in the delivery of public services (cf. Question 12 "To what extent do you think that the private sector should enter the public domain?"). Indeed, more than 80% of respondents expressed the view that the private sector should operate and own more than 20% of public services and infrastructure.

However, some slight differences appear between Poland and Russia on one hand, and between Western countries and China on the other hand.[2] While the respondents from the first two countries seem to be in favour of a large privatisation of public services (respectively 50% and 52% of the respondents think that the private sector should own/operate more than 50% of the public services), respondents in Western Countries and China seem much more balanced. Indeed, only 36% of the Western respondents believe that the private sector should own/operate more than 50% of the public services, and only 8% believe the same in China.

Although both China and Western countries show similar results with regard to privatisation of public services, the justifications are quite different. One can interpret the Western responses by recognising their much longer experience with the privatisation of public services. In addition, Western countries had more time to discover the flaws in the "New Public Management" approach, which is not yet the case with Russia or Poland.

The very small percentage obtained for China could be explained by the importance that Chinese respondents give to the public sector and its central role in sustaining and orienting economic development. Furthermore, the Chinese attach more political and social importance to basic infrastructure and services. They thus have high expectations for a fair and reasonably priced access to these services, and for their contribution to stabilizing society. This interpretation is even more plausible if we remember that the development of the middle class in China, which now enjoys a fair economic purchasing power, is still limited, with a few exceptions, to the coastal and urban regions.

An analysis by sector reveals a different perspective: quite logically, a majority (52%) of respondents from the private sector in China think that private companies should be very much involved in the delivery of public services, while only 28% think similarly in the public sector.

Questioning the Advantages of PPPs

While the previous section aimed at presenting the general degree of confidence that respondents have in the private sector involvement with public services and PPPs, this next section exposes the reasons given by the respondents to explain their position.

Question No. 14 provided the opportunity for respondents to express their views on the ability of PPPs to improve the quality of public services.[3] The results for both public and private sector respondents is very similar to the question above: more than 75% of them consider that PPPs can improve the delivery of public services, in relation to four elements.

First, 76% of respondents asserted that PPPs can improve the price/quality relation of public services. However, 30% of people with a second university degree expressed doubts (i.e. answered "don't know," "disagree," or "strongly disagree").

Second, 77% of respondents agree or even strongly agree that PPPs are more readily able to keep costs down and stick to budgets than the current public procurement system. Some doubts were emitted, however. Russian respondents were the most sceptical since only 44% of them agree. If we consider the answers by sector, 46% of the people working in NGOs/universities recognize that they don't know, disagree or strongly disagree with this proposition. These answers are confirmed by the results to our question on transaction costs (see below).

Third, very few objections were raised against the time-related efficiency of privately delivered public services. 83% of respondents agree or strongly agree to designate the timing of delivery as an important advantage of PPPs.

And fourth, a very high percentage of people believe that PPPs can facilitate the modernization of infrastructure. 80% of them support this proposition, independently of their country, sector, or degree of knowledge. Nevertheless, this optimism was balanced by responses to Question 55, which asked whether PPPs are a more or less costly way to finance infrastructure modernization. Here, a large group of respondents (43%) showed reluctance with regard to the ability of PPPs to provide cheaper infrastructure modernization and public services. Similarly, 40% of people working in NGOs/university, and 46% of people with a university doctorate emit the same doubts.

In contrast to the general positive opinions, one response stood out due to the high number of doubts expressed. This was question number 14, which touched on the subject of transaction costs in PPPs. Here, 57% of respondents said they don't know, disagree or even strongly disagree with the idea that PPPs can improve the quality of public services in relation to overall cost efficiency.

An analysis by sector does not give more positive answers; surprisingly, the strongest doubts come from the private sector, which gathers 63% of negative or neutral answers (61% for NGOs/universities). A cross-country examination shows that the results are no different, with the exception of China, that gathered a majority of positive answers for this question (60% agree or strongly agree). In addition, looking at the results according to the degree of knowledge of respondents does not indicate contradictory opinions: a large proportion (61%) of those who are very acquainted with PPPs recognize that they doubt the capacity of PPPs to reduce transaction costs. Thus, to summarize our respondents' stated opinions, PPPs are more likely to improve the delivery of services in relation to price-quality, stick to budgets, respect the timing of delivery, and modernize infrastructure. However, most respondents believe that PPPs will generate higher transaction costs than traditional public procurement.

Obstacles to the Development of PPPs

All the advantages that have been exposed so far are nonetheless counter-balanced by a number of barriers, that can generate unwanted effects on the implementation process of PPPs. These barriers were identified by our respondents and can be divided in two different categories: the "soft" obstacles, linked to the lack of knowledge, experience or political will, and which are often the main reasons why PPPs are not developed in transition economies; and the "hard" obstacles, that refer to suboptimal institutional and legal conditions in a country.

The "Soft" Obstacles

From the one-on-one interviews carried out in Poland, Ukraine, Russia and China, the psychological or political obstacles are the most important ones. They explain the small number of PPPs within what we call "pre-PPP countries." The public sector, especially local administrations, still has little confidence in the private sector. This perception is illustrated here by the lack of political will to develop PPP structures (see Table 4.4).

The second interpretation can be based on the lack of experience and knowledge on how to draft PPP projects. In the countries used in our study, between 70% and 90% of respondents think that the lack of experience and the lack of knowledge are important or very important factors respectively, in explaining the low development of PPP structures.

In addition to the lack of political will and the lack of experience, a third obstacle—situated somewhere between "soft" and "hard" obstacles—can be mentioned. Indeed, 77% of our respondents in Russia, 80% in Ukraine and

Table 4.4. Respondent's Opinion About the Lack of Political Will as a Barrier to the Implementation of PPPs

Evaluation by the respondents of the lack of political will as a factor that may explain the absence (or the little number) of PPPs in their country.		Sector in which respondents are primarily active			Total
		Public sector	Private sector	NGO, university	
Strongly disagree	Frequency	5	0	0	5
	Percent	8.6%	0%	0%	4.4%
Disagree	Frequency	9	3	3	15
	Percent	15.5%	10.0%	12.0%	13.3%
Agree	Frequency	14	2	10	26
	Percent	24.1%	6.7%	40.0%	23.0%
Strongly agree	Frequency	30	25	12	67
	Percent	51.7%	83.3%	48.0%	59.3%
Total	Frequency	58	30	25	113
	Percent	100.0%	100.0%	100.0%	100.0%

54% in China believe that corruption is an obstacle to the development of PPPs (45% in Western countries, 23% in Poland). Once more, we must underline that these numbers may not be in line with reality: the actual influence of corruption on the creation of PPPs is probably different from what is perceived by the respondents; however, these perceptions are probably at the root of a general reluctance to develop PPPs.

The "Hard" Obstacles

Adding to the soft obstacles, most respondents identified their national legal and institutional frameworks as a main cause of the low or slow development of PPPs.

In the questionnaires distributed in the five geographical areas for this research, many questions dealt with the juridical framework and its influence on the creation of PPPs.[4] Two of them can be presented here to illustrate the respondents' opinions about this subject. The first one shows quite a strong difference between Western countries, that have a relatively long experience of developing and operating PPPs, and the so-called "pre-PPP countries," where such experience is minimal.[5] In the West, only 8% of respondents think that the legal framework is insufficiently developed to allow for a wide creation of PPPs. In contrast, more than 60% of respondents in Poland and Russia believe that the legal system is not developed enough in their countries. The Table 4.5 contains the responses to this question: "Are the existing framework (i.e. institutional and legal infrastructure) sufficiently developed in the country to allow the creation of PPPs?"

Table 4.5. Respondents' Opinion About the Adequacy of the Existing Institutional and Legal Framework

Are the existing framework (i.e. institutional and legal infrastructure) sufficiently developed in the country to allow the creation of PPPs?		Country of respondent				Total
		Western countries	Poland	Russia	China	
Yes	Frequency	14	7	9	4	34
	Percent	66.7%	26.9%	39.1%	16.7%	36.2%
No	Frequency	2	17	14	15	48
	Percent	9.5%	65.4%	60.9%	62.5%	51.1%
Don't know	Frequency	5	2	0	5	12
	Percent	23.8%	7.7%	.0%	20.8%	12.8%
Total	Frequency	21	26	23	24	94
	Percent	100.0%	100.0%	100.0%	100.0%	100.0%

In spite of these heterogeneous results, the majority of our interviewees agree on the lack of clarity in the decision-making process with regard to the creation of PPPs, independently of their country or sector (more than 90% for Western countries, and an average of 74% for the other four countries). It therefore seems that even when there is a functioning juridical framework in place, the creation process of PPPs still seems very complex to the decision makers. These two features, combined with the lack of expertise and experience of the public sector, are often considered as the main reasons why PPPs are still underdeveloped or ineffective in pre-PPP countries.

However, as the previous sections show, most respondents believe that PPPs are intrinsically more efficient and able to provide higher quality public services and infrastructure than the traditional public sector.

PART III. THREE CRITERIA: SUSTAINABLE DEVELOPMENT, EQUITY AND SECURITY

From the debate on the efficiency of PPPs and their ability to provide high-quality public services, this research also analyses and evaluates the potential for public-private partnerships to contribute to sustainable development, human security and equity. In other words, one of the goals here is to answer the following question: to what extent can PPPs contribute to sustainable and equitable development, and to human security?

In contrast to the expressed views about efficiency, the respondents showed a relatively higher degree of scepticism towards the capacity of PPPs to promote these three criteria.

PPPs and Sustainable Development

Two of our questions directly deal with the capacity of PPPs to respect the natural environment.[6] Their analysis shows two different aspects. First, all the respondents—indifferently of their country or sector—expressed strong doubts (i.e. they gave a negative answer or a "don't know") with regard to a superior ability of PPPs to respect the environment, in the development and maintenance of infrastructure. The second aspect shows that 55,4% of respondents think that PPPs are more efficient in the use of natural resources. This second result can be interpreted as an effort from PPPs to become more productive and efficient; quite logically, it is in their interest to use efficiently their resources—natural or not—in order to lower production and maintenance costs. At the same time however, respect for the natural environment may also be a more costly constraint for the private partner, who has to comply with national regulations that impose specific requirements. This argument could explain why the answers to question 17 reveal such strong scepticism (see Table 4.6).

As can be seen from Table 4.6, some important differences appear between the private and public sectors. Respondents in the former expressed more confidence in the ability of PPPs to respect the natural environment. Indeed, 60% of the respondents working in private companies think that PPPs are more respectful of the natural environment than the public sector. Only 22% of the respondents who work in public institutions share the same opinion.

With regard to the criteria of familiarity with PPPs, and irrespective of their affiliation, 58% of respondents well acquainted with PPPs doubt of the superior capacity of PPPs to respect natural environment.

In order to ensure that the natural environment is truly preserved, respondents from all countries and sectors agree on the necessity to invite third party organisations to evaluate and report the way in which natural resources are used (around 80% of favourable opinions independently of any criteria). Such evaluations are expected to increase best practices and allow the creation of a knowledge synergy between public and private partners. In this respect, it is significant to acknowledge that most respondents believe that a good cooperation could favour the transfer of technologies from private companies to the local economy.[7]

In sum, the answers given about PPPs and sustainable development are not as overwhelmingly positive as they were with regard to economic effi-

Table 4.6. Respondents' Comparison Between the Capacity of PPP and Government's Provision of Public Services to be Respectful of Natural Resources

Are PPPs more respectful of natural resources than the traditional government infrastructure and services?		Sector in which respondents are primarily active			Total
		Public sector	Private sector	NGO, university	
Yes	Frequency	11	15	10	36
	Percent	22.4%	60.0%	50.0%	38.3%
No	Frequency	19	7	8	34
	Percent	38.8%	28.0%	40.0%	36.2%
Don't know	Frequency	19	3	2	24
	Percent	38.8%	12.0%	10.0%	25.5%
Total	Frequency	49	25	20	94
	Percent	100.0%	100.0%	100.0%	100.0%

ciency. A degree of scepticism came to the surface concerning the capacity of public and private actors to improve respect for the natural environment.

For many respondents, the expression "sustainability" is not understood as referring only to the natural environment. The word can also include aspects like the lasting quality of human life, as well as of social, political, economic and technological development. As we have just shown above, respondents seem to strongly believe that third-party evaluations can improve at least one of these aspects of sustainability, and thus be beneficial for the partners and, most importantly, for society as a whole.

PPPs and Equity

The questions concerning equity allowed a comparison between the services and infrastructure delivered by government, and those delivered by private companies. The diversity of answers is quite representative of the distribution of opinions about equity: they are often unclear, ambiguous, and sometimes contradictory. One principal question was: "Can you state how the realization of PPP projects influenced the living conditions of the population?" Table 4.7 provides an overview of the answers to the ques-

Table 4.7.   Respondents' Opinion About the Impact of PPPs on Living Conditions

Can you say how the realization of PPP projects influenced the living conditions of the population?		Sector in which respondents are primarily active			Total
		Public sector	Private sector	NGO, university	
Much worse	Frequency	7	1	0	8
	Percent	12.7%	3.7%	.0%	7.8%
Slightly worse	Frequency	5	2	2	9
	Percent	9.1%	7.4%	9.5%	8.7%
Remained the same	Frequency	6	7	10	23
	Percent	10.9%	25.9%	47.6%	22.3%
Slightly better	Frequency	20	12	8	40
	Percent	36.4%	44.4%	38.1%	38.8%
Much better	Frequency	17	5	1	23
	Percent	30.9%	18.5%	4.8%	22.3%
Total	Frequency	55	27	21	103
	Percent	100.0%	100.0%	100.0%	100.0%

tion; "Can you say how the realization of PPP projects influenced the living conditions of the population?"

PPPs and the Equitable Access to Public Services

To the question 29, asking respondents whether they think PPPs improve the service delivery to all social groups, 68% of the them answered positively.[8] From this group, a significant majority (more than 70%) live in Western countries, in Poland and in Ukraine. There are however some strong doubts among certain categories of people as follows: 40% of respondents holding a higher university degree are unsure or disagree about a better ability of PPPs to distribute services equitably. 48% of people working in NGOs/universities share the same opinion.

Moreover, some contradictions appear from the answers to question 30, as 56% of respondents agreed that some people could be excluded from PPP services.[9] This implies that of the 68% who think that *PPPs can improve services more efficiently for all social groups*, some respondents think as well that some social groups will remain excluded from such public-private service deliveries. When looking at the distribution of answers by sector, we find that 48% of the respondents who work in the public sector and 59% of the respondents who work in university think that some social groups could be excluded from PPP services (40% in private companies).

Some similar doubts appear for question 31 in the following way: 47% of the respondents answered negatively (meaning that they think that PPPs are less costly).[10] A more detailed analysis shows some differences depending on the professional sector, the country, or the level of knowledge of the respondents.

Generally, the public sector and NGO/universities are much more sceptical than the private sector towards the ability of PPPs to provide cheap services (50% and 72% of respondents working in the public sector or NGO/universities respectively doubt of it, while the rate is only of 43% for the private sector).

If nationality is taken as an independent variable, then it appears that the highest rates of confidence come from western respondents (only 36% of doubt), while the lowest ones are found in Russia and China (72% of doubt for Russia, 54% for China). In the middle, there is Poland with 47% of doubt and Ukraine with 40 %.

In a similar way, the level of knowledge does not generate more homogeneous results: 52% of the respondents holding a Ph.d question the capacity of PPPs to propose cheaper services than traditional public procurement. However, only 37% of the people very acquainted with PPPs do so.

As shown by the answers to questions 29 and 31 particularly, the opinions concerning equity are far from being homogeneous: there is no clear consensus among our respondents on whether PPPs can favour the development of cheap public services for the population.

Civil Society and the Development of PPPs

The second part of our section on equity deals with the perception that civil society has developed about PPPs, and whether their involvement should increase in the creation and evaluation of such projects. From the start, we must note a difference in the perceptions of civil society between Western countries and Poland on one hand, and Russia, Ukraine and China on the other hand (see Table 4.8). The very high rate of neutral opinions in the last group of countries could be interpreted as a lack of information about PPPs. In "pre-PPP countries," PPPs are often considered as a way of privatising public services, which could explain the higher rate of negative opinions.

A second explanation could be that the opinions given by our respondents actually correspond to the reality: the implementation of PPPs could have caused some perverse effects to the local population (increase of prices, low quality, etc.).

A possible way to increase the positive opinions on PPPs can be to involve more actively civil society in the development and the evaluation of these projects; this assumption can be deduced from the very positive answers to questions 37 and 38.[11]

PPPs and security

Question 41 of the survey aims at identifying the priorities with regard to the security issue. Out of the seven propositions offered to respondents, all were considered to have become increasingly important, with more than 70% of favourable answers.[12] The two exceptions were the issues of

Table 4.8. Respondents' Evaluation of Public Opinion Towards PPPs

Overall, how would you evaluate the public opinion about PPPs?		Country of respondents					Total
		Western countries	Poland	Russia	Ukraine	China	
Very bad opinion	Frequency	3	1	0	0	0	4
	Percent	13.6%	4.0%	.0%	.0%	.0%	3.4%
Slightly negative opinion	Frequency	10	15	3	2	9	39
	Percent	45.5%	60.0%	11.5%	13.3%	30.0%	33.1%
Neutral opinion	Frequency	5	5	15	8	10	43
	Percent	22.7%	20.0%	57.7%	53.3%	33.3%	36.4%
Slightly positive opinion	Frequency	3	3	8	4	10	28
	Percent	13.6%	12.0%	30.8%	26.7%	33.3%	23.7%
Very positive opinion	Frequency	1	1	0	1	1	4
	Percent	4.5%	4.0%	.0%	6.7%	3.3%	3.4%
Total	Frequency	22	25	26	15	30	118
	Percent	100.0%	100.0%	100.0%	100.0%	100.0%	100.0%

"security of social services" and "corruption," which only gathered 50% of positive answers.

Conversely, two topics gathered an exceptionally large amount of positive answers. The "security of vital infrastructure" gathered more than 70% of favourable answers in every country, with an incredibly high rate of 100% in Western countries. Similarly, the "security of clean water" gathered more than 90% in Western countries and China, and more than 70% of favourable answers in the other countries.

In general, the Polish respondents were the ones who had the relatively lowest percentages: only 40%, 37% and 37% respectively think that natural disaster protection, violence due to inter-ethnic conflicts and security of social services has become more important in the last 10 years. In spite of these small differences, the answers which refer to the ability of PPPs to provide safe infrastructure and services are usually more homogeneous than those regarding sustainable development or equity.

PPPs and the Improvement/Degradation of Security

In reference to question 42, a distinction has to be made between Western countries, where respondents seem to be more optimistic, and respondents in "pre-PPP countries."[13] Table 4.9 provides an overview of the answers: "Do you think that sharing the responsibility for security between the government and the private sector makes security more difficult to achieve?"

An interpretation of these differences can be that Western countries had a longer experience with PPPs, and consequently they developed a better ability to draft PPP contracts and deal with the security issue.

A similar distinction can be found in the difference of opinions between the private sector, which believes that sharing the responsibility for security does not lower the security level (60% of favourable opinions), and the public sector and NGOs/universities (respectively 44% and 52%).

The asymmetry of information between the public and private sectors, combined with a better ability of private companies to draft PPP contracts could be at the origin of such differences.

Corruption and PPPs

The results given to question 44[14] indicate that the only ones who consider that PPPs increase the risk of corruption are the Russian respondents (50% agree with our proposition).

Table 4.9. Respondents' Opinion About the Impact on Security if Government and the Private Sector Share the Responsibility

Do you think that sharing the responsibility for security between the government and the private sector makes security more difficult to achieve?		Country of respondents				Total
		Western countries	Poland	Russia	China	
Strongly disagree	Frequency	7	5	5	3	20
	Percent	31.8%	19.2%	22.7%	12.5%	21.3%
Disagree	Frequency	6	8	7	6	27
	Percent	27.3%	30.8%	31.8%	25.0%	28.7%
Agree	Frequency	7	7	9	7	30
	Percent	31.8%	26.9%	40.9%	29.2%	31.9%
Strongly agree	Frequency	2	6	1	8	17
	Percent	9.1%	23.1%	4.5%	33.3%	18.1%
Total	Frequency	22	26	22	24	94
	Percent	100.0%	100.0%	100.0%	100.0%	100.0%

If we look at the answers by sector, then 56% of NGOs/universities answer positively to our question. The opinions given here are quite opposed to the ones revealed by question 8 (analysed in part II.3.a: The "soft" obstacles), in which 77% of respondents in Russia, 80% in Ukraine, and 54% in China considered that corruption is an obstacle to the creation of PPPs. Two different interpretations can be given to explain these inconsistencies: either there is a contradiction, or the respondents consider that corruption is an obstacle to the creation of PPPs, but that PPPs themselves do not engender corruption.

PPP Contracts, Security Measures, and Conflict Resolution Procedures

Two questions refer to this subject. The first one, question 43 gathered a very high rate of positive answers, with respondents from Western countries, Russia, Poland and Ukraine answering at more than 75% that security measures can indeed be included in PPP contracts.[15] The only exception is China, for which the rate of "don't know" is very high (54%). This can be explained by the new character of drafting PPP contracts in that country, and by the low experience of the respondents in this domain. The second question, referring to the legal character of security and PPPs is question 59, for which three observations can be made (see Table 4.10).[16] First, a high rate of positive answers from Western countries and Poland. Second, a high rate of "no" in Russia. And third, a high rate of "don't know" in Ukraine and China.

Table 4.10. Respondents' Opinion About the Existence of Conflict Resolution Procedures for Mediation or Arbitration Available to PPP Partners

Are there conflict resolution procedures for mediation or arbitration by the PPP partners?		Country of respondents					Total
		Western countries	Poland	Russia	Ukraine	China	
Yes	Frequency	17	17	1	4	11	50
	Percent	77.3%	63.0%	4.0%	28.6%	33.3%	41.3%
No	Frequency	0	1	17	3	4	25
	Percent	.0%	3.7%	68.0%	21.4%	12.1%	20.7%
Don't know	Frequency	5	9	7	7	18	46
	Percent	22.7%	33.3%	28.0%	50.0%	54.5%	38.0%
Total	Frequency	22	27	25	14	33	121
	Percent	100.0%	100.0%	100.0%	100.0%	100.0%	100.0%

The overall low level of knowledge of such procedures in "pre-PPP countries" can be interpreted as an expression of the low acquaintance with PPPs in general and even more so with the problems they can generate and the solutions to resolve them.

All respondents seem to agree, as it will be shown in the last section, on the necessity of developing trainings on PPPs, as well as evaluating the projects.

PART IV. CONCLUSION: POLICY RECOMMENDATIONS

Independently of opinions about PPPs economic efficiency and their ability to promote sustainable development, equity or security, a wide consensus was formed on the ways of improving the implementation of these structures.

Three of them will be mentioned in this conclusion: the development of technical training, the involvement of civil society in PPPs projects, and the evaluation of the infrastructures and services provided.

The Organization of Technical Training

Probably due to the low level of knowledge and to the intrinsic complexity of PPP contracts, most respondents (between 70 and 90%) think that some technical training would be necessary for a wider development of PPPs.

According to the answers given to our question 9, respondents are not so clear about the preferred form of the training (we have proposed 4 possibilities: 1. Establish consulting companies, 2. Organize research and practical conferences, 3. Organize seminars for civil servants and businessmen, 4. special courses in universities.).[17] All of our propositions gathered between 70% and 90% of positive answers, indifferently of the country, the sector, or the level of knowledge. This general claim for the development of technical training is the consequence of the very low number of training institutions in these countries, or of their lack of visibility.

However, a clear difference appears between Western countries and the four other ones (see Table 4.11.)

Western countries are the only place where training institutions exist or are well known by respondents.

Furthermore, it seems that the information provided by international institutions very seldom reaches practitioners in the different countries of our study. There are however a few exceptions, mainly in Russia, where a majority of people recognize that they benefit from the information provided by UNECE, the EBRD and the World Bank. In the other countries (i.e. in Poland and Ukraine), the World Bank is the only one which seems to be visible.

Table 4.11. Respondents' Opinion About the Existence of Training Institutions Providing Training in PPPs

Are there training institutions in the country that provide training on PPPs?		Country of respondents					Total
		Western countries	Poland	Russia	Ukraine	China	
Yes	Frequency	13	14	5	0	1	33
	Percent	61.9%	50.0%	19.2%	.0%	3.1%	27.0%
No	Frequency	4	5	9	8	7	33
	Percent	19.0%	17.9%	34.6%	53.3%	21.9%	27.0%
Don't know	Frequency	4	9	12	7	24	56
	Percent	19.0%	32.1%	46.2%	46.7%	75.0%	45.9%
Total	Frequency	21	28	26	15	32	122
	Percent	100.0%	100.0%	100.0%	100.0%	100.0%	100.0%

The Involvement of Civil Society in the Development of PPP Projects

As already mentioned in the analysis on equity, a way of increasing favourable perceptions of PPPs could be to involve more actively civil society in the development and the evaluation of PPP projects. This assumption can be deduced from the very positive answers to questions 37 and 38: between 60% and 80% of the interviewees agree that civil society should be more involved in the development of PPP projects.

The Evaluation of PPP Projects

Only 18% of our respondents actually know the existence of an office in charge of the control of PPPs (50% in Western countries, 28% in Ukraine, 21% in Poland, 0% in Russia and China!); on the other hand, more than 60% of them think that a special agency or NGO should be created to do so.

In question 63, we asked which should be the criteria of evaluating PPP projects.[18] While almost all propositions gathered more than 50% of favourable answers, some differences appear among the sectors and the countries.

If we consider the sectoral repartition of the answers, the NGOs/universities are always the most concerned by the evaluations of PPPs, independently of the criteria (there is only one exception: the private sector is the most concerned when it comes to the *financial cost/benefit efficiency*).

A cross-country analysis shows that the answers are usually quite homogeneous (average superior to 70% of favourable answers) between Western countries, Poland, Ukraine and Russia, but there are some differences with China. For the protection of natural resources, Western countries are the most concerned by this aspect (90% of the respondents think that the protection of natural resources is important or very important), while China gives a very low importance to it (only 28% of favourable answers).

For corruption, the Chinese respondents seem to be the less concerned: only 45% of favourable answers versus 60% for the other countries. The same proportion appears for cost-benefit efficiency: with 43% of favourable answers, the Chinese seem to be once more the least concerned of the group (100% for Western countries, 98% for Poland, 83% for Russia, 87% for Ukraine). The structure of results is similar for equity (53% for China, while more than 75% for the other countries).

These last distinctions on the form of the evaluation do not modify the high degree of homogeny in the answers given with regard to policy recommendations. In summary, all respondents, independently of their country, professional sector or degree of knowledge, believe that some training institutions should be created and made visible to policy makers, that the civil society should bring more contributions to the development of PPP projects, and that some evaluations should be conducted to guarantee the respect of the contract and the fulfilment of public interest.

NOTES

1. This data is taken out from the analysis of question 2: *"How acquainted are you with PPP(s)?"* Due to the small number of answers on this question in Ukraine, this country is not taken into account here.

2. For this question No.12, we did not receive enough answers from Ukraine to take them into account.

3. Question 14: "Do PPPs improve the delivery of services?"

4. These are Questions: q8c, q8d, q8e, q8f, q47e, q47f, q60, and q61 (see next footnote).

5. Due to the small number of answers to this question in Ukraine, this country is not taken into account here.

6. Question 17: "In comparison to traditional government infrastructure and services, are PPPs more respectful of the natural environment" and question 18a: "Are PPPs more efficient in the use of natural resources?"

7. Question 23: "Do you think that the cooperation between public and private sectors can increase the transfer of innovation and technology to the local economy?"

8. "Do you think that PPPs can improve services more efficiently for all social groups?"

9. "If not, do you think that some social groups could be excluded from PPP services and infrastructure?"

10. "Are the services provided by PPPs more costly for the population?"

11. Question 37: "Do you think that the general public should have a greater influence on how public infrastructure and services are created and developed concerning the following issues?," and question 38: "Do you think that the general

public should have a greater influence on the quality of the service delivery?" An exception to these very positive answers comes from the Ukrainian respondents, who do not think that the general public should have a greater influence on how the quality of the service delivery should be in what concerns hospital and health care, social housing and transportation.

12. Question 41: "What specific security issues have become more important for the infrastructure service that you know in the last 10 years?" The seven propositions are: 1. Natural disaster protection 2. Prevention of human accidents and protection 3. Violence due to inter-ethnic conflict or terrorism 4.Security of vital infrastructure 5. Security of clean water 6. Security of social services for people who are economically marginalized or part of ethnic minorities 7. Security with regard to preventing corruption.

13. "Do you think that sharing the responsibility for security between the government and the private sector makes security more difficult to achieve?" Due to the small number of answers for this question in Ukraine, this country is not taken into account here.

14. "Do you think that private participation in infrastructure through PPPs increases the risk of corruption in comparison with the government-operated public sector?"

15. "Can security measures be included in the original PPP contract?"

16. "Are there conflict resolution procedures for mediation or arbitration by the PPP partners?"

17. "How is it possible to overcome barriers hindering PPPs and what methods could be used?"

18. a. cost/benefit, b. Equity in distribution, c. protection of natural resources, d. security measures, e. anti-corruption measures.

Part III

PPPs IN TRANSITION
COUNTRIES: FAVOURABLE
CONDITIONS AND
CONTRIBUTIONS TO
EFFICIENCY, SUSTAINABILITY,
EQUITY, AND SECURITY

5

The Future of PPPs in Poland: A Preliminary Assessment

Thomas Zacharewicz

INTRODUCTION

Over the last 18 years, Poland experienced two main historic events, which have highlighted the country's need for infrastructure modernization. These are the introduction of the market economy beginning in the early 1990's, and the entrance into the European Union in 2004. Another decision adds to the urgency, namely the decision by the UEFA executive committee to grant Poland and Ukraine the organization of the football Euro Cup in 2012. Although of less political and national importance than the first two changes, this sporting event offers a huge opportunity for the country to upgrade its infrastructure.

These changes that affect the development of Poland's infrastructure coincide with the emergence of a new economic trend: the liberalization of public services and the introduction of private capital as an alternative to traditional public procurement. In particular, the notion of public-private partnership (PPP) has often been considered as a novel way to compensate for the lack of domestic public resources by allowing a modernization of infrastructure with the input of private capital. This approach to the improvement and operation of public services and infrastructure was developed into a nation-wide public policy option in the United Kingdom, where it is often referred to as Private Finance Initiative (PFI).

Poland—and more generally all Central and Eastern European countries—are considered as outstanding candidates for the development of PPP structures. They have very low public financial capabilities, but have enormous needs in terms of infrastructure and services in all economic sectors. In addition, these countries show great economic potential to absorb financial investments offered by international companies, and thus investing in PPPs is considered in a favourable light.

However, and in spite of all these *a priori* encouraging considerations, the attempts to establish PPPs as a widely used tool for economic development have not been very successful in Poland yet.[1] Whether this is because of external causes (lack of appropriate legal framework, administrative inefficiency), or due to internal factors that are inherent to PPPs (complexity of the contract, inadequacy of these structures for a specific sector), many projects have been delayed, while others have failed or never reached the expected outcomes.

In this context, this study aims to improve our understanding of the extent to which PPPs can be a viable alternative to traditional public procurement in Poland. More specifically, it will analyse and evaluate the potential of such cooperation between the public and private sectors, as they contribute to the promotion of economic and social development in Poland that is at once cost efficient, sustainable, secure, and equitable. For this study, these four aspects have been examined through qualitative (i.e. face-to-face interviews) and quantitative analyses (i.e. closed questionnaires) that were addressed to Polish civil servants, representatives from private companies, non-governmental organizations and universities.

The results from this research are presented in the following manner: a first part provides a survey along with some general information on the development of PPPs since the country's transition to a market economy. The aim is to identify the reasons why PPPs have not found the success they were expected to have. The second part of this study, based on theoretical research and on the data gathered from our survey in Poland, will aim at analysing the intrinsic capacity of PPPs to promote sustainable, secure, and equitable development in Poland. Indeed, although many opinions assert the superiority of public-private partnerships over traditional public procurement with regard to economic efficiency and service delivery (quality and costs), both the theory and the empirical evidence conclude to a more ambiguous result. Finally, the third part of this study deals with policy recommendations for improving the implementation of PPPs.

THE DEVELOPMENT OF PUBLIC-PRIVATE PARTNERSHIPS IN POLAND: GREAT POTENTIAL, FEW ACHIEVEMENTS

The Current Situation of PPPs in Poland: A Slow Development

Two features are usually combined in discussions that explain the benefits of public-private partnerships or, more generally, the participation of private companies in the delivery of public services and the operation of public infrastructure in Poland. The first one is, 18 years after the transition to a market economy, the still strong need for infrastructure modernization. In a report published in 2004, the World Bank estimates the infrastructure investment needs for the new EU member States to amount to €65 billion over the next 15 years. It cites Poland as the country with the highest infrastructure investment needs (€21.4 billion). In particular, at the municipal level, some 70% of these investments are required for the country to develop its public infrastructure up to adequate standards for modern economic development.[2]

At the same time, the level of the public debt in Poland is particularly high. Both national and local governments are severely limited in their capacity to finance new investments.

Although these two indicators should encourage public authorities to look for alternative ways to finance infrastructure other than through traditional public procurement, the number of existing PPPs in Poland remains very low. To estimate the exact number of PPP projects in Poland is not an easy task for several reasons. As a centralised PPP office or unit is missing, State institutions that focus on specific infrastructure sectors cannot inform a central authority.

However, there is a useful survey conducted by the World Bank on Private Participation in Infrastructure (PPI). It provides information gathered through a database on the evolution of PPI projects in low and middle income countries.[3] With a focus on four sectors: water and sewerage (treatment plant and utility), telecommunications, transport (airports, roads and seaports), and energy (electricity, natural gas), the World Bank study numbers 47 PPI projects in Poland. These were created between 1990 and 2006, and they contain the sectoral distribution presented in Table 5.2.

As a comparison, the Czech Republic counts 67 projects, and Hungary 58 for a population almost four times inferior to that of Poland. Moreover, there is no remarkable progression in the creation of new projects on a time-scale frame: the number of PPIs created before the year 2000 is equivalent to the ones created after that date. In comparison to the World Bank PPI database, most other available studies dedicated to private participation in the delivery of public infrastructure and services do not present the same level of quantitative precision; however, they are more focused on PPPs in the narrower interpretation. Two reports published in 2004 and 2006 by PriceWaterHouse Coopers and Ernst&Young, identify a couple of principal

Table 5.1. Evolution of the Polish Public Debt

	2003	2004	2005	2006	2007
Public debt of Central and Local institutions, in percentage of GDP	47.1	45.7	47.1	47.6	46.8

Table 5.2. Private Participation in Infrastructure (PPI) in Poland

Sector	Sub-Sector	Number of Projects*
Energy	Electricity	18
	Natural Gas	1
	Total Energy	19
Telecom	Telecom	13
	Total Telecom	13
Transport	Airports	2
	Roads	3
	Seaports	3
	Total Transport	8
Water and sewerage	Treatment plant	1
	Utility	6
	Total Water and sewerage	7
Total		47

*Source: World Bank, PPI database.

sectors in which PPPs are relatively developed in Poland. These are water and transport (mainly highways).[4] Several reasons explain this.

First, water and transportation were particularly underdeveloped in the early 1990's. Most of the supplied water was not drinkable and the national highway network only comprised 200km. It is widely recognized that both of these infrastructures are of fundamental importance for economic development.[5] Their modernization is therefore particularly urgent. Second, some political constraints bore on Poland and Central and Eastern European countries in general; these relate to the main conditions for the integration of these countries into the Western European economy. This political change implies a drastic improvement of the quality and security standards regarding public infrastructure and services.[6] Third, the modernization of this infrastructure is particularly costly, and public authorities lack the necessary liquidity to develop the country's services quickly. Finally, private operators benefit—as they did with initial investments in the 1990s—from the outcome of several successful international projects dedicated to water and highway networks.[7]

In this context, it is quite significant that the first PPP project in water and sewage disposal services started as early as 1992 in the city of Gdańsk. Further BOT concessions for the highways A2 and A4 started in 1997. To date, the PPP formula for water supply and waste water treatment, recognized as a success in Gdańsk, keeps developing in other cities.[8]

The experience has not known such a wide success for highway construction (see Box 5.1). In 2003, the Polish network counted only 404km, or a mere 2% of the national road network.

At a lower scale, some other PPP projects were developed in Poland, mostly at local level, and in the following sectors: local transportation (cities of Tczew and Warsaw), wastes (Bielsko-Biała, Częstochowa, Płock) and central accommodation and housing (Słupsk, Walbrzych).[9] Discussions are now underway for the creation of PPPs for prisons. However, as previously mentioned, the most important opportunity for PPP development in infrastructure lies in the upcoming organization of the European football cup in 2012, and the need for modern infrastructure this event calls for.

In spite of past and future plans for great infrastructure development, Poland's experience with PPPs is still low. This is particularly noteworthy

Box 5.1. Highway Construction in Poland

At the beginning of the 1990's, the Polish highway network counted 200 km, and was very underdeveloped, even in comparison with other Central European Countries. In order to reduce this backwardness, the Polish government revealed a plan in 1993 according to which 2,600 km should be built by 2005. However, by 2003, the entire network comprised 404 km. According to several different reports, the main reason for this slow development lays in the lack of a consistent long-term policy framework. *

Originally, three projects were drafted, that were to be realised through a concession system and fully financed by toll revenues: the A4, between Cracow and Katowice (project started in 1997), a part of the A2, between Nowy Tomysl and Konin (project started in 2000, concession for 40 years), and a section of the A1 (originally between Gdańsk and Toruń, and then from Gdańsk to Nowy Marzy) in 1997. However, in light of the very low use of these highways—users were reluctant to pay the tolls—the government had to change its approach.

The toll-payment system has progressively been abandoned and replaced by contractual payments (through State financing, and a vignette system). Furthermore, an overall institution—the General Directorate of Public Roads and Motorways (GDD-KiA)—has been created in order to favour the expansion of the highway network while maintaining the existing road infrastructures.

*See for example PWC, Partnerstwo publiczno-prywatne, Wydawnictwo C.H. Beck, Warszawa, 2007, p. 177, or Benck and al., Public-private partnerships in New EU member countries of Central and Eastern Europe: an economic analysis with case-studies from the highway sector, op.cit., p. 97.

when compared with other Central and Eastern European countries such as Hungary or Czech Republic. The latter have already developed programs for prisons, hospitals or schools.[10]

The Obstacles to the Development of PPPs in Poland

Given the emerging market that Poland represents within the EU, the large gap between the potential for PPP development and the actual results bring up some questions. This aspect is even more striking if we consider the evolution in terms of the absolute number of projects or if we compare these to PPPs in other Central European countries. The second part of this study, therefore, presents the reasons why PPPs are still underdeveloped in Poland. In order to do this, the results obtained through the qualitative and quantitative analyses are evaluated against relevant international theoretical studies.

The institutional framework in which a country conceives and develops its public services and infrastructure can be defined as a set of both formal (i.e. judicial and political system) and informal rules (social norms, values and beliefs). These determine the actors' behaviour (e.g. private companies and public institutions) in economy and polity, as well as the general framework and points of reference which constitutes the preconditions and points of reference for the economy.[11] In central and eastern European countries, these structures have been submitted to considerable transformations over the past 18 years; the transition to a market economy and later the entrance in the European Union have imposed constant modifications of all the formal rules. A need to constantly adapt and re-adapt laws and regulations has become a characteristic of the economic and political transformations taking place in the Poland.

The emergence of Public-Private Partnerships is one of the many manifestations of this new set of rules. This new kind of cooperation between public and private sectors requires the creation of an appropriate judicial framework in order to function properly. It also necessitates that political and economic actors adapt to new practices. In this context, two main features have been widely identified when it comes to explaining the slow development of PPPs in Poland.[12] The first concerns the legal framework and the law on PPPs. These are particularly criticized for their lack of flexibility regarding PPP creation. The second feature is the intrinsic complexity of PPP agreements, combined with the low level of knowledge, which explains the persistant reluctance of government representatives to apply such new structures of cooperation or to use them in a sub-optimal manner.[13]

The Legislative Framework: Complete, but Rigid

Two main phases can be identified within the Polish judicial history of PPP development: one before the publication of the law on PPPs of July

2005, and one after that date. Until 2005, the creation of PPP contracts was regulated by the law on public procurement, completed by some specific laws, the application of which depended on the sector in which the PPP had to be created. As a consequence, the sector in which the PPP had to be created determined the application of the law on public procurement or of the specific laws. The system was usually criticized for its lack of clarity, especially regarding foreign companies. In July 2005, a law specific for PPPs was published. It was then amended in June 2006 with the addition of three bylaws. The aim of this PPP-specific law is to clarify the process of the establishment of PPPs o allow a wide development of such structures. So far, however, no PPP has been created in accordance with this law. It is criticized for the complex analysis which it requires, and above all, for its rigidity that makes the creation of PPPs almost impossible.

The Judicial Framework Before 2005

In 2004–2005, the European Bank for Reconstruction and Development (EBRD) undertook an assessment of concession laws in transition countries. The bank considered all key characteristics that were estimated necessary for the development of PPPs. These included: i) the general policy framework; (ii) the general concession legal framework; (iii) definitions and scope of the concessions law; (iv) selection of the concessionaire (the entity to which a concession is awarded); (v) the project agreement; (vi) availability of security instruments and State support; and (vii) dispute settlement and applicable law in relation to PPPs.

The final report by the EBRD evaluated the Polish legal regime as "partly conforming to internationally accepted principles of concessions law" and stated that "contrary to general perception regarding the relative good quality of their investment climate and private sector development legislation, a number of countries [including Poland] were rated as having a low level of compliance."

The main reason given for this rating on Poland was the lack of standardised regulation for PPP creation. The bank criticized the existing legal system in which the regulations concerning PPPs were separated in different judicial acts. Similarly, one of the other justifications provided by the EBRD was the lack of clear PPP policy established or published by the Polish government.

Indeed, two different regimes coexisted that were meant to regulate the creation of PPP contracts.[14] The first one was based on a number of regulations that were only applicable to a specific sector (for example, the law of 1994 on toll highways). The second one was founded on the traditional capacity of public authorities to contract out public work to some private companies on the basis of the usual rules of public procurement.

Table 5.3. Compliance with International Standards in Poland

Compliance with internationally accepted standards or principles				
Very high compliance/ Fully conforms	High compliance/ Largely conforms	Medium compliance/ Generally conforms	Low compliance/ Partly conforms	Very low compliance/ Does not conform
Lithuania	Bulgaria Czech Republic Slovenia	Bosnia and Herzegovina FYR Macedonia Moldova Romania Russia Serbia and Montenegro Slovak Republic Ukraine Armenia Azerbaijan Estonia Kazakhstan	Albania Croatia Hungary Kyrgyz Republic Latvia Poland Turkmenistan Uzbekistan	Belarus Georgia Tajikistan

Source: EBRD, Assessment of concession laws, 2005.

Although a majority of the Polish respondents judged that these regulations were more efficient than the subsequent law of 2005, and that they allowed a wider development of PPPs, many private companies criticized the lack of clarity, as well as the restrictions they imposed. In a report published in 2002 by the American Chamber of Commerce in Poland, the many judicial barriers that limited the expansion of PPPs were identified.[15] The most restrictive regulations concerned the obligation for the project initiators (for example, a city or a region) to obtain the formal agreement of the president of the public procurement office before signing any contract that exceeded a period of three years.[16] Furthermore, such a signature was necessary in case the contractual deal would exceed 200.000 €, or in case the contract was made with a foreign company. While the sum mentioned is low for most infrastructure development work, the regulation regarding deals with foreign companies was perceived as particularly discriminatory for potential investors. Another restriction considered detrimental for the creation of PPPs was the obligation for private companies to apply the Polish law on public procurement in the case of sub-contracting, although the European Union allowed more permissive regulations. In the end, the Polish legal framework for PPPs lacked the clarity and transparency necessary to encourage the development of infrastructure. It was considered too restrictive for a fast and efficient development of PPPs.

The Polish Law on PPPs: A Complex and Rigid Document

When drafting the law on PPPs—published in July 2005 and complemented by three bylaws in June 2006—the Polish government had three main objectives in mind.[17] First, the law was supposed to create an appropriate legal framework that could stimulate public investment through private finance. Second, its aim was to provide guidelines and benchmarks for the elaboration of optimal contracts that would significantly lower the risks for both public and private partners. Third, the law aimed to demonstrate that cooperation between public administration and private companies could serve the public interest. Almost two years after its publication (and one year after the publication of the explicative bylaws), the number of PPP projects created under the prescription of this law remains very limited.

In parallel, the results from the quantitative survey carried out in June and July 2007, show that some 80% of Polish respondents considered that the country still lacked legal structures and procedures to inspire confidence, and that the decision-making process remained unclear.[18] However, the analysis also indicates that the more educated the Polish respondents were, the less pessimistic they were about the law on PPPs, with only 60% of them expressing their concern about the country's legal structures.

The debate on the PPP law of 2005 and its adequacy for Polish economic reality is based principally on two different arguments. First, arguments expressed by opponents, particularly government representatives at the local level, stressing that there is no need for a specific law. They point towards the United Kingdom as an example. The leading country in the development of Private Finance Initiatives does not offer a specific legal framework for PPPs. In the case of Poland, so the argument goes, it was merely sufficient to modernize the existing regulations (the law on public procurement and the law on public finance) that allowed the development of PPPs. Moreover, the law published in July 2005 introduced too many administrative constraints. These compeled public partners to provide many complex, costly and time-consuming analyses, that discouraged public institutions—above all at the local level—to propose and create new projects.

It should be mentioned here that the Polish law of 2005 on PPPs does not invalidate the pre-existing regulations. The previous law on public procurement and the law on public finance, along with other specific regulations, are still in force and applicable to cooperation between public and private sectors. However, contracts signed under the previous legal framework cannot officially be referred to as Public-Private Partnerships, as they are not based on the regulations created by the law of 2005 on PPPs. Subsequently, Poland faces a paradoxical and sub-optimal situation, in which PPPs can continue to develop outside the legal framework of 2005 that was specifically drafted to allow their development.[19]

The second and opposite argument is held by those who see in the 2005 law a necessary dimension that provides greater visibility to PPPs in Poland. In their opinion, the new law on PPPs has two complementary functions, in addition to its main role of regulating the creation of complex PPP structures. These are the provision of benchmarks and guidelines in order to avoid badly drafted PPP contracts and the ability thereby to promote best practice. Nevertheless, one has to note that by the end of 2007, almost three years after the publication of the new law, no PPP was created according to its prescriptions. One of the main reasons for this lies in a specific article of this law (Art.13), which makes its implementation impossible. Before examining what Article 13 contains, a short presentation of the main notions of the new law is necessary.

The law on PPPs of 2005, along with its amendments, defines several fundamental ideas, including PPPs.[20] It presents the institutions which can act as a public or a private partner, the procedure which has to be followed f to select a private partner, and specifies the period of validity of the PPP contract.

One of the key notions introduced by the law is the idea of value-for-money. This calls for an analysis on the part of the public sector before selecting its private partner. Thus, Article 3 states:[21] "A public-private partnership can become a way of executing a project if it provides the public entity more benefit than if it were executed in another way."

The benefits for the public interest are: an economy of expenditure for the public partner, an increase in the quality of the service provided, or a reduction of the damages to the environment.

Theoretical literature and international institutions commonly recognize that the key justification for implementing PPPs is the notion of value-for-money. This contrasts with the general perception that PPPs will compensate for the lack of finance capabilities on the part of the public sector.[22] From this perspective, the intentions of the Polish legislators seem to be in line with what was identified as PPP best practice.

In spite of this, the concrete implications of the requirement for value-for-money are becoming the focal point in this polemic. Article 11 states that the financial evaluation is compulsory and that without this, the public office is not allowed to sign a contract with a private partner (Art.21). This preliminary analysis has to provide the following:[23]

11.1.1 The risks associated with the implementation of the contemplated undertaking, taking into account different methods of sharing these risks between the public entity and the private partner and the impact on the level of public debt and deficit of the public finance sector;

11.1.2 The economic and financial aspects of the contemplated undertaking, including a comparison of the costs of implementing the undertaking within public-private partnership with the costs of its implementation in another form;

11.1.3. Comparison of the benefits involved in the implementation of the undertaking within public-private partnership with the benefits and social threats involved in implementing the undertaking in another form;

11.1.4. The legal status of the asset components, if the legal title to the asset components is to be transferred or established by the public entity for the benefit of the private partner or a company [...].

These provisions were further defined through the addition of a bylaw by the Ministry of finance, published in June 2006. However, these have been particularly criticized for their very general and restrictive character, as well as for their complexity and for the increased transaction costs they impose on the public partners. Moreover, the law does not define a size limitation of the PPP project below which these cost analyses would no longer be necessary; this last feature is especially discouraging for small municipalities.

More importantly, Article 13 renders the creation of a PPP close to impossible.[24] This was demonstrated in a project led by the city of Wągrowiec and the consulting company Investment Support. This case was revealed at the end of the year 2007 by the judicial review *Gazeta prawna*.[25] After having provided all the compulsory analyses legitimating the implementation of a PPP, the city of Wągrowiec started to look for a private partner. As defined by Article 13 of the law on PPPs, the call for tender proposals concerning the PPP project has to be published in the *Biuletyn Zamówień Publicznych* and in the *Biuletyn Informacji Publiczne*.[26] Normally, the format of such a call for tenders is defined through a bylaw from the ministry of economy. The problem is that three years after the creation of the law on PPPs, this bylaw was not provided. Therefore, this makes impossible the publication of the procurement process and the call for tenders, nor does it allow for the selection of a private partner through an open bidding process.

In an article published in the review "Law in transition," the EBRD stated that "Concession legislation [...] can create a clear framework for the public-private partnership in question, providing ready-made solutions for what could otherwise prove very difficult questions of scope and structure. On the other hand, the legislative framework can sometimes seem inflexible, obscure or politically skewed."[27] This statement is particularly applicable to the Polish situation; the law on PPPs seems to have corrected the main flaws of the pre-existing legal framework, namely the lack of visibility and transparency. However, in spite of these improvements, no PPP were created according to the prescriptions of this law. One must then conclude that the legislator was not successful in meeting the objectives of stimulating investments and reducing psychological barriers. Two reasons can be invoked to explain this.

First, the compulsory analysis which the law requires prior to the implementation of a PPP is undoubtedly very general (even with the explanations provided through the bylaw), complex, time-consuming and costly. It potentially increases transaction costs, and penalizes particularly small public authorities, with low financial capabilities. In this sense, the Polish law on PPPs can be criticized for its rigidity. However, this feature does not mean that a preliminary financial cost analysis would be unnecessary before the call for tenders and the signing of a PPP contract.

As this study will portray, strong doubts exist about the ability of PPPs to be applicable across sectors. If no preliminary cost and feasibility analyses are carried out, then a risk exists that PPPs can be developed on the basis of either opportunistic or ideological considerations. As these partnerships are by nature complex agreements, the possibility remains that financial mismanagement or idealism might introduce perverse effects both for the society and the public partner.[28] Preliminary feasibility studies are thus recommended, as is further explained below.

The second reason for the lack of investment stimulation is more fundamental. Article 13 impedes the publication of the procurement offer, and makes the entire law unusable.

The Lack of Knowledge

In Poland, as in most developing countries, national and local public officials often lack experience and comprehensive understanding of the intrinsic complexity of PPP contracts. This was discovered thank to the survey done for this study: 85% of respondents considered that lack of knowledge of contractual arrangements is a main obstacle to the development of PPPs.

More precisely, this lack of understanding touches on two different realities.[29] First, the adaptation of Polish law and policy to EU norms has resulted in an insufficient administrative capacity for public officials to be informed about contractual deals and to adapt their work to the institutional changes taking place. Second, there is a lack of historical experience of private involvement and sub-contracting for the delivery of public services. This lack of knowledge of contractual arrangements and of PPPs stands in stark contrast to the level of expertise that private companies have gathered from their work in other countries or industry sectors. This informational asymmetry is all the more important when it appears to be one of the main determinants of the quality of PPP contracts. In turn, this influences the quality of the services provided to the general public.

The knowledge gap between public and private partners has strong repercussions on the elaboration of risk-sharing, and more generally on the capacity of the two partners to draft comprehensive and optimal PPP contracts.[30] The literature on the subject consents that shortcomings in PPP agreements are often the source of many negative effects during the operation of a project.[31]

Two series of consequences can be identified that are directly linked to the partners' lack of knowledge and experience, as well as to the incompleteness of PPP contracts. The first one, defined by Williamson, refers to the opportunistic behaviour of one partner in order to maximise its own profit, and subsequently shows a lack of concern regarding the side-effects generated for the other partner or for society in general.[32] One such perverse consequence of an incomplete PPP contract has been described in the Polish review *Gazeta Prawna*.[33] It is described that a PPP contract with a BOT (Build-Operate-Transfer) model based on a joint venture of 100 years, was signed between the city of Wilanów and the Turkish company Deniz IC in order to build and manage a new town hall. After the project collapsed, the public authorities of the city explained: "the joint venture contract between the city *Ratusz Wilanów* and Deniz IC [the foreign investor] was particularly unfavourable for the public interest [because] no penalties were defined in case the agreement would not be fulfilled or would not be fulfilled adequately."[34]

The foreign investor did not finish the construction of the building and managed to take back the capital invested in the project. The joint venture ran into debt and the building still stands unfinished in Wilanów. This example is representative of opportunistic behaviour as a perverse effect that stems from fundamental errors in the drafting PPP contracts. Such a case presents an illustration of the possible consequences caused by the lack of experience and knowledge about PPPs in the public sector, and the commercial logic within which private companies generally operate.

Ideally, sub-optimal measures included in an initial contract can be corrected through renegotiation.[35] Estache and Serebrisky (2004) show that this renegotiation process seems to be the rule rather than the exception with regard to PPPs; Public-Private Partnerships are complex agreements and it is almost impossible to draft optimal contracts prior to changes or unforeseen events. Amendments or new clauses often have to be defined in the contract once the project has started, even if this incurs additional transaction costs.

As this study will further show, it would be abusive to assert that the lack of knowledge on the part of State representatives or government officials is the only factor leading to the renegotiation of contracts. It remains, however, one of the main causes of such problems, especially in developing and transition countries.

The Political a priori

The lack of technical knowledge and experience regarding the drafting of PPP projects often goes with a strong politicization of public decisions and policy-making. Throughout the survey conducted for this study, a very strong correlation appeared between the following two features: knowledge and political will. Thus, 85% of the respondents who pointed out the lack of knowledge also mentioned the lack of political will as an obstacle to the development of PPPs.

A second result confirms this tendency: around 90% of the total number of respondents qualified the lack of political will as one of the main features that slows down the creation of PPPs. Two main reasons can be identified as being at the origin of such a high score: habit and tradition on one hand, and public opinion on another hand.

Habit and tradition are reflected by public authorities that show a reluctance to surrender control of infrastructure and services. P. Wróbel and T. Aziewicz show that this is particularly the case for local public authorities.[36] The privatisation process is usually slower in cities than at the national level. It is interesting to point out in this context that this reluctance to organisational and managerial change is often based on irrational and ideological preoccupations, such as the idea of a supposed link between PPPs and corruption. An illustration of this was revealed in the survey: although 80% of the respondents considered that "private participation in infrastructure through PPPs does not increase the risk of corruption in comparison with the government-operated public sector," they also recognized that the perception of corruption is much stronger than its real manifestations. It is in this regard quite significant that PriceWaterHouse Coopers outlines corruption as one of the common *myths* linked to development of PPPs, in the article "7 myths and 3 truths on Public-Private Partnerships."[37]

In Poland, a high number of PPP projects were cancelled before their implementation because of traditional beliefs, preconceived opinions and habits. In a conference given in September 2003, M. Krzysztof Siwek, from the PPP department of the Ministry of infrastructure, gave the following example of a PPP project failure:[38]

"In a small Polish town there were three thermal power stations; two of them worked for two big industrial companies and the other one for the town. All three were ineffective, obsolete and not environmentally friendly. In addition, due to the low productivity of the industrial parks, the potential of the thermal power stations were under-exploited. Nevertheless, the competition and excess supply did not keep the price of heat low for local consumers. On the contrary, the price covered unjustified costs incurred by the three stations, as well as the heat distributor. The latter was inefficient, under-capitalized, and not restructured. Apparently, the local government was unable to implement the appropriate heat policy, and lacked necessary resources to do so."

At that point, a potential investor suggested a solution based on the PPP formula:

1. The investor would buy and sell off the three thermal power stations, and replace them with a small, environmentally friendly electro-ther-

mal station that would produce heat and electricity by association. Then he would buy the local heat network.

2. According to a long-standing contract, the town and the industrial companies would receive heat and electricity at a fixed price.
3. Once the period of the contract expired, the investor would give the electro-thermal station to the municipality.

The project was never put in place. This was not because of any legal limitation. Rather, there was a lack of political will on the public partner's side; the municipality, the industrial parks (a public company and a state treasury company) and the heat distributor (also a public company) did not manage to reach an agreement. The simple fact that the investor was going to make profit from the project was perceived as a disadvantage."

A second reason which could determine the public sector's lack of political will to develop PPPs lies in the influence that public opinion has on political authority. This is particularly true at the local level, where markets are designated as "socially sensitive" and information circulates very easily between city councils and the population.[39] The data gathered through the survey in Poland confirms this tendency: some 53% of respondents considered that Polish society has a "slightly negative opinion" regarding PPPs. This result also reveals that PPPs are often understood as a kind of privatisation that opens the door to a price rise for public services. In this context, many local authorities prefer not to propose any changes in the structure and management of public services, rather than face opposition from their electorates.

The effects of the politicization of decisions regarding the creation of PPPs have been presented thus far from the point of view of government authorities and public opinion. Obviously, private companies also have to deal with such non-technical considerations and take these into account when they assess the "political risks" of a PPP project. Indeed, the tendency to justify the implementation or the refusal of a PPP project through ideological views rather than empirical feasibility assessments, introduces a high level of uncertainty of public actors' decisions, especially in election periods. In Poland, as in most transition countries, the development of democracy implies relatively frequent changes in government formation, which can lead to greater uncertainty for private companies. This is all the more true for PPPs which need political stability, as they usually have a long-term life cycle of 20 years and more. In an article written on PPPs in transition countries, P. Snelson asserts that: "The swing from a positive approach to PPPs to a negative approach and cancellation of PPPs after an election is unfortunately, commonplace in some countries. This has occurred in many countries and has become a watchword for concession companies, which now look at how the procurement of a particular PPP will fit into the election cycle."[40]

The effects of such changes of the procurement process are not only negative for private companies, but also for the public administration and society as a whole. They generate high, unnecessary transaction costs, delay the implementation of public services and the modernization of infrastructure. Conversely, it would be beneficial to all the partners to make their decisions on whether or not to implement PPPs, based on technical and value-for-money comparisons rather than political considerations.

THE CONTRIBUTION OF PPPS TO EFFICIENCY, EQUITY, SECURITY AND SUSTAINABILITY

Most of the obstacles presented above which slow down PPP development, are mainly due to the relative newness of Public-Private Partnerships in Poland. The creation of an appropriate judicial and institutional framework is indeed a lengthy process, and the adaptation of economic actors—especially at the local level—to the new economic approaches can take even longer. However, as it was shown earlier, international institutions such as the EBRD have noted some remarkable improvements in the procurement process since the publication of the law on PPPs in 2005. In a similar manner, the lack of technical knowledge and the assessment of political risks are issues that can be improved, and for which ameliorations can reasonably be expected in the next few years. In this context, an overwhelming majority (93%) of respondents think that the participation of private companies in the delivery of public services will increase over the next 10 years. They also expressed significant hope regarding a rapid settlement of Poland's political instability and lack of judicial clarity.

A common opinion expressed in Poland, and more generally in developing and transition countries, is that most of the inefficiencies related to PPPs are due to sub-optimal ways of governance, as previously mentioned. Once these problems are resolved, PPPs become the best solution for a faster and high-quality delivery of public services. In other words, many respondents seem to believe that Public-Private Partnerships would be intrinsically more efficient than the public sector.

However, neither the theory nor the empirical evidence supports such a categorical assumption. At the same time, there is no conclusive evidence of a systematic inferiority of private sector delivery of public services, when compared with traditional public procurement. What studies do show however, is that there is a need to question beliefs and revisit politically skewed opinions that assume that either the private or the public sector is always more efficient than the other.

Public-Private Partnerships certainly have the capacity to correct some of the flaws of public administration, but it would be wrong not to recognize that they can also generate new problems. Based on the opinions gathered in Poland through the survey carried out for this study, relevant theoretical debates and empirical evidence, this next section will present a reflexion on the capacity of PPPs to promote efficiency, equity, security and sustainable development in Poland.

General Perceptions and Evidence of Public and Private Efficiency

It is widely assumed in Poland that PPPs have the potential to provide better services and to allow a faster infrastructure development than through traditional public procurement. Almost 90% of respondents thought that the introduction of private capital in the traditional public sphere can improve the quality of public services.[41] 64% of them also believed that PPPs are a less costly way to finance infrastructure modernization, compared to traditional provision by the government.[42] Two main reasons are invoked when it comes to justify these opinions.

The first one is both directly linked with the historical changes that occurred at the end of the 1980's in Eastern Europe, and with the emergence of a new ideological trend in the United Kingdom, named "New Public Management." Indeed, although 18 years have passed since the change of political regime in Poland, the public administration is still very often considered to be chronically inefficient and unable to conduct large-scale projects. It is quite significant that more than 80% of respondents in the Polish survey declared that they are "little" or "not at all" satisfied with the current delivery of public infrastructure and services. At the same time, the British model of market oriented public services has found a wide echo in Poland. The privatisation, or at least the introduction of private governance and market incentives into the management of traditional public spheres, would *per se* allow the modernization of obsolete structures. It is frequently seen as the only way to improve the delivery of public services.

This assumed superiority of private companies over the public sector was broadly criticized, even by institutions well known to be in favour of economic liberalisation. The best example of such strong doubts comes from the International Monetary Fund (IMF). In a paper written in 2004 in collaboration with the World Bank and the Inter-American Development Bank entitled *Public-Private Partnerships*, the organisation recognizes that: "the key issue is whether PPPs result in efficiency gains that more than offset higher private sector borrowing costs. [...] Much of the case for PPPs rests on the relative efficiency of the private sector. While there is an extensive literature on this subject, the theory is ambiguous and the empirical evidence is mixed."[43]

Most of the World Bank policy papers confirm these doubts about the greater efficiency of the private sector. In a research paper dealing with

infrastructure performance in developing and transition countries, Estache
and colleagues recognize that: "for utilities, it seems that in general ownership often does not matter as much as sometimes argued. Most cross-country papers on utilities find no statistically significant difference in efficiency
scores between public and private sectors."[44]

The European Investment Bank is also uncertain about an absolute superior efficiency of the private sector. A. Riess, the deputy head of the economic and financial studies division of the EIB admits that: "one can safely
claim that the drive towards PPPs over the last decades has been fuelled
not only by economic efficiency considerations but also by governments
budget constraints, and—more generally—a sometimes uncritical, if not
ideological presumption that private sector participation in the provision
of public services can do no harm. But perhaps it can, and the fiscal motivation for PPPs might have pushed them into sectors where they do not
add value."[45]

Some of the most well known academic institutions and pertinent theoretical research conclude as well that there is no general evidence of superior private sector efficiency. In an article published in the *Oxford Review
of Economic Policy*, P. Grout recognizes that PPPs can bring some positive
results in some sectors, but they can also cause some economic and social
damage in other sectors: "Sectors, and projects within sectors, will have different characteristics, and for some the PFI model will bring large efficiency
gains and for others the approach . . . may be positively harmful."[46]

The research centre of the University of Greenwich (PSIRU), which
has published many papers on PPPs, concludes broadly that there is no
systematic or intrinsic advantage to private sector operation in terms of
efficiency, just as there is no evidence that allows one to assume that a
public sector operator is automatically less efficient and effective.[47] In these
circumstances, policy makers should not consider the introduction of private sector operators into public services as an objective or a desirable issue,
but should rather evaluate them as neutrally as possible. Particularly, PPPs
should not be considered as a way to automatically improve the quality of
service delivery.

The second reason invoked by Polish respondents to justify the necessity
of a shift from public to private management and financing of services, is
less ideological and more pragmatic. The debate about private involvement
so far has been based on the question whether public services should be
provided through traditional public procurement or through PPPs, according to the criteria of quality and cost efficiency.

The pragmatic response in Poland was surprising at times. As in many
developing countries and emerging markets, the criteria of quality and cost
are sometimes subordinated to volume and timing; this can be seen as
the urgency to have rapid public use of infrastructure that is important for

economic growth, such as highways or airports. In this case, the question is not whether PPPs could be an alternative to public procurement for the modernization of infrastructure. Rather, the issue is whether any infrastructure project can be financed and implemented at all! For, without private funds, very little or nothing can be built by the government. In this pragmatic consideration, a PPP project can offer a way forward for infrastructure construction, which the public sector would otherwise be unable to provide within the desired time horizon.

As shown by M. Brusis and C. Zadra-Veil, the Polish decentralization process, along with the adhesion to the European Union, have transmitted new responsibilities and competencies to local public authorities.[48] This provoked a sharp increase of their debts. Since 1999, their expenditures have been increasing faster than their revenues. As most of the public enterprises do not have the financial capacity to ensure the maintenance of their infrastructure, governments have been slowing down investments, and service coverage rates have been stagnating.[49]

In the short-term, if government judges that there is an urgent need to modernize their assets, then private financial investment through PPPs is often considered to be a useful alternative.[50] This is all the more true when public authorities have to face additional external temporal constraints, such as the organization of the European Football Cup in 2012 for example. The decision to grant Poland and Ukraine the organization of such an event was taken by the UEFA executive committee in April 2007. This leaves these two countries a time horizon of just five years to modernize their sports and transportation infrastructures. It is a huge challenge for both Poland and Ukraine that cannot be taken up without at least partial financial participation from the private sector.

However, when there is no external time constraint –as this is most often the case—and when there is, in a short-term perspective, no alternative to PPPs, then the choice of the partner is purely political. In other words, governments have to decide whether it is worth or not modernizing their assets, knowing that a fast modernization could have some perverse effects on the quality, equity, or security level of the infrastructure, but also knowing that a more equitable, higher quality solution could take several years.

Whether envisaged as the only possibility of modernizing infrastructure because of budget constraints or as an alternative to traditional public procurement, PPPs present some endogenous factors that are likely to affect society and the environment. This is so, particularly through perverse effects in the quality and/or the security level of the infrastructure and services provided, and also through an increase of prices of services.

Three main causes of these possible side effects were identified through the inquiry in Poland, and more generally by the theory on the subject. Before examining the impact of these intrinsic characteristics of PPPs on equity, security and sustainable development, a general presentation of them is essential.

The first one of these causes deals directly with the essence of PPPs. Public and private partners usually have conflicting views about the quality of the infrastructure to be built and of the services to be provided. The public side tends to favour allocative efficiency, i.e. to provide safe and good quality public services and infrastructure, available to all the citizens; on the other hand, private companies aim at maximising benefits and productive efficiency, i.e. minimising the costs of building and operating the infrastructure and services.

This feature would not produce any unwanted effects if both partners were able to draft perfect PPP contracts. However –and this is the second main cause of the appearance of perverse effects—PPP contracts are by nature imperfect. We have shown in Part II that sub-optimal PPP contracts may be the consequence of a lack of technical knowledge or asymmetric information between partners.

Nevertheless, analysis of risk sharing and PPP contract design has demonstrated that PPP contracts are intrinsically imperfect. In particular, O. Williamson and O. Hart insist on the complexity of the contract and on the difficulty of defining, measuring and guaranteeing the quality of some of the infrastructure services.[51] Moreover, the long-term duration of PPP contracts implies that potential technical innovations improving the service quality could become available. This intrinsic imperfect character of PPP contracts obviously has some unwanted effects on the quality and the safety of infrastructure and service, affecting citizens and society in general.

The third point being at the origin of unwanted side effects of PPPs is strongly linked to the previous: the high degree of contract incompleteness conduct almost systematically to renegotiation. This feature increases transaction costs, which are already higher than in the case of public procurement, due to the complexity of the contract. These costs, as T. Valila shows it, prevent potential bidders from entering the bidding process, which undermines *ex ante* the competition (competition *for* the market, and not *in* the market).[52] This, in turn, can lower the productive efficiency of the private partner, and therefore the value-for-money of the PPP project.

PPPs and Equity

Two main results stand out from the inquiry, which deal with the capacity of PPPs to provide an equitable development in Poland. First, a majority of the respondents (53%) believe that the services provided by PPPs are less costly for the population than usual public services. Second, the proportion of people who share this opinion is inversely proportional to their degree of knowledge about PPPs. In fact, while 71% of the respondents who recognize being little acquainted with such a cooperation think that it can provide services at a lower cost than the public sector, only 20% of the most experienced people agree with this proposition. Inversely, about 60% of these most experienced people admit that it is difficult to give a clear and definitive answer to this question.[53]

Indeed, many parameters contribute to the high degree of uncertainty of PPPs, and the comparison between the services and infrastructure provided by them and traditional public procurement is not always possible. C. Thomson recognizes that there is no generalized answer *ex post* as to whether PPPs are more or less expensive than public procurement projects.[54] *Ex ante*, the task is not easier, since under a PPP structure, the private partner bears more risks than under public procurement, justifying the higher cost of the project.[55] Furthermore, PPPs cannot be analysed as an homogeneous entity, but one should look at their ability to provide infrastructure and services at a lower cost according to the sector they belong to, and sometimes even according to the projects.

In Poland, we have shown earlier that PPPs have mostly been developed in road and water infrastructure. It is in this last area that they were most successful. In particular, the example of the cooperation between the company SAUR (owned by the French company Bouygues) and the city of Gdańsk is often designated as a reference in the country. With a concession contract signed in 1992 for a period of thirty years, the PPP allowed a drastic improvement of the quality of the supplied water. In a report published by the company in 2007, it is shown that in 1992 only 8% of the supplied water fulfilled European quality standards, while in 2006, the average rate rose to 86%.[56] At the same time, the price stayed close to the national average, when the exploitation costs were higher than in the rest of the country.[57] As we previously pointed out, it is not possible to compare *ex post* what would have been the outcome of publicly procured services, but the good results of this PPP are clearly undeniable.

The case of the city Bielsko-Biała presents similar data, but brings some other information in the debate on equity. The cooperation takes the form of a joint venture between the city of Bielsko-Biała (and some other smaller towns) and the private company United Utilities. It proved to be successful both in terms of quality standards and prices: while the water was not drinkable in 1991, it now fulfils the European standards (ISO 9001) and the prices proposed are the lowest in Śląsk (the region of Bielsko-Biała). Additionally, the company introduced in 2004 a price discount policy depending on the level of consumption.[58]

However, the Urząd Ochrony Konkurencji i Konsumentów (Office for the defence of competition and consumers) denounced the company for using monopolistic practices, and enforcing some financial conditions which were

not included in the original contract. More precisely, in case of a late payment from the consumer -after half a year of non-payment-, the company
can take the right to ask for an "adequate insurance," such as the delivery of
a financial guarantee as a condition for future water supply.

This case-study can be used as a basis for a wider reflection on the change
of perception of consumption and citizenship, implied by PPPs, and more
generally by the New Public Management. Indeed, this example illustrates
the existence of conflicting objectives under public or private procurement,
which are prone to be at the origin of practical inconveniences for citizens/
consumers, especially when coupled with contract incompleteness and
natural monopoly.

Under public procurement, water tends to be considered either a public good, characterised by non-excludability and non-rivalry (individual
consumers cannot be excluded from consuming it, and the consumption
by one individual does not reduce consumption possibilities for others),
or a merit good, for which public intervention is needed to improve the
economy's efficiency to allocate resources. This allocative role of the State
is directly linked to a conception of society and citizenship: the individual
is considered a member of a community, and his/her consumption of basic
goods—such as water—is seen as a right, for which market failures may
have to be corrected by public intervention.

Inversely, the introduction of private techniques of ownership/operation
of public services has a potential to question these assumptions, presuming
that the acquisition of goods should rather be linked to consumers' purchasing power than to citizens' rights. In this regard, PPPs -or other forms
of New Public Management—could be used as an alternative to traditional
procurement in any sector of the economy.[59]

These opinions are usually based on assumptions such as the perfect
character of market and on its intrinsic capacity to provide an equitable
repartition of resources. However, on the basis of Hart's and Williamson's
writings and as it is illustrated by the example of Bielsko-Biała, we have
shown that PPP contracts are by nature incomplete, and that the conflicting preferences of the State (more inclined to prioritise allocative efficiency)
and the private sector (benefit/productive efficiency) can lead to sub-
optimal outcomes for citizens. This is all the more true in a case of natural
monopoly—such as water supply—for which there is no alternative but to
consume the services provided. In this regard, a UNDP World Report on
Human Development asserts that: "Private involvement is not the bright
line between success and failure in the water provision. Nor is it a guaran-
tor of market efficiency. Water provision through a network is a natural
monopoly, reducing the scope for efficiency gains through competition
and making effective regulation to secure consumer interests an imperative.
[...] Decisions about the appropriate public-private mix have to be taken

case-by-case on local values and conditions. The challenge for all providers, public and private, is to extend access and overcome the price disadvantage faced by poor households."[60]

The case of the Polish highways provides another focus of the possible implications of a lowering equity on the economic efficiency of a PPP, in absence of a monopoly.[61] Three highway projects were originally planned to be fully financed by toll revenues paid by the users: the A4, between Cracow and Katowice (project started in 1997), a part of the A2, between Nowy Tomysl and Konin (project started in 2000, concession for 40 years), and a section of the A1 (originally between Gdańsk and Toruń in 1997, but the project has been reduced in 2004 to Gdańsk—Nowy Marzy).

Two complementary problems were at the roots of the failure of these projects. First, the traffic forecasts were too optimistic. Second, the tolls were only implemented on some segments of the highways, which resulted in strong traffic relocations. Indeed, different roads were available between cities, and this explained drivers' reluctance to pay the tolls. Consequently, this traffic relocation resulted in the development of congestions on smaller roads, as well as low revenues for the private operator.

The situation described here is thus quite opposite to the one presented in Bielsko-Biała. Indeed, under a situation of natural monopoly, the citizens/consumers were penalized by a lowering of equity. In the case of the Polish highway program, in which alternative solutions were offered to the users who were unwilling to pay tolls, it was the private operator which had to face the negative consequences of a price rise. Today, the government gave up the idea of levying tolls for financing the development of its transport network, renegotiated the PPP contract in order to create a country-wide vignette system and a national highway management program.

The two examples given here do not demonstrate neither the inferiority nor the superiority of PPPs or of traditional public procurement, with regard to equity. The case of the highway program and the bad results which came out of it are an illustration of the consequences of a mistake in the design of PPPs. The example of PPPs in water supply, on the contrary, allowed an improvement of the quality of the service, while avoiding a drastic rise of prices. However, the case of Bielsko-Biała shows the potential perverse effects of the trade-off between benefit/productivity and allocative efficiency implied by PPPs. What is shown however, is the need to question both forms of public service provision.

PPPs and Security

The opinions about the ability of PPPs to provide secure infrastructure and services are more balanced than the opinions concerning social equity. Thus, 46% of the respondents agree with the fact that sharing responsibility between government and private sector makes security difficult to achieve, but another 46% think the contrary.[62]

These results are in line with the theoretical discussion presented above, namely that it is difficult to give a general answer about which between traditional public procurement or PPPs is the most likely to propose the highest degree of security. As with the question of equity, the three factors identified, namely the trade-off between productive and allocative efficiency, contract incompleteness and renegotiations, are key determinants when it comes to justifying this level of uncertainty. However, they have to be looked at jointly with four other inter-related characteristics: the lifetime of the PPP, the need for additional investment, the role of innovation, and the externalities they presuppose for the private partner and for society in general.

Taking into consideration that PPPs in Poland are mostly implemented in "hard" infrastructure, the longer a project will last, the higher the probability that additional investments and technical innovations could improve the security level of the infrastructure.[63] As the duration of PPP contracts is generally above 20 years, the necessity of such unforeseen (and often unforeseeable) additional investments is almost systematic.

The nature of such investments into security provisions is the focal point that determines which procurement process is best to develop safe infrastructure, that can be socially enhancing. In the model based on contract incompleteness, O. Hart establishes a distinction between two kinds of investments that influence the cost and the quality of the services provided.[64] The first one, named "investment *i*," presents a situation in which the investment has a positive influence on (i.e. reduces) the operating cost of the infrastructure and improves the quality of the service; it is therefore both productively and socially efficient. The author takes the example of a prison, for which an investment made at the building stage would make management easier. This illustration is completed by A. Riess with the example of a building in which an energy-efficient heating system would lower fuel consumption, to the benefit of both the operator (lowering costs), and society (less environmental pollution).[65] This argument is often used to justify the implementation of a PPP: because the builder and the operator of an infrastructure are joined in a unique entity, there is a common interest to make such an investment. In other words, the private partner would benefit from the positive externalities induced by the expenditure realised at the building stage.

On the contrary, under pure public procurement, such mechanical synergy is more difficult to establish. As the builder and the operator are two different companies, there is less interest in making an investment at the building stage that will lower operating costs afterwards, even if it improves the quality of the asset.

The second type of investment presented by O. Hart, named "*e*," would lower operating costs as well, but instead of improving the quality and/or security of the infrastructure, it may actually reduce it. The same example of a prison is taken: "in the process of building a prison, the builder might realise that he can install an electric fence that reduces the likelihood of escaping. This in turn decreases operating costs, since fewer guards have to be hired, but may not be what the government has in mind (it reduces quality)."[66] This case illustrates the potential outcomes of the conflicting preferences between the public and private partner under a PPP structure (with the intrinsic characteristic of contract incompleteness). While the private company is more prone to prioritise cost reduction, there is a risk that this lowers the quality of the infrastructure provided. In that case, a PPP would internalise the financial benefits of the investment, but the result may not fulfil public interests in terms of quality and security.

With public procurement on the other hand, this investment "*e*" may not be made for the same reasons than for investment "*i*": the lack of synergy between the builder and the operator would prevents them from lowering operating costs. Therefore, this situation would imply a fulfilment of public interest, but on the long-term, the cost of operating the infrastructure may become higher than under a PPP (and would consequently have a negative impact on the economic efficiency of the project).

In this perspective, the PPP solution would lead to a faster modernization of infrastructure and to a more economically efficient management. However, this could potentially be at the cost of lowering the quality and security of the service provided. Conversely, public procurement could possibly result in under-investment, a slower modernization and higher operating costs, but prioritising security. This ambivalence of both structures illustrates the assertion given in the introduction of the second part of this chapter: PPPs certainly have the capacity to correct some of the flaws of public administration, but it would be abusive not to recognize that they generate new problems as well.

The approach used by O. Hart focuses on investments made at the building stage of a project and which lower operating costs. Later on, J. Benett and E. Iossa develop his model by including cases in which the safety of infrastructures is of particular importance.[67] In this respect, they introduce some additional types of investments. More precisely, they consider an unforeseeable investment that is therefore not included in the original contract, and which, while increasing the safety of the services, may have the negative externality of increasing maintenance costs. In this case, the answer is (once more) complex, although perhaps favouring a public procurement process. The existence of a negative externality is very likely to discourage a PPP to make such an investment, but this does not mean that traditional procurement is automatically more adequate. According to the authors, "If the externality is negative, the case for bundling is weakened and, if the externality is weak, either public and/or private ownership with unbundled provision is preferred. PFI is more likely to be preferred (a) the more positive (or the less negative) is the externality; (b) the stronger the effects that innovations in building management have on the residual market value of facilities; and (c) the weaker the effect that innovations have on the benefit from provision of the public service. With a weak negative externality, if the period over which the service is to be provided is lengthened, public provision is favoured relative to private provision."[68]

In other words, certain cases where safety of infrastructure is of particular concern may require many costly investments that do not increase the residual value of the infrastructure, but instead make it expensive to operate. In such cases, public procurement and ownership is more likely to meet public interests than the PPP model. This is all the more true when the projects have been conceived to run for 20 years or more.

An evaluation of the existing PPPs in Poland supports this theory: whether PPPs or traditional public procurement are more likely to provide secure infrastructure in particular cases does not mean that there is a definitive categorisation in favour of either side. However, one has to recognize that the existence of a trade-off between cost-savings and quality/security was not often an issue. While examining highway concessions in four Central European Countries (Poland, Hungary, Czech Republic and Austria), Brenck and colleagues found only one case in which different preferences of public and private partners could have raised some problems.[69] In the Polish A2 project, they noted that the concessionaire proposed a kind of road surface that was "slightly thinner than specified in the contract." However, the *ex post* verifications showed that this unilateral deviation from the contract did not jeopardize the project nor the general quality of the infrastructure. The security of its users is neither threatened, but this positive result does not invalidate the fact that these verifications should have been made *ex ante*. In a conference given in October 2006 about PPPs and the Polish motorway development program, Marek Ratajczak (from Poznan University of Economics) confirmed that there is no empirical evidence favouring the superiority of PPPs above traditional procurement methods. He further stated that: "PPPs should not be considered in every case as a better solution to traditional public investment" and that: "PPPs do not give guarantees to be successful."[70]

With regard to the water sector, PPPs usually score well in meeting the objectives established for quality and security of the infrastructure. To take the example of Gdańsk and Bielsko-Biała again, both projects fulfil the criteria of quality, security and respect of the environment established by the European norms ISO-2004.[71]

Finally, a debate about the opportunity of building and operating prisons under the PPP model was also taken up in Poland. There is indeed a strong need to both modernize existing penitentiary infrastructure, and build new prisons.[72] If the government decides to pursue its plan to build four new prisons, most of the discussions will touch on the ability of PPPs to deliver good quality and safe infrastructure and services.

PPPs and Sustainable Development

In the theoretical chapter of this study, Paolo Urio defines the sustainability of economic development by referring to: "Human, social, political, economic and technological development that meets the needs of the present without compromising the ability of future generations to meet their own needs. Sustainable development is intimately linked to human security; without security, development is impossible. However, sustainability also includes another element, namely the fair distribution of economic and social development to all members of a community or country—hence the emphasis here on equitable access to resources and infrastructure. In addition, sustainable development can also be taken to mean the protection of existing assets as well as future assets still to be developed, such as infrastructure that is vital for economic and social development and for the preservation of the natural environment."[73]

As it appears here, the notion of sustainability includes different aspects, such as human and infrastructure security, equitable access to resources and the preservation of the natural environment. As was shown earlier, there is no definitive answer to whether PPPs are more or less able to improve equity and security than traditional public procurement. The results are similar concerning the preservation of the natural environment.

The analysis of the research survey in Poland indicates that 44% of the respondents believe that PPPs are more respectful of the natural environment, in comparison to traditional government infrastructure and services. At the same time however, 66% emitted doubts (i.e. they answered "no" or "don't know") with regard to the issue of environmental sustainability.[74] And indeed, neither the theory nor the practice allows to provide any general assertion.

As what concerns the theoretical discussion on PPPs, the argumentation based on Hart's model of investment, described in the section above on security, is perfectly applicable to sustainable development as well. Thus, assuming contract incompleteness, we can presume that the nature of the investment and its influence on the infrastructure operating costs, are fundamental conditions for the improvement of a project's sustainability. If the investment is likely to bring positive financial externalities to the private partner, then its realisation is reasonably foreseeable, but it may reduce the quality of the infrastructure.[75] On the contrary, as J. Benett and E. Iossa consider, if the investment is likely to produce negative financial externalities, then the traditional public procurement may be more appropriate to meet the public interest.[76]

The analysis of practical case-studies neither helps to provide certainty on PPPs and sustainable development. Some cases, such as Gdańsk or Bieslko-Biała in water supply, seem to show that PPPs (or more generally private participation in the delivery of public infrastructure and services) were able to fulfil the European criteria of environment protection.[77] However, based upon its study of water-supply around the world, the UNDP Human Development Report of 2006 insists on the impossibility of establishing a mechanical correlation between the participation of a private partner and the success of a water-supply distribution system, in terms of equity and sustainable development.

Once more, there is no general "certainty" which can guarantee the ability of PPPs to better promote sustainable development than the public sector. At the same time, nothing proves that PPPs are less able to do so than traditional public procurement. Therefore, the only solution remains a case by case assessment and evaluation of feasibility, economy, equity, security and sustainability.

CONCLUSION: POLICY RECOMMENDATIONS

This last section provides a number of policy recommendations and guidelines that could be useful for an appropriate implementation of PPPs in Poland. Throughout this chapter, we have shown that there are many factors which have slowed down the development of PPP structures and rendered them less than optimal. Furthermore, some elements intrinsic to PPPs should lead to a more balanced discussion, whether in favour PPPs or supporting traditional public procurement.

A main outcome of this research is that there is no general formula which always guarantees the success of PPPs. However, we can provide some indications on how to avoid important problems and reduce the potential perverse effects of this kind of cooperation. They can be divided in two categories.

The first one concerns the measures which can be taken *ex ante*, before the implementation of the project. Such measures deal mostly with deciding whether or not to implement a PPP, the process of selecting a private partner and how to draft the contract. The second category refers to the regulation and the evaluation of the project during its implementation (and eventually, at the end of it), in order to protect public interest and to guarantee the fulfilment of the objectives as defined in the contract.

The Need for Prophylactic Measures: The *ex ante* Regulation

The use of the term "prophylactic" refers to the protection of public interest through the prevention of perverse effects. These measures can take two main forms: up-stream, a State investment in human capital and education that helps to reduce the errors caused by decisions based on politically skewed opinions, ideology or opportunism. And inversely, down-stream, the State could favour the development of projects based on technical considerations and feasibility studies. Later, at the time of deciding whether or not to create a PPP, while selecting the private partner, or eventually at the critical moment of drafting the PPP contract, independent advice can help with the conciliation of public and private goals, while guaranteeing the protection of civil society.

We have seen earlier that 85% of the respondents to the survey consider the lack of knowledge as one of the main obstacles to the development of PPPs.[78] The lack of understanding and experience has led to some non-economically justified refusals and also to the implementation of PPP structures on the basis of short-sighted agreements. In turn, these effects often result in a late modernization of the infrastructure, or the development of unwanted side-effects such as a high renegotiation rate, a rise in transaction costs and sub-optimal quality.

Consequently, 80% of respondents are in favour of seminars for civil servants and businessmen, as well as research in parallel to practical conferences that would serve to inform a larger number of people.[79] The widest consensus was obtained with regard to education and information on PPPs at university level. From the survey, more than 90% of respondents agreed that more specific courses should be offered in universities, completed with other educational activities.[80] These very high rates of responses are strengthened by the fact that 50% of the people in Poland are unaware of the existence of training institutions. Moreover, most respondents asserted that they do not benefit from information provided by international organisations such as the EBRD, the World Bank, the IMF, or the United Nations Economic Commission for Europe.[81]

Based on the example of Western European countries, an investment in human capital, combined with the promotion of information and training, will help to improve the quality of the procurement process and the development of PPPs in transition countries.

These up-stream educational measures have to be completed by an external regulation provided by public institutions, both at national and local level. This could help during the modernization of the infrastructure network. This institutional State intervention can take several complementary forms. First, the legal framework should define the scope of PPPs and the procedure in which they can be implemented. Secondly, the creation of specific "PPP units" with the task of advising the parties engaged in the development of PPPs. Such a PPP information centre could help with the preliminary costs or feasibility analyses that are required by law. Later, these PPP units can help with the drafting of contracts, aiming to reducing the risks inherent in the conflicting preferences of the public and private partners. Through intervention, the PPP unit would help prevent inconveniences such as moral hazard, abuse of confidence, or financial opportunism during the realisation of the project, by limiting the asymmetry of knowledge and information between partners. This would ideally also help to reduce the number of renegotiations and transaction costs.

As previously stated, the Polish law on PPPs published in 2005 introduced in its article 3 the notion of value-for-money. One of the key justifications for the creation of a PPP should be its capacity to meet public interest better than any other means of providing public services. This prescription is in line with the theory and with the recommendations of key international organizations. However, its very general character and the complex, time-consuming and costly analysis it implies, has discouraged many public institutions, especially at the local level, to develop PPPs.

However, the suppression of such preliminary analyses would favour the development of perverse effects. At worst, these could be less transparent procurement processes, even though the European Union imposes strict transparency measures on public procurement. At best, such perverse effects could mean a strengthening of the intrinsic flaws of PPPs, like incomplete contracts or unfavourable trade-offs between allocative and productive efficiency.

A much better solution would be the creation of a specialised "PPP unit" in Poland. Its aim could be to help with the provision of the necessary preliminary analysis, and to advise the public entity as it negotiates the PPP contract. This could lower the potential for renegotiations (but not suppress them), as well as reduce transaction costs, and therefore increase the economic efficiency of projects.

Monitoring and Evaluating PPP Projects

At least three components were mentioned in the Polish study that are both inherent to PPPs and at the root of some unwanted effects. These are the conflicting preferences of public and private partners, contract incompleteness, and renegotiations.

A public investment in human capital, an appropriate legal framework and the creation of a PPP unit could reduce the potential and the frequency of these perverse effects. However, they cannot avoid them completely. In this perspective, the regulation of the projects that are implemented could represent an additional guarantee for the fulfilment of public interest.

The survey carried out for this study revealed that respondents in Poland think that the evaluation of PPPs should focus on three different aspects: cost/benefit efficiency, the equity in distribution for the entire population, and security measures. In the survey, each one of these propositions gathered more than 80% favourable answers.

So far, the control of the fulfilment of PPP projects was discussed mainly as a task for the public partner. Nevertheless, some independent regulatory authorities do exist, but their competencies are usually limited to one sector or one aspect of a public service.[82] The creation of an institution whose role would be specifically to follow the evolution of PPP projects could help in dealing with the intrinsic negative aspects mentioned earlier. It could furthermore improve the achievement and preservation of public interest. However, all measures aimed to prevent and correct unwanted effects from PPPs have a cost, which must to be included in the debate on public and private efficiency.

Through this chapter, theoretical literature and empirical evidence, prevalent opinions were questioned and evaluated to determine whether PPPs offer better and more efficient services that those delivered by State authorities through traditional public procurement. The experience in Poland shows that PPPs have the potential to improve some aspects of public services, and that they are generally more able to modernize infrastructure in a more timely and economically manner. This aspect can sometimes be of vital importance, especially in the context of time-bound commitments, such as the organization of the football Euro Cup in 2012. However, one should not forget that PPPs have intrinsic flaws, which have the potential to be counter-productive to public interest whose fulfilment is, after all, the main goal of public policy.

NOTES

1. A. Brenck, T.Beckers, M.Heinrich, and C. Von Hirschausen, Public-private partnerships in New EU member countries of Central and Eastern Europe, EIB Papers, Vol.10, No 2 (2005), pp. 82–112.

2. Information taken from PWC, Developing PPPs in New Europe, p. 7

3. A definition of the methodology used for the creation of the PPI Database is given by the World Bank, and focuses on the following aspects: "The database records contractual arrangements with and without investments in which private parties assume operating risks in low- and middle-income countries (as classified by the World Bank). Projects included in the database do not have to be entirely privately owned, financed or operated. Some have public participation as well. [...]For projects that involve investments, the database figures reflect total project investments encompassing the shares attributable to both the private and the public parties." http://ppi.worldbank.org/resources/ppi_methodology.aspx. There

are some slight differences between PPI and PPP: PPI focus on private financial involvement, whereas the main criteria for PPP lays on effective investments. All PPPs can therefore be considered as PPI, but the contrary is not always true (especially in what concerns telecommunications).

4. PWC, Developing public-private partnerships in New Europe, 2004, and Ernst&Young, Partnerstwo publiczno prywatne. Nowe możliwości realizacji projektów infrastrukturalnych, 2006.

5. For the water sector, see UNDP, Human Development Report 2006: Beyond Scarcity: Power, poverty and the global water crisis, United Nations, New York, 2006. For transportation, see Hirschhausen, Modernizing infrastructure in transformation economics, Edward Elgar Publishing, Cheltenham, UK, 2006.

6. See A. Brenck, T. Beckers, M. Heinrich, C. von Hirschausen, Public-private partnerships in New EU member countries of Central and Eastern Europe: an economic analysis with case-studies from the highway sector, EIB papers, vol. 10, No. 2 (2005), p. 82–102.

7. Brenck and al. declare indeed that "water and sewerage have been prime targets for PPPs, mainly due to the backwardness of the water sector in the region and the urgent need for financing, but also because project developers in the water sector rode on a wave of successful international projects [...]. The highway sector lends itself particularly well to an analysis of the experience with PPPs in Central and Eastern Europe because investment needs in this sector were considered to be exceptionally large and urgent. International experience—especially from the United Kingdom—seemed to indicate substantial efficiency gains of PPPs in the highway sector." Ibidem, p. 88.

8. The other most well known PPP projects in water supply are located in Bielsko-Biała, and Piaseczno.

9. This information is based on J.Zynarski, Partnerswo Publiczno-Prywatne w realiach polskich, Conference given in Lublin, April 21st 2004.

10. For a comparative overview, see PWC, Developing Public Private Partnerships in New Europe, 2004 p. 11.

11. North, D. C., *Institutions, Institutional Change and Economic Performance*. Cambridge: Cambridge University Press, 1990.

12. See in particular C. Zadra-Veil, *Les PPP en Europe Centrale*, XVI Internacional RESER conference, Lisbon, September 28–30, 2006, and P. Snelson, *Public-Private Partnerships in transition countries*, in Law in transition, EBRD, 2007, pp. 30–38.

13. Part III will discuss the possibility/impossibility of drafting optimal PPP contracts. Here, the argument given aims at showing that a higher level of knowledge of the legal and institutional framework would improve the quality of the PPP contract, reduce perverse effects, and subsequently improve service delivery.

14. See M. Kulesza, M. Bitner, A. Kozłowska, Ustawa o Partnerstwie Publiczno-Prywatnym, Dom wydawniczy ABC, Warsaw, 2006, p. 22.

15. American Chamber of Commerce in Poland, Partnerstwo Publiczno-Prywatne jako metoda rozwoju infrastuktury w Polsce (PPP as a method of infrastructure development in Poland), Warszawa, 2002.

16. The public procurement office is, in Polish, the *Urząd Zamówień Publicznych*.

17. See Ernst&Young, Partnerstwo Publiczno-Prywatne, Nowe możliwości realizacji projektów infrastrukturalnych (PPP, New possibilities of infrastrcutre projects realisation), October 2006, p. 15, and M.Kulesza and al., op.cit. p. 25.

18. This data is taken out of the analysis of questions 8 and 47 from the research questionnaire for the survey in Poland.

19. See, K.Siwek, Ministry of regional development, Możliwości łączenia środków UE i PPP w perspektywie 2007-2013 (The possibility of combining EU funds with PPP in the 2007-2013 perspective), Conference on PPP best practice, June 21st, 2007, Warsaw.

20. "The public-private partnership, as understood in this law, is a cooperation based on a contract of public-private partnership between a public subject and a private partner in order to execute a public service [...]." Author's translation of the law, Ustawa z dnia 28 lipca 2005 o Partnerstwie Publiczno-Prywatnym, opracowano na podstawie Dz.U z 2005r. Nr 169, poz. 1420.

21. Author's translation of the law, Ustawa z dnia 28 lipca 2005 o Partnerstwie Publiczno-Prywatnym, opracowano na podstawie Dz.U z 2005r. Nr 169, poz. 1420.

22. Among many others, see the report on PPPs published by the International Monetary Fund, *Public-Private Partnership*, March 2004: "The decision whether to undertake a PPP project should be based on technically sound value-for-money comparisons. It is particularly important to avoid a possible bias in favour of PPPs because they involve private finance, and in some cases generate a revenue stream for the government," p. 18.

23. Author's translation of the law, Ustawa z dnia 28 lipca 2005 o Partnerstwie Publiczno-Prywatnym, op.cit.

24. Of any PPP which respects the prescriptions of the law. However, as we have shown earlier, the Polish law on PPPs does not invalidate the pre-existing legislation. It is therefore possible to create PPPs out of this specific law.

25. Gazeta prawna, *Przepisy o zamówieniach publicznych blokują inwestycje partnerskie*, Gazeta prawna nr 217 (2087), czwartek 8 listopada 2007r.

26. According to art. 21, the non-publication of the public office's call for tender proposals leads to the invalidation of the PPP project itself.

27. C. Clement-Davies, Fullbright&Jaworski International, *Public-private partnerships in Central and Eastern Europe: structuring concession agreements*, in Law in transition, EBRD, 2007, p. 40.

28. The already mentioned report of the IMF states in its very first lines that "it cannot be taken for granted that PPPs are more efficient than public investment and government supply of services. One particular concern is that PPPs can be used mainly to bypass spending controls, and to move public investment off budget and debt off the government balance sheet, while the government still bears most of the risk involved and faces potentially large fiscal costs," IMF, Public-Private Partnerships, op.cit., p. 3.

29. See C. Zadra-Veil, op.cit., p. 17.

30. The knowledge gap between partners has undoubtedly a strong influence on contract shortcomings. However, the more general question of whether it is possible or not to draft optimal PPP contracts will be discussed in Part III.

31. See in particular: J. L. Guasch, *Granting and renegotiating infrastructure concessions. Doing it right*. The World Bank, Washington D.C., USA, 2004, and A. Estache, T. Serebrisky, *Where do we stand on transport deregulation and PPP?*, World Bank Policy Research Working Paper No.3356, 2004.

32. Williamson, Oliver E., *The Economic institutions of capitalism*, The Free Press, New York, 1985.

33. See Gazeta Prawna, *Miejsce dla 107 tysięcy mieszkańców*, nr 212 (1830), 2006-10-31.

34. Author's translation, ibid.

35. J. L. Guasch defines the renegotiation as "a significant change or amendment not envisioned or driven by stated contingencies in any of the following areas: tariffs, investment plans and levels, exclusivity rights, guarantees, lump-sum payments or annual fees, coverage targets, services standards, and concession period." J. L.Guasch, Granting and renegotiating infrastructure concessions. Doing it right, op.cit., p. 12.

36. See P. Wróbel, *Zachowania inwestorów uczestniczących w prywatyzacji podmiotów komunalnych*, Conference given on November 4th 2004, Warsaw, and T. Aziewicz, *Transformacja gospodarki komunalnej w Polsce*, in J. Majewski and al., Program Prywatyzacji Podmiotów Komunalnych—materiały z konferencji i sympozjów, DORADCA consultants Ltd. I Gdańskie Towarzystwo Naukowe, Gdańsk-Gdynia 2004.

37. PriceWaterHouse Coopers, 7 mitów i 3 prawdy o Partnerstwie Publiczno-Prywatnym, 2006, p. 24.

38. Author's translation of K.Siwek, *Koncepcja Partnerstwa Publiczno-Prywatnego*, 30.09.2004, available at http://www.ippp.pl/instytut/temp/koncepcja_ppp_30.09.03_wgk.pdf

39. P. Wróbel, Zachowania inwestorów uczestniczących w prywatyzacji podmiotów komunalnych, Conference given on November, 4th 2004, Warsaw, available at http://www.komunalne.info/repository/files/Piotr_Wrobel_-_Inwestorzy_w_PPPK.pdf

40. P. Snelson, *Public-Private Partnerships in transition countries*, in Law in transition, EBRD, 2007, p. 36.

41. Data taken out of the question 13 of the research questionnaire: "Do you think that the introduction of private capital into the traditional public sphere could improve the quality of public services?"

42. Data taken out of the question 55 of the research questionnaire: "Is the PPP a more costly or less costly way to finance the modernization of infrastructure as compared to provision by the government?"

43. International Monetary Fund, Public-Private Partnerships, op.cit., pp. 12–14.

44. A.Estache and al., Infrastructure performance and reform in developing and transition economies: evidence from a survey of productivity measures, World Bank Policy Research Working Paper 3514, February 2005, p. 21.

45. A. Riess, *Is the PPP model applicable across sectors?* EIB papers, vol.10, No 2 (2005), p. 11.

46. P. Grout, *The economics of Private Finance Initiative*, Oxford Review of Economic Policy, (13:4), p. 53–66.

47. See, for example, D.Hall and E.Lobina, *The relative efficiency of public and private sector water*, PSIRU, Business School, University of Greenwich, September 2005.

48. M. Brusis, L'échelon régional en Europe Centrale et Orientale: Institutions, compétences et ressources, Revue comparative Est-Ouest, Vol. 34, No. 2, p. 145–171, C.Zadra-Veil, Les partenariats publics-privés en Europe Centrale, op.cit., et C.Zadra-Veil, Les enseignements du modèle britannique de PFI dans le cadre communautaire pour un nouveau membre comme la Pologne, conference given at the occasion of the international symposium "Formes de concurrence et enjeux de régulation des services d'intérêt général, Université Paris 8 Saint-Denis, September 29th–30th 2005.

49. This situation is not particular to Poland; most of developing and transition countries have experienced a similar fiscal crisis in the mid-1990's, making harder the maintenance—and therefore the modernisation—of public infrastructure. For a detailed description of infrastructure reform in developing and transition countries, see A. Estache and al., *Infrastructure performance and reform in developing and transition economies: evidence from a survey of productivity measures*, op.cit.

50. As it is of purely political nature, this aspect of PPPs will not be discussed in this paper.

51. See among others O. Williamson, The Economic institutions of capitalism, The Free Press, New York, 1985, and O. Hart, Incomplete contracts and public ownership: remarks and an application to Public-Private Partnerships, in The Economic Journal (113), 2003, p. 69–76.

52. T. Valila, How expensive are cost savings? On the economics of public-private partnerships, EIB papers, vol. 10 (2005), no. 1, p. 94–119.

53. Data taken out of the question 31 of the research questionnaire "Are the services provided by PPPs more costly for the population?"

54. C. C. Thomson, Public-Private Partnerships: prerequisites for prime performance?, EIB papers, vol. 10, No. 2 (2005), p. 126.

55. PWC admits for example that the cost of a highway kilometre under traditional public procurement is inferior of a few or even tens of percent in comparison with a PPP, but that the higher remuneration of the PPP is justified by its extra obligations and costs, such as: the risks of delay, of operating and modernizing the highway, the costs of technological innovations, etc. . . . PWC, *7 mitów I 3 prawdy o Partnerstwie Publiczno-Prywatnym*, op.cit., p. 17.

56. Saur Neptun Gdańsk S.A., *15 lat PPP*, 2007, p. 6, www.gdansk.pl/g2/2007_10/16991_fileot.ppt?PHPSESSID=9afe2ef33b2eb1b52b48

57. According to the declarations of Szczepan Lewna, Vice-President of the city of Gdańsk, *"PPPs in particularly sensitive areas" (PPP w obszarze szczególnie wrażliwym)*, CEO, March 1st 2004, http://www.cxo.pl/artykuly/39014.html. This information about prices has been confirmed by S.Zysnarski, who asserts that the increase of the prices of the water supplied has been inferior to the evolution of inflation. S.Zysnarski, *Partnerstwo Publiczno-Prywatne w realiach polskich*, op.cit., p. 5.

58. See Aqua Bielsko-Biała, Annual report 2006, p. 15.

59. Sharing these views, Smith writes that "The operation of a toll road is not conceptually very different from operating a railway, a hospital or a prison, [...] all must provide specified services to a guaranteed and measurable standards." A. J. Smith, Privatized infrastructure: the role of the government. Thomas Telford, London, 1999. Quoted by A.Riess, Is the PPP model applicable across sectors?, op.cit., p. 12.

60. United Nations Development Programme (UNDP), Human Development Report 2006: Beyond Scarcity: Power, poverty and the global water crisis, United Nations, New York, 2006, p. 89.

61. This part is mostly based on A. Brenck, T. Beckers, M. Heinrich, C. Von Hirschausen, Public-private partnerships in New EU member countries of Central and Eastern Europe, Bak and Burkewicz, country study—Poland, Polish program of motorways constructions—Barriers of implementation, Bergamo, November 26th-27th 2004, and Agnieszka Gajewska-Jedwabna, Partnerstwo Publiczno-Prywatne, PriceWaterHouse Coopers, Wydawnictwo C. H. Beck, Warsaw, 2007.

62. Answer to question 42: "Do you think that sharing responsibility for security between government and private sector makes security more difficult to achieve?"

63. This notion is defined by P.Urio as "[referring] to physical resources and services (like roads, railways, energy, housing, etc.)" and is opposed to "soft" infrastructure, "whose aim is not to develop anything physical, but to directly improve human capital, namely attitudes, knowledge, skills, as well as physical and mental health. It is the domain of education, science and technology (including the dissemination of innovation and best practices) health, and more generally, the development of safety nets." See further the theoretical chapter 2 above.

64. O. Hart, Incomplete contracts and public ownership: remarks and an application to Public-Private Partnerships, op.cit.

65. A. Riess, Is the PPP model applicable across sectors?, op.cit., p. 16.

66. Ibidem.

67. E. Bennett and E. Iossa, *Building and managing facilities for public services*, CMPO working paper Series n°05/137, December 2005. For a very good summary of their argumentation, see A. Riess, op.cit., pp. 19–25.

68. E. Bennett and E. Iossa, Building and managing facilities for public services, op.cit., p. 27.

69. A. Brenck, T.Beckers, M.Heinrich, C. Von Hirschausen, Public-private partnerships in New EU member countries of Central and Eastern Europe, op.cit.

70. M. Ratajczak, Advantages and threats of Public-Private Partnerships in larger infrastructure projects: Polish motorway development program," Presentation given at the European week of regions and cities, Brussels, 11.10.2006.

71. See Aqua Bielsko-Biała, Annual report 2006, and Saur Neptun Gdańsk S.A., 15 lat PPP (15 years of PPPs), op.cit.

72. PWC evaluates Poland's needs to around 50 new prisons. PWC, *Partnerstwo Publiczno-Prywatne*, Wydawnictwo C.H.Beck, Warsaw, 2007, p. 247.

73. P. Urio, Under What Conditions Can Public-Private-Partnerships (PPPs) Improve Efficiency, Equity, Security and Sustainable Development in Countries at the Pre-PPP Stage?, Ch.2 of the present volume.

74. This data is taken out of the analysis of question 17: "In comparison to traditional government infrastructure and services, are PPPs more respectful of the natural environment?"

75. See the argumentation proposed by O. Hart on the two kinds of investments "i" and "e," pp. 188–189 above.

76. See pp. 189–190 above.

77. See p. 190 above.

78. p. 16.

79. Data taken out of the question 9 of the research questionnaire: "How is it possible to overcome barriers for PPPs and what methods could be used?"

80. Ibidem.

81. Data taken out of the question 27 "Are there training institutions in the country that provide training on PPPs?" and 28 "Do local employees benefit from information and training given by international organisations" of the research questionnaire.

82. For example, the Urząd Ochrony Konkurencji i Konsumentów (or Office for the defence of competition and consumers) deals with monopolistic practices and more generally with the protection of consumers. Similarly, the role of the Chamber of water infrastructure (Izba Wodociągów i Kanalizacji) is to control the quality of water infrastructure and services

6

PPPs in the Russian Federation: A Preliminary Assessment

Tatiana Chernyavskaya and Vladimir Varnavsky

BACKGROUND INFORMATION

The concept of Public Private Partnerships (PPPs) was introduced for the first time in Russia during the summer of 2004. In September-October 2004, Mr. Fradkov, Prime-Minister of Russia at that time (from 14 September 2007, the Prime Minister was Mr. Zubkov), used this concept in his description of the future of the country—as one of the main tools to further strengthen economic development. Since then, a lot of efforts on both Federal and regional levels were made to integrate the concept of PPPs in the existing economic relationships between the government and the private sector. It appears that PPPs were already used in some sectors, including water and transportation. However, they were operated locally, under exceptional conditions and privileges provided by the government in partnership with the private sector. These partnerships were, of course, not called by the same name. In the beginning of 2008, in many regions of the country and, especially at the Federal level of the government, PPPs became one of the most used concepts in economic strategies and plans.

In this chapter we are going to talk about public-private partnerships in the Russian Federation, in view of their wide usage at different levels of authority in the country. We will keep the main target of this research project in mind, which asked the following questions: can PPPs contribute to sustainable development? Can they benefit all the groups of society? Can PPPs ensure the security criteria, when compared to projects operated by the public or the private sector individually? And finally, can PPPs in Russia deliver more efficient public infrastructure and public services through the involvement of private finances and business-like operations?

We will begin by briefly discussing the overall situation and progress of PPPs as they are introduced in the economy of the Russian Federation. An analysis of the main questions of the research will be provided in Part 2 of this chapter. To begin, we will look at an overview of the current situation in the country, namely the: Political context; Legal context; Economic context; Social context; Security context; and Governance.

The last three of these aspects are a part of the main focus of this research and will be discussed in the second part of this chapter. The concluding pages are devoted to summarising the Russian context and offering some recommendations that can be considered for future policy formulation on PPPs.

1. THE CURRENT SITUATION

Russia already developed its own history in PPPs since 2004. The legal context appears to be well advanced, in terms of positioning partnerships in the socio-economic structure of the country's development. Underlying the legal context, the main driver for implementing the partnerships is political will. This has also proved to be the case, compared to the experience of other European countries where PPPs were also introduced. It requires strong political will on the part of government ministries or parliamentary authorities to introduce new approaches to infrastructure development and to public procurement, for which strong State support is a precondition.

The role of PPPs in the Russian Federation was formulated to be that of an instrument in the improvement of infrastructure. It includes the possibility to pay less for the necessary economic development through available oil revenues. It also mentions ways to increase foreign direct investment (FDI) in economy and the fulfilment of the State's social responsibilities, through raising employment, improving government policy and increasing the contributions of science and technology to innovation.

The current high revenues from Russian natural resources are used to further the economic development of the country, improving the well-being of the population, and strengthening the competitiveness of the market. Investment funds, Special Economic Zones, the Bank for Development and Foreign Economic Affairs[1], combined with strong PPP component, could be of a great benefit to the country, although a lot is still to be done.

1.1. THE POLITICAL CONTEXT

Policy Towards Private Enterprise and Competition

It is important for this discussion to remember that Russia introduced a more liberal and open market economy only in the early 1990s. This is one of the reasons why the country is still behind the level of economic development of Western countries in areas such as the freedom of entrepreneurship, maturity of civil society institutions, and the market-based relationships among small and medium size enterprises. For example, Russia ranked in the middle of the World Bank's Ease of Doing Business index in 2005 (79th out of 155 countries covered).[2] The overall ease of conducting business in Russia is thus significantly lower than the comparative global national level in terms of GDP per capita. According to the World Bank, Russia held the 11th place for GDP in the world.

The country made further progress in the recent years in easing the conditions for setting up businesses. There has been considerable progress in recent years in deregulation—in particular with regard to the ease of setting up businesses, an area where Russia records its highest global rank on the WB index (31st). The number of procedures and the time taken to start a new business were further reduced, as was the minimum capital requirement and the cost of setting up a business.

Policy Towards Foreign Investment

As is well known, Russia does not attract the same capital inflows in the form of foreign investment as other emerging markets do. For example, in comparison to China, the level of annual FDI in Russia is not that high. In 2006, it was just a bit higher than USD 20 billions (see Table 6.1). At the same time, it is eight times more than it was in 2001, which shows a significant rise in the attractiveness of Russian markets for foreign investors in recent years.

An article published in *The Economist* in July 2006, shows that there is still a good potential for FDI in Russia. The country's peaks in investment were seen already in 2003. Natural resources being significant for the world economy, along with an educated but low-cost workforce, and a fast growing consumer market are some of the attractions for investors. The continuation of reforms, started during the two terms of Vladimir Putin's federal administration, were recently reconfirmed by the current President Dmitry Medvedev. He placed an even stronger accent on the social side of reforms, and promised further improvements in the investment climate for both internal and external investors. The law on foreign investment (which dates from 1999), with its amendments of 2002 and 2003, has contributed to improving the investment climate in the country.

Table 6.1. Direct Foreign Investment in Russia

Foreign direct investment

	2001[a]	2002[a]	2003[a]	2004[a]	2005[a]	2006[b]	2007[b]	2008[b]	2009[b]	2010[b]
Foreign direct investment (US$ bn)										
Inward direct investment	2.7	3.5	8.0	15.4	14.6	21.5	19.5	20.1	23.5	25.0
Inward direct investment (% of GDP)	0.9	1.0	1.8	2.6	1.9	2.3	1.8	1.7	1.8	1.8
Inward direct investment (% of gross fixed investment)	4.7	5.6	10.0	14.3	10.5	12.4	9.2	8.4	8.7	8.3
Outward direct investment	-2.5	-3.5	-9.7	-10.3	-13.1	-12.9	-13.1	-13.4	-14.2	-15.5
Net foreign direct investment	0.2	-0.1	-1.8	5.1	1.5	8.6	6.4	6.7	9.3	9.5
Stock of inward direct investment	23.7	27.2	35.2	50.6	65.2	86.7	106.2	126.3	149.8	174.8
Stock of inward direct investment per head (US$)	162.6	187.3	243.2	351.5	454.7	606.8	746.0	890.5	1,060.1	1,241.8
Stock of inward direct investment (% of GDP)	7.7	7.9	8.1	8.6	8.5	9.2	9.6	10.7	11.6	12.4
Memorandum items										
Share of world inward direct investment flows (%)	0.39	0.61	1.59	2.68	1.72	2.45	2.00	1.93	2.12	2.11
Share of world inward direct investment stock (%)	0.39	0.37	0.40	0.52[c]	0.61[c]	0.75	0.85	0.93	1.02	1.11

[a]Actual. [b]Economist Intelligence Unit forecasts. [c]Economist Intelligence Unit estimates.

Box 6.1.   Competition Among Foreign Companies for the Concession of the "Western High-Speed Diameter" in Russia*

In Russia this project is simply seen as a way for foreign investors to enter the design of toll-roads. It is necessary to note that, in total, during the selection of participants in the open competition for the right to conclude concession agreements about the building of the toll-road "Western high-speed diameter" in Saint Petersburg in March 2007, only 4 consortiums had access to the competition process at the end. The most important transnational companies in that list were:

- MLA Lieferasphalt GmbH (consortium composed by companies: ALPINE Mayreder Bau GmbH, FccC-Construccion S.A., Deutsche Bank AG);
- "ZSD" the Neva meridian "" (Strabag A.G., Bouygues Travaux Publics, Hochtief PPP Solutions, Egis Projects, JOINT STOCK COMPANY "mostootryad No. 19");
- "Vincida Grupo de Inversiones 2006, S.L." (Obrascon Huantre Lain, S.A. (OHL), OHL Concesiones S.L.);
- "St. Petersburg high-speed main B.V." (Bechtel International Inc, Enka Holding, Intertoll Infrastructure Developments).

The projects which are about to start in the next few months are mostly of a big scale and important for the economy of the regions concerned, as well as for the country as a whole.

*Here "diameter" means "ring road"; from author's translation into English.

Russia's market is not entirely open to foreign investment and, like most other countries, some sectors are closed because they are considered of national importance. There are legal limits and restrictions on foreign investments in some sectors in Russia, which are considered of strategic importance for the country. These include defence, aviation, railways, electricity, gas and some service sectors like banking and telecommunications. These restrictions were recently strengthened through the adoption of Federal Law No. 57–FZ on April 29, 2008. It is entitled "On the Procedure for Making Foreign Investments in Economic Companies of Strategic Importance for Ensuring the Country's Defence Capacity and State Security," and it contains a list of "strategic sectors" in which foreign investment are to be restricted, including most defense-related activities, aviation and natural monopolies. The list of more than 100 "strategic enterprises" that cannot be privatized was also identified. The latter includes oil and gas giants, among other companies.

At the same time, 7.5% of the capital shares of Gazprom belong to foreign investors, and more than 40% to the Russian private enterprises and individuals.[3] We should also point out that, as in most other countries, Russia also limits bringing in foreign investments for mergers and acquisitions for particularly big deals.

The Administrative Aspect

The concept of PPP has become increasingly popular in Russia, and is now gaining the necessary political support. President V. Putin declared in November 2007 in one of his statements that: "The head of State also considers that, despite the increased amounts of funding that the State has allocated to modernizing the transport infrastructure, capital investments from private investors must complement these budgetary funds. And this public-private partnership must be attractive and beneficial not only for the State, but also for those investing their personal funds."[4]

Thus, government at both federal and local levels is promoting policies and regulations in favour of partnerships with the private sector. At the meeting of the Government of the Russian Federation on 7 February 2008, it was pointed out that the "mechanism of public-private partnership is new for the Russian legislation," that is why there is still a lot to be done for its development.[5]

The formulation of the PPP administration system began in 2004 in Russia. The Council on Competitiveness and Entrepreneurship was created in June 2004, to provide advice to the Government of the Russian Federation in the format of interactive discussions between federal authorities, the business sector and the scientific community. The Council consists of 42 members: ministers, deputies of the State Duma, representatives of the Central Bank, CEOs of major corporations, and experts from the Academy of Sciences and other research institutions. One of its tasks is to evaluate the problems in the implementation of PPPs in Russia. The questions of public-private partnership in the transport sector were examined for the first time during the session of 7 October of this Council. In accordance with the decisions made at these meetings, advisory bodies on PPPs were established in the ministries and other official governmental bodies.[6]

After the officially announced political intention to develop this kind of public-private cooperation in the country, a number of authorities were assigned with the responsibility for the development of PPPs at the national level. The very first was the Ministry of Transport. Another very important authority in the PPP development was the Ministry of Economic Development and Trade, and its Department of Investment Policy. Other bodies, including the Ministry of Regional Development and the Ministry of Culture and Mass Communications, also took the PPP initiative as instrumental for attracting investments into their projects. An Expert Council on PPPs was created in three ministries which are: Transport, Regional Development and

Culture, and Mass Communications. But the fact is that, all the above new expert organs are consultative. They do not make directives or executive decisions on PPPs. Their sphere of activity is limited to the examination of projects and the preparation of recommendations for the public bodies.

The formation of the PPP administration system continued in Russia in 2006–2007. Public-private partnerships were included in the priority list of the governmental Programme of socio-economic Development of the Russian Federation for the mid-term perspective (2006–2008).[7] This Programme was approved by the Government on 19 January 2006 (Decision No. 38-p). It identifies a development of management and coordination of PPP activities on the federal and regional levels, including monitoring of results and distribution of best practices.

In addition, one of the basic instruments of management and coordination of PPP development at the federal and regional levels will be the creation of departmental, regional and sectoral plans on PPPs. The Federal Program for the Modernization of the Russian Transport System for the years 2002–2010, contains the idea of using PPPs and, in particular, concession schemes for the purpose of financing transport infrastructure projects. A number of important projects which shall be structured as PPPs are currently being developed, namely the Western High-Speed Diameter (highway around the city) of Saint-Petersburg, the Central Peripheral Motorway in the Moscow Region, and the toll road from Moscow to Saint-Petersburg.

The need to develop the departmental plans during the years 2007–2008 is determined by the special decree of the government. The Government Decree on the systematic recommendations regarding the progress of regional plans of action on PPP development was issued in 2008. In addition, special systems of administration were created for the management of the Investment Fund and Special Economic Zones.

The Investment Fund

Based on the extra revenues earned from the Russian oil and other successful industries, a new administration system was developed to become the Investment Fund of the Russian Federation (see further below). The Investment fund was created on 23 November 2005, through the government Decree No.694. Its purpose is to provide State support for investment projects, which have national importance and take the form of public-private partnerships. This Fund provides an administrative scheme of the selection of investment projects over several stages as shown in Figure 6.1.

Before the submission of the proposal to the Ministry of Economic Development and Trade of the Russian Federation (MEDT), the initiators of investment projects must obtain the consent of the following istitutions: Body of

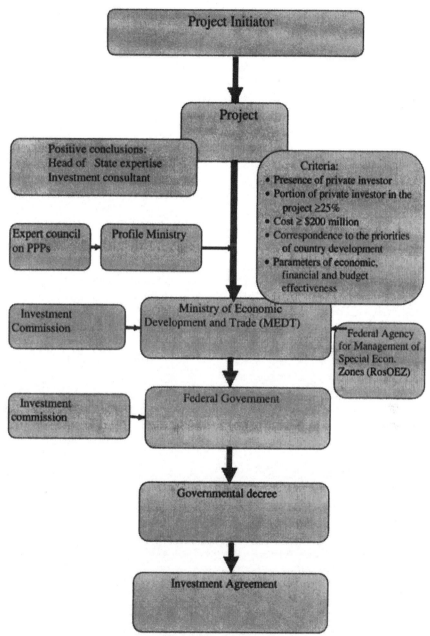

Figure 6.1. Scheme of Project Development for Obtaining Financial Resources from the Investment Fund of the Russian Federation.

the Main state expertise of Russia; Investment consultant; Federal ministry, which provides State policy and the normative/legislative regulation in the sector of the proposal.

The projects which satisfy these criteria are then examined by the Investment Commission of the MEDT on the selection of investment projects. This Commission makes a list of investment projects which have State value, and transfers it to the government commission for further examination. The projects selected by the government commission are then included in the list of investment projects liable for receiving State support from the Fund's financial resources. This list, along with the "passports" (i.e. short descriptions) of the selected projects, are subject to approval by the government of the Russian Federation through issuing the corresponding order. The order of the government of the Russian Federation is the base for the conclusion of the investment agreement on behalf of the government.

Money from the Investment Fund is provided only to those projects that have a direct participation of the business sector in the investment. The basic criterion for Investment Fund financing is that at least 25% of funds must be contributed by the private sector. The minimum cost of a project is 5 billion roubles (about USD 200 million). Priority is given to projects where the regional authorities are also participating in the funding. The size of the investment fund in 2006 was approximately 2,5 billion USD, while in 2007 its value increased to 4,4 billion USD. According to the government decision, this money can only be provided for infrastructural projects.

On 20 May 2006, the Ministry of Economic Development and Trade (MEDT) concluded its acceptance of the first proposals for the use of funds from the Investment fund. There were more than 50 proposals from federal and regional authorities, as well as private companies. Among these,

Box 6.2.   Investment Fund of the Russian Federation

The volume of the Investment fund has increased from 69.7 billion roubles in 2006 to 89.2 billion roubles in 2008. The Investment fund becomes an instrument for the State's participation in investment projects of all types. The modalities of investments through the Fund are:

First, the funding of up to 75% of total project costs as equity investment, or the financing of certain assets in exchange for an ownership title of the assets; or

Second, a guarantee on 60% of the borrowings for the project purposes.

Finally, to qualify for IF support, an investment project must comply with clearly defined public sector priorities and generate social benefits. Economic parameters of the project include mandatory economic profit.

23 investment proposals concerned the transport sector and seven were for power engineering. Nine of these proposals were presented by industry, and another six were for housing and communal services. Three dealt with the agriculture sector, and finally, the last six involved the national economy.

At the beginning of the process, the Federal Agency for Management of Special Economic Zones (RosOEZ) and the MEDT declined 31 proposals for different reasons. Nevertheless, these declined projects were not prohibited from participating in the subsequent competitions to receive financial assistance from the Investment Fund. The projects could be finalized in order to obtain State support during the years to come. Table 6.2 gives the complete list of the projects which received the right for financial support through the Investment Fund as of 15 September 2007.

The new investment process for public-private partnerships in Russia is obtained as follows: in the European part of the country support is provided

Table 6.2. Projects that Received Support from the Investment Fund of Russia. (As of 1 January, 2008)

Project and its region	Investments, billion roubles	
	Total	Investment fund
Construction of toll road "Western High-Speed Diameter" (Saint Petersburg)	99,95	32,1
Building of high-speed automobile road Moscow - Saint Petersburg (section 15-58 km) (Moscow, Moscow region)	54,93	25,8
Complex of oil refineries in Nijhnekamsk (republic Of Tatarstan)	130,3	16,5
Complex development of lower Priangar'e (Krasnoyarskiy Kray)	358,71	34,4
New output on MKAD from the federal highway "Moscow - Minsk" (circuit of Odintsovo)	17,26	10,0
Building of Orel tunnel under Neva river	31,67	10,33
Creation of transport infrastructure for the development of mineral resources in the south-east Chita region	142,181	40,95
Automobile road M-4 "Don" (Moscow, Lipetsk and Voronezh region, Krasnodar region) – development of project documentation	19,9	0,17
Building of toll-road Krasnodar-Abinsk-Kabardinka (Kabardinsky region) – development of project documentation	112,98	59,9
Complex programme of building and reconstructing the water supply and drainage items of Rostov-on-Don city and south-west of Rostov region	19,5	5,13
Construction of railway line "Kyzyl-Kuragino" (Republic of Tyva)	74,63	52,24
Building of a multifunctional trans-shipping complex "South-2" in the seaport Ust-Luga (Leningrad region)	8,41	2,1
TOTAL	**1070,42**	**289,62**

Sources: First, V. Varnavsky. "PPP in Logistics", *Logistics and Management*, 2008, C. 27; and second, data for the Session of the Government of the Russian Federation on 7 February 2008. Also available at: http://www.government.ru/government/governmentactivity/rfgovernmentsession/2008/i070208/materials/

to infrastructure development, particularly road construction, which is the biggest weakness in transport infrastructure. The motor roads of Moscow and Saint Petersburg are the two main priorities. However, the government commission for the Investment Fund also discussed the construction of roads in other regions of the country, namely in the Krasnodar region in central Russia, where the highway "Don" is located.

In the Eastern part of the country preference is given to the construction of large industrial complexes, comparable in scale with the Soviet "interbranch programs" for territorial and productive complexes. These are, first of all, industrial clusters in the lower Priangar'e and Chita regions. Among all projects financed by the Investment Fund, these projects are the largest, with total capital investments amounting to 8,2 and 5,4 billion USD respectively, for period that can last up to 2015.

The first experience of creating public-private partnerships in industrial infrastructure within the framework of the Investment Fund is quite positive. We shall see how it develops in the future.

Special Economic Zones (SEZ)

In 2007, the Sate Duma adopted amendments to the Federal law No.116–FZ "On special economic zones" (SEZ). The creation of these geographic zones in sea ports and airports were allowed in Russia under the law "On Special Economic Zones" to guarantee the functioning and control of these special zones. To do this, in April 2006 the government reorganized the federal state unitary enterprise "Foreign economic association" (Vneshstroyimport) into the joint stock company "Special economic zones" with 100% participation of the State. The maintenance and coordination of activities related to SEZs is administrated by the Federal Agency for Management of Special Economic Zones (RosOEZ). This agency was established in accordance with the Decree of the President of the Russian Federation called "On Federal Agency for Management of Special Economic Zones."

The further adoption of the following normative and legislative base for the SEZs gave rise to more active PPP investment policies at the regional and municipal levels: Decree of the President of the Russian Federation of July 22, 2005, No.855 called "On Federal Agency for Management of Special Economic Zones"; Decree of the Government of the Russian Federation of August 19, 2005, No.530, "Regulation of Federal Agency for Management of Special Economic Zones." The status of SEZ gives privileges to company directors in three areas of economic policy: tax and customs exemptions, State financing of infrastructure, and reduction of the administrative barriers. The combination of these tools is a typical example of public-private partnership, which made the regime of SEZs attractive for business.

The first six SEZs were created at the end of 2005. Two of them were created in the industrial production sector: one in Lipetsk, in the production of consumer electronics, and in Tatarstane (Yelabuga) in the production of automobiles and their utilities, as well as one in the highly technological petrochemical production sector. The other four SEZs relate to innovation: one is on the development of information and nuclear physics technologies (Dubna); a second on the creation and production of articles of micro- and nano-electronics (Zelenograd) in the Moscow region; the third on the development of highly technological production in Saint Petersburg; and last is on the development of new materials in Tomsk.

The first Special Economic Zone (SEZ) of an industrial type was created in November 2007 in the city of Elabuga (Republic of Tatarstan). The business management centre, customs terminal, and the system of "single window" (a system which allows the applicants to submit regulatory documents at a single location and/or single entity) were established in this SEZ. The start-up of resident conveyer SEZ entitled "Alabuga" of the limited company "Severstalavto-Elabuga" also took place. In 2006, the very first projects on developing tourism and recreation zones were initiated. There are seven such zones now.

The RosOEZ (Federal Agency for Management of the Special Economic Zones) has representations in all special economic zones—Territorial Administration of the agency. There is also an Expert council for "technology-introductory zones" created under the RosOEZ.[8] Its goal is to organize and conduct expert evaluations of the business plans, presented by those who claim to obtain the status of resident of the SEZ. It also issues evaluations on the projects of the residents who would like to change the agreement conditions of their technical-introductory activities. The council consists of important Russian scientists, economists and experts.

Aside from the Investment Fund and Special Economic Zones (SEZ), other PPP institutions were also created in Russia. These include specially created governmental bodies, such as Institutes of Development, that will play important roles in the PPP development process. These bodies comprise the following: the Venture Innovation Fund, the State Corporation Bank for Development and Foreign Economic Affairs (Vnesheko-nombank), and a Support Fund for Housing and Communal Services. Such mechanisms should help during the first stages of the realization of PPP projects.

According to the recent messages from the Ex-President Putin and current President Medvedev, one of the key elements of a new development strategy will be the investment into human capital. Details of specific instruments oriented towards support of PPPs are discussed in the part dedicated to legal framework for PPPs in Russia.

1.2 The **Institutional Context: Actors Involved in the Investment, Infrastructure and PPP Sectors**

There are a number of actors working in the area of investment, infrastructure and PPPs in particular. The main governmental body in the area of investment is the Foreign Investment Advisory Council (FIAC). Since 1994, it is lead by the head of Government of the Russian Federation.[9]

Box 6.3.   Information in the Investor's Guidebook to Russia

The MEDT coordinates the FIAC and its working groups' operations. These working groups which include representatives of federal and regional agencies, as well as foreign investors, are an essential part of the FIAC mechanism. They review such issues as improvement of the tax legislation and economic conditions for foreign investors in Russia, according to the target of each group. This can include: state regulation; tax and accounting; financial institutions and capital markets; industry, construction and High Tech; natural resources; food and agriculture; image of Russia. The main form of FIAC operations is conducting a direct dialogue between the Government of the Russian Federation and foreign companies and banks on issues related to the establishment of a favorable investment climate in Russia, and the mobilization of foreign investment for the Russian economy.

The main objective of AmCham (American Chamber of Commerce) is to promote favorable conditions for commercial, industrial and investment cooperation between US businesspeople and their Russian counterparts.

The Investor Protection Association (IPA)—a non-profit organization established in April 2000, includes approximately 30 major Russian and foreign investors with a total investment of over USD 20 billion (as of May 2005). It provides assistance to its members through expert advice; represents their interests in legal conflicts; represents the joint position in government agencies; and offers network opportunities and IT support.

The Association of European Businesses (AEB)—a non-profit organization of European companies and entrepreneurs dealing with Russian companies and operating in the Russian market. It has represented European businesses interested in Russia and promoted European companies in Russia since 1995.

Other investment-related organizations are National league of Management Companies for Non-profit Partnership (NLU), ROTOBO (Japanese Association for Trade with Russia and Eastern Europe), Russian-Chinese Business Centers etc.

Source: Investor's Guidebook to Russia-2006 by MEDT and FIAC. Endorsed by Ministry of Economic Development and Trade of the Russian Federation, 2006.

Several federal ministries and agencies, primarily economic, take part in its operations from the Russian side. The Ministry of Economic Development and Trade, with the support of the Foreign Investment Advisory Council, has developed an Investor's Guidebook to Russia that contains information as presented in Box 6.3.[10]

With the liberalization of the Russian economy in the 1990s, there was a progressive improvement in the State's regulatory mechanism, which oversees the structures and people engaged in economic and business activity. In addition to State control bodies, oversight of labour conditions and safety may be performed by public organizations that have the appropriate authority. Public monitoring of compliance with the rights and lawful interests of employees in the area of labour safety may indeed be performed by professional unions and other representative bodies that are entitled to form their own inspectorates for these purposes and to elect labour safety officials.

There are a number of business associations that are monitoring investment regulations of the government. Two main organizations are the Chamber of Trade and Industry, and the Russian Union of Industrialists and Entrepreneurs. Both of these organizations are involved in advisory groups to the Government, focusing on investment policy formulation, including PPPs.

For the moment there is no pure PPP organization or association, although tendencies exist in some investment-related companies to create specific branches that work with PPPs and monitor them. One of the ways to mobilize civil society to better understand PPPs is through the creation of a National Centre on the Development of Private-Public Partnerships (NCPPP). It is headed by Alexander Bazhenov, member of the board of governments in the Eurasian Water Partnership. This effort was not supported by the government and was opposed by some other potential candidates for this position in the organization. Until now, the Centre developed as an NGO with a clear focus on PPPs, but without any formalized role for civil society.

Another organization that focuses on PPPs is the Centre of Strategic Research (CSR). Its mission is to facilitate the nation's successful development by granting expert and normative legal support for the reforms undertaken in the economical and social sphere.[11] In cooperation with the World Bank (WB), CSR conducted a number of PPP-related workshops, as well as research on different aspects of PPPs and their implementation in the Russian Federation since 2004. This organization is specialized in PPPs in the transport infrastructure—highways, toll roads, ports and railways.

Some international consultancy agencies, such as KPMG, PWC, etc. are very much interested in the promotion of their services and in the centralization of PPP offices based in their premises. However, thus far, they have only conducted a limited number of country-level and regional conferences on PPPs.

The financial sector is also very interested in the managerial role for PPPs in Russia. A number of banks, including the Vneshekonombank and the Vneshtorgbank, have shown their readiness to lead in the financial approach to PPPs. However, they have not received clear support from the Government, which is dubious of any private financial institution in Russia. There are a number of academic centres within major Russian universities where PPPs were seriously studied within special advisory groups. Projects and proposals to study PPPs provided consultative support and training for governmental bodies on different levels (i.e. High School of Economics, IWEIR Russian Academy of Sciences etc.).

The role of international organizations in the development of PPPs in Russia should not be underestimated as it is quite critical for awareness raising, networking, knowledge sharing and exchange of best practices. Some governmental requests are addressed, for example, to the UNECE for such cooperation.

Types of PPPs in Russia

The most commonly used forms of PPPs in Russia include joint ventures, lease of public assets, public contracts and purchases.

There are thousands of joint ventures in the public and private sectors in Russia. These are, for example, Gazprom (state ownership is 50,002%)[12], Russian Public Corporation of Energy and Electrification[13] "RAO EES" (state ownership 52,3457%) and a number of other companies.

Revenues of the federal budget in 2007 amounted to USD 1 billion just from selling State and municipal properties. Every year, the federal and regional governments, as well as municipalities, conclude many contracts in the areas of public procurement, research & development, and management. At the same time, in spite of the laws "On Concession Agreements" and "Production Sharing Agreements," there are still no concessions or new production sharing agreements in Russia.

Impact of PPPs

In Russia, so far only the first humble steps were made towards the promising future of PPPs. Along with traditional forms of PPPs, Russia also has specific forms of cooperation, which do not exist in developed countries: these are the Investment Fund and Special Economic Zones. However, the new PPP tools which appeared in 2005–2007 in Russia are only the first step in the general industrial policy. The preferred direction of State financing is clear: infrastructure (transport, electricity, trunk pipelines, housing and communal services), innovation projects, the development of small cities, mortgage financing, human capital (education, public health), and small and medium-size enterprises. However, Russia seriously needs a long-term strategy for social and economic development for the next 20 years to come. In order to have a balance between resources and production capacities in Russia in 10–20 years, it is necessary to develop long-term plans of geographical distribution of manufacturing and productive forces.

1.3 The legal Context

The legislative base for PPP development in Russia is scarce. Currently, there is only one Federal Law "On concession agreements" (August 2005) and a number of governmental resolutions on standard concession agreements that address PPP issues in a number of sectors (seaports, roads etc.). The most important fact is that there are not enough subordinate legislation norms for concessions (instructions, standard agreements, State guarantees to investors, mechanisms of arbitration, methodology of concession payments derivation, etc.) and hardly any new ones are developed.

There is no lack of investment resources in Russia for implementing big infrastructure projects. Money is not an issue for either the State or the business sector, but the lack of norms and legislative base, combined with the high risks of non-return of private investment is pushing project costs upwards. Just to demonstrate: in a business plan for the construction of the "Western High-Speed Diameter" automobile road in St. Petersburg, the cost of constructing 1 km of the road is 180 million USD, which is much higher than in similar projects in the EU or the United States. At the same time, the price of building land, as well as wages of Russian workers are two to three times lower than in the West. For example, in the USA the construction of 47 miles of toll road E-470 (segments II, III and IV) in Colorado cost USD 408 million (5,4 mio USD for 1 km of the road).[14]

The Law on Concessions

The Federal Law "On Concession Agreements" No. 115 (the "Concession Law") was adopted on 21 July 2005. It governs the process of launching a concession—from the formulation of an agreement and tendering, to risk allocation, and government support possibilities. Nevertheless, the euphoria that followed the Law's adoption in 2005 was curtailed by a number of obstacles in the regulation of relations between parties involved in concession projects.

Features of Concession Agreements

The objects owned by the Government that can be transferred into a concession are determined in Article 4 of the Federal Law "On Concession Agreements" as follows: motor roads, bridges, tunnels, other road infrastructure, items of rail transport and pipeline transport, sea and river ports (including the water-engineering constructions of ports, items of their production and engineering infrastructure), seagoing and river vessels, airports; items for production, transfer and distribution of electric and thermal energy; municipal service system (including: water, heat, gas and power supply, water-drainage, cleaning of waste water, processing and the utilization (burial) of household trash); the subway system and another transport of general use, the institutions of public health, education, culture, sport, and leisure.

According to the CA-Project Consulting,[15] the concessionaire (a company from the private sector) can reconstruct or even construct any infrastructure, and/or provide specific services related to this infrastructure under the concession agreement. This infrastructure will then be owned by the state. According to the Russian law, some of these objects (like public transport infrastructure, for example) cannot be privately owned. For such cases, concessions are the only way to attract private investment into these businesses.

It is probable that engaging into infrastructure projects under the responsibility of local and regional authorities (above all—transportation and utilities) is easier for investors than it would be for the Federal Government. The reasoning behind this is related to more flexible legislation and a shorter decision-making process at the local level. Moreover, an investor could even get involved in the decision-making process, alongside the local authorities.

The Concession Law establishes a clear tender procedure for concession-type PPP projects, which could be either open or closed.

The general rule is an open tender; a closed tender is only conducted if the concession agreement involves an object of strategic significance for the country's defense or information, which constitutes a State secret. The tender winner is determined by the tender commission. The criteria for selecting the winning bidder are not set up in the Concession Law; they shall be identified in the tender documentation on a case-by-case basis. In case of any infringement of the tender procedure, any third party may file a claim to invalidate the tender results and, as a consequence, the concluded agreement. The Law does not provide any scale of severity for such procedural breaches, so any violation may lead to the cancelation of a project.[16]

The Law "On Concession Agreements" is a law of direct action. This indicates, first of all, the need for its concrete definition in other laws and normative reports. It also means that it can be used by any State body regarding its property, as indicated in Article 4 immediately after the Law entered into force. One may assume that the normative and legislative base will be developed in proportion to the realization of the pilot projects of concession in roads. It is absolutely possible that after several years this form of PPPs will no longer cause bewilderment among entrepreneurs and the population in Russia.

However, almost three years have passed from the adoption of the Law "On Concession Agreements," and not a single concession project was concluded in Russia. The main reason for this is the slow development of subordinate legislation normative base for concessions. The Government only adopted standard concession agreements in different sectors of the economy in 2006: for motor roads (decision of the Government of 27 May, 2006, No.319), for railroads (No.744), for sea and river ports (No.745), for seagoing and river vessels (No.746), for water-engineering constructions (No.747), and for municipal infrastructure (No.748).

The Concession Law does not cover all types of PPP projects; it was neither intended to do so, nor to restrict them to concessions alone. For example, such forms of PPP ownership as BOOT, DBOT, DBF[17] and others are beyond the scope of the Concession Law, which prohibits a private party to sell the constructed or modernized facilities. But this does not mean that such types of PPPs are impossible in Russia.

Existing obstacles for the implementation of concession projects in Russia include the lack of legal practice and practical experience in running common projects with the State and private investors; moreover, expert say that there is no adequate definition of concessions, as a separate economic category in the Law "On Concession Agreements" and this worsen the lack of essential provisions for ensuring the adequate protection of the property rights of the concessionaires.

The concessionaire's rights are also under legal pressure, as a concessionaire may not guarantee the project assets or rights to a third-party under the concession agreement. This is expected to hinder the financing of concession projects in Russia, as such guarantees are conventional forms of security for financing a loan. Moreover, provisons related to the compensation of the concessionaire are non-existent, should the project fail for economic reasons. An early termination without any mandatory compensation for investors increases a project's credit risk, and reduces incentives for the government.

It seems that the rights of the State are more protected then the rights of the private stakeholder—there are ambiguities in the procedure for extracting land from private owners, including an unclear approach to the calculation of compensation and extremely long periods (usually more than 25 years) for opposing the withdrawal conditions. Property rights with respect to numerous objects of State and municipal infrastructure are not clearly defined. Given that a clear property regime is an essential prerequisite for the structuring of all PPP arrangements, steps should be taken and funds allocated for the resolution of this issue. The important issue of taxation is uncertain: it is not determined whether concessions should be subject to a common or special tax system; taxation benefits (exemptions, discounts, tax holidays, tax credits, etc.) are not identified.[18]

Other PPP Legislation

PPPs could also be classified under general public procurement legisla-
tion. The Federal Law "On the Placement of Orders for the Procurement of
Goods, Performing Works, and Rendering Services for State and Municipal
Needs" No. 94–FZ dated July 21, 2005 (the Law on State and Municipal
Tenders) is one of the laws which gave equal rights to domestic and foreign
bidders, thus promoting competition in the area of PPPs.

In 2005, after the adoption of the first PPP law, a regulative framework
and legislative base was created, and a number of basic PPP mechanisms
were developed for the implementation of infrastructure projects. These
mechanisms can be divided into two separate investment categories: concession agreements and project support through the Institutions for Economic
Development (Investment Fund, Special Economic Zones and others).

An important step towards PPPs was the adoption of the State Investment Fund rules (Government Regulation of 23 November 2005 No.694).
There were changes regarding the use of concessions, the improvement of

Box 6.4. Progress and Barriers for PPPs in Russia

Progress:
   Adoption of the Federal Law "On Concession Agreements" (2005) is
seen as a big progress towards introduction of PPPs in the country. It
took a while, but the development of regional, municipal and sector-
specific policy frameworks is also taking place, it includes the adoption
of the regional law "On the Participation of the City of Saint Petersburg
in the Public-Private Partnerships" (2006) and the creation of bodies
responsible for PPPs (for example: Government Council on Competitiveness (2004), Expert Council for PPPs by the Ministry of Transport
(2006).

Constraints:*

• Lack of traditions
• Political issues
• Incapacity of the government to develop PPPs—difficulties for the private
  sector to act in tandem and in a coordinated way
• Lack of financial resources
• Bureaucracy and the absence of a legal framework
• Lack of incentives from both sides
• Limited demand and low prestige among potential participants

*Public Private Partnerships in Vocational Education—experiences from Russia and
Ukraine, *Fourth ECA Education Conference Timo Kuusela*, Tirana, 26 October 2007.

transparency, as well as increasing effectiveness (State Government Regulation N 732, 31 October).

At the beginning of 2006, the officials from the Ministry of Economic Development and Trade (MEDT) and the Ministry of Finance formed the normative base for the Investment Fund.

There is also law-making activity in the area of PPPs at the regional level. In Saint Petersburg for example, on 20 December 2006, the law "On the Participation of the City of Saint Petersburg in the Public-Private Partnerships" was adopted. The law pertained to the realization of socially significant projects, the attraction of private investments, and the improvement in the quality of goods and services provided to the local consumers. This law concretely defines this position of the Federal Law "On Concession Agreements" and its development.

1.4 The Economic Context

Government Promotion of PPP Development

According to Professor Varnavsky (IWEIR RAS, Moscow)[19] there are several different ways to achieve PPP goals and to solve the problems identified by the Government with regard to PPP development in Russia.[20]

PPP projects in infrastructure have become increasingly popular in Russia during the last four years. Before that, the usefulness of PPPs existed mainly as a topic of hot discussions. Now words are replaced by actions, and the progress of PPPs in developing the Russian infrastructure is undeniable.

Government promotion of PPPs can be seen particularly in the following three areas. First, the Russian government is striving to improve the environment for PPPs by introducing new legislation. This includes the recently adopted Federal Law "On Concession Agreements," which will be briefly discussed further down. Following the introduction of this law, the Russian Federation has embarked on a journey of great importance. As well as in many other transition countries, this law is the foundation of PPPs. Second, the introduction of PPPs in many sectors is happening at the same time as the underlying legal structure is also being developed. Regional, municipal and sector-specific policy frameworks are put in place. A Federal law on roads was adopted by the State Duma in October 2007 (No.257–FZ). Bills on concessions in public utilities were submitted and are currently waiting an approval of the State Duma.

Third, many ministries and governmental agencies are forming special bodies that are to be responsible for the implementation of PPPs.

As suggested by Alexander Bazhenov,[21] the main difficulties for PPPs in Russia are the limited number of quality projects, the lack of funds, and insufficient expertise in the public sector to prepare long-term investment programs for PPPs. Public property is not fully registered and requires time, as well as significant investments to become part of a PPP arrangement (either for transfer or for security). Public procurement contracts can be financed with public funds for no longer than 5 years. Risk of early termination of public procurement still goes unsecured without coverage from the budget (an implication of the Public Procurement Law) and early termination risk can not be properly covered by municipal budgets (an implication of the Budget Code). It is clear that the regional budget level is not sufficient to assume risks on investments of major size and federal policy limits issuance of long-term guarantees—these and other regulations are not streamlined to support the necessary PPP arrangements.

In spite of all these financial and regulatory barriers towards PPP development, the need and vision for a national PPP unit is emerging. "The lack of quality PPP projects pushes public assets away from market-based investments (through financial markets) and/or limits the use of available long-term assets to investments in financial bonds.," as inicated by Alexander Bazhenov.[22] The mission of a national PPP unit would be to supplement existing management of long-term public assets with quality projects, risk profile of which is appropriate for market-based investments of long-term assets such as Pension Savings, etc. The unit should be project driven, initiating quality projects for market based long-term investments. It should also accumulate experience and disseminate it to public authorities. Furthermore, the unit should be closely linked to the Ministry of Finance and banks, in order to receive financial support for PPP initiatives. The recent initiative of the Vneshekonombank to create such a unit in its structure was welcomed by both the authorities and the private sector.[23]

1.5 Government Capacities to Offer Investors a Stable Investment Environment

Current State of Economic Growth in Russia

Russia's economic growth was quite robust for the last five years, particularly if we compare it to those of major developed countries. The Russian economy showed an average annual growth rate of over 6%. In 2006, the Russian GDP increased by 6.3% and in 2007 by 8.1%. The rapid economic growth in Russia was driven by three main factors. First, the rising oil and gas production in the country. Second, a surge in world oil prices. And third, the devaluation of the rouble in 1998, which led to improved competitiveness for domestic industries.

Other factors also contributed to promote an economic upturn in the country. The Russian Government pursued a tight fiscal policy, and kept the

Table 6.3.   Money Indicators of Russia. (US$ bn., Current Prices, GDP for 2007 = 32 Billion Rub., or ~ 1300 US$ bn.)

Years	Stabilization Fund	Federal budget surplus	International reserves	External Debt
2003	3	+ 8	77	98
2004	18	+ 25	125	97
2005	45	+ 59	182	71
2006	88.7	+ 77	289	45,7
2007	89.13*	+ 57,3**	476,4*	39,6***

*as of 01.01.2008
**Federal law "On the Federal Budget 2007"
***as of 01.10.2007
Source: PPP in Russia—infrastructure issues. V. Varnavsky. October 2007.
Presentation at the conference in the High School of Economics. Available at:
www.hse.fi/NR/rdonlyres/D40BF349-2AE2-4CF1-B75F-0B5898755AE5/6100/Varnavskiy.pdf

federal budget in surplus in the last ten years. As a result, the Russian government and many regional authorities have accumulated huge reserves.

The Federal Government transferred a significant part of oil export income to the so-called Stabilization Fund, in which the Government holds now almost 90 billion dollars. This is the equivalent of 7.5% of GDP. The currency reserve of the Russian Federation has surpassed 470 billion USD. At the same time, the Russian Government started to pay its foreign debt ahead of the original schedule. As a result, external debt of the Russian government was reduced to only 40 billion USD. This encouraged all key international credit rating agencies to raise the country's credit rating.

Several Russian companies have also accumulated large amounts of capital due to their very high incomes. For example, most of the major energy companies in Russia are now more profitable than their foreign rivals. During the last year, the price of shares rose, and market capitalization of these companies reached a record level.

However, despite the substantial resources accumulated in both public and private sectors and the rather robust investment activity, modernization of industrial and social infrastructure in Russia still requires much more investment.

Under the current structure of public ownership of infrastructure in Russia, PPPs remain one of the most important ways to involve private (corporate) funds in infrastructure modernization.

The trend in Russia towards PPPs follows the track of other countries with similar structures, but the history of planned economy and the resulting market limitations create real obstacles for private investors and banks to contribute to the development of PPPs in the country. PPPs are supposed to have interactions between public and private sectors in the long term, whereas the tendency among Russian companies is quite the opposite. There are no guarantees for companies on their investments for more than 10 years, and a history of such guarantees does not exist. Only the ownership of property rights for the objects to be constructed might be of interest to the private investors, but in PPP projects all infrastructure construction remains public ownership. It is becoming more and more clear that only through support of the government at federal and regional levels, could Russia create the conditions for the investment flows of long-term PPPs, with profits and secured rates of return.

Transport infrastructure and municipal services are on the front line of projects available to develop PPPs. These projects need large investments, and they could serve as an ideal framework for cooperation between public and private sectors. Social infrastructure, including education, health, recreation and prisons may be later involved in PPP schemes.

Transformation of public unitary enterprises (municipally or state owned) into commercial enterprises in the utilities sector (water, heating, public transport, gas in the City of Moscow, for example) was an incentive to expand the areas of PPP application. The social application of PPPs could be seen through the increase in public spending on social services, and the devolution of responsibilities to local authorities in areas like affordable housing (special Investment Fund programmes for youth, for example), hospitals, schools and colleges, and museums. Government investment in infrastructure increased, namely in infrastructure for special economic zones, new development of mineral resources and toll roads schemes.

PPP Financing Issues

Banks and other financial institutions are not yet organized to support PPPs in Russia. There is almost no experience in project bonds, or in medium and long term lending, and there is only a limited number of capital-intensive models in Russia. Most commercial banks work only with short-term obligations. Co-financing PPP projects can only be done through

Box 6.5. St Petersburg's Southwest Wastewater Treatment Plant

Since the end of the 1990s, the State and private investors implemented some projects jointly. Most of these projects concern water supply and sewage water treatment. Among them, the following should be mentioned: the creation of the St Petersburg's Southwest Wastewater Treatment Plant, the Aeration Station in the Moscow Micro-district Yuzhnoe Butovo and in Zelenograd, and the reconstruction of a garbage incineration plant, which recently commenced in Moscow.

The St Petersburg's Southwest Wastewater Treatment Plant is the most significant environmental investment and the first major PPP project carried out in Russia. This EUR 190 million project is financed by the Nordic Investment Bank (NIB), the European Bank for Reconstruction and Development (EBRD), the European Investment Bank (EIB), Finnfund and Swedfund, the Northern Dimension Environmental Partnership (NDEP), Finland, Sweden and the European Commission. Nordic construction companies (NCC), Skanska and YIT Consulting Ltd., the Nordic Environment Finance Corporation (NEFCO), and Vodokanal of St Petersburg set up a special company LLC Nordvod, and invested risk capital in the project. NCC, Skanska and YIT established a joint venture, SWTP Construction Oy, to handle the design and construction of the plant. Construction started at the beginning of 2003. The treatment plant was completed according to the agreed schedule in September 2005, with EUR 2 million under budget. The project includes a 12-year operation agreement.

Source: Anastasia Rusinova, Attorney, LL.M. PPP in Russia: An overview, CA—project consulting, Ltd., p. 1–2.

the federal Investment Fund and solely for projects over USD 150 million. Various industry related funds and regional investment funds are still under discussion. However, the nature of infrastructural investment requires at once large scale long-term lending, state financial support and the attraction of international capital.

Russian PPP projects are lacking transparency in the preparation and implementation phases, as well as clarity on the rate of return and risk sharing.

The basic principles of the Federal Law "On Concession Agreements" do not work due to the low sustainability of concession legislation. The Law does not set out any detailed frameworks for private and State participation in financing concession projects. Some of the new PPP institutions were created in Russia to solve the financial issues (see information on the Investment Fund and SEZ in the relevant part of this paper).

1.6 PPPs by Economic Sector

It is clear that businesses from the private sector should participate in industrial and social infrastructure only if they are more effective. However, efficiency as an economic category is very complex. It could be mathematically derived as a ratio of valued work accomplished per rouble expended, reduction of prices on service, steady development, increase of safety, change in ecological compatibility, etc.

In different sectors of infrastructure, various tendencies can be observed. On the one hand, communal services and roads are deteriorating. On the other hand, some seaports, especially in the Leningrad region, show substantial improvement. New ports such as Ust-Luga, Primorsk, and Visotsk by St.-Petersburg are under construction. Nevertheless, the situation with the communal services is critical.

Water and Wastewater

Compared to other infrastructure services in Russia, water-supply and wastewater services are actively engaged in PPPs schemes. The Ministry of Regional Development is responsible for the improvement of water and waste services to the population. They use PPPs as a main source of financing and providing such services. A branch on PPPs was created in the Department of Housing and Communal Services specifically for solving issues related to social infrastructure (utilities). The issue of equal access to the outcomes of these projects is still being elaborated. A number of regions, although having the money for social development and housing, still cannot regulate legislatively the complex systems of distribution and payment for the construction, energy and water supply for social needs. Regions and

Table 6.4. Private Companies in the Utilities Sector in Russia

Company/Operator	Cities
«RKS» (Holding "Integrated Energy System")	Tambov, Tomsk, Volgograd, Kirov, Petrozavodsk, Krasnoarmeysk (Perm region), Novorossiysk
« RosVodokanal» (Holding "Alfa-Group")	Orenburg, Orsk, Barnaul, Kaluga region
EuroEsian Water Partnership	Omsk, Rostov-on-Don
Novogor-Prikam'ye (Holding Interros)	Perm, Berezniaki

Source: V. Varnavsky. Private captial in the housing service of Russia. "World economy and international relations", 2007, 1, page 30.

municipalities are solving this problem independently according to their current needs and resources. This could create problems in the future.

PPPs were developed locally in a number of cities in Russia, long before the Law on Concessions was approved. For example, some municipal utility system projects of the RosVodokanal Company were developed as a PPP scheme in several Russian cities (Orenburg, Orsk, Barnaul, Kaluga region).

Since the end of the 1990s, the first water and sewerage private operators started to appear in Russia. This process slowed down with time. The main reason is that private companies do not want to invest into communal systems with high levels of deterioration (exploitation for more than 15 years). This fact is very common for most Russian cities. At the same time, private companies are ready to operate new communal systems, but such arrangements are not profitable for the State or the Municipalities.

There is no normative and legislative basis for concessions in the communal sector. There is no law on concessions in housing. There are 25,000 municipalities in Russia, and they do not all have statutory acts to transfer water supply networks and sewerage systems to private companies for long periods. These municipalities were not able to develop such norms and legislations because it is a prerogative of the federal legislature.

Transport Infrastructure

Long before the adoption of the Federal Law "On Concession Agreements," toll roads in Russia already existed (i.e. roads transferred into concession). In the Pskov province for example, since spring 2002 a number of roads covering a total length of 226 km, were collecting payments from the automobiles registered in other regions. In the Lipetsk region, there is a section on the federal motor road "Don" around the village Khlevnoye that was imposing tolls on drivers since 1999. Similarly, in the Altai region

Box 6.6.   Transport Strategy of Russia

A promising way of attracting non-governmental resources to finance transport infrastructure is the public-private partnership.

The main format of PPP is a concession in the area of toll-roads, railway construction, development of airports, and public city transportation.

One of the priorities is to develop a regulative and normative basis to ensure clear lawful distribution of rights, responsibilities and risks between the State and the investor. Identification of priority areas for the application of PPPs in transportation is also crucial.

Source: Transport Strategy of the Russian Federation until 2020. Approved by the order of the Ministry of Transport of the Russian Federation No.45 of 12 May 2005.

a section of the motor road "Altai-Kuzbass" with the length of 137 km was functioning on a paid basis for seven years.

At the same time, concessions were given a legal basis in 2007. During February 2007, the tender for the concession on the building and maintenance of Saint Petersburg toll road "Western High-Speed Diameter" (46 km) was declared. The building of toll roads Moscow—Saint Petersburg, Moscow—Minsk, and others were next. The first concession contracts involving automobile roads are in the process of preparation now and should be signed by the end of 2008.

In the area of port economy, PPPs are more actively developed in the Baltic region. The Seaport Ust-Luga received an investment from the Investment Fund of the Russian Federation. The very first Special Economic Zone in seaports will be opened in 2008.

The public corporation OAO RZD (Russian railroads, 100% owned by the State) is the only operator of the entire network of public railroads. There are initial plans to build private railroads (mainly to link with perspective mineral deposits), but it is premature to speak about them. In seaports, the docks, coastal waters and local railways are owned by the State. Sometimes, these are transferred to private companies for rent or operating control. There are yet no concessions in seaports, nor are any planned for the near future.

Electricity/Energy

Corporatization (the transformation of state assets into state-owned corporations in order to introduce corporate management to their administration) or joint venture development is the most actively developing form of PPP in the electricity sector in Russia. RAO Unified Energy System of Russia

(RAO UES) was established in 1992 by the Presidential Decrees of August 15, 1992 No. 923 and November 5, 1992 No. 1334. In 2008, RAO UES provided 70% of electricity generation and about one-third of heat delivery in Russia. It also controlled 72% of generating capacities and 96% of the total length of Russia's trunk transmission lines. As of 31 December 2006, the State owned 52.68% of shares in RAO UES, which account for 54.99% of issued ordinary shares. 45% of issued shares are traded on the stock market of the Russian Federation.

The State will soon own only the Federal Network Company (main networks of electricity) and power system dispatching.[24] The private sector on the other hand, will own the generation, distribution and marketing of electricity. This process was already initiated in the spring of 2008.

There are no PPPs in the transportation of oil. This sector is financed through the State-owned company Transneft.

PPPs in Social Infrastructure

There is little or almost no information about PPPs in the social infrastructure in Russia (i.e. in education, health, culture etc). With regards to the development of social infrastructure the situation of Russia is still worse than that of Eastern European countries. The comparison between Russia and Eastern Europe is quite interesting, given the similarities of their economic and social development.

If PPPs in social infrastructure of post-industrial economies, such as the UK or Australia appeared in the mid-1990s, this knowledge came to Russia only in the first decade of the 21st century. The Ministry of Culture and Mass Communication of the Russian Federation sees the idea of private financing of cultural and historical heritage as one of the possibilities to support museums, historical villages, parks and other cultural monuments through PPPs. Vice-Minister of culture Dr. Dmitri Amunts developed this idea while taking part in various international and national conferences and meetings.[25]

Transfer of state social infrastructure into private hands is very sensitive in public opinion. So, according to the results of the analysis prepared by the KROK Severo-Zapad,[26] PPPs should be implemented, first of all in the industrial infrastructure, such as the utilities sector (63% of respondents), road infrastructure (49%), and building of municipal housing (42%). Socially sensitive areas mentioned as potential sectors for PPPs were public transport and health, with 31% of positive responses.

As the social situation is still tense in Russia, it is very dangerous to implement PPP mechanisms for the social infrastructure. They should be well developed in the other infrastructure sectors first. The reason behind this is that while the issues of huge infrastructure projects are mostly of

Table 6.5. Social Indicators and Living Standards of Russia

Social indicators and living standards

	2005		2010	
	Russia	Eastern Europe (av)	Russia	Eastern Europe (av)
Health				
Healthcare spending (% of GDP)	5.3	5.5	5.1	5.8
Healthcare spending (US$ per head)	282	297	510	514
Infant mortality rate (per 1,000 live births)	16.6	14.8	14.6	13.1
Physicians (per 1,000 population)	4.2	3.5	4.1	3.5
Food and beverages				
Food, beverages & tobacco (% of household spending)	45.9	37.6	39.8	34.1
Meat consumption (kg per person)	55.5	64.0	65.5	71.7
Milk consumption (litres per person)	157.1	174.2	183.9	195.0
Alcoholic drinks, sales volume (litres per person)	80.4	70.2	103.6	85.9
Coffee & tea consumption (kg per person)	3.6	3.5	4.2	3.8
Consumer goods in use (per 1,000 population)				
Passenger cars	162	228	202	259
Telephone main lines	296	305	385	375
Mobile phone subscribers	877	667	1085	944
Television sets	600	552	758	674
Personal computers	130	156	213	228
Retail sales volume (per 1,000 population)				
Refrigerators	19.1	20.9	25.1	26.6
Video recorders	5.5	5.4	4.2	3.7
Washing machines	13.0	16.8	18.0	22.2
Households				
No. of households (m)	53.3	106.8	53.9	108.1
No. of people per household (av)	2.7	2.7	2.6	2.6

Source: Country Report: Russia. Economic Intelligence Unit, The Economist. - 2007

pure economic significance for the country, the already problematic social area where government is traditionally the only responsible player, would immediately react to any negative changes. Unfortunately, the presence of private sector revenues is sometimes seen as a negative factor per se.

Housing and PPPs

A national project named "Social housing" was started in 2004.[27] The State, municipal governmental bodies, banks, building companies and the population participated in building such houses for young, numerous families, rural population, military personnel and other social categories. There are different forms of PPPs: housing certificates, subsidies, hypothec (mortgage) etc.

Health, Education, and Environmental Protection

There are almost no PPP projects in these areas. Services of education or health are provided either by the State or private companies. Environmental protection is completely under State competence (Ministry of Natural Resources).

Still, there is discussion going on in each of these sectors regarding the ways of attracting private investors to ongoing projects, but even when these projects are taking place, they are based on ad hoc agreements among stakeholders. For example, although private insurance companies are interested in providing good services to their clients, and in sipte of serious discussions going on about projects aimed at linking high-quality medical services and insurers, active systematic initiatives for the introduction of PPPs into the health sector are still under question mark.

PPPs and Innovation

A study on PPPs for innovations was conducted by the Ministry of Education and Science of the Russian Federation in cooperation with the OECD in 2005. This study examines how relations between science and industry, and more specifically partnerships between the public and private sectors, can be developed in Russia to foster innovation to strengthen the basis for sustainable long-term growth; to mprove the international competitiveness of Russian firms and to enable the Russian Federation to better respond to domestic demand for high technology and sophisticated production.

The recommendations of this report, mainly concentrate on the improvement of conditions for innovation, and the increase in the contribution of science and technology to innovation. They include parts on the importance of securing finances for the maintenance, revamping and development of

research infrastructures through PPPs, on a demand-driven basis. It is encouraged to launch new initiatives like Pilot PPP programmes of long-term
collaborative research, helping firms to develop their R&D and technological competences.

PPPs and SMEs

The question of SMEs in Russia is quite complex. The niche of SMEs is
education, health and environmental protection. They could not work in
automobile and railway roads or in shelf as the main players. Their role
would mostly be in companies serving big infrastructure projects, due to
their financial scale. At present time, there are only large-scale PPP projects
at the national level under discussion. There is yet no discussion on the
SME involvement, although understanding on having SMEs as subcontrac-
tors in big projects is understood as an area of potential growth.

1.7 Perspectives for PPPs

From the very beginning of PPP development in the Russian Federation
in 2004, PPPs were understood as a key solution for main infrastructure
issues of the country. Some regions were more and more active in this area
even before the notion of PPPs appeared at the federal level. For example,
the St. Petersburg administration and the Governor of the city were per-
sonally involved in close cooperation with the representatives of Finland
business society on the question of water treatment in the city. This project
(South-West sewage treatment plant) together with the reconstruction of
the energy system by Gazprom, were the pioneer PPP projects at the regional level in Russia. The St. Petersburg administration was also a pioneer
in developing its own local law on PPPs.

At the same time, the future of PPP development in Russia does not look
as successful as in Europe. The trust in the State remains low. The biggest
PPP deal in Russia today is the Western High Speed Diameter (WHSD)
project to construct a motorway linking St Petersburg's trade ports with
the national road network. The implementation of this pilot project will
be a practical test for the legal PPP framework in Russia. It will give investors greater insight into the credit strengths and risks involved. Most of the
projects financed by the Investment Fund must be finalized by 2015–2020
(toll roads, railways, territorial and productive complexes). They will give
power pulse for development of Western territories of Russia, Siberia and
the Far East (extreme east parts of Russia, between Siberia and the Pacific
Ocean).

PPP structures are currently considered as a tool for (re)constructing
railways, airports and seaports. Current infrastructure projects in this area,

as announced to the public, include reconstructing the Moscow airport system, rebuilding the Tolmachevo airport in Novosibirsk, and constructing a passenger terminal and port in St. Petersburg (the Morskoy Fasad project), among other projects.

Despite a number of obstacles for the private investor to conclude a PPP agreement with representatives of the government in Russia, the PPP concept is becoming more popular and common in the country, at both federal and municipal levels.

2. PPPS IN RUSSIA: ASPECTS OF EFFICIENCY, SUSTAINABILITY, EQUITY AND SECURITY

Information in this chapter is based on the research questionnaires and interviews organized in the course of 2007 in Russia. In total, 26 representatives of academia, NGOs, as well as public and private sectors working with PPPs, were asked about the contributions of PPPs to the main elements of this research.

It should be noted that PPPs are seen as a new mechanism for infrastructure development in the country, and therefore it was rather difficult to speak about them in real terms as almost no PPP projects have a lasting history in the country. Even more difficult was to discuss the results and impact of PPPs in different sectors and, particularly with regard to efficiency, sustainability, equity and security. Some questions had to be explained, when it was possible during the face-to-face interviews, others remained unanswered as the respondents did not want to make unfounded inferences.

2.1 Efficiency

According to the experts interviewed for our research, the infrastructure in Russia is mostly provided by the government (according to the opinion of more than half of our respondents) and there is clear indication that our respondents think that the private sector should have a greater influence on the realization of public tasks.[28] Indeed, 80% of our respondents are unsatisfied with the quality of public services, and 70% think that the private sector operates less than 20% of it.

Furthermore, more than 80% consider that PPPs can improve the quality of public services with regard to: the price-quality, the timing of delivery, and the requirements of the final user, in an innovative way. However, 50% of the respondents disagree or strongly disagree with the fact that PPPs can improve the quality of public services in relation to the ability to keep costs low. At the same time, 73% of them think that PPPs do facilitate the project's financing.

The question on whether PPPs are more efficient in the use of natural resources than traditional government infrastructure gave about equal number of positive and negative answers, although more detailed discussion on energy efficiency shows the uncertainty about real interrelation of PPPs and effective use of energy.[29]

In general, the question about efficiency produced ambivalent opinions: aside from the lack of experience, the tendencies on public-private cooperation are very specific in nature and much welcomed by the parties, thus making it difficult to judge the real level of efficiency. The real question is whether the public sector can afford to sustain the project on its own. Equally important is the question of value for money to be respected by "credit card" projects like PPPs and, at the end, the willingness of the parties to measure the impact of the project on the economic situation before and after the project implementation.[30]

Thus, surprisingly, an important part of the potential efficiency is connected with the political will to implement the project and the sufficient number of private bidders to participate in a competitive tender to have the project implemented for the best price.

Public Opinion and Participation

A number of factors were mentioned during the interviews[31] that define the conditions for the development of PPPs. Presented in order of priority as expressed by the respondents from the business sector, the following are considered most important: government guarantees, profitability, access to finances to leverage exiting funds, and reducing risks.

From a social and economical point of view the following factors were mentioned: improving the service level and quality, better value for money, and additional benefits from know-how of private sector.

Respondents also mentioned some important barriers to overcome for the development of PPPs; these are: lack of normative and legislative bases, corruption, absence of due regulation, insufficiency of skills and knowledge, complexity of contracts.

In contrast, a number of benefits which are most often mentioned in the literature are the following:

- speedy, efficient and cost-effective delivery of projects;
- value for money for the taxpayer;
- the optimal risk transfer and risk management;
- creation of added value through synergies between public authorities and private sector companies, in particular, through the integration and cross-transfer of public and private sector skills, knowledge and expertise;

- alleviation of capacity constraints and bottlenecks in the economy through higher productivity of labour and capital resources in the delivery of projects;
- competition and greater construction capacity (including the participation of overseas firms—especially in joint ventures and partnering arrangements);
- innovation and diversity in the provision of public services;
- effective utilization of State assets to the benefit of all users of public services.

2.2. Sustainable Development

According to the interviewees' opinion[32], PPPs could be more efficient in the use of natural resources (water, petroleum, gas, agricultural land, forests and wood) than traditional government infrastructure. As all infrastructure projects have direct and indirect effects on natural resources, it remained unclear how exactly such projects would be better with regards to their impact on the sustainable development. Some respondents, which provided negative opinions, had as a main argument the complexity of the mechanism for establishing the risk allocation for damage to nature.

Many transportation and energy projects can encourage or discourage ecology. Environmental remediation for critical ecological impacts should be considered as part of a public-private partnership agreement. The Government might require the private sector to include an adaptive management feature to monitor the environmental impact into the contractual agreement. If the environmental standards are not met, the government imposes penalties. In Russia there is a special agency for these tasks. This is the Federal Supervisory Natural Resources Management Service.

As discussed by Dr. Hill, PPPs must often satisfy the diverse needs of two primary constituencies—the funding organizations and the service recipients.[33] While this close attention is both appropriate and essential, the investigation demonstrates the necessity to monitor service delivery and implementation of the contract. In order to prevent the waste of natural resources or pollution, an independent observer should be invited to evaluate the project and report on its development. A broader vision of service provision is a necessary condition of the success of such PPP projects.

In the Russian Federation, there are many independent ecological movements which initiate public control for the implementation of infrastructure projects. These include among others: the Russian ecological party "The Greens," the Russian society for the protection of animals "Fauna", the Constructive ecological movement of Russia "Kedr," "The Russian ecological independent expertise," the Non-governmental ecological centre "Dauria," the Interregional public foundation "Siberian Civic Initiatives Support Centre."

To take an example, in 2006 a new non-governmental ecological organization "Save Yuntolovo" was created in Saint-Petersburg. This organization deemed that the environmental impact assessment of the PPPs project "Western High Speed Diameter" was unsatisfactory, because it was calculated on the basis of smaller figures.[34] This illustrates the importance of local public opinion in the implementation of partnerships. Unfortunately, such projects of national and regional importance are not always publicly available and accessible. This issue could be solved by developing a mechanism to increase public awareness and, thus, response.

2.3 Equitable Access

The desire of private companies to participate in infrastructure is not defined by geographical parameters, but institutional ones. In particular, by the legislation, management, regulation, dispute resolution, and government support. For example, the important factors to construct a toll road are the level of incomes of the drivers, the intensity of movement, etc. In small cities nobody will build toll roads. At the same time, more intensive investments in Russia can be observed in the North-East part of the country, in Siberia, and in the Far East regions.

As a rule, PPP projects touch upon limited groups of the population. Therefore, they might improve the delivery of goods and services only for some social groups. PPPs in roads might improve the life of drivers, while PPPs in hospitals might improve the health of invalids, and so on. The negative impact of these partnerships also relates to a limited number of people to be affected by them.

In the case of profit-making PPPs, their focus may be on particular groups of consumers. PPPs in the water sector sometimes lead to discrimination between citizens, especially of the poor. This was the case in water concessions in Buenos Aires, Lima and other cities. High rates for the connection to the water system infrastructure also may cause discrimination. Some services may become inaccessible for certain social groups due to a sharp rise in the price of delivery (PPPs in stadiums, swimming pools, skating rings, and other sports and cultural activities).

However, it is clear from the opinions of the experts interviewed[35] (both sectors—public and private) that the realization of PPP projects must improve the living conditions of the population sooner or later. The factors that justify such an optimistic opinion are mostly based on the expectations from both sectors of the partnership. Public sector representatives are searching for ways to improve the economic situation in the country and in specific regions. Additional infrastructure creates a more viable economy, which in turn, brings welfare to the citizens—the original target of the State. PPPs clearly bring additional options for the private sector as it is interested in additional profits. The opinion of the nongovernmental organizations is less straightforward: while representing the general public and/or a specific initiative within the society, NGOs are deeply involved in a system of interdependencies and provision of conditions for a "better life" of each citizen or groups of citizens. This makes NGOs more an independent observer of the PPP initiatives on a case by case basis, conditions of which may vary.

It is becoming more and more clear that the discussion on partnerships in general and their contribution to the sustainable development in particular, is directly linked to the sustainability of the projects themselves. If there is any doubt about the need of a specific project, its economic viability or on-going demand for its outputs, the question of the project's contribution to sustainable development is becoming ambivalent. Partnerships for the sake of partnerships could not be sustainable in any way.

2.4. Security

According to the data gathered through the interviews, PPPs are not seen by the respondents from both public and private sector as infrastructure projects with special security aspects. These projects should not be treated more specifically than pure public or private projects as the security standards should be monitoried by specialised agencies which are respondible for them. As was stated at the OECD Global Forum for International Investment, "No actor can replace government weakness in policy formulation, security, regulation and risk management. Security of infrastructure is supported by the related norm and standards, system of police and courts; norms and regulations for production and services."[36]

During the last fifteen years, all levels of government in Russia concentrated more on such economic problems as privatization, commercialization, and management. At that time, infrastructure issues were almost not addressed at all. Industrial and social infrastructure was not renewed for a long time, and since 1991, only aesthetic efforts were taken to improve the situation. Nowadays, both the public and private sectors consider the questions of safety and security in infrastructure as important issues.

Russia's vital infrastructure, such as electricity, railways and roads, water systems, central heating, etc. is in an obsolete state up to 50–70%. The deteriorating state of the infrastructure causes various damages and increases the possibility of a catastrophe. That is why it continues to constrain economic development in the country very significantly. Rehabilitation and modernization of existing infrastructure is probably one of the main economic problems in Russia.

Currently, there are also many problems with new constructions especially in big cities like Moscow and Saint Petersburg. Controlling construction, respecting norms and standards, and monitoring quality have become essential tasks for the federal and local governments.

It is necessary to note, that many security measures are not directly related to PPPs, and include questions of safety and prevention of corruption. One of the important goals of the transportation sector is to protect the public, the transport facilities and those employed in this sector from acts of terrorism. Authorities responsible for security aspects in the country include the Security Committee of the Russian State Duma, the RF Transport Security Fund and others.

Security and Safety in Russia Including Infrastructure Aspect

According to the point of view of Ariel Cohen (publication in Heritage Foundation), "problems of security in Russia could be divided into a number of categories:[37] 1. Non-proliferation and terrorism; 2. Energy security, cooperation and investment; 3. Resolving of "frozen" conflicts in the former Soviet Union; 4. Democracy and human rights; 5. Infrastructure security.

Better monitoring of new constructions and reconstruction/updating of old infrastructure are the core parts of this category."

The security aspect in PPP projects could be linked to all of the above categories to a certain extent. The overall opinion of experts is that security aspects should be clearly fixed in the contractual agreement as the area of joint responsibility. Nevertheless, each category of security (i.e. technical requirements for norms, environmental security and safety) is protected by different laws and regulations, which could not be regarded together as a common "security aspect" of the PPP contract in general. Here, the question is how these contractually agreed points would be respected by the private sector—and the general opinion of expert is more in favour of mutual trust between sectors, with the presence of controlling authorities. Private sector experts confirm that in big infrastructure projects it is not in their interest to break any rules. Thus, once again the regulatory function of the controlling bodies becomes one of the most important instruments for ensuring the smooth implementation of security norms in partnership agreements on infrastructure.

"Frozen conflicts" and terrorism remain specific issues for security in the country. According to the expert opinion, partnership agreements could be a special category in this regard, due to the entry of private sector into traditionally public areas of responsibility. This requires additional regulations to be added to the contracts.

Anti-Terrorism Measures

Energy security and anti-terrorism measures are becoming one of the most important matters of concern inside and outside Russia. The internal threat and the cooperation with other countries in the discussion and resolution of these issues are very important.

The vital role of the private sector in cooperation with governments to prevent and combat terrorism, and the role of the media in this fight are now openly recognized. The Russian Federation is taking active steps to counter terrorism. In the fourteenth meeting of the OSCE economic forum[38] which took place in Prague in May 2006, the Russian Ministry of Transport stated that "the resolution of this difficult problem requires [...] the appropriate changes in the approaches to the technology involved in transport processes to make it more reactive and also improvements in transport security with regard to terrorism." The Russian delegation proposed to make use of the transport and transit potential of the Russian Federation in the interests of the economic development of the OSCE participating States. The delegation reassured participants from other countries that a comprehensive State system for ensuring transport security is currently being created by the Government. The combating of terrorism is of high importance, supported by technical facilities and procedures implemented in this System.

It is also important to notice the willingness of the State to cooperate with the international community (countries and organizations) on raising the standards of all transport facilities, including underground and regular railways, car parks, bus stops, river stations etc. In this regard, cooperation between organizations and within the NATO-Russia dialogue, defined as a priority the smooth operation of international transport corridors. The business communities are also involved, because security of enterprises is not guaranteed any more.

Corruption

Corruption is seen by the experts interviewed for this research as one of the main aspects of financial insecurity for PPP projects. The opinions are quite different, but there was no neutral reaction to this question[39] during interviews. Moreover, the issue of security in PPP projects is seen by experts as the question of financial security.

Corruption is a negative social and political phenomenon, not only in Russia but in all countries of the world. According to the presentation at the OECD Global Forum for International Investment, "infrastructure is particularly vulnerable to corruption, which degrades quality, increases costs, keeps honest investors away and undermines public trust and public support to PPPs."[40] Private participation in infrastructure through PPPs, according to interviewees, could increase the risk of corruption in comparison with the government-operated public sector. Improved governance and the rule of law are the core aspects for raising awareness of decision makers and the general public. Financial management based on internationally recognised standards and a transparent procurement system could help prevent abuses at the project level.

Russia remains one of the most corrupt countries in Europe, according to a recent report published by Transparency International.[41] According to the Anti-corruption Gateway for Europe and Asia[42] "Partnerships against corruption," workshops were held in some regions of Russia already in 2001 to develop an Anti-Corruption Action Plan, as well as mechanisms of cooperation and coordination within and among sectors of society. Unfortunately, these actions are still organized on an ad-hoc basis and addressed very specifically.

With regard to the PPPs in infrastructure, it is clear that corruption should be addressed in an explicit manner. Each stage of the project implementation, starting from competitive bidding, should be part of a transparent process, with reporting mechanisms to the wider public. Higher risk of corruption during direct negotiations and non-transparent bids should be avoided wherever possible. At the same time, as was stated by one of the experts from the private sector "...most citizens consider PPPs as the next corruption mechanism which has been thought up by the State. In reality, PPPs are one of least corrupted mechanisms existing in our country with participation of the State."

3. CONCLUSIONS AND RECOMMENDATIONS

PPPs were introduced in Russia in 2004. They were accepted by the governmental authorities and included in all the strategic plans at the federal and regional levels, which demonstrates that they will be further developed and implemented. While Russia began to develop public-private delivery methods of public services and infrastructure already in the late 1990s and early 2000, the tendency shows that the interest of foreign companies to bring their best practices and the ability of Russian authorities to adopt this experience remains limited. Russia has a huge potential for PPPs, including financial resources in both public and private sectors. Russia also has a great need for further investments in the industrial and social infrastructure. The legislative background of PPPs is undergoing active development, and the creation of PPPs is demand-driven from the federal level to regions and municipalities.[43]

Despite these positive factors, the country is still poorly prepared institutionally to realize large-scale PPP projects. This is due to the specific economic environment of the country, high risks for private investments, a lack of transparency, issues of legislation, weak regulation and management, the presence of corruption at all levels of government, as well as poor business regulation and support systems. Here are some critical tendencies for PPPs in Russia:

- Management of the PPP process should include the establishment of a Special Federal Agency, with the authority to unify the legislation and rules of application for PPPs in the regions. At the same time, this Agency should encourage various forms and methodology of PPP application, according to particular local needs.
- Development of sector-specific policy frameworks for PPPs, as well as an appropriate normative base in regions and municipalities. As a Federation, Russia has 84 regions (Oblasts, Krais Republics) and more than 24 thousand municipalities. All of them have a significant property that can be used in PPP agreements with private companies.
- Compliance with international rules and standards. Russia has a potential for thousands of PPPs projects (big and small) to be realized in the nearest future. Obviously it will require participation of foreign companies which, in turn, should fully comply with international norms and standards.

The main spheres for PPP projects in Russia remain the industrial and social infrastructure. For the development PPPs, the Russian government can use traditional instruments (joint ventures, lease of public assets, public contracts and purchases), as well as create special mechanisms to finance infrastructure projects (in particular, Investment Fund, Special economic zones and others).

As private participation in infrastructure through PPPs can increase the risk of corruption in comparison with the government-operated public sector, the rule of law and transparent procurement processes should be at the heart of PPP projects. In particular, corruption needs to be addressed in a more systematic way.

The monitoring of service delivery and implementation of contractual obligations should be seen as key to the process of PPP implementation and operation. In order to prevent the waste of natural resources or pollution, an independent observer should be invited to evaluate all projects and report on their development. Thus, a broader vision of service provision is a necessary condition for the success of projects. These should promote the transfer of innovation and technology to the local economy in many ways, such as:

- The creation of public-private partnerships should contribute a transfer of skills, know-how, information, regulatory norms and mechanisms, strategy design and implementation methods;

- PPPs can facilitate technology transfers from the federal level to the regional and municipal levels due to the combination of joint funding with local small and medium firms;
- PPPs should involve cooperative R&D among industry, universities and government laboratories, and thus encourage technology-based local economic growth;
- Partnership outcomes such as patents, or commercial products and services may be transferred to the local economy.

Having access to best practices of PPPs in Western Europe, Australia, USA and Canada, it would be useful for Russia to study the potential difficulties of implementation of such projects at different scales and levels. Many countries around the world are successfully adopting the PPP concept for public procurement, public utilities and public ownership and management. However, at the same time enough projects were cancelled or are in financial or managerial distress, and can offer important lessons for the future.

The financial crisis in 1997 and 1998 caused stress in many PPP projects, and a number of them were canceled, as governments proved incapable or unwilling to meet their obligations. The decline in investment commitments was driven mainly by a reduction in privatization and in investments in licenses or concessions to provide infrastructure services. The local currency revenues of PPP projects could no longer service foreign currency debt, which was made more expensive by steep currency devaluations. Other projects were affected by political controversies and serious environmental problems.

The main causes of the cancellation of PPPs include mistakes in concepts and management in specific PPPs scheme, the absence of good data or of incorrect assumptions by governments and private operators and, as a result, lower than expected revenues from end-users (such as lower traffic on transport routes). These lead to problems with revenues and financial stability of the projects. In the water and sanitation sector, these problems add up on top of issues such as handling the pricing policy and its sustainable reforms, and an inappropriate quality of services. In addition, issues of political preferences and policy decisions that are incompatible with the real market economy are also among the main obstacles. Finally, the issue of risk allocation among sectors and the incentives for corruption which are created by an unclear design in PPP contracts should also be mentioned.

Deep understanding of the main PPP principles, as well as errors in their implementation in other cases around the world, can allow the Russian government to avoid many mistakes in the future by introducing clear PPP concepts. A systematic and coordinated approach to PPPs, with strong reference and support to a legislative base, would reduce the risks of cancelation of such projects in the future. Furthermore, a centralization of efforts through the special PPP Unit at the federal level should be considered as crucial for partnerships, sharing information on best practices and support. One of the main tasks for the development of PPPs in Russia should also be considered on the basis of the following:

- a development of the human capital and potential through training and preparation of civil servants in Russia to deal with the concept of PPPs at each level of authority;
- setting up education and training seminars on best practices in the world of PPPs to be organized in collaboration with leading international organizations such as the UNECE and others, for all concerned Russian governmental bodies, regions and municipalities; and more generally,
- preparation of guidelines to promote good governance in Public-Private Partnerships, to improve the awareness, capacity and skills of the public sector in developing successful PPPs in Russia.

These are the main requirements for the development of PPPs in Russia. They should be fully supported by the government's legislation, its institutional framework, as well as economic and organizational principles. This is a very big and new change in the economic relationship among public and private actors in the Russian Federation.

ANNEX: CASE STUDIES

Project 1 Building of Toll Road Highway "Western High-Speed Diameter"

Purpose of the project: the connection of St. Petersburg transportation hub, which includes large seaport and basic transport—logistic complexes of the city, to the network of federal and territorial highways in the direction of Finland, Estonia, the Ukraine, Belarus and adjacent regions.

Optimization of transport streams, an increase in the effectiveness of intra-urban transportation, the guarantee of the shortest highway connection between the northwestern, central and southern regions of Saint Petersburg.

The urban arterial high-speed toll road "Western high-speed diameter" (WHSD) with the 46 kilometres of 4 to 6 driving lanes with the addition of 14 transport junctions at different levels.

Total volume of investments on the project: 99,95 bln.rub., including:

Means of the federal budget of 32,1 billion rub.
Form of PPP—concession for the period of realization—2008–2010.

Project 2 The Comprehensive Development of Lower Priangarje

Purposes of the investment project: strengthening the industrial potential of territories in the east of the country (lower Priangarje, Eastern Siberia) on the basis of the creation and development of transport and energy infrastructure, management of natural resources and building of industrial units. The plan should have an essential positive effect on the pace in the dynamics of the basic macroeconomic indices of the development of the country and improve the parameters of its economic safety on the principles of public-private partnership. This defines the state importance of the project.

Participants in the investment project: Joint Stock Company "Corporation of the Krasnoyarsk region development," and also commercial organizations—investors of the industrial projects: Joint Stock Company "Russian Aluminium," Joint Stock Company "hydro-OGK," Vnesheconombank.

Estimate cost of the project: 359 bln rub, including costs of the private investors—325 bln rub, resources of the federal budget—34 bln rub.

Resources of the Federal budget will be provided for the development of infrastructure (automobile and railroads, electric power lines). This makes it possible for commercial organizations to invest into the building of the new industrial units of the metallurgical, timber processing, petrochemical and other sectors.

Period of the realization of the project: 2006—2015.

NOTES

1. http://www.veb.ru/en/
2. World Development Indicators database, World Bank, 1 July 2007.
3. http://www.gazprom.ru/articles/article2449.shtml.
4. http://www.kremlin.ru/eng/text/themes/2007/11/132136_151062.shtml.
5. According to the press release from the meeting of the Government or the Russian Federation on 7 February 2008 http://www.government.ru/government/governmentactivity/rfgovernmentsession/2008/i070208/materials/5529292.htm
6. this information have been taken from an article published in 2007 by the European PPP center: http://www.epppc.hu/russia
7. See further: http://www.government.ru/government/governmentactivity/rfgovernmentplans/17e7eecfa113438f801532aa0c19379f.doc
8. http://eng.www.rosoez.ru/oez/oez_types/engineering_oez/
9. Constituted by the Governmental Regulation No.1108, of 29 September 1994.
10. Investor's Guidebook to Russia-2006 by MEDT and FIAC. Endorsed by Ministry of Economic Development and Trade of the Russian Federation, 2006.
11. www.csr.ru
12. http://www.gazprom.ru/articles/article2449.shtml.

13. http://www.rao-ees.ru/ru/investor/str_share/show.cgi?sc_struct.htm

14. Report to Congress on Public-Private Partnerships. US Department of Transportation. 2004. p. 44.

15. PPPs in Russia: An Overview. May 2007. CA-Project Consulting, Ltd. P. 2.

16. Source: PPPs in Russia: An Overview. May 2007. CA-Project Consulting, Ltd. P. 3.

17. Build Own Operate Transfer, Design Build Operate Transfer, Design Build Finance

18. Source: A. Bazhenov "PPPs in Russia,"—presentation at the Fourth UNECE PPP Alliance conference, London, October 2005.

19. Institute of World Economy and International Relations of the Russian Academy of Science

20. http://www.hse.fi/EN/cemat/seminar/2007/seminar_2007.htm

21. A. Bazhenov, Presentation at the 4th UNECE PPP Alliance conference, London, October 2005.

22. A. Bazhenov, National PPP Center (Russia),—presentation at the 4th UNECE PPP Alliance conference, London, October 2005.

23. Bank of External Economy (translation by the author)

24. According to the status when the report was written (Spring 2008).

25. Among the most recent—at the International Conference on Knowledge Sharing and Capacity-Building on Promoting Successful Public-Private Partnerships in the UNECE Region, Tel Aviv, Israel, 5–8 June 2007

26. According to the results of questionnaire distributed by the company "KROK Severo-Zapad" among 67 participants at the Round Table on "PPPs as an instrument of investment attraction" research at the IX St. Petersburg Economic Forum, 2005

27. More information is available on the web page of the programme of national projects at http://www.rost.ru/

28. Question 1 of the Face-to-Face interview: "Are infrastructure and services today in your country provided mostly by: the government, the private sector, PPP, or other types of public and private cooperation in the following sectors: water, transport, housing, health, energy, innovation, other?"

29. Question 10 of the Face-to-Face interview: "Are PPPs more efficient in the use of natural resources (water, petroleum, gas, agricultural land, forests and wood) than traditional government infrastructure?"

30. PPPs are seen by some experts as "credit card" projects as they assume no free money provided by the investors to the public sector or vice versa, they are formulated with clear understanding that all the investments should be returned sooner or later through certain modality. It is an analogy with the "credit card" concept where by definition the money are not unlimited, not free and, by definintion, not given to the creditor forever. See Chapter 3, under "Cost efficiency."

31. Probe question under question 5 of the Face-to-Face interview: what will be the factors favourable to PPP?

32. Question 10 of the Face-to-Face interview: "Are PPPs more efficient in the use of natural resources (water, petroleum, gas, agricultural land, forests and wood) than traditional government infrastructure?"

33. Social Service Delivery through Public-Private Partnerships: Implications for Faith-Based Organizations. R. P. Hill, University of Portland, USA, p. 5—paper at Spring Research Conference, 2003.

34. Western High Speed Diameter: Strategic Risks of a Strategic Project. EBRD Annual Meeting, May 2008 (http://bankwatch.org/documents/ebrd_agm08_ip_whsd.pdf)

35. According to the opinions from question 14 of the Face-to-Face Interview: Can you say how the realization of PPP projects influenced the living conditions of the population in your country?

36. Private Participation in Infrastructure: Lessons Learned. Enhancing the Investment Climate: The Case for Infrastructure. OECD Global Forum for International Investment Istanbul, November 6–7, 2006.

37. "Dating with the Putin Challenge." By Ariel Cohen, Ph.D., The Heritage Foundation,—2006. (http://www.heritage.org/Research/features/issues/issuearea/Putin.cfm) and: www.heritage.org

38. Talking Points of the Ministry of Transport of The Russian Federation at the Second Session of the Fourteenth Meeting of the OSCE Economic Forum, Prague, 23 May 2006. See further: http://www.osce.org/documents/eea/2006/05/19209_en.pdf

39. Question 15 of the Face-to-face questionnaire: "What specific security issues have become more important in your country for the infrastructure service that you know in the last 10 years? Example:—*Security with regard to preventing corruption?*"

40. Private Participation in Infrastructure: Lessons Learned. Enhancing the Investment Climate: The Case for Infrastructure. OECD Global Forum for International Investment Istanbul, November 6–7, 2006.

41. See further: http://www.transparency.org/

42. According to information from http://www.nobribes.org and projects by USAID (ttp://www.usaid.gov/policy/budget/cbj2006/ee/pdf/ru_118-0231.pdf)

43. These remarks were also published by author (Prof. Varnavsky) as part of discussion at: http://www.hse.fi/NR/rdonlyres/D40BF349-2AE2-4CF1-B75F-0B5898755AE5/6100/Varnavskiy.pdf

7

The Future of PPPs in Ukraine: A Preliminary Assessment

Tatiana Chernyavskaya and Oleg Gurynenko

INTRODUCTION

This chapter is the result of research on Public-Private Partnerships (PPPs) in Ukraine and the potential for their development. Ukraine, like its neighbouring post-communist countries, has only very little experience with open capital markets and private industrial investment, let alone private investment in public services and infrastructure. However, this vast country with substantial natural resources has not only the potential to be one of Europe's "bread baskets," but also one of its producers and suppliers of vital resources such as energy, fresh water, wood and minerals.

Ukraine was chosen for this study because of the potential it represents for the development of PPPs and the great need its population has today for improved public infrastructure and services. Few other studies currently address the private involvement in Ukraine's public sector services, and this report should therefore be read as a first attempt to shed some light onto this new field. Opportunities, challenges, potential benefits and obstacles are discussed here with regard to PPPs, which represent an original approach to an area that is undergoing great change. Like other Central and Eastern European countries, Ukraine is heavily investing in the development of its infrastructure in order to enhance its economic potential.

The research for this study was done in three phases. First, a review was carried out, evaluating the existing economic, legal and policy context affecting the development of PPPs. Secondly, a number of respondents were asked to fill in a standardised closed-question survey, while an additional selection of individuals were interviewed by the authors. These one-on-one meetings were held with Ukrainian representatives from various government offices and agencies that are involved in the management of public infrastructure. Furthermore, among those interviewed featured academics and private businessmen, knowledgeable about the possibilities for private involvement in the delivery of public services and infrastructure. Finally, the third phase in this research was empirical in nature, analysing the information obtained in the country and assembling this information into the research based on secondary sources. The result of this combined effort is presented in the discussion that follows.

It is also necessary to add to this introduction that the notion of PPPs is very new in the country. Despite the ambitions of the Government to implement this mechanism, it is necessary to point out that some obstacles, including political instability, have a strong influence on decisions that favour the development of PPPs in Ukraine. This chapter reviews some of the possibilities of introducing public-private partnerships as a mechanism to leverage additional financial means into infrastructure development. Regardless of the current difficulties with their implementation, most experts interviewed in this study agreed that PPPs should be used widely by different sectors of the economy, but stressing that the approach and needs may vary from sector to sector.

1. ECONOMIC DEVELOPMENT IN UKRAINE

There is no doubt, Ukraine is at a very important moment in its history: the transition from a centralised administration of public services and infrastructure to a liberal market with international competition. The government in general, and some departments and regional administrations in particular, have realised the potential that economic growth brings to the development of public infrastructure. The national and international private sector is not blind to this potential and has begun to enter the Ukrainian market.

Ukraine's economy expanded by almost 50% between 2000 and 2004, according to the Economic Performance Review of the Economic Intelligence Unit (EIU).[1] Such extraordinary growth slowed down dramatically at the end of 2004, due to a radical change in government, combined with fluctuations in the price of steel. This could not but influence the living conditions of large parts of the population, that only just started to recover from the poor economic policies practiced during the communist period. According to the same EIU Report, "in 2000–06 real wages increased at an average annual rate of 19%, before they decreased sharply to around 12% at the end of 2007, due to the acceleration of inflation in the second half of the year." The distribution of financial resources is concentrated mostly in Kiev, the capital, and in other large cities. Poverty remains one of the biggest problems in the country. The wage gap and, thus, the gap in standards of living between the newly-rising middle class and the rest of population continue to widen.

Ukraine's economic transition from Soviet central-planning is moving forward only very slowly. In spite of the declared willingness of the country's elite and authorities to introduce market reforms, industrial and agricultural sectors still lack appropriate financial inflows. The reason is that economic uncertainties and political instability continue to plague business leaders.

According to the EIU, the diversification of the Ukrainian economy is gradually developing. In order to experience sustained economic growth, relying on resource-based improvements is not sufficient. A shift from a resource economy to a technology-driven growth is necessary. However, the vested interests of traditional trade partners such as Russia and countries in Central Asia, combined with the very slow governmental reform to assist these improvements, still hamper a fuller development of the country's enormous economic potential. Unfortunately, reform has not yet established a public policy approach that stimulates the development of trade in manufactured and processed goods, bringing a higher added value to the country. The positive effects of such an approach are already visible in the food-processing industry. It is one of the growing sectors, which enjoys significant development because it benefits from established connections with its traditional clients in the domestic market, as well as in neighbouring countries. Table 7.2 provides an overview of economic indicators related to GDP:

The Privatization Process in Ukraine

One can see a less rapid engagement in the privatization process and the acceptance of foreign investments in the country. To a large extent, this results from a lack of economic restructuring and from the overwhelming

Table 7.1. Main economic country indicators of Ukraine (2007)

Real GDP growth (%)	7.3
Consumer price inflation (av; %)	12.8
Current-account balance (US$ m)	-4,070.0
Exchange rate (av; HRN:US$)	5.1
Population (m)	46.2
External debt (year-end; US$ m)	60,783.2[a]
Economist Intelligence Unit estimates.	

Data is actual unless otherwise indicated, from: Economic Intelligence Unit (EIU), Country Data, The economy: Economic performance; Main report: February 1st 2008, www.eiu.com

Table 7.2. Basic Economic Data of Ukraine (2007)

Subject Descriptor	Units	Scale	2004	2007	2008
Gross domestic product, constant prices	Annual percent change		7.2	7	6.5
Gross domestic product, current prices	U.S. dollars	Billions	591.861	1,223.735	1,480.180
Gross domestic product per capita, current prices	U.S. dollars	Units	4,104.444	8,611.672	10,467.503
Gross domestic product based on purchasing-power-parity (PPP) valuation of country GDP	Current international dollar	Billions	1,438.395	1,908.739	2,068.083
Inflation, average consumer prices	Annual percent change		10.9	8.1	7.5
Current account balance	U.S. dollars	Billions	59.514	72.543	49.181

International Monetary Fund, World Economic Outlook Database, October 2007

presence of the State in the national economy. In general, the government has not managed yet to deepen the reforms sufficiently. Difficulties continue to hamper industrial investment, such as problems in the application of the rule of law, poorly conceived taxation laws, or corruption and organized crime. These have all contributed to create an unfavourable business climate.

Infrastructure is one of the main pillars for economic development in transition countries. Research at the OECD shows that an increase in economic development occurs in regions that undertook infrastructure modernization.[2] In Ukraine, the construction sector receives only very limited financing from the State. According to the EIU, "in 2007, housing construction was the only part of the construction sector that still grew."[3]

Ukraine is geographically located on the border of the former Soviet Union and Eastern Europe. It has borders with a number of former Soviet republics (Russia, Belarus, Modlova) and countries that are new members of the European Union (Poland, Hungary, Romania and Slovakia). This location gives Ukraine a huge potential market in trading goods and services between East and West. However, its transportation and communications infrastructure, including sea and river ports, roads etc., do not allow an efficient use of this potential. The result is that poor infrastructure and the lack of investment slow down the development of the country.

It is also important to mention that in 1994, the government of Ukraine and officials from international donor organizations, such as the World Bank and the European Union, signed a Memorandum of Understanding to govern Ukraine's mass privatization program. This set forth the commitments undertaken by the government of Ukraine to implement privatization and, on the basis, the international donors agreed to provide technical and financial assistance for the program. The process of privatization of

Ukraine's industry in the early 1990's was more "spontaneous," with the *nomenklatura* appropriating itself a great number of State assets. Conversely, the new privatization programme overseen by the international community had as a main target the stabilization of the country's economy. Today, privatization is still taking place but in a more controlled fashion. However, with regard to the population's welfare, it has done very little to reduce poverty. Indeed, the low standard of living remains one of the main barriers for the introduction of more private sector entrepreneurship and investment in the development of State infrastructure and maintenance.

The next section of this chapter introduces the concept of public-private partnerships in Ukraine, within the legal and administrative context of public infrastructure and services.

1.1. Political, Legal and Administrative Context

There is no single conceptual approach to understand PPPs and their main characteristics. A project Law on PPPs does exist, but is not registered nor approved, and its draft versions are still under development. The development of this law was initiated by international organizations such as the World Bank and the European Bank for Reconstruction and Development (EBRD). In fact, the latter is today's largest investor in the country.[4]

The main theoretical and regulatory basis for PPPs in Ukraine is the new draft law proposed by the Ministry of the Economy, called "On Public-Private Partnerships."[5] It serves as a starting point for elaborating "the Concept of Public-Private Partnership Development 2008–2012" in the country.[6] In March 2008, the concept and the project were accepted by the government and were sent to the parliament for ratification.

According to this Law, the main forms of PPPs to be realised in the country are joint ventures or forms of agreement such as: rent, leasing, concession, management, and cooperation. This legal concept also stipulates that private property can also include the physical property or physical objects within a PPP. This may include the construction (or reconstruction) of physical infrastructure, property acquisition, as well as the use, operation and management of such physical objects.

This proposed legal concept does not answer some of the main questions regarding the forms of agreement and the guarantees for investors. Moreover, it disregards questions such as: what are the benefits of PPPs and how are they different from rental, leasing, concession or management contracts? The proposed concept just makes reference to these forms of agreement, but does not explain the particularities of PPPs, nor their differences from other forms of cooperation between public and private sectors.

The draft law states that PPPs can be seen as a particular form of agreement on mutual rights and responsibilities. Such agreements can be made on the basis of a legally-binding relationships, in which private investors take on concrete responsibilities while the State gains related rights. This gives a specific characteristic to the partnership that can include continuity or long duration. It means that these relations are not single-stage operations that resulted from the termination of previous legal relations between parties. In this perspective, the State will preserve its control of regulating economic and social relations, and will also be a partner, along with the private investor. The presence of the government at different stages of a project constitutes a basic principle of the State's authority as regulator, but it does not mean that its presence and influence should be a principal characteristic of a PPP.

For the purposes of defining PPPs in Ukraine, it can be assumed that through a PPP contract, the State and the private sector sign long-term cooperation agreements. In addition to the characteristic of the long duration of PPPs, two other characteristics can be mentioned. These are, first, the guarantee of a balance of rights of State and municipal property; and second, the presence of a private investor (or a number of investors), selected through a specific tendering process. Furthermore, an investment programme for development under the strict control of the State should be introduced.

The Main Forms of PPPs in Ukraine

Overall, the situation in the country is characterized by the slow growth of private financial investments in infrastructure and public services. Legislation on concessions was introduced more than 10 years ago, but it was not used due to problems of political instability and the lack of regulation in legislation. This includes issues of State guarantees on two concession road projects that were initiated in the late 1990s. The new wave of interest in PPPs started in 2005, from initiatives taken by the authorities in the transport sector.

After defining the main characteristics of possible PPPs in Ukraine, we can describe its main actors. The agents of PPPs in Ukraine are, on one side, the private investor or company, and on the other side, the State, that is often represented by a central, regional or local authority. The third party would be the end user of public infrastructure and services (the end-product). While the latter does not formally participate in a PPP project, its role includes, among others, the socio-economic evaluation of potential for the creation of a successful partnership (i.e. on the demand side of the road project). It also evaluates the acceptance of the project and its services by the wider audience.

Private investors can either be a physical private person (resident or non-resident) or a legal entity (with its office in Ukraine or outside, i.e.

resident or non-resident). A regional or local authority is represented by various councils at the rural, town, or city level, through its executive committees or specially-created bodies (economic administrations, State-run enterprises, divestitures (the term "divestiture" can be used here to imply the sale of entire public operations and assets and is a process by which the government sells the right to operate the property), or other models of government decision-making). The public sector can be represented by a number of governmental bodies, including Cabinet of Ministers, Ministries, departments (Ukrautodor, Ukromorport, Ukraeroput etc.), regional State administrations, or State enterprises (Ukrpochta, Ukrrailroads, Ukrtelecom).

The objects (government infrastructure and property) of PPPs in Ukraine may be enterprises (property itself). The different forms of PPPs that can be created include agreements of civil responsibility such as leasing, management, rent, concession and licensing. We did not include pure privatization into this list, as it assumes a sale of State rights on property. However, it must be considered that pure privatization also involves investment obligations much like any other private investments. These can be the completion of construction in the agreed time frame, modernization and maintenance, a certain level of production, specialization, fixed or regulated price levels and workplaces. A good example of this kind of privatization is Metal Steel Krivoj Rog, where a lot of investment liabilities were introduced in the contract. This example shows the limits of foreign investor participation, as the parameters of evaluation of these privatization agreements are not well defined, and can be changed by the government at any time.

Taking into consideration that the development of private involvement in the delivery of public infrastructure and services is still in its early stage in Ukraine, the main possible forms of "private sector cooperation" for public procurement are still limited. They can be described as follows.

Government Procurement

The traditional method to develop public infrastructure was through government-operated enterprises. The procurement of goods and services by the government from the private sector came about later, and is driven by economic needs of the State. The main disadvantages of this limited involvement of the private sector are the reduced business freedom and the strict hierarchy of relations between State authority and private supplier. The parameters of such cooperation are well defined, but there is no stimulation for improvement—this format is peculiar for a social economic system. It is regulated by the law "On Purchase of Commodities, Works and Services for State Means,"[7] of the Civil Code of Ukraine. It demands a specific procedure for procurement (compulsory tender) and involves the activity of specific State owned bodies, like the Tender chamber for the final authorization of the project.

1. *Joint public-private enterprises* are a form of collaboration that is similar to public-private partnerships. However, the actors may have different interests that can result in a tendency to aggravate relations, especially in management issues. One reason is that State-founded companies cannot be completely independent from government. They are more disposed to political ambitions in their management, and can be influenced by political powers during elections, crises, public policy changes, etc. The result is that these enterprises are less entrepreneurial and more dependent on State subsidies or grants; and they do not stimulate development nor innovate in favour of reform.

2. *Joint activity* is realized through an agreement regulating the joint activity by common norms within the Civil Code (CC[8]). There is a compensation rule for such relations, and taxation is regulated in relation to the contract itself. It is a way to avoid the requirements of rent legislation. The agreement is signed on the basis of direct negotiations with interested parties. Recently, a flourishing of these schemes caused the new government to prohibit this kind of joint public-private activity. Thus, it has forbidden joint activities that cause the acquisition of State property.

3. *Long-term crediting or subsidizing* are not seen as a PPP in Ukraine. This is a form of transferring control over public assets that is not optimal for infrastructure development. The main reason is that the development or modernization is not carried out as expected, but delayed to the time when the credits should be returned to the government. Furthermore, there are no guarantees of achieving the targets for which the credit was offered by the government. Actually this is a way of financing projects and then not implementing them.

4. *Zones of economic development* are specific territories or sectors, for which the State approved the granting of certain special advantages. There are 11 such zones in Ukraine today, and they border onto 72 depressive regions or parts of regions in Ukraine "which level of development by the indices is the lowest among the territories of respective type,"[9] where poverty is high and economic development is low. The purpose of special economic zones (SEZ) is to attract investment from the private sector. The objective may be to improve conditions in particularly underdeveloped areas or to stimulate growth in areas where proximity with strategic transportation and population centres are key to economic development.

The existing 11 SEZ currently include the special economic zone "Zakarpattya," created on the territory of the Zakarpattya region according to the Decree of the President of Ukraine "About a special economic zone Zakarpattya" as of December 9, 1998 □1339/98, adopted as the Law of Ukraine □2223– III in March 22, 2001.[10] There is also another SEZ, "Reni," created in Odessa region at the end of 2000.[11] These zones provide advantageous conditions for private sector development. The State also created a cooperative environment for business development through its inner and outer controlling organs. These can be considered as a partnership between public and private sectors. However, recent analysis of SEZ shows a big neglect of duties on the part of the government for the SEZ and its controlling agencies. The idea to undertake certain activities in depressive territories was unique, but implementation was faced with problems such as corruption, the absence of infrastructure (some SEZ were not even measured or territorially delineated), fake investment programs, or tax evasion. The bill on the creation of new SEZ, their expansion, and acceptance of new investment programs in existing SEZ, is still under moratorium since 2004. This moratorium is still valid and the results of SEZ activity are under dispute.

5. *Leasing, rent, management, product-sharing agreements, concessions; construction, projecting, assembling contracts; R&D contracts and commissions.* These forms of procurement by the government allow the involvement of the private sector in the delivery of public infrastructure and services. Some of them (like product-sharing agreements) are seen as a PPP in the country. As the most frequent form of private involvement in public work is through concession agreements, these are discussed in greater detail below, in the section on the legal context.

Other forms of private sector cooperation include: the sale of property shares in the country (land or property shares), free privatization of land, and corporate rights of the State. The last form of cooperation is quite difficult to understand. At the time of Ukraine's independence from the Soviet Union, there was no private property to speak of and only some forms of individual property existed. The spreading ideas on the use of private property, and the absence of primary capital accumulation lead to a process of free privatization of State property. This property was then passed on to private investors and workers without any compensation mechanisms. This process was introduced for agricultural grain, meat and milk production, as well as for river ports and other small manufacturing firms. The State kept shares in the form of corporate rights. Further free privatization of housing and real estate is still going on to this day.

Taking into consideration the importance of the agricultural industry in the country, special privatization processes were introduced at the village-forming enterprises (*kolkhoz, sovkhoz*). Here, property rights were spread equally among workers (in average between 400–500 people). Legislative ignorance and misunderstanding among a majority of the population brought about the redistribution of property shares and further reforming of these enterprises. The specificity of these enterprises in Soviet times was that they owned social and production infrastructure, in addition to lands. These enterprises were constructing roads, houses, club-houses, hospitals, kindergartens, as well as gas and transmission facilities. Only social infrastructure was not subject to privatization after the country's declaration of independence. This brought large numbers of owners to each piece of property and created difficulties in the management of their rights. For example, an investor can rent property rental fees or can purchase them. But it is very hard to accumulate 100% of rental fees to use the property itself. The processes of privatization are still going on.

1.2. Legal Context

The regulatory framework in Ukraine is not yet adapted to the involvement of the private sector in the delivery of public services and the development of public infrastructure. An OECD country Survey in 2007 stated that "the state of affairs not only constrains the ability of policy makers to implement their initiatives, it imposes direct costs on citizens and entrepreneurs in their day-to-day interactions with public officials." Although some progress could be seen in some areas, the most sensitive and important ones, like constitutional changes remain uncertain. The possibility of political interference into the legislation is very high. Accountability in decision making was supposed to be improved through the introduction of a system of administrative courts in 2005. The law on administrative procedures was approved in July 2005 and came into force in September of that same year. The legal jurisdiction between administrative and economic courts was not clear enough for about 3 years. Some problems in classifying cases still occur. Also the total cancellation of foreign investor benefits in 2000 by "The Bill of Ukraine" caused a contraction of investments which led the OECD to declare that: "the investment climate also suffers from a high degree of legal confusion and uncertainty."[12]

The contract's environment is unclear due to a bias introduced by two basic legal codes that govern commercial affairs in Ukraine. These are the Civil Code and the Commercial Code (Grazhdansky Kodeks and Kommerchesky Kodeks) that entered into force in 2004. The latter still keeps Soviet legal traditions, based on a more administrative rather than commercial approach. It limits freedom of contract and provides basis for minor technical deficiencies. The Civil Code on the other hand, can better adapt itself to the market economy, despite some weaknesses of formal regulative character. The main problem is seen in the overlap and sometimes contradiction of these codes with each other. The regulation of property rights is also affected by the introduction of these Civil and the Commercial Codes, with the consequence that disputes cannot be solved in a court of law.

Taking into account the above-mentioned overall legislation that concerns the private sector's involvement in public infrastructure and services, we can expect to see deficiencies in legal support for a completely new form of commercial interaction. The "Ukrainian Law Firms"[13] was published as *"A Handbook for Law Clients"* that explains that there is a developed framework for the implementation of PPPs in the country, which is especially advanced for road infrastructure projects. However, the Handbook claims that "due to the lack of governmental support and insufficient protection of investors' rights there is practically no record of PPP transactions in Ukraine."

As a recent experience with the initiation of road infrastructure project and facilities shows, the State's initiative is key for a real implementation of public infrastructure and services projects. Concessions remain the most common form of PPPs in the country. This is for the following logical reason: concessions are seen as the instrument of financing development of roads and they are already used in practice. It is not easy to see the potential of other forms of partnerships when they are still under discussion.

The President's Decree regarding the "Measures in the Area of Investment Activities" defined the primary measures of project realization. It concerns short-term strategic intentions of the State for the implementation of concessions in the transport infrastructure. This decree states that concessions are to be seen as a special regime for the stimulation of investment. The need to facilitate the introduction of concession mechanisms in the areas of construction, reconstruction, repairing and maintenance of the road system (i.e. transport system) was also pointed out. Further expansion of the use of concessions was also included in public utility projects in big cities (more than 1 million people) for heating, water supply and waste removal.

Concessions

The single conceptual approach to the realization of long-term State policy in the area of concession activities is the Law "On Concessions (O kontsessijah.)," supported by the special law regarding the development of road infrastructure "On Concession for Construction and Exploitation of Automobile Roads (O kontsessijah dla stroitelstva I ekspluatatsii avtomobil-nyh dorog)," both adopted in 1999. Supportive subordinate legislation was also developed to implement these laws. The Programme of development of investment activities for 2002–2010, adopted by the Cabinet of Ministers of Ukraine in 2001, targets among others, the modernization of the transport infrastructure, through the intended use of concession and leasing mechanisms. Thus, the concept with the main components was introduced: the transport infrastructure would be developed through investors, in order to target the achievement of social guidelines. There is also supportive legislation for the introduction of concessions in areas such as heating, water supply, wastewater and sanitation.

There is an extensive number of norms and regulations for the realization of the Law on concessions. It includes the list of concession objects, the standard concession agreements, the procedure of concession tendering, the order of the establishment of maximum pay for the use of concession highways, on the procedure of the assignment of privileges, grants, compensation to concessionaires, etc. At present, only two concession agreements dealing with road infrastructure development have been signed. According to experts, almost no progress from them is visible (as of May 2007). In addition to road concessions, two agreements are under develpoment, concerning cultural heritage in the region of Lviv (led by Lviv regional State administration), and wind power plants (led by Donetsk and Kcherson regional State administration).

Other forms of PPPs were introduced later, including rent, management and licensing. Looking at the legislation support for other PPP forms in Ukraine, we can name the following:

Renting is regulated by the Civil Code of Ukraine, the Economic Code of Ukraine, the Bill of Ukraine "On land rent," the Land Code, and the Law "On Rent of State and Public Property," which is introduced through tenders even though there are some difficulties. It remains difficult to involve new investors in already existing contracts, due to legislation gaps. There are also issues with regard to the possibility of privatization of rented property/objects, as the regulation is subject to different interpretations of the applicable law. In such contracts, the State is represented either by the Fund of State Property, its territorial branches for national public assets, or by the local authorities for public property. In addition, market assessments of property vary significantly from evaluations confirmed by the State bodies.

Leasing could also be organized through PPP agreements within the Ukrainian interpretation. However, we do not examine this form of collaboration here, because leasing concerns only individual property objects, and not infrastructure or public service systems, which are usually larger and more complex. The main regulation for leasing agreements is made by tax laws, the Bill of Ukraine "Of financial leasing," as well as the Civil and Economic Code.

Management contracts are regulated by the Civil Code of Ukraine and the Law "On Management of State Property Objects." The property object of these contracts includes corporate public rights, as well as physical property, provided by the State authorities. Recently, contracts on property management were introduced with regard to State assets that are considered as key assets of national importance. These are: water territory of ports, docks, and hydraulic engineering constructions of different purposes. Examples exist in the cities of Chernigov, Kherson, Zaporozhje and Dnepropetrovs, where the State was represented by branches of the Ministry of Transport and Communication. The granting of the contract includes a tendering process, although competition for such contracts is limited.

Licensing could also be considered as a form of PPP, as such contracts can be acquired through competitive tenders. There is a long list of activities liable to licensing—it has 77 types of activities, including, among others, licensing of banking activities, oil transportation, conveyance of passengers by air, sea, river and land transport, including railways; fire safety services; etc. (as listed in the Law of Ukraine as of 01.06.2000 □ 1775-III "About the Licensing of Certain Types of Economic Activity" –Zakon Ukrainy ot 01.06.2000 g. □ 1775-III "o licenzirovanii opredelennyh vidov hozajstvennoj dejatelnosti."). Their quantity is increasing. It is regulated by the Bill of Ukraine "On licensing certain types of economic activity." Furthermore, other forms of activities such as rental, management or building agreements might be based upon receiving a license.

Production-sharing agreements are regulated by the Law "On Production-Sharing Agreements," the Code "On Earth Interior" and the Law "On Oil and Gas." There is also a system of subordinate legislation. These agreements were included into concession agreements from the very beginning and they are mentioned in the project Law "On PPPs."

1.3. Economic Context

For Ukraine, the overall economic situation has improved since its independence. Substantial economic growth was observed recently. Real GDP average growth amounted to 7.4% for the years 2000–06. However, difficulties remain with attracting foreign direct investment (FDI). According to the OECD Economic Survey, "the stock of FDI per capita reached only 372 USD in 2005, just over 16% of the corresponding figure for neighbouring Poland."[14] This figure is definitely too low for a country with such human capital potential and other comparative advantages (like its neighbourhood with EU markets). Structural reforms in the country are very slow, with progress only visible in the telecommunications (Ukrtelecom) and power supply sectors. At the same time, important sectors like roads (including railroads) and water (including wastewater) have worsened over the years.

The EIU reports that transport infrastructure, which was not particularly good even during the Soviet time, has deteriorated since 1991 due to the

Box 7.1.   The Example of Vanco International Limited, Ukraine

Only one agreement was signed for 30 years in October 2007. The information was disclosed due to the internationally known issue with Vanco International Limited.

The new government accused the previous government of handing over such a vast territory to a private company for mineral resource exploitation without fulfilling appropriate investment obligations. As a matter of fact, the government itself annulled its decision to pursue with this contract, and cancelled the license for exploiting the mineral resource base. This hindered the fulfilment of mutual obligations.

This example shows that:

1. Even when a civil contract is signed, the parties still face the possibility to go to court in a case of dispute over property or rights. In this case, the government annulled the contract.
2. Data concerning this project was not available and only few people knew about it.
3. The problem of transferring rights and obligations through such an agreement came to light.
4. Much time was wasted from the moment the tender was won in 2006, and until the fulfilling of the contractual obligations actually started.

absence of financial inflows for maintenance, repair and modernization.[15] The country is quite far from fulfilling its potential as a gateway between central Europe and the other members of the Commonwealth of Independent States (CIS). However, the selection of Ukraine to co-host the Euro 2012 football tournament is acting as an important incentive to improve transportation networks, both within the country and between Ukraine and Poland. The condition of regional airports will also benefit from this initiative. The latter issue is discussed in more detail below.

Data from the EIU analysis (EIU, Main Report on Ukraine, February 2008: www.eiu.com) shows that the network of roads, with about 170,000 km across the country, is underdeveloped. The government lacks the necessary funds for maintenance, not to speak of modernization and expansion. Moreover, the lack of road maintenance influences car ownership and driver behaviour, which affects private sector participation in the development of the road network. Indeed, the private sector sees little potential in earning returns on investments when the overall road conditions are bad, opportunities for toll highways are lacking, and legislative and regulatory questions remain unresolved.

The rail network consists of 22,000 km and is inherited from the Soviet times; serious investments are also necessary in this case to modernize the system. At current usage, the revenue that is collected suffices merely to cover operating expenses and hardly anything is left for capital investment. Nevertheless, some improvements were made possible through an increase of cash payments in 2000 and through private sector investment in carriages. As a result, there are high-speed, inter-city rail links between Kiev and the eastern cities of Kharkiv and Dnipropetrovsk, to name a few. The government is also slowly permitting passenger rail tariffs to rise, which should have a positive influence on rendering the rail network more attractive for investors.

The airport network of Ukraine consists of 32 civilian or dual civilian/ military airports. Of this number, 19 have an international status.[16] Most of these airports were built in the Soviet era, and have fallen into decay since the country's independence in 1991. Today, the capital's airport Kiev-Borispol is the main international airport of the country. It has been under reconstruction for many years in order to introduce infrastructure improvements, which significantly improved its capacity.

State of Infrastructure by Sector in View of the Implementation of PPPs

A review of the main actors in infrastructure by sector is divided among (A) transportation and communication, (B) communal services, (C) energy, and (D) social housing. These include the following sub-categories and descriptions:

(A) Transportation and Communication

The main institute of State regulation and management is the Ministry of Transportation and Communication. The main operator is an open join—stock Company called "Ukrtelecom" (95% of which is in State ownership). Its affiliated company is "Utel," a natural monopoly of the State with licenses for communication and broadcasting. There are also a number of privately owned mobile telephone operators.

Transportation

Automobile roads and bridges are mostly owned by the State. The Ukrautodor, or the State Inspection of Automobile Roads, is the government operator in this sector. However, in local settlements it is the municipal councils who own the roads. Due to the recent need for more State funds to repair and improve the road system, many municipality-owned roads were transferred to State ownership, except for the city of Kiev. This facilitates the work of local authorities, but puts the burden on State finances.

Two concession agreements were signed already in 1999 for the re-construction of transport corridors, but they are still not developed. The current legislation envisaged the introduction of toll-roads to increase the revenue flow, but only in areas where alternative highways are available. Ukrautodor attracts credits based on State guarantees, and constructs roads, covering the tendering procedure, appointing winners, investment inflows, controlling and taking on maintenance contracts and other project-man-agement activities.

Bridges, viaducts and tunnels are also part of the road infrastructure, but PPPs are not foreseen in such cases. However, a recent project of construct-ing a tunnel under the Dnepr River was approved due to a concession granted by the City administration of Kyiv (Kiev). Until now, such projects remained only at the level of discussions and never actually implemented, due to the high costs involved.

River Ports in the country are mostly located on the Dnepr River and contrary to other transportation infrastructure, most of these are privatized. Ukrre-chflot[17] owns Zaporozje, Dnepropetrovsk, Chernigov and Kherson ports, and acts as a monopoly in the sector of passenger and cargo conveyance. A specific issue here is that hydraulic engineering construction remains in State ownership (docks, piers, quays). The Ministry of Transportation and Communication approved the option of introducing management agree-ments with the local ports.

Regarding seaports, most of them cannot be privatized according to the current legislation. However, their surfaces are so big that private structures are operating in different parts, under renting or joint activity contracts. While these contractual agreements allow for the private and commercial use of the facilities, they do not allow investments for the development of the ports' infrastructure.

Airports after 1991 in local regions were mostly left without clear owners. Parts of such airports were reorganized, but could not be privatized, and the remaining parts were either sold (privatized) or placed under rent contract with local holders. The case of the country's main airport, the Borispol Airport near Kiev, shows the failure of the introduction of private capital in order to develop the new terminal. The reason behind the failure is the lack of understanding between the administration of the airport and the private owners of the land; furthermore, operation in this area is subject to licenses provided by the State.

Railway roads are developed and managed by the State enterprise "Ukrzaliznitsya." It owns all rail lines and related infrastructure such as stations, booking facilities, bases, depots, etc. It also oversees all types of revenue-earning means of cargo and passenger transportation. However, the lack of government investment in the improvement of the rail infrastructure and new rail cars is causing a gradual decrease of the quality of services that are already low. User fees and ticket prices were raised to increase revenues. This brought about two consequences. First, tensions appeared between end-users and operators. And second, cargo was gradually transferred from the rail onto the road—the latter being an expensive answer to the need of a more reliable transportation solution.

In addition, another reason for the transfer of cargo from rail to road is that the operator Ukrzaliznitsya does not offer efficient transport services for goods that require refrigeration—a glaring lack of investment into the rail service for a country that sees food production as one of its principal industries.

(B) Communal Services

The water and sewage system is provided by utility enterprises that were traditionally managed by the government, but are now partially operated by a private investor, especially in municipalities.

Waste treatment involves the segmentation of the treatment of solid waste collection, transportation, disposal, incineration through combustion and recycling. The latter is mostly covered by the private sector under license. The service itself includes only transportation, as the only combustion plant in Kiev is the plant "Energy." It has obsolete equipment, and causes serious damages to the environment. It is owned by the Kiev energy enterprise, and its re-equipment and modernization is plagued with administrative difficulties, as well as with a lack of heating and electric power in the region. The reconstruction is under development by the owners, the price is going to be covered by credits from international and local sources.

What worsens the current situation is that Kievvodokanal, the only strategic enterprise in Kiev that provides the city with water, is at risk of bankruptcy and does not have the necessary financial, technical and human resources for further operations.[18] This adds to the threat of an ecological catastrophe that is already quite acute in Kiev, due to the poor sanitation of the city's waste water treatment.

Heating is provided by centralized local stations, such as boiler-houses, which are mostly in private hands. They were sold through divestitures to private companies, or through the creation of mixed enterprises with a certain percentage of shares remaining as public property but under the control of local investors.

All gas pipelines are under State property. The distribution of gas in the different regions is organized through privately owned local gas companies. These only have the right to sell gas and to operate the pipelines. They have management contracts of all pipelines with certain regions operated by the State-owned enterprise Naftogas and are obliged to prolong it each year. Recent damage caused by a gas explosion revealed the very low level of servicing of local gas companies. Construction of new pipelines is organized through financing by the State or municipal government (i.e. State program for the development of gas pipelines in the regions). In order to purchase gas, consumers need to get the product from private firms and pay for its transportation to the State company.

Other public utilities are provided by the traditional housing operational offices (abbreviation in Russian is ZhEK). This structure has its roots in the old Soviet system of centralized administration, and has not changed since. There are some examples of changes in favour of better and less-costly services, but they are mostly public-owned administrations. Nonetheless, the general tendency is to introduce new private ZhEKs. This is happening due to new private constructions and the need for new public utilities in these houses. It is important that the services are less expensive for the end user. Private companies realize that by installing full services in new privately managed houses, they can earn profits and a return on their investment. So far, this was only done by big companies constructing numerous buildings. Another option for residents in existing traditional ZhEK housing is to create associations of apartment-owners. Today, the law allows them to be co-owners of apartment houses and organize their own servicing contracts with external companies.

(C) Energy (Regional Energy Systems, Main and Local Networks)

Every region in Ukraine has it own energy-supply bodies, except for Kiev where there is a company with mixed ownership rights called "Kievenergo." It is very hard to identify the real owners of this company, because all shares of the municipality were transferred to a newly created company called Kyivenergoholding. All municipal shares of previous companies Kyivvodokonal, Kyivgas and Kyivenergo were transferred to the new holding entity as well. The other shareholders and their percentages of shares remained within municipal property, but the quantity is difficult to define.

Most of the energy producing companies (including nuclear power plants) are owned by the State and cannot be transferred to the private sector, although discussions about it come up quite often. This concerns hydroelectric power stations, heat and power plants. Some of these were already transferred to private investors for management and operation. Regional electricity supply companies are also partially State owned. Electricity production remains for the most part in public hands, but its transportation is now semi-private. Electricity lines are essentially owned by local energy companies that are partially private, but the main electricity lines are still owned by the State. This shows that private operation is already well underway, and the possibility of passing main electricity lines into private operation also exists.

Thermal stations and local plants belong to the municipal sector and could not all be privatized. However, the tendency is towards their transfer into renting, joint ventures or cooperation agreements.

Social infrastructure, which includes hospitals, education and the social development sector (libraries, archives, etc.), some private operations are being introduced. Public education is provided free in Ukraine, although some limits exist, depending on the university. There are private Universities, accredited by the Ministry of Education and Science. This form of partnership is introduced through licensing of educational services, such as the provision of licenses to private universities, based on their educational activities and performance.

With regard to the medical sector, both State and private operators exist, subject to licensing. Legislation ensures free access to medical services, although in reality it involves payments for specific additional services. The tendency is that internal operations remain the prerogative of State hospitals. There is also a small sector of private medicine (family doctors), although it is still unique for the sector. The system of social insurance is voluntary and remains therefore quite weak at this time.

(D) Social Housing

Social housing for pensioners (retirees), low-income families and other low-income groups of the population are paid entirely by the State and the local municipality. Recently, the schemes of 50% financial participation of a low-income family in construction was introduced, but this is still limited only for the city of Kiev. At the same time, the regulation transferring 7–15% of privately-build houses in big cities to municipal property, has also taken place. These accommodations are to be used for low-income families and other categories of individuals, subject to State support in housing issues. In case of elite property, this property could be sold at the market price in exchange for social housing support in other regions. In addition to delivering a certain percentage of square meters to the municipality, the builder participates as an investor in the city infrastructure development. This is done through obligatory payment of a certain amount of money to the municipality—the condition for starting construction of the elite property. Moreover, if the private builder tends to construct flats, he is obliged to include certain social infrastructures.

There are also other State Programs of construction and reconstruction. However, all of them are based on the idea of budget financing and low-rate long-term credit resources.

Evaluation of PPPs in Ukraine

The dire need for economic development, combined with the risk of losing its transition potential as a gateway between the former Soviet East and the European Union, is leading the Ukrainian Government to consider other means to improve its infrastructure. Political will for the introduction of PPPs in the economy creates a preferential environment for the development of new legislation on PPPs, including the creation of a PPP agenda by the Ministry of Economy. These changes are in part due to the economic situation in the country, which is becoming worse with the lack of current investment in infrastructure maintenance and modernization.

A major role in the initiative of introducing PPPs as an instrument for improving the financing for infrastructure is played by international organizations. These include the European Bank for Reconstruction and Development (EBRD), the World Bank (WB) and UN Development Programme (UNDP). The EBRD is the biggest financial investor in Ukraine and has committed over EUR 2.87 billion through more than 130 projects, since January 2007. The bank's support is for a number of projects, some of which are related to financing infrastructure in the region.[19] For example, the Ukraine Third Project "Kiev-Chop M06 Road Rehabilitation," provides financial support for the completion of the highway in accordance with European standards. It was started with the first and second EBRD road projects in Ukraine, and benefits from an EBRD loan of EUR 200 million that is supplemented by the European Investment Bank (EIB). This activity was initiated through the joint efforts of the EBRD and Ukrautodor. It targets the restructuring of road network management, the financing strategy, developing benchmarks for efficiency and setting goals to encourage private sector participation, by improving the legislative framework and initiating various road projects on a PPP basis. In addition, the EBRD and Ukraine signed an agreement that is intended to boost public sector investments through financing in the transportation and communications sectors. It also supports the power sector, municipal infrastructure, natural resources (compressor stations and gas storage facilities) and energy efficiency (to introduce Carbon emission Finance). The overall cost of the programme is expected to reach one billion EUR. This cooperation is organized in order to support both parties in the promotion of PPPs in the road sector, amongst others.

The forthcoming Euro 2012 football championship provides an important impetus to pay special attention to the huge investment needs in public infrastructure and services. The organization of the tournament was awarded on the initiative of the Ukrainian soccer federation, in joint partnership with Poland. The task of successfully preparing for the tournament is huge, and includes the building of roads, hotels and sport infrastructure. The situation cannot be compared to that in Poland, where infrastructure is largely already in place and merely needs renovation and modernization. In Ukraine, the preparations for the championship include the complete construction of new stadiums for 32,000 spectators in Dnepropetrovsk, and 50,000 spectators in Donetsk. Additionally, the Olympic Stadium in Kiev needs to be reconstructed and further related constructions are needed in Lviv, Kharkov and Odessa. The plan is to designate USD 750 million for the development and reconstruction of the sporting infrastructure in the country, and a National Agency for Euro 2012 was set up to serve this purpose. The combined expected value of all projects in Ukraine for the Euro 2012 championship will be around USD 25 billion. The private sector is expected to invest some USD 20 billion of this sum. The Government clearly announced its willingness to test PPPs on pilots for the tournament.[20] This is seen as a unique opportunity to boost the economic development of Ukraine and attract sustainable investments into infrastructure modernization and construction.

Taking into consideration the very early stage of introduction of public-private partnerships in Ukraine, an evaluation of the main questions regarding their efficiency, sustainability, equity and security involves a number of difficulties. The next section is dedicated to this evaluation.

2. PPPS IN UKRAINE: RESEARCH FINDINGS FOR EFFICIENCY, SUSTAINABLE DEVELOPMENT, EQUITY AND SECURITY

The next section presents a discussion on the contribution of PPPs to the four main aspects of this research: efficiency, sustainable development, equity and security. The last two points of this section will discuss equity and security of PPP projects not only from the point of their inclusion into sustainability evaluation, but also as individual characteristics of PPP projects.

Due to the lack of PPP projects in Ukraine and the difficulty this posed for the research interviews, other information sources had to be incorporated in the interview questions that referred to PPPs in other countries. Additional research was also done to analyze the current situation in the country.

2.1 Efficiency

Discussing the efficiency of PPP projects in Ukraine cannot be based on practical examples, as there is no statistical information on the number of projects that are officially recognized as PPPs. Nevertheless, while the introduction of this form of private involvement in public services and infrastructure is taking place, some existing activities can be seen as partnerships.

The general perception regarding the efficiency of PPPs among interviewed experts from both the public and private sectors is generally positive. All the respondents were trying to avoid judgments on the potential of the infrastructure projects realized through partnerships. Public sector representatives for example, explained their expectations on private sector participation through contractual obligations, which will improve the delivery of services. Business representatives argued in favour of potential efficiency of partnerships, and based this on their experience with pure private projects. This refers to industry models with lower costs for management, greater innovative approaches to operations, improvements in the use of financial resources, and better accountability of projects.

The expectation about the efficiency of PPPs is based on a simple observation that, for the moment in Ukraine, the proposed PPP projects are still non-existent. As one respondent put it: "there is a good quality road between Kiev and Odessa, but its technical characteristics do not allow drivers to travel at speeds higher than what is possible on other regional roads." The State lacks resources to modernize this strategically important road.

With regard to the efficiency of the economy in Ukraine over the last 10 years, it declined according to the research of Anatoliy G. Goncharuk, and fell to the level of 1995 in the year 2004.[21] Dr. Goncharuk explains this through the financial crisis of 1998, which caused a decline in productivity of all four production factors (labour, capital, inventory and entrepreneurship) and with a decline in productivities of fixed capital investments, material resources and innovations in 2003–2004.

The public perception of PPPs shows the need to develop and modernize infrastructure, in order to provide a certain level of quality services in the fields of vital activities, especially in public utilities. The recent rise in prices for all public services is seen as unacceptable, when taking into consideration the inability of local municipalities to regulate tariffs. This was openly admitted by the Ministry of Economy. In 2006, all regional municipalities raised the prices for public services including water supply, heating, building maintenance, infrastructure servicing, waste disposal, and other municipal services, except for electricity supply. This resulted in many litigations. Most of them were lost because the tariffs were not changed since Soviet times, which made the municipal authorities insolvent. The changes in tariff were different in all cities and were adopted individually by each local council, without coordinating with the central authorities. The administrative issues are not of interest to most of the population; their interests reside in the quality of services, their sufficient quantity, and the effective use of resources.

Recent practice shows that, for example, in public utilities services, private individuals form initiatives to control the provision of basic utilities, such as heating, water, waste, security and cleaning services. This can be seen as the beginning of popular non-governmental and non-profit associations that work in partnership with public utilities or private providers. This shows that efficiency of public services is questionable and improvement of services in this area is necessary. The creation of such small private service companies is stimulated by the recent transition to full payment for all public services by the end-user. All public services were previously subsidized by the government, and the increase in prices has raised the expectations of consumers. Thus, according to the opinion of both public and private sector representatives, efficiency in the provision of public utilities services can be achieved through a transfer of operational functions into the hands of private associations or small service companies.

Another example that confirms the partnerships-related expectations in both government and private sector regarding the transport networks is the following: according to the opinion of interviewed experts, private companies could be more efficient in the provision of conveyance services of both cargo and passengers connections because of their greater flexibility. The flexibility of the private sector is driven by the market competition, where clients prefer individual treatment and tailor-made services. The presence of a number of private enterprises on this market already creates a high competition among them, as well as for the public companies.

However, the private sector does not necessarily fulfil expectations for equity. It is worth mentioning here that private sector interests are mostly allocated to the profitable markets, whereas low-profit transportation services remain with the public sector. This situation creates or reinforces the traditional bias for partnerships with the private sector. Indeed, this follows what most Western experts will readily admit, namely that PPPs are not a panacea to the distribution of public services, but merely an instrument to render this sector more dynamic through private-sector involvement. The value of such private interests is particularly important in potentially profitable market segments, where the public sector remains inert and lacks flexibility, speed of reaction, or response to end-user needs. As for many Ukrainians, the mentality of the old socialist society with its devotion to pure public property is gradually being replaced by high competitiveness for a provision of services within profitable markets.

We know from the analysis produced by the IMF, the World Bank and the European Investment Bank that there is no single opinion about the efficiency of PPPs.[22] The idea of efficiency in the case of transition economies rests not only on the objective to maintain a fixed (and low) level of cost in the public budget, and to maximize benefits for the population or vice versa.[23] The idea of efficiency also rests on the objective to have investment in infrastructure happen at all.

Bearing in mind that the public and the private sectors have different interests, evaluating the efficiency remains difficult. In Ukraine, the public sector's interest lies in delivering infrastructure services that are of good quality and affordable prices, while the private sector by definition seeks to increase its profits. Generally speaking, effective cooperation could be based on the introduction of a value for money evaluation in the contractual agreements for PPPs.

Most private sector respondents admitted their readiness to follow the "rules of the game" in partnerships, as they would be established in the contract. At the same time, public sector representatives expressed their willingness to introduce efficiency parameters in contractual agreements as well. Thus, according to our respondents for this research in Ukraine, the contract becomes the only source of regulation for the evaluation of efficiency. However, the current lack of knowledge on how to draft contracts that provide a full coverage of all necessary aspects of cooperation, including efficiency, may damage the best intentions of both parties.

2.2 Sustainable Development

Sustainability is a complex concept, which includes parameters of human, social, political and technological development. It reflects the need to preserve our resources and the environment for the needs of future generations, and introduce development without compromising them. The theoretical chapter of this book by Paolo Urio (Chapter 2) refers to such components of sustainability like equity for all members and protection of resources, including security of infrastructure. The latter can be understood in view of the preservation of the natural environment, which can be damaged by insecure infrastructure built with a lack of respect for stability, safety and durability. This means that it will have to be reconstructed at a later date, incurring additional environmental and financial costs.

According to the opinions of public sector representatives, PPP projects do not cause a greater threat to the parameters of sustainability than other traditional construction or infrastructure projects. The role of the State at this stage of development in Ukraine is to use the momentum of growth in the economy. This includes the need to fulfil the promise of implementing the necessary infrastructure for the Euro 2012 football championship. However, establishing or upholding regulations is not without its challenges. A recent example of privatization and pollution of the environment can be found at the Odessa port factory. There was a leak of ammonium on its territory and within the ammonium tube line itself. This is why the potentially dangerous activities of certain enterprises must be under strict control of the State.

Another more political change has also raised expectations. This is the orange revolution of 2007. If expectations for modernization are not met over time, frustrations among the population can lead to political instability. Ukrainians have a simple wish, to live better. The chance for Ukraine to become the gateway between the CIS countries and Europe in terms of service transportation should not be lost. Failure to do so would damage the well-being of future generations and throw back the country's economy. The comparative advantages of Ukraine should be moved from the traditional agricultural sector to more competitive areas. Due to the global food crisis, we could use the idea of further development of the agricultural sector on the base of PPPs with local land owners, available property and infrastructure.

According to the authorities, the successful implementation of the infrastructures for the Euro Football Championship 2012 also works for a better image of the country in the world. It brings the element of preservation of better perception of the country to improve living standards of future generations. There are already a number of cases where local private sports clubs volunteered to participate in the development of the sports infrastructure for the 2012 games. However, the willingness of the private sector to enter partnerships with the State should be strictly controlled. The euphoria of the possibility to construct the new infrastructure should not influence the practical calculation and concrete responsibilities of the parties as the future payments from the public sector to cover expenses of the private sector should be always taken into consideration. The games will be over and the debt will stay on the public side.

It is necessary to mention that while the development of infrastructure itself is perceived by both sectors as a positive intention, the private sector sees it as a new business opportunity and a way to improve living conditions. In addition, the public sector is expected to cover the financial costs because of its direct social function. In this light, the parameters of environmental protection are seen by both private and public sectors as non-related to the partnerships. In other words, either through partnerships or individually, the requirements of environmental protection, respect of standard norms and regulations, and the control over it is organized by special governmental institutions. These include agencies of the Ministry of Environmental Protection, Sanitary Inspection, Geological survey, Department for the protection of labour, as well as industrial and other supervisory agencies. Furthermore, the municipal governments also play a great role in overseeing the development of public and infrastructure services.

To conclude, the issue of sustainable development through its concrete factors is seen by both private and public sectors as a parameter which will by no means be neglected by cross-sector partnerships. At the same time, these projects are not more damaging for the environment in comparison to any other traditional construction project. The development of the transport network, combined with the creation of better public utility services is seen by the experts as a main reason to introduce infrastructure projects now, for the benefit of future generations.

2.3 Equity

In this book, equity is seen as a characteristic of the distribution of goods and services, as well as the access to vital resources and infrastructure. The issue of equitable development is seen as the idea to protect certain groups of the population that are more vulnerable to discrimination. In the case of Ukraine, these groups can be low-income communities, including retirees (pensioners) or Tatar minorities that live mostly in the Crimea region.

The issue of discrimination of low-income groups was seen by the representatives interviewed from the public sector as a question with an existing solution: for the time being, only the projects on toll roads are to be realized through concessions by the government. No other projects, including PPPs in hospitals and schools, are to be developed through such partnerships. This might be subject to negations after the pension reform is finished and the idea of obligatory medical, social and pension insurance starts to emerge.

The issue of toll roads, according to government officials, is covered by the introduction of such roads only in the case where an alternative free road is available. This means that if the low-income population will not be able to pay for the toll road, they will have the option to travel on the existing free roads. Possible discrimination here could also be seen as an alternative choice for an individual. For example, by introducing conditional prices during hours of high traffic, drivers would prefer the less expensive hours in the day. At the same time, payment is introduced to guarantee a better service over the long-term, but does not include the service itself.

Representatives of non-governmental organizations mentioned the concept of paid service versus free service as a way to subsidize low-income groups. Free access does not give the people the feeling that they are granted with something special, whereas the alternative choice would be either to use the service and pay for it (less than other groups) from the special governmental grant, or to choose not to use this service at all. The only concern would be raised in the case of an instable economic situation, where compensations will not cover the real prices of services, especially when these are increased by inflation. In Kiev for example, the city council and the city administration rejected the construction of bridges and part of a ring road (road around the city) on the basis of a PPP. The scheme of government credits and granting guarantees was preferred instead.

As for other sectors where PPPs could be potentially introduced, or where the partnership already exists, the parameter of equitability could still be improved. For example, there is a general expectation that after private sector innovation lowering the costs of the project, the low-income consumers will be able to use the services as well. However, private sector representatives believe that, taking into consideration the state of the current infrastructure in Ukraine such as in the public utility sector, this will not allow the costs to decrease through the introduction of privately initiated technologies and innovative schemes, as expected. The issue here is that the renovation of existing infrastructure is a priority, which cannot be compensated by the limited budgets available in municipalities. Hence, costs to end-users will very likely rise, even with the introduction of private sector innovation and technology. At the same time, the improvement of paid services could be connected to the improvement of services provided for free as they will be provided through the same establishments.

To conclude, the issue of equitable access is not seen by the respondents as a feature of PPPs. As experience is lacking, opinions on the potential of these partnerships tend to be rather positive. One main reason is that as people face the choice of having PPPs as an alternative in services, the option of private-sector involvement in public services and infrastructure remains attractive. The reason for that is that people hope for better quality for their money, as opposed to not having any improvements at all or have them with poor quality that will not be improved in the near future.

2.4 Security

According to the OECD analysis, "improving framework conditions for business, particularly by strengthening the rule of law and the security of property rights, should be seen as important priorities in this context. Surveys of foreign and domestic entrepreneurs and investors consistently show that unstable institutions, high levels of legal and regulatory uncertainty, and weak property rights are among the most important obstacles to doing business in Ukraine."[24] Moreover, its report on corruption states: "while Ukraine has a rich array of legal instruments and broad strategic documents, efficient coordination, implementation and enforcement remain insufficient. Currently, the adoption and enforcement of corruption provisions needs to be channelled to a greater extent towards prevention."[25]

The OSCE project co-ordination in Ukraine reported that until recently most of its projects in the country "aim at supporting Ukraine in the adaptation of its legislation, institutions and processes to the requirements of a modern democracy, based on the rule of law. Hence, a special emphasis has been laid so far on strengthening the ability of Ukraine's institutions to promote and implement the rule of law."[26]

With regard to security, both public and private sector perspectives have relevance in their contribution to this issue. The spectrum of security parameters vary however, by sector and approach. For example, security of the infrastructure, security of financial services and guarantees for foreign investors at the entry point into the country, security in terms of criminal elements and conflicts, as well as safety nets and a fair policy of income (re)distribution, or the security provided by an understandable, clear tax system etc.

The relationship between security and PPPs was not easily understood by the respondents in Ukraine. It was difficult for them to compare whether traditional public procurement or PPPs will have a higher degree of security. To most respondents, the issue is one of clarifying what is necessary in contractual agreements and clarifying government regulations on safety, health and prevention of accidents. As for securing the process of contract negotiations or renegotiations in the course of project implementation, the likelihood that insecurity may arise is high, since inexperience leads to poorly formulated contracts. The issue of understanding security measures by public and private parties and thus, introducing respective measures to enhance it, should be organized in a different way which, if not agreed in the terms of contract, might not be accepted by either of the parties.

It is easier to speak about security of hard infrastructure like roads, where technical requirements for quality of materials and their use come with a clear engineering specification. In this case, innovative approaches of the private sector, if not corresponding to the national norms and standards, will be seen as a violation of contractual agreements. However, there are some cases in other types of infrastructure where such violations will not as easily verifiable. For example, in areas where the law is unclear on structural security, or where the possible insecurity of the infrastructure poses risks to the health of employees or end-users, or even where pollution and accidents may damage the natural environment.

Overall, the evaluation by respondents from both sectors agreed that the private sector could bring innovative approaches and flexibility to projects. At the same time, these innovations could be seen as a barrier to the fulfilment of security requirements of partnership agreements. It was further agreed that pure public sector procurement does not stimulate innovative approaches. This might lead to the obsolescence of provided infrastructure, even when it is provided in a less-costly way.

Finally, the issue of insecurity through corruption was not seen by respondents as a parameter for major concern under PPP agreements. However, some experts expressed their belief in a decrease of corruption due to "less involvement of the public sector."

Taking into consideration the very preliminary stage of PPPs in the public infrastructure improvement in Ukraine, it is quite understandable to see that both public and private sector representatives were not completely sure about the security aspects of such partnerships. There are some expert estimations that operating the infrastructure with such a high level of deterioration with minimum State budgetary support can put the security both within the country and for the neighbouring countries under question mark.

CONCLUSION AND POLICY RECOMMENDATIONS

An evaluation of the current legal, economic and political situation in the country, combined with the economic need to fulfil the promise for Euro 2012, and recent improvements in the legislation, shows that the country is becoming ready for the introduction of public-private partnerships on selected infrastructure areas. The possibility of developing pilot projects is currently being studied.

There are a number of legislative acts, including the Law "On Concessions," which open the door for the introduction of toll road projects. In addition, the economic preconditions are in favour of projects with any kind of private involvement in public infrastructure, and specifically PPP concessions agreements. Although the project of the law "On PPPs" is still under development, its concept is already introduced by the Ministry of Economy, which is responsible for defining PPPs in Ukraine.

The main problem for private capital in PPP partnerships remains the absence of a long-term strategy to attract investments from the private sector into the infrastructure sectors of economy. This requires that the mechanism of interaction with the State regarding the retention of the right of property is defined more clearly. The absence of clear policy leads to systematic underinvestment from the public sector in the development of public services and infrastructure.

Strategic long-term goals to attract foreign investments through the mechanisms of public-private partnership were not introduced in the short-term and remain unrealized. The differences between concessions and other contractual partnerships of the State and private capital were not identified. Among other forms of contracts are leasing, renting, management, license, control—all of these are seen as the alternatives to concession. Privatization is also quite visible in this list. The object of a concession could not be privatized until today, but amendments to the bill of Ukraine made it possible. This is the condition for concession activity, which provides for concession only the exceptional areas of activity of the State and local authorities. Current legislation defines such spheres but does not stress them as exceptional.

Until now, there was no clear answer on what to do with unprofitable public enterprises, especially housing and communal services, or sectors of government monopoly, in terms of private sector participation in them.

The main issue in Ukraine regarding the introduction of concessions is the concretization and detailing of its mechanism. The steps on improving concessional legislation, developing special laws on different economic areas, and unifying this legislation with the international legislation, are priorities recognized by the Government.

If public authorities have alternatives when making decisions about PPP contracts, especially when it is not necessary by law to follow specific regulations, the way is open to abuse and corruption. Moreover, these situations do not favour the attraction of foreign investments, as they create a variety of contractual forms that introduces ambiguous understanding of mutual rights and responsibilities. In this regard, our respondents have stressed the need to monitor the action of officials and to establish strict rules, with the aim of avoiding this type of problems

Availability of plain and clear data on PPPs and their trends is also crucial for the success of the mechanism in the country. This could benefit from involving international organizations, independent auditors, lawyers, experts and other profile specialists into data analysis, and make it accessible to all interested parties.

Ukraine continues to develop infrastructure exclusively through credits with international financial organizations. This might lead to the situation that from the budget outlays planned for roads in 2011 summing up to HRN 35 (EUR 4,6) billion, HRN 10 (EUR 1,3) billion will have to be paid for obligations raised in 2007–8.

The trend of development of special forms of international economic collaboration is also strengthened by the forthcoming final part of the Euro 2012 football tournament in Ukraine. The Government has approved a State Special-purpose Programme for the preparation and conducting of Euro 2012. On the basis of this program, the attraction of investment is more than HRN 100 billions, from which 82% fall under other sources of funds (not coming from State and local budgets). Infrastructure is taken as the main object of investment, but the concession mechanism is introduced only for the road infrastructure (road Lvov -Krakovec, Lvov- Brody, Brody-Rovno, main ring road around Kiev, Odessa -Monashi). The mechanism of the realization of other infrastructural projects is not determined. It must be also based upon local municipality programs, although it is indicated in the program that the mechanism of public-private partnership is to be one of the main special conditions to attract investments. However, sufficient institutional environment for the implementation of such mechanism is not created, and completely left to the efforts of the private investor.

Passing the responsibility and functions to the Ministry of Economy is also not the best way out. This might be useful to create an absolutely new State authority, coordinating the activity with the State, local bodies and municipal power—a so-called PPP unit. This authority might control or at least guide the activity of local bodies. Therefore, the system of certain institutions must be created with a clear understanding of their structure and responsibilities.

Recommendations

A concession policy might be realized through the concrete program (plan) of organizing concession activity, which should determine control of concessions, monitoring of their activity, analysis based on industrial and economic activity, preparation of yearly reports about the realization of concession projects and publication of its results.

This programme should provide the boundary of the concession organization of production over the short -term, the priority directions of concession activities, identify territories for the organization of concessions, development of the directions of concessional activity. It should build the system of concession mechanism for the administrative-territorial units, taking into account the specific character of each region. The improvement of legislation at the level of State and normative—lawful reports at the level of region should be taken into consideration.

Development of infrastructure (in particular transport), power industry, including non-traditional and renewable sources of energy, and development of housing and utilities should become the promising trends of concession activity.

It is necessary to introduce an understanding of the difference between concessions and other forms of cooperation between public and private sectors, as well as to identify a clear role of privatization in the State economy. This concerns, in particular, the laws on rent and management of State property.

It might be necessary to introduce a pilot project on implementation of PPPs or concession mechanisms in a particular municipality or a city. The next stage could include the realization of a bigger concession project, in the limits of the national jurisdiction of State. It should strongly rely on the level of development of international infrastructure and take into account the already existing international experience. In the last stage of the programme, it is necessary to extend the PPP mechanism to the socio-cultural area, as it was naturally done in the western countries.

This program must include the introduction of an efficient mechanism of monitoring and control of the concessional activity.

NOTES

1. Economic Intelligence Unit (EIU), Economic Performance Review; Main report, 1 February, 2008. See further: www.eiu.com.

2. For more details, see "The sources of Economic Growth in OECD countries," OECD, 2003; ISBN 92-64-19945-4—© OECD 2003.

3. Economist Intelligence Unit, "The economy: Economic performance; Main report," published February 1st 2008 at www.eiu.com.

4. According to the country information on the official web page of the EBRD at http://www.ebrd.org/country/country/ukraine/index.htm.

5. O derzhavno-privatnom partnerstvi.

6. According to the Ministry of Economy of Ukraine, the first draft of the Concept was reviewed already in November 2007 by the Committee on Economic Policy and European Integration. http://www.me.gov.ua/control/uk/publish/printable_article?art_id=109167

7. In original language: "Pro Zakupivli Tovariv, Robit I Poslug za Derzhavni Koshti."

8. Grazhdansky Kodeks.

9. The Law of Ukraine "On Stimulating the Development of Regions," date of Entry into Force: January 1, 2006.

10. http://www.ogrsez.uzhgorod.ua/.

11. http://sez-reni.narod.ru/eng/index.htm.

12. OECD Economic Surveys: Ukraine: Economic Assessment; ISBN 978-92-64-03753-3,—OECD 2007.

13. Based analysis provided at www.ukrainianlawfirms.com ; 2008, Yuridicheskay Praktica Publishing.

14. Ukraine: Economic Assessment,—OECD Economic Surveys, Volume 2007/16, September 2007. ISBN 978-92-64-03753-3; p. 9-10.

15. EIU, Main Report on Ukraine, February 2008: www.eiu.com.

16. EIU, Main Report on Ukraine, February 2008: www.eiu.com.

17. http://www.ukrrichflot.com/cgi-bin/eng/history/view.cgi?id=2.

18. http://www.vodokanal.kiev.ua/new/index.php.

19. Ukraine homepage on the web page of EBRD at www.ebrd.org.

20. Speech of Ms. Slusarenko, the vice-Minister of Economics at the Jacobs Fleming Annual PPP in CEE Conference on 15–16 October 2007 in Prague, Czech Republic.

21. Anatoliy A. Goncharuk, "Economic Efficiency in Transition: The Case of Ukraine," in Managing Global Transitions journal, Volume 4, Number 2, Summer 2006; p. 129–43. Article provided by University of Primorska, Faculty of Management Koper in its journal Managing Global Transitions.

22. See further the chapter on PPPs in Poland by Thomas Zacharewicz on PPPs in Poland in this report for examples.

23. As stated in the theoretical Chapter 2 of this book by P. Urio, the rational foundations of cost-benefit analysis have been established for example by Anthony Downs, Inside Bureaucracy, Boston, Little, Brown & Co., 1967, Herbert A. Simon, Administrative Behavior. A Study of Decision-Making Processes in Administration Organization, New York, The Free Press, 1997 (4th ed.), and Aaron Wildavsky. "The Political Economy of Efficiency: Cost-Benefit Analysis, Systems Analysis and Program Budgeting," Public Administration Review, December 1966, pp. 292–310. Tevfik F. Nas, Cost-Benefit Analysis. Theory and Application, London, Sage, 1996. A bibliography referring to practical application can be found in Gilles Gauthier and Framçois Huppé, Cost-Benefit Analysis, An Extensive Bibliography, Boucheville (Québec, Canada), Morin, 1991).

24. OECD Economic Surveys: Ukraine: Economic Assessment—ISBN 978-92-64-03753-3 -OECD 2007, p. 42.

25. Fighting Corruption in Transition Economies: Ukraine—ISBN 92-64-01081-5—OECD 2005, p. 15.

26. Factsheet of the OSCE Project Co-ordinator in Ukraine,—9 November 2004: www.osce.org/ukraine.

8

The Future of PPPs in China:
A Preliminary Assessment

Yongheng Yang and Wankuan Zhang

INTRODUCTION

Public private partnerships (PPPs) may be defined as the partnership between the public sector and the private sector for the purposes of designing, planning, financing, constructing and/or operating projects, which would have been traditionally regarded as being in the sphere of competence of the public sector.[1] Public Private Partnerships (PPPs) in China have developed only in recent years. While PPPs are relatively new in China, there is a great potential for their application, due to the strong demand for public facilities and services.

The emergence and development of PPPs in China were accompanied by a market liberalization reform of public facilities and services. There are four major reasons why the Chinese government needs to reform the provision of public facilities and services.

The first reason is due to an inadequate investment in public facilities and services. China is undergoing a high rate of urbanization. Since 1998, the urbanization rate has grown at 1.4% per annum. Each year, there has been an influx of 20 million rural residents into cities. This unprecedented urbanization naturally creates an ever increasing demand for urban facilities and services. Traditionally, the investment in public infrastructure relies heavily on the government's funding. In 2002, the total investment in public facilities amounted to RMB 315 billions, 80% of which was from the government and the remaining 20% from the private sector.[2] Tax, the major source of government income, is increasingly inadequate to meet the demand for infrastructure investment. For local governments, bonds and loans are strictly forbidden, which further narrows their financial channels and limits their expenditures to fund infrastructure investment. Expenditure on public facilities only accounts for a small portion of the GDP, about 0.8% and 1.7% during the 8th and 9th Five-Year Plan Period respectively. In 2003, it increased to 3.82% with a total expenditure of RMB 446.2 billions. With the speedy growth in urbanization, reliance on government expenditure is insufficient to make things happen. The government should widen the funding sources, particularly from the private sector. Therefore, PPPs have become a supplementary strategy for the Chinese government, especially at the local level, to raise funds in hard infrastructure.[3]

The second reason is the poor provision of public facilities and services by state-owned enterprises. A high proportion of state-owned enterprises, coupled with their obsolete management systems, lack of market competition and social responsibility, all resulted in inefficient use of capital and poor public service delivery. In 2003, 80% of public transportation companies in 66 cities and 60% of water supply companies in 89 cities were operating at a loss.[4] Only 86% and 42% of cities have water supply and sewage treatment respectively. The road area coverage ratio is only 8.6%, which is fairly low compared to the international norm of not less than 20% .[5] The per capita area of paved road in China was 11.04m^2 in 2006, which is far below the average 20–40m^2 of the developed countries.[6] Thus, there is a huge potential for improvement of the efficiency in the provision of public facilities and services by the private sector.

The third reason is the structural change of government expenditure. With the ongoing socio-economic development, China is striving to build a harmonious society, which calls for a more balanced growth between economic and social development. The "Soft" infrastructure, like education, health care, social security, and public welfare, are given top priority in government investment. Therefore, the government needs investments from the private sector to fund traditional "hard" infrastructure, such as transportation and water supply.

The fourth reason is to increase the efficiency and effectiveness by introducing competition. Traditionally, the government held the responsibility of investing, building, and operating infrastructure projects in China. However, for government, preserving its roles in infrastructure operations only gave rise to monopoly on provisions of public facilities and services, which leads to poor public service delivery,[7] and brings great harm to public welfare.

So, starting in the late 1980s and early 1990s, more and more Chinese cities opened up their public facilities and service markets to local and international investments, in order to speed up urbanization. A great number of private companies were established during the 1990s. Since 2000, market mechanisms increasingly matured in most cities. PPPs have been introduced as one of the government's strategies for providing public facilities and services, which increased the market competition among both local and foreign investors. The government has also begun strengthening its control systems, by monitoring public facilities and services provided by the private sector. According to the World Bank, there were 691 infrastructure projects with private participation from 1990 to 2006, with a total investment of US$ 91.7 billions, as shown in Table 8.1.

1. THE CURRENT SITUATION

1.1 The Political Context

Traditionally, China operated under a socialist planned economic system, under which all companies were owned by the Government and no private companies or free markets existed. Starting in the late 1970s, China introduced its reform program, which began to open up the market to more competitive forces, and, in the early 1980s, limited market competition emerged in some major cities. However, the Chinese economy was still dominated by state-owned enterprises.

Table 8.1. Total Infrastructure Projects by Primary Sector and Sub-sector in China (1990–2006)

Primary Sector	Sub-sectors	Number of Projects	Total Investment (US$ million)
Energy	Electricity	132	29,349
	Natural Gas	164	3,790
	Total	296	33,140
Telecom	Telecom	4	14,518
Transport	Airports	15	2,448
	Railroads	7	5,314
	Roads	125	20,504
	Seaports	51	10,349
	Total	198	38,615
Water and sewerage	Treatment plant	176	3,888
	Utility	17	1,617
	Total	193	5,505
Total		691	91,777

Source: http://ppi.worldbank.org/explore/ppi_exploreCountry.aspx?countryId=50

From 1984 to 1992, the government began to expand its institutional reform by contracting out the management of public enterprises and converting grants into loans. First, the previous factory managers were put in charge of public utilities. Second, the government began reforming the institution financing the public enterprises, and loans, rather than grants, became the major funding channel. At this stage, many medium- and long-term loans from international financial organizations, such as the World Bank and the Asian Development Bank, were utilized to upgrade and expand the infrastructure.

From 1992 to 1998, modern enterprise systems were developed, and funds from foreign direct investors were flowing into public utilities companies. With the introduction of China's *Company Laws*, state-owned enterprises were restructured into companies with limited liability, which could be owned by local and foreign investors. As some state-owned enterprises became private companies, public facilities and services were no longer monopolized by the government. Many famous foreign companies, such as the Sino-French Water and Thames Water, were investors in the public utilities companies.

From 1998 to 2002, the stock assets of public utilities were activated by the capitalization operation of municipal goverments. Many local governments sold part or all of their high-quality assets of public utilities to private or foreign companies, and thus acquired large amounts of funds which were then used to speed up the urbanization process. This phase of public utilities reform was characterised by the structural change of property ownership, implying an inflow of various domestic and foreign capital, which contributed to the operation of public utilities.

From 2002 onward, the central government embarked on a large-scale policy and institutional innovation of public utilities, and many regulations and policies were formulated. For example, the Ministry of Construction (at present the Ministry of Housing and Urban-Rural Construction) issued the "The Circular on Accelerating Marketization of Urban Utilities (2002)" and "The Administrative Method of Urban Utilities Concessions (2004)".

Policy Towards Private Enterprises, Foreign Investment and Competition

With its rapid urbanization, China has made remarkable progress in urban infrastructure. Central and local governments are currently deepening the internal reform of companies in the urban infrastructure sector. From a political point of view, market liberalization reform has gained ground everywhere in China. Governments are withdrawing from asset operation and daily management, believing that preserving their roles in enterprises give rise to further monopolies of public facilities and services.

Starting from the late 1980s and early 1990s, many local governments opened up their public facilities markets, attracting a wider range of local and overseas investment, to speed up urban development. Many private companies were established during the 1990s. According to the first economic census in 2004, state-owned enterprises (SOEs) accounted for only 5.5% of the total number of companies.[8] In addition, China launched a new round of reforms and adopted more liberal policies for foreign investment in the early 1990s. After that, China experienced a dramatic increase in foreign direct investment (FDI). Attracted by high expected returns and tax exemptions, FDI inflows have increased by almost 50% annually from 1992 to 1996. The trend continued even after the Asian financial crisis. In 2007, the utilized FDI flowing to China was US$82.66 billions,[9] second only to the United Kingdom and the United States.

In addition to enhancing market liberalization reform, in October 2003 the Third Session of the Sixteenth Central Committee of the Communist Party of China decided to allow social capital to invest in the public utilities sector, in order to meet the demands of national socio-economic development. Furthermore, the Third Session also intended to broaden the market economy to monopolized sectors and to introduce the competition mechanism.

With this aspect in mind, the State Council, the National Development and Reform Commission (former State Development Planning Commission), the Ministry of Construction (at present the Ministry of Housing and Urban-Rural Construction), and the State Environmental Protection Administration (at present the Ministry of Environmental Protection) issued a variety of policies and documents to promote the industrialization and market liberalization reform of the infrastructure sector. Some provinces and cities also issued corresponding regulations, yet there is no legal document addressing the reform of China's public utilities sector, and the existing policies are not systematically implemented. With the rapid urbanization taking place, China has a tremendous demand for investments in the construction and upgrade of infrastructure facilities.

Administrative Aspects

Conflicts generally exist during an institutional transition period. For the Chinese urban infrastructure sector, market liberalization is a revolutionary reform, and is inevitably subject to the impediment of interest groups. It is therefore critical to redefine the relative role and the responsibilities of the government in public service delivery. In order to promote market liberalization in the infrastructure sector, the relevant central authorities, including ministries and commissions, issued regulations to facilitate the separation of government functions from enterprise management. However, local authorities and public utility enterprises, the interest groups under traditional institutions, are blocking the progress of market liberalization. For instance, the Ministry of Construction has discharged most of its responsibilities in operating business, but the separation of government functions from enterprise management with local construction authorities has been moving very slowly.

It is also necessary to balance the interests of all parties or actors involved in PPPs. In the Chinese infrastructure sector prior to reform, all related agencies, and particularly government departments, were competing for power and profit, and no clear classification of responsibilities exists among them. For example, the Ministry of Water Resources (MOWR) took charge of water resource management and became a major power in the reform of China's water management system. Within the market liberalization reform in the water sector, the MOWR plans to make use of this opportunity to expand its influence to water industries, such as urban water suppliers. Moreover, with its dominant position in the water management sector, the MOWR has set up its own water supply enterprises to compete with others, which contravenes the market competition principles. The internal strife for power and interest among government agencies has severely exhausted the system and hindered the healthy development of the infrastructure market.

A typically occurring phenomenon is local protectionism, by which local governments impose barriers to prevent foreign or national companies from freely entering the local market, in order to protect either business and/or the government itself. Of course, such actions are not scarce in Western economies as well, but, given the weaknesses in China's PPP system, the motivations behind these actions are all but admirable.

Another issue is political risk. Given the long-term nature of PPP projects and the large capital investments they require, political continuity and stability are very important for their success. Unpredictable changes of government policies may result in great losses for the private companies involved. Political fluctuations are considered the biggest risk for foreign enterprises to invest in China, whether through PPP projects or otherwise. The specific problem appears to be the difference between the textual terms of a policy and its actual implementation. The policies of the central government may not be fully complied to or implemented by local governments. When PPP projects are negotiated with the local government, several aspects of the policy are likely to be changed by the local governments to meet their interests.

There has been a lack of administrative framework for PPP projects. In China, a PPP project may generally involve many different government departments, such as the Development and Reform Commission, the Bureau of Environmental Protection, the Bureau of Land Resources, and so on. A government authority has the right to approve projects in its administrative field. For example, the PPP project of road construction should be approved by the municipal transportation department, and, the PPP project of creating a water plant should be approved by the municipal construction department. If a project is relevant to the domains of several authorities, it also requires the approval of all related government departments. Amongst these departments, it is not clear which one has the authority to negotiate and sign a contract. It is quite arbitrary whether the promise given by an appointed government representative is enforceable. In addition, nearly all projects need the approval of the local Development and Reform Commission. For those projects which involve larger investments or which engender cross-provincial impacts, they must be submitted to central authorities for approval. Thus, some overseas investors may insist on the implementation of the relevant rules or regulations for a PPP project, to insure that the signed agreement will be enforceable.

In order to attract foreign investment, some local governments also tend to promise more than they are capable of delivering. When government officials change, the new officials may look for ways to terminate those agreements which seem unfair or unreasonable. Even if the previously signed contact is still beneficial to the local economy, the new officials may require changing or renegotiating the contract terms to align with their new plans. Therefore, the frequent replacement of government officials brings risks or uncertainties to private companies in operating PPPs.[10]

Types of PPPs in China

There are three main types of private involvement in public services and public infrastructure in China.

The first one is the *outsourcing project*. Outsourcing is suitable for a task or project that is easily monitored and measured, such as trash collection. Usually, the investment in outsourcing originate from the public sector, and, accordingly, all risks lie with them. Outsourcing contracts do not normally last for more than eight years, and sometimes the contract is put up for bidding amongst private companies every year.[11]

The second is the *concession project*. In a concession, the government grants a special permission to the private sector, allowing it to manage public facilities. A typical concession project usually runs on a 20- to 30-years contract. The concession model is applied to new projects, to upgrading facilities, and to extending the life of old facilities. The most common mode of operating the concession model in China is the build-operate-transfer (BOT) model. In this mode, the private sector designs, finances, and constructs a new facility under a long-term concession contract, and operates the facility during the term of the contract. After that, ownership is transferred back to the public sector. With this approach, private companies are responsible for part or all of the investment, but they share both risks and benefits with the public sector.

Generally, there are two types of BOT modes in PPPs in China. The first type is defined as the B-SO-T (build-subsidize in the course of operation-transfer), which is a mixed public-private system that allows investors to reap more than they invested in the building and operating process. Hence, they generate a profitable return while still meeting public needs. For example, in Beijing a metropolitan railway project is divided into two parts—one meant for the public good, that is to be operated on a not-for-profit basis, and the other is a profit-making line. The government covers the cost of capital construction (non-profit), while the private company invests in the purchase or development of other operational items (profit). The second type is the SB-O-T (subsidize in the course of building-operation-transfer). B-SO-T obliges the government to share possible risks with investors during the operational phase, while SB-O-T necessitates risk sharing during the construction period. In both cases, a government subsidy is necessary. The investor seeks profits and the government is responsible to ensure that the investor is properly rewarded, and that public needs are met.[12]

The third type of collaboration is the *public/private joint venture infrastructure project*. Under this arrangement, private companies and government or state-owned companies, are jointly responsible for the initial investment, earning their profit from fees or charges paid by end users under the supervision of the government. One typical example is the Hefei Baima Bus Company Ltd. The HK Baima Group and Hefei Bus Group invested RMB 50 millions to set up the Hefei Baima Bus Company Ltd. While each partner holds 50% of the stock, they are jointly responsible for the operation of the company over a 30-year period. Another similar example is the Nanning Baima Bus Company Ltd. in the Guangxi province, which is funded by the HK Baima Group and the Nanning Bus Corporation. The advantage of these projects is that the government can maintain considerable control over the company's operation and thus implement more easily regular supervision, while at the same time sharing some of the risks with the private company.

As for the parties participating in PPPs in China, it is mainly municipal governments or local governments that usually stand for the public interest, and hold the responsibility of public services provision. The private sector consisted mainly of foreign private companies in the 1990s, but private Chinese companies also began to enter this market after the year 2000. Recently, many state-owned companies have also been taking part in PPP projects, especially large ones that demand much funding, advanced technology, and special expertise. Non-profit agencies in China rarely serve as a private partner to the government.

Anti-Corruption and Government Credibility in PPPs

Managerial and administrative problems represent risks for private companies wishing to invest in public facilities and services. There is currently little information reporting how these risks are addressed in Chinese PPP projects. But two issues are very important for the successful application of PPPs in China: anti-corruption and government credibility.

Corruption easily occurs when bidding for PPP contracts takes place under obscure circumstances. It is very important to make the selection of the partner as transparent as possible. Although China's *Tendering and Bidding Law* clearly specifies that the tendering process should be open and fair, in reality it is far from satisfactory, evidenced by many cases of bribery. In one of the most notorious cases, a vice-mayor of Kunming City was sued for the Kunming East Link Expressway project in the Yunnan province. The expressway project adopted the BOT model. The vice-mayor in charge of this project was accused of receiving bribes exceeding the sum of RMB 30 millions in 2007.

Corruption and bribery frequently appear in PPPs where the government department responsible for supervision, or its affiliated agency, is also an investor of the project company. In this scenario, the heads of the government department would generally be part of the board of the project company. The conflicting roles of government in the PPP project would inevitably increase the difficulty of supervision, and result in harming the public interest. Moreover, the infrastructure sector is an area with high corruption risk. Anti-corruption efforts in PPPs should be enhanced by improving the openness, fairness and transparency of the bidding process, encouraging public participation in the decision-making process, enforcing the regular supervision of the operation, and strengthening performance evaluation and audition, to hold the participants accountable.

An important concern of many investors in PPP projects is whether or not the other partners will comply with the signed contract terms during the whole project. Violations of the terms of contract may arise for a number of reasons, including a poor understanding of the terms themselves and their possible consequences. These often happen due to a lack of proper financial analysis by the government or Public Utility Company before signing the contract.

The general literature on this subject consents that government credibility is crucial for private investment in public facilities and services. There are several key contributors for guaranteeing government credibility: political checks and balances, an independent juridical system, and independent regulations.[13] In less democratic countries like Singapore, the government guarantees its credibility by compensating production investors, demoting or replacing its representatives or agents, and increasing private sector participation in monitoring, evaluating, or amending government policies.[14] However, none of the above key contributors has matured in China up to now. China's government lacks a sufficient degree of credibility, and this is a critical factor hindering the further development of PPPs in China. One professor we interviewed said: *[Government credibility] is the biggest problem in nowadays China. Many BOT projects failed in the 1990s, mainly due to the lack of government credibility.*

In southeast China, particularly in the Zhejiang Province, local government is considered trustworthy, from the private sector perspective. The private partner can require the government to provide assurances, such as financial guarantees. Generally, local government will not violate its own contractual agreement when its financial capacity is relatively better and its solvency is serious. Its primary target is to make the PPP project very successful and to provide better services to the public. In addition, the suspension of daily operations of public facilities, such as a garbage disposal factory for example, will result in serious pollution and worsen the living conditions of urban households. Therefore, it is wise for local government to comply with its commitments and provide the private partner with a foreseeable operational environment.

The government's credibility varies greatly in different regions of China. Generally, local governments with a more developed economy and better financial capacities are perceived to be more serious in keeping promises. Furthermore, the project itself may urge the government to keep its promises. For example, garbage and wastewater treatment plants would suspend their operation if they did not get timely and adequate payment. This could lead to serious results that the government may not expect, like severe environmental pollution and the disorder of urban life. To secure its own interest, the private company generally requests a promise from a government financial department, as a supplementary guarantee to the formal signed contract. Sometimes, private companies also seek guarantees from a third party, like the upper level government or an international organization.

1.2 The Legal Context[15]

With the development of economic reform in China, market liberalization in the urban infrastructure sector has become a primary consensus among central and local governments, and a series of policies at various levels have been implemented to facilitate the progress. The government has actively promoted successful PPP practices in order to better provide public facilities and services.

Since the year 2000, the government introduced a series of policies, guides, and rules to govern the provision of public facilities and services by the private sector. The Ministry of Construction issued the "Opinions on the Acceleration of the Privatization Process of Public Facilities" in December 2002 and the "Rules on Management of Urban Utilities Concessions Operation" in May 2003.

Based on the above directives from the central government, local governments started to establish operational rules regarding the scope, procedures, and relevant guidelines for opening up the market to the provision of public facilities and services. For instance, the Shenzhen Municipal Government issued the "Rules for the Operation of Urban Utilities Concessions" in May 2003, and the Beijing Municipal Government issued the "Rules for the Operation of Urban Basic Utilities Concessions" in October 2003. The above rules lay down important steps regarding how political direction turns into practice for the privatization of public facilities. It touches upon such issues as:

- How to use a concession operation to provide public facilities and services;
- How to determine the property ownership of newly constructed facilities;
- How to determine the period of concession operation;
- Whether the concession operator needs to pay any fees for the right of operation;
- How to deal with the property after the expiry of the concession period;
- How to reform the existing state-owned enterprises in line with the concession operators, particularly on the relevant service charge/fee;
- How to set a reasonable fee to balance the investor's return on his investment;
- How to set up a subsidy mechanism where necessary;
- How the government exercises an effective control on the quality of public facilities and services?

In 2004, the Ministry of Construction also issued a "Sample Document for the Concession Operation of the Urban Water Supply, Gas Supply and Waste Disposal" to provide a more detailed arrangement of public utilities concessions. This document only sets down some guidelines; both parties have more or less the freedom to negotiate the detailed items of the concession contract according to the actual circumstances. More recently, the

Beijing Municipal Government issued the "Regulations for Concession Operation of Beijing Basic Urban Facilities" on 1st March 2006. This is the first formal regulation providing an exemplary legislative framework addressing the provision of public facilities by the private sector. At the current stage, most PPP projects in China mainly adopt the traditional build-operate-transfer (BOT) model.

In order to accelerate the liberalization of the urban infrastructure market, the State Council, the National Development and Reform Commission (the former State Development Planning Commission), and the former Ministry of Construction have jointly issued a series of related rules and regulations since the 1980s, which have accelerated the unified consensus of local governments and the public sector towards the reform of the urban infrastructure sectors. Major laws and regulations relevant to BOT/PPP projects are listed below:

- *The General Principles of Civil Law (1986)*
- *The Circular Concerning the Issues of Absorbing Foreign Investment through BOT (1995)*
- *The Circular on Several Issues Concerning the Examination, Approval, and Administration of Experimental Foreign-Invested Concession Projects (1995)*
- *The PRC Security Law (1995)*
- *The Interim Provisions on the Administration of Project Financing Obtained from Overseas (1997)*
- *The Contract Law (1999)*
- *The Notice on Views of Promoting and Introducing Private Investment (2001)*
- *The Foreign Investment Catalogue (2002)*
- *The Circular on Accelerating Market Liberalization of Urban Utilities (2002)*
- *The Circular on Accelerating Industrialization of Urban Wastewater and Solid Waste Treatment (2002)*
- *The Administrative Method of Urban Utilities Concessions (2004)*

1.3. The Economic Context

The Current State of the Economic Growth in China

In the late 1970s, China embarked on a major program of economic reform. In the following two decades, China experienced remarkable economic growth. Since 1978, GDP growth rates have averaged around 10% per year, reaching 10.7% per year in the 1990s. The last two decades have witnessed a dramatic transformation of the Chinese economy. During this period, real GDP growth averaged 9.5% per year. In 1980, the per capita GDP in China was RMB 463 per year, and, in 2007, this figure reached RMB 18934, with major cities such as Beijing and Shanghai exceeding US$8,000.[16] Even when taking inflation into consideration, the Chinese people's living standard increased almost six times in the last 20 years. If calculated on the basis of purchasing power, the increase in the size of Chinese economy is even more impressive. According to IMF reports, the Chinese economy in 1990 accounted for just over 6% of world output, ranking third behind the United States and Japan. More recent research by the World Bank suggests that, based on purchasing power parity, China has the world's second largest economy, exceeded only by that of the United States.[17]

The links between economic growth and infrastructure are without a doubt important. All of the World Development Report (1994) studies show some degree of positive correlation between infrastructure spending and growth, which indicates that infrastructure spending and economic growth may happen simultaneously or infrastructure spending simply may follow economic growth. China is a good example to view these relationships. For example, China's inter-city transport network was one of the least developed networks in the mid 1990's. Its total route length per capita, in terms of railways and highways was lower than that of Brazil, Argentina and India. This lack of infrastructure hampers the production and mobility of raw materials, and this has a negative impact on Chinese competitiveness, consumption and economic growth. The quality of infrastructure—hard infrastructure like transport, telecommunication and energy or soft infrastructure like education—will have an impact on an economy's ability and capacity to respond to global change. Therefore, the high-speed economic growth requires corresponding development of infrastructure.

In addition, China is currently undergoing rapid urbanization and industrialization, leading to a dramatic increase in the demand for public facilities and to a need for investment in infrastructure, both of which are great opportunities for the development of PPPs.

Initially, the total investment is insufficient, and the gap between supply and demand is large. The development level of urban utilities is still low, and is far below that of developed countries. For example, in 2006, national average coverage rates of urban population with access to tap water and gas are 86.7% and 79.1% respectively, which are inadequate to satisfy the need of Chinese citizens.[18] Furthermore, China is experiencing rapid urbanization, and urban residents increase by 20 millions every year, which significantly increases the demand for public utilities. However, the investment in infrastructure is still inefficient. The investment was less than 1% of GDP before 1991. In 2007, the percentage rose to 5.67%, but was still much lower than the international average of 7%.[19]

PPPs by Economic Sectors

In China, PPPs started in the early 1990s and developed rapidly in many sectors and cities, such as Zhejiang, Beijing, Nanjing, and Shezhen. In the past two decades, PPPs in China generally concentrated in three "hard" infrastructure sectors: the water industry, transportation, and environmental projects. There are also a few cases in "soft" infrastructure sectors like health care and education.

PPPs in the Water Industry

In the previous planned economic system, China's water supply system, like other public utilities, was dominated by the government. The water was offered by the government to the public at a nominal price. The government used to be the sole actor responsible for designing, constructing, financing, and operating water plants.

In general, China's water supply capacity falls short of the current demand. The economic growth and population expansion, together with an accelerated urbanization, further lead to the water shortage in today's China. To address the growing water demand and simultaneously to utilize the water resources in a sustainable way, a huge amount of investment is required, which may be beyond the affordability of government. At the present time, the Chinese government realized that it cannot solely support the huge capital investment in the water industry, and therefore, it might have to find other ways to adequately finance the required investment. Since then, many PPP projects have seen the day and operated very successfully in this sector.

The first PPP water project with a BOT mode started in 1996, when the British Thames Water Company invested US$ 73 millions to provide water to Dachang in Shanghai City, acquiring a concession of 20 years. After its successful implementation, this mode was copied and transplanted in a large number of other Chinese water projects.

Another successful example is Plant B of the Chengdu No. 6 Water Supply Plant, which is one of the BOT projects approved by the former Chinese Planning Commission (the present National Development and Reform Commission). In September 1997, this project was officially opened to international bidding. Foreign companies and company unions from 33 countries participated in the bidding. A French company, the Veolia and Marubeni Corporation, finally won. In August 1999, the BOT project agreement was officially signed, with a concession period of 18 years, including a construction period of over two years. The project company, formed by the French company, Chengdu General Water-Marubeni Water Supply Ltd., was to be responsible for financing, designing, constructing, and operating during the concession. At the end of the concession, the water plant was to be returned to the Chengdu Municipal government without any charges. The construction was finished in December 2001, and the plant started to supply water on February 7th 2002, with a daily water supply of 400,000 m3.

Many PPP operations also took place in the wastewater treatment industry, where a large number of plants were set up in terms of PPPs. The Shanghai Youlian Zhuyuan Wastewater Treatment Plant is a good example. Its construction can be divided into two phases. The planning of Zhuyuan Plant I (Zhuyuan wastewater phase I), with a design capacity of 1.7 million tons/day and an advanced treatment technology, commenced in 2001. In May 2002, Shanghai Youlian Group won the bid with a price of 0.222 RMB/ton and a concession period of 20 years. The bidding price covers total cost, including depreciation and profit, with a rate of return of 6%. The project began in June 2002, and was put into construction in October that same year. Now, the plant is running.

Technologically, wastewater treatment can be divided into two major types, one dealing with industrial wastewater and the other dealing with consumption wastewater. The biggest problem faced by the government when dealing with industrial wastewater, is how to balance local economic development and environmental protection. The biggest challenge in consumption wastewater treatment, however, is the inadequate collection system and supply network for the treated wastewater. In the short term, the government has to bear a significant part of the costs for operating the wastewater treatment system, and leave the construction of a sewage process plant to private investors.

In fact, the water industry in China has been gradually opening up to the private investors. To attract private funds, the government tried different models, ranging from the first negotiated BOT water project, the Shanghai Dachang water project, to the first competitively bid BOT project, the Chengdu No. 6 water plant. To date, there have been many BOT/PPP cases in the water industry, but these pilot projects have generated mixed results.

PPPs in the Transportation Industry

In China's transportation industry, PPPs were extensively used in the past two decades, particularly in highway construction. PPP funding plays a crucial role for the high speed expansion of China's highway network. BOT is the most popular PPP mode in China's transportation industry. For instance, the Suining Segment of the Miansui Expressway, whose construction will begin in late 2008, is a joint highway project of Sichuan Suining municipal government and the China Railway Erju Co. Ltd. The latter will invest RMB 3.76 billions in the project and obtain a charge concession of 28 years and 5 months. Another example is the Hangzhou Bay Bridge Project in Zhejiang Province, which was just put into use on May 1st 2008. In Sept. 2001, the Ningbo municipal government, the Jiaxing municipal government, and some private enterprises jointly set up a project company and invested RMB 11.8 billions in it.

PPPs are also widely used in the construction of urban transportation systems. One typical example is the Beijing Subway Line 4 funded through a joint-venture with Hong Kong MTR Corporation with a total investment of RMB 4.6 billions. According to the agreement signed in April 2006, Hong Kong MTR Corporation undertook the construction of major equipment for this line, including the trains, signals, and telecommunication service, and will operate the line for the next 30 years. The new line is expected to be put into use in 2009. This is the first time that Beijing invited a non-governmental investor to operate its monopoly metro line system. The project is also the first one in China to use the Public-private partnership model in urban transportation construction.

Another example is the Second Phase of Shenzhen Metro Line 4. The Shenzhen Municipal Government and the Hong Kong MTR Corporation will jointly invest RMB 6 billions in the Second Phase of Shenzhen Metro Line 4. The Hong Kong MTR Corporation will design and construct the project, as well as operate this line for a 30-year term. According to the new agreement signed in January 2004, the Hong Kong MTR Corporation set up a project company in China Mainland to construct Phase 2 of Line 4 and to operate Line 4.

In Shanghai, since 1993, the concession of many transportation projects, such as Nanpu Bridge, Yangpu Bridge, Xupu Bridge, Tunnel of Dapu Road, Tunnel of Yanan East Road, and Hujia Express, were awarded to private companies under PPP projects.

In brief, the PPP model was widely used in transportation projects, as an additional way for the Chinese government to raise funds in hard infrastructure. Indeed, PPPs proved to be an efficient way to operate the transportation infrastructure. Although, it must be admitted that both the public sector and the private sector play significant roles in China's transportation industry, there are obvious differences in terms of funding sources. In the south-eastern coastal cities, most of the highways are built by PPPs, while in western China most of the highways receive investment from the government. One possible explanation is that the relatively high economic development level in south-eastern China makes the PPP projects more profitable and attractive for the private sector. In addition, in the railway sector, the Ministry of Railways and its affiliated public utility agencies are still the major players, and only some PPP projects can be found in this sector.

PPPs in the Environmental Sector

In the environmental sector, most PPP projects are found in the waste-water treatment industry, which was discussed earlier in the water industry section. This section mainly discusses PPP operations in solid waste management with two illustrative examples. One is the Beijing Gaoantun Trash-burning Co. Ltd, and the other is the Shanghai Environmental Recycling Energy Co. Ltd.

In 2003, the Golden State Holding Group Corporation, together with several other companies, set up the Beijing Gaoantun Trash-burning Co. Ltd. The total investment amounted to RMB 750 millions. Golden State Holding Group Corporation would be responsible for the operation of the plant.

On June 18th 2005, Golden State Holding Group Corporation and Shanghai Environmental Investment Co. Ltd. signed a contract and launched a joint investment of RMB 600 millions, to set up the Shanghai Environmental Recycling Energy Co. Ltd. This newly-established company will start its operations mainly in solid waste recycling, including the investment, construction, operation, and maintenance of a trash-burning generating plant.

PPPs in the Other Sectors

Whereas all housing was provided by the government in the past, the market has now undergone major transitions. The main share of housing is now provided by real estate developers, making the current government share less than 20%. Some future problems may occur with this model. For example, housing prices have been rising very rapidly recently, and became unaffordable for most urban households.

The health sector, including the infrastructure and services provided by hospitals, is currently dominated by the government, with only a few services operated through PPPs. However, the institutional environment is more and more adapted for private companies to operate in soft infrastructure sectors, like health care and education.

As for renewable energy, no PPP wind power project has been undertaken until now. Most relevant efforts are still under discussion.

In brief, PPP projects, generally with large investments and scales, are frequently found in "hard" infrastructure sectors like transportation (particularly highway), power supply, water supply, and sewage treatment. In addition, there are a lot of PPP projects in the sectors of railway and ports, in spite of the dominant role of the public sector in these areas. About a quarter of the Olympic stadiums were constructed through the PPP model. The implementation of PPPs in "soft" infrastructure sectors like health and education is still at its very beginning.

2. THE CONTRIBUTIONS OF PPPS IN CHINA

PPPs have Raised Substantial Funds for China's Public Facilities and Services

In recent years, as the Chinese economy developed rapidly, the demand for public facilities and services greatly increased, but the government lacks the funds to build sufficient infrastructure. PPPs played a prominent role in public service provision, and thus facilitated the social and economic development. Many of our interviewees, especially government officials, stress the importance of PPPs to promote social and economic development. As one official said: *We don't have enough money to build enough facilities for people, and a PPP is an effective way to overcome the difficulty, although people still have to pay for the services.*

PPPs have Significantly Improved the Efficiency of Public Service Delivery

The improvement is reflected in two aspects: the quantity of physical facilities and the quality of public service delivery. The involvement of PPPs in public facilities and services has increased the coverage of physical infrastructure, improved the physical quality of facilities, and enhanced the service quality of public utilities. The most significant improvements were found in sectors like water and transportation, the bottlenecks in the past. The openness of China's real estate industry to private companies encourages the industry's prosperity, and has improved the housing condition of citizens to a large extent. However, the absence of government in social housing and the lack of government supervision on the real estate market stimulate the development of serious bubbles in China's real estate industry, making the housing price unaffordable for most common households.

In addition, the introduction of PPPs improves the quality of public facilities and services dramatically by introducing advanced technology, a customer-oriented business philosophy, and highly-efficient operation methods in public sectors.

PPPs Promoted the Market Liberalization of Public Utilities and Re-established the Role of the Government

To date, PPPs have mainly focused on the new establishment of infrastructure, which is called incremental reform. The success of an incremental reform in turn encouraged the reform of the traditional infrastructure in that domain. Therefore, the introduction of PPPs resulted in the upgrading of both hard infrastructure, like facilities and soft infrastructure, like management. In reality, the Beijing municipal government adopted the strategy that incremental reforms are to be carried out first, followed by a reform of the present assets owned by the government. Such strategies have made considerable progress in reforming the management of the traditional infrastructure.[20]

PPPs also helped to redefine the government's role with regard to public facilities. The private companies involved in the PPP projects are not the subordinates or affiliated agencies of the government. The government has no direct power to intervene in the regular operation of PPPs. All the government may do is to supervise and regulate the operation of PPPs, according to the law and the contract. This raises a big challenge for China's government. Therefore, it will have to update its knowledge and switch its working style in order to be successful.

PPPs have Facilitated Technology Transfer and Management Innovation

The company that wins the bidding phase usually has advanced technology and efficient management in the PPP project considering that technological and managerial innovation can make the project much more profitable. Such advantages inevitably exert a positive influence on the local companies and economy. Most of the interviewees agree that PPPs can stimulate the technological development of local economy, while some are concerned that some private companies may use out-of-date technologies that could potentially worsen the local environment.

PPPs have Improved the Institutional Transparency and Accountability in China

Generally, the selection of private partners in PPP projects is made through an open and fair bidding process. Such institutional arrangements promote the transparency and quality of government decision-making in infrastructure construction. Most of the people whom we interviewed believe that PPPs can reduce corruption during the construction of public facilities, via an enhanced transparency. However, a concern remains that the manipulation in the bidding process may increase the possibility of corruption.

PPPs can also enhance accountability in public projects. The traditional evaluation of public projects is subject to criticism because of hasty and careless investigations. In fact, it is also difficult for the government to strictly assess its own performance, and use the result for punishment or reward. In PPP projects, the government has to evaluate the performance of public facilities and services against the signed contract, and hold the private enterprise accountable for the evaluation results.

3. PROBLEMS WITH THE
IMPLEMENTATION OF PPPS IN CHINA[21]

Past experience has indicated that a number of problems were encountered with the implementation of PPPs in China. PPPs are relatively new to government officials, private investors and consumers, and there is an apparent lack of experience in the commercial, technical, legal and political aspects of PPPs. Even foreign investors with substantial experience in PPPs may not be able to understand all relevant practices and procedures instantly, because China's market has only been opened up since a relatively short period of time.

In October 2007, we conducted interviews among the government officials, practitioners and academics in several major Chinese cities, asking the different groups about their perception on the development of PPPs in China. A majority of those interviewed believed that attracting funds was the government's main motivation for implement PPPs, especially in less developed areas. PPPs are an alternative tool for facilitating economic development. However, in developed areas such as Beijing, improving the efficiency of public service delivery is always considered the most important reason for PPPs. Reforming the investment institutions and enhancing the investment efficiency is considered the best way to alleviate the need for infrastructure investment in these areas. The implementation of PPP projects in Beijing demonstrated that at least the building cost is reduced considerably at an early stage of the PPP. Of course, nearly all of the interviewees mentioned these two aspects.

There has been too much emphasis on attracting investment from the private sector and too little attention to market competition. The main objective of PPPs is to make use of market competition in order to ensure the effective use of resources in the provision of public facilities and services. However, some local governments have placed too much emphasis on attracting private investments, by offering very favourable conditions compared to the normal national status, sometimes at the cost of the public interest.

PPPs have also been treated as the privatization of public facilities/services, focusing on short-term returns without a spirit of long-term partnership. In order to achieve a high return on investment, both the government and private investor tried to charge a high fee for the facilities and services provided. In this case, the financial risk and burden are shifted to the public, who faces a high price for the public facilities and services without getting the corresponding increase in service quality.

Moreover, there has been inadequate knowledge on PPPs. Both the government and private investor have made decisions which were not based on thorough and objective technical and financial analyses. There was also no proper risk assessment. When problems arose, parties looked for ways of escaping from their responsibility. In addition, compared with the private sector, the government has less expertise, knowledge and information on particular PPP projects, which places them in a disadvantageous position when negotiating with a private company. This is especially true for the Chinese government considering that China is moving from a planned economy to a market economy, and most government officials lack knowledge and experience on the responsibility of government in a market economy.

The government's risk-control capability is still weak. When a PPP project is launched, the government is normally reluctant to take on any risks, even though it is in the best position to mitigate such risks. The government sometimes ignores the fact that it holds the ultimate responsibility in providing public services. Regardless of who receives a concession or joint venture, the government cannot avoid such responsibility. An imbalance of risk allocation will result in an increase of overall risks for private investors, thus making investments less attractive for the private sector and adding extra costs for the government. This reflects the need for the government to study more PPP schemes and understand how a PPP scheme can help, as well as detract from projects.

Furthermore, there has been a lack of administrative framework for PPP projects. Amongst various government departments, it is not clear which has the authority to negotiate and sign a contract. It is quite unpredictable whether or not the promise given by an appointed government representative is enforceable. Thus, some foreign investors may insist on the passing of relevant rules or regulations for a PPP project, to insure that the signed agreement will be enforceable.

In order to attract foreign investment, some local governments have promised more than they are capable of delivering. When the government officials change, the new officials may look for ways to terminate those agreements which are found to be unfair or unreasonable.

The price control system is still not perfect. The public has no effective channel to voice its opinion on PPP projects. If there is a dispute, it is not clear whether or not the matter can be resolved under the administrative and contract law.

The failures of some PPP projects discourage foreign investors and ruin the investment environment, which in turn fails to attract foreign companies. One example is the Changchun Huijin Beijiao sewage treatment factory. On March 8th 2000, the Huijin Company signed a contract with the Changchun municipal draining water company to build a joint venture. On July 14th, the Changchun municipal government formally approved the concession of the Changchun Huijin Sewage Treatment Plant and guaranteed the Huijin Company a fixed return. At the end of that year, the project was put into operation. However, in September 2002, the central government feared that the local government might take excessive risks and required the local government to liquidate the PPP project. On February 28th 2003, the Changchun municipal government withdrew its previously issued approval. At that point, the Huijin Company sued the Changchun municipal government and required compensation. Finally, the Changchun municipal government bought back the factory and settled the dispute. However, this issue had negative effects on the investment climate, and harmed the government's credibility.[22]

Some local governments suffer heavy losses from PPP projects due to poor preparation and a lack of competency. In fact, there are many failed PPP cases in China. However, no severe negative consequences can be noted due to the failed PPPs, because most of the failed projects have been bought back by the government, and returned to traditional public services delivery.

Of course, the failure of a few PPP projects in the past two decades is unable to mask the overall success of PPPs in China, as well as their significant contributions to improve the quality and efficiency of public facilities and service.

4. CONCLUSIONS AND RECOMMENDATIONS

PPPs are gaining popularity in China, and there have been many successful projects in sectors such as water, transportation, and the environment. The adaptation of PPPs to public facilities and services is not only a strategy to raise funds, but also an effort to improve decision-making and make it more transparent. Most PPP projects play an active role in social and economic development. Some experts say that in China, the second wave of PPPs is coming now. The first wave of PPPs occurred in the 1990s, when foreign investors played a major role. In the approaching second wave, the domestic private sector and state-owned enterprises will increasingly dominate PPP projects in China.

However, many problems still remain. Many institutions, laws, and mechanisms require establishment and further improvement. China should draw on the lessons learned from past experiences with PPPs, and take effective actions to facilitate the development of these structures. With the introduction of some guides, rules and regulations, it is expected that many of the problems discussed should be overcome. However, there is still room for improving the PPP system in China.

Introducing Competition in the PPP Process

According to China's Tendering and Bidding Law, all construction projects related to public interest and security should be subject to open competitive bidding. Competition in the bidding process can reduce construction costs, encourage technology innovation, and improve project quality. For example, in Beijing, five wastewater treatment plants, namely Beiyuan, Dingfuzhuang, Wulituo, Daitou, and Dongba, were put into use in April 2004. All the private partners in the five projects were selected through competitive bidding, which reduced the overall construction cost to RMB 230 millions, a sum lower than the government expected.

The Phase I of the Lugouqiao sewage treatment plant is the first wastewater treatment project in Beijing to be opened for global bidding. The bidding winner was a foreign private company, named Veolia Water Corporation. It introduced advanced technology and management expertise in the operation of the plant, thus achieving a very successful performance.

The introduction of competition in PPPs, such as open bidding and competitive bargaining, will lead to successful PPP operations with cost-saving, high efficiency, advanced technology and modern management.

Adopting Standardized and Detailed Contracts

The PPP contract is a legal document by which the government monitors, supervises and evaluates public facilities and services provided by the private sector. Considering the complexity and importance of PPP contracts, the government should pay a great deal of attention to detail when drawing up such contracts. The more detailed a PPP contract, the less likely the probability of future conflicts between the public and private sectors. Of course, the government should balance the efforts spent on negotiation and dealing with future uncertainties. For the purpose of simplifying the contract preparation, it is worthwhile to design a standardized formatted PPP contract, which can easily be adjusted to particular PPP projects.

Ensuring an Integrated and Coherent Legal System

In China, there are many regulations related to PPPs enacted by different levels of government. The State Council formulated the Decision on the Reform of Investment Institutions in 2004 and the regulation entitled *Some Opinions on Encouraging, Supporting, and Guiding the development of Non-state-Owned Economy* in 2005. The Ministry of Construction promulgated a series of regulations, such as the *Opinions on Accelerating the Market Liberalization of Public Utilities* in 2002, the *Measure on Public Utilities Concession Management* in 2004, and the *Opinions on Strengthening Regulation of Public Utilities* in 2005. The Ministry of Construction (MOC) also issued the *Sample Concession Agreement Document for Urban Water Supply, Gas Pipeline, Urban Garbage Disposal* in 2004.

All of these recent regulations provide guidelines for the private sector to take part in public service delivery. However, no specific laws regulating PPPs have been issued yet. Almost all the people we interviewed mentioned the lack of an integrated and coherent legal system in China.

Some local governments also formulated some regulations, such as the *Measure on the Beijing Municipal Infrastructure Concession Management* in 2002 and the *Measure on the Shenzhen Municipal Public Utilities Concession Management* in 2003.

China's Bidding Law came into effect as of January 1st 2000. This law was designed initially for the tendering processes of engineering procurements, and prohibits any amendments to the terms and conditions specified in the bidding document. It also prohibits any form of negotiation after the bidding evaluation has ended.

One of the biggest advantages of the PPP model is that the tender is designed to provide bidders with a certain flexibility, allowing them to come up with innovative proposals that will create additional value or help reduce project costs. Consequently, there is a need for some flexibility in the Bidding Law.

While some flexibility is important, it is fair to say that, in many bidding processes in China, a major difficulty is the insufficient planning and development of the contracts prior to the bidding process. While there is a need for more flexibility than the Bidding Law allows, it should not allow so much flexibility that there is insufficient pressure to encourage the preparation of proper bid documents and contracts.

In addition, the laws and regulations should be consistent. The marketization must be guaranteed by an integrated and coherent regulatory framework. The enforcement of new laws or regulations will not only address new situations, but also remain consistent with existing regulations.

There is no specific law for PPPs in China. The regulations are discreet and even sometimes mutually contradictory, which has hindered any further development of PPPs in China. Based on the experiences and lessons learned from PPPs over the past two decades, now is the right time to set up a specific law for PPPs.

Finally, a proper judiciary system for dispute resolution is important to protect the private sector's investments in capital intensive PPP projects.

Further Enhancing the Anti-Corruption Efforts

Corruption imposes a heavy transaction cost on the private companies involved in PPPs. Usually, the PPP is achieved through a public bidding, and the process is relatively open, transparent, and fair. But the success of PPP operation requires close cooperation between the public and private

sectors, and, in many cases, the private sector needs the government's coordination and support. This situation provides government officials with
plenty of opportunities to seize a bribe. One interviewee from the private
sector complained: *They (government officials) always find a chance to come
here to seek entertainment. All the profit is eaten out by them.*

Clarifying the Procedures for Securing the Authority's Approval

The biggest difficulty for private investors to invest in infrastructure
projects is receiving the approval from the authorities. Just as in all other
countries, getting permits and approvals for infrastructure projects in
China is complex and time consuming. But in China, the decision-making process is very obscure and unpredictable, which makes the process
of securing approvals especially difficult. Moreover, once an application
has been submitted to the authorities, it is very difficult to make amendments, even if the amendments reduce costs or improve the quality of the
project. Such an application and approval process increases the risk and
uncertainty for the investors, which will be ultimately reflected in a higher
overall project cost, making the venture more expensive for both private
and public sectors.

Furthermore, the activities requiring the approval of different government departments are frequently uncoordinated, even repetitive and mutually contradictory, which brings much inconvenience and extra costs to
the private companies involved. As one interviewee from the private sector
said: "Some procedures are unnecessary; some are outdated conventions
and can be avoided. As for a project, from initiating the project to getting
the final approval, it will take us two years, which may be relatively rapid
compared with others. In some areas, projects have not received any approval after three to four years. Therefore, the approving procedures should
be redefined to eliminate some unnecessary intermediate steps."

Private enterprises need clear guidance on how to obtain approvals from
government agencies. When multiple government agencies are involved in
the approving process, the responsibilities of each agency should be clearly
defined. Otherwise, investors will have to spend a lot of time finding out
which agencies should be in charge of approving their projects.

Standard procedure for undertaking a PPP project should be established
at the central level of the government, to provide a guideline on infrastructure project implementation. The procedure should establish the steps that
a PPP project has to go through in order to assess its suitability and feasibility. The procedure should also define general criteria including project
economics, public service comparisons, risk allocation mechanisms, as well
as model concession agreement. Once the procedure is developed, every

infrastructure project undertaken must follow the procedure in order to get approval from the authority.

Improving the Government's Capacity in the Areas of Negotiation, Enforcement and Supervision

For China's government officials, the successful application of PPPs in public facilities and services requires upgrading their professional skills in negotiation, operation and supervision. The government should improve its capacity in PPPs operations by training its officials and following some international PPP best practices. It is also important for government to recruit professional consultants to provide specific expertise, so as to make up for its inadequate knowledge on particular technical aspects.

In 1998, the Beijing municipal government selected Consortia of Mitsubishi and Angeli through an open bidding process, as a private partner to fund Beijing No. 10 Water Factory BOT project. The cooperation was smooth at the early stage. However, the private company withdrew from this project before the construction formally started for undisclosed reasons. Fortunately, the Beijing municipal government recruited professional consultants to participate in the whole process. The consultants helped the municipal government to establish a set of clear and concrete rules to secure the government's interests, especially when the foreign investor withdrew at the construction stage. The involvement of professional consultants has become a necessary component of many domestic PPP projects.

The government needs to strengthen its capacity in regulating and monitoring PPP projects. The launch of a pilot project will help government officials to better understand PPP projects. Technical support provided by PPP professionals is critical to a successful PPP project. Other countries have already adopted good practices when developing a PPP project, and these should be carefully studied and tailored to China's current situation. Interactive communication between government officials and experienced PPP professionals to develop pilot PPP projects can benefit the development of PPPs in China.

First, the government's supervision of PPPs needs to be transformed. Traditionally, the government is more accustomed to using directives, administrative authority, inspection and approval to manage business activities. In order to promote the development of PPPs in a market-oriented China, it has to turn to professional supervision by contract, law, and regulations.

Second, the organizational framework and the distribution of responsibilities should be clearly specified. It should be made clear whether the PPP is supervised by a separate government division, an independent special department, or a combination of the present regulation with the conventional planning, administration approval, and funds management function.

Thirdly, the concrete government supervision technique should be improved. With the private sector engaging in public infrastructure and services, the circumstances faced by the government are becoming more complex. The government has to match its increasing responsibilities with corresponding skills.

In addition, the government should be fully aware of and pay more attention to the risk allocation between the public and private sectors. Depending on the economics of the project, the government's objective, and the market's initial response to the project, an appropriate risk-sharing structure among involved parties needs to be carefully designed. However, this principle has not been well understood by the various government agencies in China.

Improving Policy Consistency

The internal coherence of government policies is vital for winning the trust and attracting the investment from private companies. It is particularly true for China during her economic and political transition. During this transition process, China undertook significant changes to realign its policies and reorganize its industries, which undoubtedly have a great impact on the ongoing PPP projects. Industrial reforms in sectors like electricity, telecommunication, and water supply, have created great uncertainty for the existing private projects.

The political climate in China has been relatively stable in recent years. But with the deepening of reforms, the administrative system and regulation framework have undergone drastic changes, which brought to light a lot of inconsistencies in the reform process. As one interviewee responded: "Private companies must keep track of these changes, and learn to respond effectively to them, in order to survive in the evolving environment. The evolution of policy is a trend that we cannot block. Obviously, policy change increases the uncertainty and risk of the enterprises to operate their business. The only thing we can do is to understand the changes and learn to respond to them effectively".

Policy consistency is an important element for private companies to invest in PPPs. The government should keep its strategies and policies as consistent as possible, and avoid any unnecessary or inconsiderate changes. Any amendment on existing polices should be carefully studied and evaluated. The voice of private companies should be taken into consideration when formulating a new policy or amending an existing one.

Reforming the Financial Market to Support the Private Sector's Financial Requirements

The banking system in China should be further reformed to meet the financing requirements of private companies involved in PPPs. The financial and insurance markets should also be improved to reduce the uncertainties and risks that private companies may encounter during their PPP operations.

There are several key areas which need further reform namely: imbalanced financing structures, limitations on debt levels, security package design, refinancing techniques, interest rate hedging, and constraints on capital injection.

Improving the Government's Planning Capability in Order to Avoid Unexpected Changes after the Implementation of a PPP, and Thus Preventing Losses to Both the Public and Private Sectors

PPPs are primarily adopted in the area of urban infrastructure, and the infrastructure sector is considered as a typical "public good", with externalities and natural monopoly. Therefore, an outright privatisation of the infrastructure sector may lead to many potential problems. For example, the charges of public infrastructures may be too high for marginal and low-income groups to afford or access these basic public services. Theoretically, PPPs can make use of the advantages of both government and market, if the government has a strong urban planning capability. Scientific planning can prevent the uncertainties which may arise in PPP operations.

A PPP project usually has a long life span of more than 15 years, during which the economic, political, and demographic environment could change dramatically. Insofar as is reasonable and possible, the contractual arrangements agreed upon at the time when the concession is granted will have to take into account these possible changes, particularly the adverse ones.

The performance evaluation on PPP projects has not been given enough attention. This could potentially lead to poorly structured PPP projects, in which the government merely seeks short-term benefits to satisfy public interests. It is therefore necessary to establish a system to benchmark the performance of a particular project and make the assessment of an operator's efficiency more objective and less subjective.

Enhancing Transparency So as to Reduce the Cost Paid by Both Government and Private Sector

Information is critical for both the government and the private sector. The private sector needs to know the laws, regulations, and procedures of

PPPs, so the government should disclose relevant information promptly. The government must be acquainted with information about the private sector and its operational mode in order to effectively make decisions and carry out regulation and supervision. However, many private companies working in PPPs are reluctant to disclose information because they want to maintain commercial confidentiality.

As consumers of the public services, citizens have the right to information from both the government and the private sector. As one interviewee said: *Transparency is the most important factor (for the success of PPPs); all processes should be transparent. The contract has no commercial confidentiality, because it involves public rather than private services, so it is unreasonable to point to commercial confidentiality. If you keep commercial confidentiality, you cannot attend to the tender.*

Transparency also helps decrease the transaction costs of PPPs, so measures should be taken to maintain and improve transparency.

NOTES

1. P. H. K. Ho, "Development of Public Private Partnerships (PPPs) in China", *Surveyors Times*, 15(10), 2006.

2. Ibidem.

3. H. Yu and H. Qin, H., The Experiment of Pubic-Private Partnerships in China: Green Book of China's Municipal Public Utilities No.1., Shanghai, Shanghai People's Publishing House, 2005.

4. Ho, loc. cit.

5. Ibidem.

6. National Bureau of Statistics of China, China Statistical Yearbook 2007, Beijing: China Statistics Press.

7. Ho, loc. cit.

8. http://news.xinhuanet.com/fortune/2005-12/06/content_3884022.htm

9. MOFCOM

10. http://www.h2o-china.com/report/salon_4/book.htm

11. J. Adams, A. Young and Z. Wu, "Public private partnerships in China: System, constraints and future prospects", *International Journal of Public Sector Management*, 2006, 19(4), pp. 384-396.

12. K. E. Haynes, K. E., "Infrastructure: the glue of megacities", *Megacities Lecture* 9, 2006

13. D.C. North, D.C. and B. R. Weingast, "Constitutions and commitments: the evolutions of institutions governing the public choices in the seventeenth century England", *The Journal of Economic History*, 1989, 49, pp. 803-832.; B. Levy and P. T. Spiller, "The Institutional Foundations of Regulatory Commitment: A Comparative Analysis of Telecommunications Regulation", *Journal of Law, Economics & Organization*, 1994, 10(2):201-246.; Moser, P., Checks and balances, and the supply of central bank independence, *European Economic Review*, 1999, 43, pp. 1569-1593.;

W. J. Henisz, W.J., "The institutional environment for infrastructure investment", *Industrial and Corporate Change*, 2002, 11(2), pp. 355-389.; D. Stasavage, D. (2002), Private investment and political institutions, *Economics and Politics*, 2002, 14(1), pp. 41-63.; C. Ménard and M. Shirley, Reforming Public Utilities: Lessons from Urban Water Systems in Six Developing Countries, *World Bank Report*, 2002, pp. 1-54.; W. J. Henisz and B. A. Zelner B.A., Explicating political hazards and safeguards: a transaction cost politics approach. *Industrial and Corporate Change*, 2004, 13(6), pp. 901-915.

14. O. Fionayap, Government's credible commitment in economic policy-making: Evidence from Singapore, *Policy Sciences*, 2003, 36(3-4), pp. 237-255.

15. This section makes a lot of references to Ho, loc. cit.

16. National Bureau of Statistics of China, China Statistical Abstract 2008, Beijing: China Statistics Press

17. F. He, "China's economic reform: Success, problems and challenges", 2007, http://www.crcpp.org/cpipphtml/hf_paper/2007-11/20/200711200925.html

18. National Bureau of Statistics, China Statistical Abstract 2007, Beijing: China Statistics Press

19. Calculated with the data published by MOHURD and NBS

20. X. Y. Ding, Theory and Practice of Marketization for Urban Infrastructure, Beijing, Beijing Scientific Publishing House, 2005.

21. This section makes a lot of references to Ho, loc. cit.

22. Asian Development Bank, *Final Report on Major Issues and Recommendations of PPP in the Water Sector in China*, 2005, http://www.adb.org

ANNEX I
PLANT B OF CHENGDU NO. 6 WATER SUPPLY PLANT

Plant B of Chengdu No. 6 Water Supply Plant is the earliest BOT project in the water industry in China. In August 1999, the Chengdu Municipal Government signed a concession agreement with the Chengdu General Water-Marubeni Water Supply Ltd. formed by Veolia and Marubeni Corporation, with a concession period of 18 years including a construction period of over two years. Chengdu General Water-Marubeni Water Supply Ltd. was responsible for financing, designing, constructing, and operating the whole project in the concession period. After the end of concession, the water plant would be returned to Chengdu Municipality without charging any payment. Total investment of the project amounted to USD107.6 millions, 30% of which was directly invested by shareholders of the project company (60% by French company Veolia, and 40% by Japanese Marubeni); the remaining 70% came from the Asia Development Bank, European Investment Bank, and another 5 commercial banks headed by Lyons Credit Bank. The construction of the project was finished in December 2001. Formal water supply started on February 7th 2002, with a daily water supply of 400000 m3.

With regard to the project evaluation, the Chengdu Municipal Government achieved the best economic results. The water price Veolia-Marubeni offered was RMB 0.96/ m³, far below the second lowest price RMB 1.10/ m³. Besides, there is a large space for compressing cost. According to the evaluation of the Chengdu Municipal Government, the investment would have totalled RMB 1.2 billion, but the actual investment of the bidder was 0.3 billion lower. During the process of construction of Plant B, special attention was paid to idea design, performance of facilities, and tight design. Compared with Chinese traditional design, investment construction and operation costs were drastically reduced, while the investment effect was increased.

From the perspective of sustainable development, Plant B applied the design idea of concentration, maximum design optimum including change of thickness of pipeline walls, tight workmanship, and decrease of land occupation area from originally designed 100 mu to 70 mu. Plant B belonged to heavy-load design, reduced considerably electricity consumption and saved much cost of the operation. To date, all the water provided by Plant B met the standard of drinkable water.

But there are also some problems, the severest of which is the Chengdu Municipal Government's guaranty of minimum water demand of 400 thousand tons each day. Plant A has the capacity of providing 600 thousand tons each day, but had to undertake the adjustment of water supply after Plant B was put into operation. Due to the imprecise prediction of the water demand, the great fluctuation of water demand led to the extreme inefficiency of Plant A.

Generally speaking, although some defects exist, Chengdu No. 6 Water Supply Plant is a relatively successful PPP project.

ANNEX II
TUOJIANG BRIDGE CONSTRUCTION
AND MANAGEMENT LTD.

Zizhong County is located in the middle of Sichuan province. The Tuojiang River flows through Zizhong Municipality and divides the city in two parts. Tuojiang bridge, built in 1980, was the only one across the river in the city. In June 1997, the Zizhong Municipal Government signed an agreement with a private enterprise, the Sichuan Jiuda Corporation, which was to invest in the renovation and enlargement of the bridge. A toll was to be charged for 16 years to earn back the investment. In 2001, the whole project was completed, and the investment checked by the Auditing Office of Sichuan Province Government totalled RMB 26.5 millions. Tuojiang Bridge Construction and Management Ltd. began to collect fees from Jan 2002, the toll rate ranging from RMB 1 to 16.

However, in the first year of operation, the Zizhong Municipal Government required the Tuoqiao Company to reduce the toll rate up to 9 times. As a response, the Tuoqiao Company decreased the rate to some extent. In June 2003, the Zizhong Municipal Government demanded the Tuoqiao Company to further reduce the toll rate for bus, taxi and pedicab, which was refused by the Company. Afterwards, many vehicles crossing the bridge refused to pay the toll, and the conflicts between the Tuoqiao Company, citizens and the county government escalated. In July 2003, the Tuoqiao Company sued the Zizhong Municipal Government, and requested the cancellation of the administrative decrees made by the Zizhong Municipal Government to lower the toll rate. After reconciliation, the Zizhong Municipal Government spent RMB 44 millions to buy back the bridge in December 2005.

Concerning the project evaluation, the amount of funds the Zizhong Municipal Government spent in buying back the bridge was RMB 44 millions, which was far more than the RMB 26.5 million the Sichuan Jiuda Corporation had invested, not to mention the fees that had been collected. So, the project completely failed from the economic perspective. Moreover, the project also gave rise to severe equity problems, and many citizens were not able to afford the high toll rate. Last but very importantly, ongoing conflicts between the Tuoqiao Company, citizens and the Zizhong Municipal Government posed a great threat to the social stability and public security of the Zizhong County. Many factors combined to cause the failure of the project, such as the inadequate capacities of the government, lack of government credibility and ineffective government regulation during the construction and operation of the bridge.

In a word, the case of Tuojiang Bridge Construction and Management Ltd. is a typical example of a failed BOT project in China's local area. It is of great significance to all local governments that may attempt to provide public services through PPPs.

IV

CONCLUSION

9

PPPs in In-transition Countries:
Prospects and Limits for
the Improvement of Efficiency,
Sustainability, Equity,
and Security

Paolo Urio

In the first chapter I explained why the choice of our four countries was based upon diversity rather than similarity: as the proponents of PPPs consider that this type of provision can be beneficial in all situations, a research like ours would be in a better position to test this hypothesis by choosing countries in a pre-PPP stage with large differences, rather than with close similarities. It is not therefore surprising that our research has revealed important differences. But, as we shall see, there are also some remarkable similarities.

For the purpose of interpreting the strategies of in-transition countries applied to introduce some market mechanisms, scholars have developed a variety of models. While it is not possible to present them here in detail, one model stands out, namely that of Ivan Szelenyi.[1] He presents three pathways out of command economy: *the Chinese path*, which is described as a path "from below" (i.e. with transition starting from the reform in the countryside) and led by a developmental state. By contrast to the Chinese model, the European post-communist countries adopted a strategy "from above," i.e. the transition started with the privatization of the corporate sector, but without the lead of a developmental state. Two different models are used for interpreting the transition of these countries: these are the neo-patrimonial and the neo-liberal models. Thus, *the Eastern European neo-patrimonial systems*,[2] of which Russia is the most interesting case for our research, is qualified as "making capitalists without capitalism," where "the transformation of property rights proceeded faster than the making of market institutions," barter remaining an important form of exchange.

Finally, the *neo-liberalism in Central Europe* model refers to a process where "the changes in economic institutions were faster, more radical (...) Public ownership was eliminated on short notice, and the economy, prices, and foreign trade were precipitously deregulated." This third model is called "making capitalism without capitalists," in which "the corporate sector was privatized mainly by turning it over to foreign investors."[3] So this typology puts more emphasis on differences than on similarities.

Nevertheless, Szelenyi recognizes in his article (written in 2007) that he developed this typology around 1997–98 when differences in the transition paths followed by these countries were in fact quite important; moreover, he points out that during the following decade there have been signs of a certain degree of convergence, especially between countries of the second and third type, as institutionalization of the market has been developed in Russia, and a new class of capitalists has emerged in Central European countries. And, maybe even more important, Central European countries, like Poland, have become members of the European Union, and therefore must conform to the criteria of market economy and liberal democracy. Even Russia "shows signs of some institutional convergence with the liberal model (...) The role of barter has declined, market institutions have become more firmly established, and the oligarchs seem to be ready to make deals with the government about taxes and seem to realize that they need a more predictable environment if they want to attract badly needed foreign capital and technology."[4] Nevertheless, Szelenyi maintains that some important differences persist, and that "there are still three worlds of post-communist capitalism": it is true that in China little remains of "capitalism from below" (i.e. from the agriculture) but the State is still playing the role of a developmental state.[5] Russia has certainly developed market institutions, but patrimonial social relations still persist, and Central European states have adapted their institutions to the liberal model, but "with a clear neo-liberal bent."[6]

What is the contribution of our research to the debate about the convergence or divergence of pathways out of command economy, and what are the prospects for the development of PPPs in this context? Let us first say that we have found both differences and similarities amongst our four countries. It is not surprising that the most important differences are based upon the particular history of each country (in spite of their common past as command economy under communist rule), which explains differences in attitudes towards western-style political democratization, as well as differences in political values and cultures, and institutional settings, not to forget differences in their physical size (in terms of surface and population) and geographical situation. The similarities appear first of all in their will to introduce market mechanisms and complete or partial privatization of some State activities (although with strategies as different as the Russian- and Polish-style shock therapy of the nineties, or the incremental path to reforms Chinese-style); second, in the technical requirements these strategies must comply with. These similarities appear in spite of the fact that technical conditions may vary considerably, especially those related to laws and regulations, as well as the practices of managing the relations between central and local authorities, and between public authorities and citizens. More generally, we must not forget, especially when we formulate recommendations, that technical requirements must be implemented within the framework of the cultural values and institutions mentioned above. Finally, the analysis of our standardized questionnaires (Chapter 4) shows that when the respondents of one of the four transition countries manifest opinions close to that of the Western experts, this country is always the same: Poland. This should not come as a surprise, as Poland is a member of the European Union and as such, as we have already said in Chapter 1, has complied with the requirements of the Union concerning the adoption of the major features of liberal democracy and market economy (and we may add with Szelenyi, with a neo-liberal flavour) and is therefore, amongst our four transition countries the one that is most likely to accept the idea of implementing PPPs.[7]

Before we go any further, it must be stressed that the implementation of market mechanisms (of which PPPs are a special case) is a very complex endeavour. Our research has not dealt in depth with all the aspects of this complexity, and more particularly the technical aspects related to risk analysis, contract law, not to speak of the technicalities of infrastructures construction and management such as roads, railways, water plants and waste water treatment. Nevertheless, thanks to the analysis of the available scientific evidence and the interviews we conducted with experts in both Western and in-transition countries, it has been possible to draw a reasonably precise picture showing the similarities and differences that appear amongst our four in-transition countries in this very complex domain. Chapters 3 to 8 have presented the situation in the West and in each of the four countries. It is now possible to summarize our findings and to formulate some general conclusion and recommendations.

In the following pages we will summarize the findings presented in the previous chapters by taking into consideration information gathered from both standardized questionnaires (analyzed in Chapter 4) and by face to face interviews, official documents and other published materials (analyzed in Chapter 3 and 5 to 8). Let us start with six remarks about the way we will summarize our findings.

First, when dealing with the answers of our respondents we will most of the time summarize the opinions expressed through both standardized questionnaires and face-to-face interviews, and we will occasionally refer to the results of the the former (already presented in Chapter 4) only when they provide some additional insights.

Second, we will distinguish the conditions that make it easy or difficult to adopt and implement PPPs and the contribution of PPPs to economic efficiency, sustainable development, equity and security. As we suggested in Chapter 1, PPPs must first exist before we can appreciate to what extent they contribute to these values: setting up PPPs does not necessarily contribute to any of these values. It is of course possible that some of these conditions make it possible not only to set up PPPs, but also to contribute to the realization of these four values. But there is not an *a priori* guarantee that this will be the case: we have seen in Chapter 1, and more in detail in Chapter 2, that very often it will be necessary to proceed to some trade-offs, for example between economic efficiency and equity. The research has shown that there might be some even more complex trade-offs, when the time factor is taken into consideration not only in the short run, but also in the long term. For example, if the Government considers that it is urgent to provide a certain infrastructure to the present generation of citizens, and if the financial capacity of the State is limited, it could decide to have recourse to private money, and this will enable the government to provide this service in a relatively short time. But, as this is generally more expensive than public borrowing (not to speak of transaction costs), this will result in the medium and long term in an additional cost, that will be paid by the next generation of citizens.[8] But on the contrary, one could also consider that this infrastructure may contribute to economic development, and when the repayment time comes, the economy (and the fiscal capacity of the State) may be in a better position to pay for that infrastructure. This example shows that efficiency and equity are at stake and that there is not necessarily an optimal decision that can satisfy all the stakeholders. In the first case, the choice of providing the infrastructure to the present generation at a higher cost can be considered as non-efficient (at least in the short and medium term) but equitable for the present population that may very badly need this infrastructure (as is often the case for in-transition countries), whereas it could be considered inequitable for the next generation that will have not only to pay a higher price, but most likely will inherit an old-fashioned infrastructure. In the second case the decision is more efficient and equitable for the next generation, but not so for the present one.

Third, we will distinguish empirical findings on the conditions mentioned above from the opinion of the people we interviewed. We will also compare these findings with the empirical evidence and theoretical considerations available for other countries, both developed and in-transition. We must remind the reader that the experience of PPPs in these countries is rather new. As a consequence, the "expertise" of the people we interviewed in our four countries is not always very high, as many of them admitted either during the face-to-face interviews or in their responses to our standardized questionnaires (see Chapter 4). Therefore, we shall consider their answers and opinions with great care.

Fourth, we will distinguish ideological-political factors, technical conditions, and contextual ones. Fifth, sectors in which PPPs have been introduced in these countries are limited to physical (or hard) infrastructures, such as transportation (roads, railways, sea- and air-ports), water provision, waste water treatment.[9] We have not found cases of PPPs in soft infrastructure, such as education, health and safety nets, except if we consider, as we have done in Chapter 2, that water supply is a soft infrastructure. Nevertheless, this does not mean that PPPs in other kinds of soft infrastructure may not be introduced in the future into these countries, as many respondents have mentioned.[10]

Sixth and last remark: as our research has been focused on PPPs, little information has been collected on the more radical forms of private intervention in the provision of public services, i.e. full privatization. As a consequence, we are not in a position to discuss and compare the merits of these two forms of private intervention, especially for soft infrastructures. Nevertheless, information already available in scientific journals, supported by information informally obtained in China shows that, at least for this country, several experiments of full privatization (or partial privatization with insufficient public control) especially in the domain of education and health, have produced some negative outcomes from the point of view of both efficiency and equity. Decisions to correct these negative outcomes have already been taken at the local level, and the central government has recently decided to take these situations very seriously, especially in the domains of health and social safety nets.[11] The available evidence (especially for health) puts some very strong doubts on the capacity of privatization, even in its less radical forms, to satisfy fundamental criteria such as efficiency, effectiveness, quality, and equity in domains where the market does not exist, i.e. when lack of competition and asymmetric information make it difficult for actors, at least those at the demand side, to behave rationally as postulated by the market model. Finally, if it is evident that the decision to attribute the provision of any kind of infrastructure is taken by the political authorities, our research has confirmed what we proposed in Chapter 2: the choice of attributing the provision of infrastructures to the market or to the State is more likely to be based upon scientific evidence in the case of private and public goods, whereas for the problematic category of merit goods the choice is more likely to be oriented by ideological, political or opportunistic considerations. This lack of clear scientific evidence explains to a certain extent why countries that have been used for a long time to the provision of all kinds of services and infrastructures by the State have been more reluctant, at least until now, to give access to private money for the provision of merit goods like education, health, and safety nets.

MAJOR FACTORS CONDITIONING
THE IMPLEMENTATION OF PPPS

What are the major factors that condition the implementation of PPPs? Before we comment upon them in detail, let us briefly try to present the logic that links all these factors. First of all, it is clear that *history* is the first determinant factor. Russia, Poland and Ukraine have been affected by the collapse of the Soviet Union in 1991, China by the tragedy of the Cultural Revolution that ended in 1976 and led the Communist party to embrace the road of reforms. In spite of the differences between the four countries, and especially the striking differences between the more cautious and incremental path adopted by the Chinese leadership (later comforted in its choice when the Communist party lost power in Russia) and the negative consequences of the shock therapy of the Eltsin years, all four countries stared to introduce market mechanisms in their economy. So, dramatic historical events may constitute the first condition that favours PPPs. Bearing this in mind, we will regroup our major findings under three interrelated headings or levels: strategic, contextual, and operational, each of them comprising a set of conditions or factors susceptible to having an impact on PPPs. It must be said that the three levels are not perfectly separated, and this will pose some problems of interpretation. But this is the inevitable consequence of an analytic approach that aims at reducing complexity by dividing reality into more simple and manageable components, whereas they are in fact imbedded into a single reality. Figure 9.1 summarizes the conditions having an impact on the adoption and implementation of PPPs.

The strategic level comprises the major components of the polity (especially the political elite or leadership, political parties, and public opinion), the public administration (especially the administrative elite), and the set of other institutions that have access to the political decision-making process (e.g. think tanks, interest groups). The contextual level comprises the conditions and factors within which the strategy is implemented thanks to the devices of the operational level. The following contextual elements are considered: the state of the economy (domestic and international), the state of infrastructures, the globalization of information, the impact of international organizations and, more generally, of the trends in the global economy, the geographical situation of the four countries concerned, and finally the occurrence of special events. The operational level comprises the more technical factors that have an impact on the adoption and implementation of PPPs, and more generally all sorts of arrangements giving to the private partner the secure institutional and legal environment it needs for accepting the investment risks, to the public authorities the institutional, legal, and expertise necessary for an effective participation in the partnerships, and to the public the necessary instruments for assuring transparency

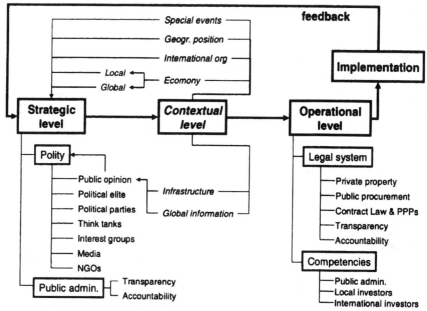

Figure 9.1. Three Levels of Conditions for PPPs' Adoption and Implementation.

and accountability of the activities placed under the responsibility of the public and private partners. In other words it is a set of "enablers" without which a correct analysis of the contextual level by the political leadership, and an effective implementation of the PPPs objectives run the risk of not producing the expected positive results, or at least may very well be the source of some major difficulties. The operational level comprises first of all the legal system: i.e. the rules governing the economy, private property, public procurement, contract law (and more specifically rules governing PPPs), as well as rules concerning transparency and accountability; second, the competencies of public authorities and local investors necessary for the mastering of the complexity of PPPs contracts and of the domains in which they are implemented.

We will conclude with an evaluation of the impact of PPPs on efficiency, sustainability, equity and security. Unfortunately, our conclusion on these important aspects will be of a very tentative nature, as the implementation of PPPs in our countries is very recent, and therefore an in-depth evaluation of their impact is not yet possible. Consequently, our discussion will inevitably be based upon the opinion of our respondents, some available empirical evidence in the four countries, and evidence from the experiences of countries with long history in PPPs. But even if we can count on the latter, that we will use with great care,[12] it is clear that the evidence we can provide will be, at best, partial and controversial.

The Strategic Level

The Political Will

The first factor in favour of the introduction of market mechanisms is certainly the political will. This can be based upon an ideological shift operated by the elites (as has been the case in Russia, Poland and Ukraine, although at different paces), or by a pragmatic attitude that prevailed in China after 1978 under the leadership of Deng Xiaoping.[13] In both cases the door was open for PPPs, but Poland and Russia (and later Ukraine) proceeded more clearly in a Western-like strategy that consists in setting up an institutional, legal and regulatory environment first (even if not entirely satisfactory) whereas China (that does not have the same institutional and legal practice) proceeded first by experimentation, and started to establish or amend the legal and institutional arrangements only after a careful evaluation of their adequacy to, and efficiency in the Chinese context.

The importance of political will has been mentioned by a majority of respondents to the standardized questionnaires and mentioned the absence of this factor as being an obstacle to the implementation of PPPs.[14] Some of the people interviewed face-to-face, who considered with favour the implementation of PPPs, complained about the traditional ideological biases and habits inherited from the command economy as factors going against the adoption of PPPs, especially at the local level, where, we may add, some well-entrenched vested interests still operate within the old ideological structure and constitute an obstacle to the adoption of other ways of supplying public services. This may be one of the major obstacles to PPPs at the strategic level. On the contrary, as we had the opportunity to witness in China, some members of the leadership are simply very careful before they make the final decision in favour of PPPs. But, as we have already said, one of the advantages of the Chinese way of managing the public sector and its progressive retreat from a certain number of activities in favour of the private sector is its strategy to experiment on a limited regional (provincial or municipal) base, before extending to the entire nation or, more likely to other regions with similar characteristics the practices that have proven good.[15]

Peoples' Trust in the State's Will to Introduce PPPs and Public Opinion

The second factor identified by many of our respondents in the four countries is the trust people (and especially those willing to embark upon PPPs) have in the will of the State to set up a reliable and consistent set of public policies making the establishment of PPPs possible. Many respondents in Russia and especially in China have complained that this trust is not yet sufficiently sustained by clear signs given to potential private investors by the political leadership. We will see hereafter that the trust in the political will cannot be satisfied by simple declarations of principles, but must be translated into a complex set of operational means favouring the implementation of PPPs, the fundamental aim being the establishment of a secure environment for private investors.

Strictly linked to the preceding factors is the state of public opinion. In the absence of a survey of public opinion in our four countries it is difficult to evaluate the level of citizens' satisfaction with the existing infrastructure. Opinions expressed by our respondents to the standardized questionnaire (already presented in Chapter 4) give nevertheless a plausible picture: almost 80% are not at all or little satisfied with the present state of infrastructure in their country.[16] And although many consider that improvements have been achieved, the gap between the high percentages of people who are not satisfied and the generally modest level of improvement means that expectations are high. And that the gap could eventually be filled by new initiatives of which PPPs could be a viable choice. Having this perspective in mind, it is clear that citizens with a high degree of confidence in their government will be willing to accept and support the decisions made by the political leadership, provided that it can prove that the day-to-day implementation of public policies favouring PPPs is in fact improving the situation of the different components of society, and this within a relatively stable environment. If this proves to be the case, the choices made for attributing the delivery of public services to the State, the market or PPPs will have a chance of being supported by the population. This will be true for PPPs, if the government can convince the citizens that in this way the quality and quantity of public services will improve compared to the former provision by state organizations. This will be easier if the population is dissatisfied by the poor performance of existing public services both in terms of quality and quantity, and even more so if the fees for having access to services supplied by the state are increasing. Political marketing becomes a necessity for the government in these circumstances.[17] The analysis of the standardized questionnaires performed by Thomas Zacharewicz in Chapter 4, shows that among our respondents in all our countries there is a high degree of confidence in the capacity of PPPs to realize this objective.[18] Moreover, the majority of people interviewed face-to-face considers that public opinion in their country is either in favour of PPPs or at least is not opposed. This is not surprising if we consider that provision of public service under communist rule has been too often of mediocre quality (in spite of its universal character satisfying the criterion of equitable access), and that after the collapse of these regimes there has been a relatively long period during which these services have considerably deteriorated. Only a few doubts have been expressed about the capacity of PPPs to improve the situation, especially by Chinese and Western respondents.

Nevertheless, some negative opinions have been put forward, that are in tune with some theoretical and empirical findings, concerning the emergence of transaction costs. As Thomas Zacharewicz has already presented in Chapter 4, while analyzing the standardized questionnaires, 57% of respondents don't know, disagree or strongly disagree with the capacity of PPPs to improve the delivery of services in relation to transaction costs. The problem of transaction costs is well known in scientific literature, but not necessarily outside academic and expert circles. That there are many people who do not know what to answer about transaction costs is understandable if we recall the expertise needed to improve the delivery of services in relation to transaction costs. In clear words these people, on the basis of experience and/or knowledge, know that PPPs can increase transaction costs. And these may more than cover the savings in production or delivery costs that private expertise is expected to provide for public services. These and similar questions will be analysed in the last part of this conclusion.

Stability

Political, social and economic stability is the—factor identified by our respondents that can support and reinforce political will. People we interviewed complained about the lack of this factor during the first half of the nineties in Russia and even later in Poland and Ukraine, but the situation considerably improved in the next decade especially in Poland and Russia, but not so much in Ukraine. It is a well-known concern of the Chinese leadership to maintain political and social stability as a condition favouring economic development.

Corruption

Another factor mentioned by several respondents, especially in China and Russia that could be an obstacle to PPPs is corruption. Internationally, corruption is considered as a negative behaviour both for private and public cadres as it is not only immoral, but also economically inefficient.[19] It is clear that in Western countries, i.e. in situations corresponding to a mature social, economic and political system, such behaviour is generally condemned without exception. But when we consider it in the framework of our four transition countries, it is more difficult to express a clear-cut judgment. Some authors even consider that in a transition situations, where both culturally and institutionally the country is not yet ready to play the game according to Western rules, exchange of favours between elites can contribute to boost the economic system by avoiding bureaucratic deadlocks.[20] Nevertheless all the respondents who mentioned this problem were very much against the corruption practices that they identified in their countries, especially in China and Russia. And this seems also to be the opinion publicly expressed by Professor Hu Angang, University of Tsinghua.[21] The conclusion we can propose is that it is possible that at an initial stage of the transition from command to market economy, there will be an intermediary period (the shorter the better) during which it will be naïve and foolish to try to avoid all forms of collusion between the members of the former public elite and the new emerging elite, or to expect that in the transition process the former elite will not try to barter its public capital for private capital or advantages, as history too often shows to be the practically unavoidable case. But, as the cases of Russia and China very well show, after the process of institutionalization of the market economy has reached a sufficient level of maturity to further tolerate corruption would amount not only to inefficient outcomes, but also to what Hu Angang calls a "black hole, which is an invisible abyss." If serious and effective measures are not taken to eradicate this "black hole" corruption may not only become a widespread economic harm, but according to the Tsinghua professor corruption has in fact already become "a major enemy of economic development and social stability in China, and has caused prodigious economic costs for the country and its people."[22] Unfortunately, this is not to say that, as many of our respondents have maintained, PPPs will diminish corruption. On the contrary, some of our respondents have declared that PPPs will not have any serious impact on corruption, as this phenomenon is rooted in some deep cultural and behavioural traits that cannot be easily eradicated by institutional arrangements alone.[23]

The Efficiency of Public Administration

But even with the support of the population, politicians alone cannot do much in any country, unless they can count on an efficient public administration. This is maybe one of the weakest points at the strategic level, as many respondents expressed doubts about the expertise of the national and, even more, the local public administrations to act as a competent partner in PPPs.[24] Now, this is one of the most important weaknesses that explains the difficulties in drafting of the contract and in setting up viable PPPs. If the public partner does not have a level of expertise that is at least equivalent to that of the private partner, the door is open for at least serious difficulties in the management of PPPs, at worst also for some failures. The importance of this factor in Western countries has been already explained by Olivier Brenninkmeijer in Chapter 3, and it is not surprising that it has also been put forward by many of our respondents in the four countries. The importance of expertise within government will become even more evident when we deal with the requirements at the operational level. There we will show that expertise by the public authorities is one of the most important factors for mastering the negotiations with the private partners, for writing the contract and for re-negotiating it when necessary, for supervising its execution, and for evaluating whether the objectives set in the contract (both for cost, quality and quantity) are being realized. This makes it necessary to organize a permanent monitoring, realized at regular intervals, to ensure the supervision and the evaluation necessary for detecting in time possible departures from the goals stated in the contract.

The Four "Prior Decisions" for Opting in Favour of PPPs

In Chapter 2 we introduced the idea of the necessity to go through "four prior decisions" as a preliminary decisional phase before deciding if PPPs are a suitable alternative to provision of public services and infrastructures by the State. It is clear that such decisions are taken in the context of the strategic level we have just described and in the contextual situation we will deal with in the next paragraphs; the success or failure of the decisions will depend on the availability of operational factors that support the implementation of PPP. Before we present the contextual and the operational levels, let us go back to the four prior decisions presented in Chapter 2, and examine how our respondents have justified the decision in favour of PPPs. We had considered that the final decision in favour of PPP must be preceded by four decisions related to the superiority of PPP compared to State provision of services in terms of (1) economic efficiency (2) management performance, (3) the capacity of PPP to provide services more rapidly, and (4) the question of who will pay for them in the end. The last question is more particularly related to the dilemma between efficiency and equity, the other three to efficiency and effectiveness.

In spite of some differences between countries and sectors, the majority of our respondents manifest a high degree of confidence in the superior capacity of the private sector in terms of efficiency, quality, and the capacity to modernize public services. And this opinion also corresponds very likely to the faith in the superior managerial capacity of the private sector.[25] Moreover, the majority think that the development of the intervention of the private sector will improve transparency, accountability and monitoring. Of course we are dealing here with opinions based more upon faith than on empirical evidence. In fact, when asked during the face-to-face interviews to provide empirical evidence sustaining their opinions, the great majority could not refer to real cases of success of PPPs. Of course this finding does not mean that in reality PPPs cannot match these opinions. It simply shows that the majority of our respondents have faith in the beneficial outcomes of more private sector intervention, although this should be confirmed by empirical research, which at the moment of our inquiry was very limited or simply not available.

The consequence is that in evaluating the actual chances of success of PPPs in our countries, we will have to go back to empirical evidence available in developed countries, as well as in in-transition countries where research has been already conducted. We will do this in the last part of our conclusion.

Little information was provided by our respondents on the question of "who will pay in the end," whereas they spent more time explaining the lack of public money, which, combined with the urgency of either upgrading the existing services or building new ones, appears to be the main argument in favour of PPPs. This opinion is further reinforced by the scant confidence our respondents have in the expertise of the public authorities (especially at the local level) and the inefficiencies of the bureaucracy. To this some respondents added the resistance of vested interests at all levels, and the difficulties in managing the relations between the central and local authorities. These final difficulties are also considered by some people, especially in Russia, as some of the major obstacles encountered when defining a governmental development strategy in which to insert the contribution of PPPs. Although we know that the same problems also exist in China, nobody mentioned the management of centre-periphery relationships as one of the major obstacles to the definition of Chinese development strategy.

The Main Reason in Favour of PPPs

Therefore, the main reason in favour of PPPs seems to be the urgency in providing or upgrading infrastructure and services, and in this respect the dominant opinion is that only the private sector can provide the huge amount of investment needed. If the availability of domestic private money is limited, the only way out is to favour foreign private investment. And this is valid also for countries like China and Poland, where the government and some domestic private investors begin to be able to invest considerable amounts of money, not only in their countries but also abroad. Nevertheless, the problem is that, according to a majority of respondents, the task is so big that private money coming from abroad is necessary at least as a complement to public investment. And this favours PPPs where the public and the private sectors share the financial investment and risks. One of the major consequences of this situation, however, is that it poses a strategic dilemma for the governments concerned, to the point that they have imposed some limits on foreign investments in domains they have qualified as strategic. These concern mainly the defence industry, natural resources, and mass media.[26]

Public Institutions for Sustaining the Implementation of PPPs

Finally, some respondents complained about the lack of a centralized unit in charge of defining a consistent policy on PPPs, and also being able to provide expertise to local government. This poses again the problem of the necessity of improving the expertise of public authorities at all levels, for the efficient management of the complexities of PPPs.[27] On the contrary, the existence of an Investment Fund is considered as a positive institutional and financial instrument favouring the implementation of PPPs, as in the case for Russia. Moreover, several Russian respondents considered as a positive evolution the increasing number of local initiatives to establish PPPs, even if some expressed the fear that this will further complicate the relationships between local and central authorities.

The Contextual Level

The decisions taken about the possibility of introducing PPPs will be conditioned by a series of factors we have regrouped under the heading of "contextual conditions," and first of all the state and trends of the economy.

The Situation and the Development of the National Economy

Here we will take into consideration the national economy, whereas the global economy will be dealt with in conjunction with the role of international organizations. Many respondents consider that stagnating economy, economic slowdowns, an immature banking system, problematic financial markets are all factors that render the implementation of PPPs difficult if not impossible. The major characteristics of the domestic economy favourable to the development of PPPs have been identified by a majority of respondents in the four countries: a robust economic development in a stable environment driving to a growing consumer market, an ongoing process of industrialization and urbanization (this being particularly important in China), the support of a robust banking system willing to lend money to private investors (and not only to big conglomerates but also to small and medium size investors).[28]

All these conditions mentioned so far sound rather positive *per se*. But there are some other conditions, that are clearly negative, that will, because of their negative character, favour the choice of PPPs: these are the persistence of public deficits and the consequent increase of public dept, that is most of the time considered in the neo-liberal theory of public finance as to be avoided at all costs (and often without regard to the nature—current consumption or investment—of the expenses that led to public debt). If, moreover, the prevailing opinion is that taxes should not be increased because they will discourage domestic demand and investments, this situation will be considered as proof of the lack of public money we referred to above, and therefore this will reinforce the option in favour of PPPs.

The Globalization of Information and the State of Domestic Infrastructure

Second, as we have already said when examining the role of public opinion, the actual state of public services and infrastructure will influence the attitudes of both political leaders and the citizens. Even if our research has not been designed to deal with public opinion specifically, it is nevertheless necessary to introduce it in this conclusion, as it is a direct result of the globalization of communication. This certainly has an impact on the way the population of in-transition countries evaluate their living conditions compared to what they know about the more developed countries. It is a plausible hypothesis that on this evaluation they address demands to their elites for the improvement of their living conditions, of which infrastructures and public services are a fundamental component.

The importance of the globalization of information for our research has been widely recognized because information technology revolution has considerably reduced the distance between nations and people. Contrary to the first globalization of the XIX century (where capital and labour mobility was not less important than now) the present globalization has this distinctive feature: it places practically all the people, even those living in the most remote places of the developing and transition countries, in a position to read, hear and see what is going on in the most developed part of the world: the high standard of living, the facilities in transportation (public and private) and in housing, with all the modern facilities such as current cold and hot water, central heating, sanitary in-house equipment, modern kitchen, domestic apparels; nice clothing, plenty of food and beverages, decent (if not generous) safety nets, and even luxury products. It is not surprising that these people are wanting all these material goods and services, and the sooner the better. It is only thanks to the ability of their national government if they can accept to limit to a reasonable level the desire to satisfy all these needs. But even so, the pressure on the national and local governments cannot be ignored by the leadership. Finally, we may add that this factor, linked to the globalization of information, is reinforcing the need for services improvement of infrastructure available in transition countries, because, as we mentioned before, the latter are generally of a mediocre quality and quantity.[29] And in the framework of this vast domain of unsatisfied needs, the state of the domestic infrastructure, as it is perceived and evaluated by both the population and the political elite, constitutes the third factor of the contextual level.

The Impact of the Global Economy and International Organizations

The impact of two interrelated factors, the global economy and international organizations, constitutes two additional conditions that favour the implementation of PPPs. As we already mentioned in Chapter 2, since the beginning of the 80' a vast movement of trade liberalization (the origins of which can be traced back to the immediate period after the second world war) occurred at the international level, based upon the revival of liberalism (later labelled neo-liberalism) of which the most operational consequences have been the "Washington consensus" and the "New Public Management." Based upon neo-classical economy and public choice theory this movement has favoured a total liberalization of the world economy (including liberalization and deregulation of financial markets), as well as the privatization or semi-privatization of large sectors of the national economies (including both hard and soft infrastructures). This trend has been powerfully supported not only by the most advanced nations (led by the US and later by the European Union) but also, and may be more significantly, by global international organizations dominated by these countries, such as the World Bank, the International Monetary Fund, the World Trade Organization and the OECD. Neo-liberalism has thus become the admitted (and imposed) orthodoxy for organizing the global economy and for boosting economic and social development in both developing and transition countries. It is in this context that the latter have been forced to implement structural reforms based upon neo-liberal orthodoxy in exchange of loans from the IMF and other organization, international and national. This meant basically two sets of measures: (1) opening their national economy to the world, and (2) privatizing large segments of their economy, including both hard and soft infrastructures. This of course has reduced the choice of these countries as to what would be the better strategy for boosting their development. As the negative consequences of these events are well documented, it is only necessary in the context of this research to direct the reader to the scientific literature that has criticized the neo-liberal movement both on its theoretical flaws and its material consequences, for both developed and transition countries.[30]

The consequences of this movement can be seen on our four countries. During the first phase of its transition to market economy Russia has followed almost literally the advice, prescriptions and guidance of neo-liberal experts, with the consequences we know. But the fact of not being totally imbedded into the global economy (Russia is not a member of the WTO) has facilitated the transition to the leadership style and the economic development initiated under the administration of President Putin. This has in part reversed some of the neo-liberal trends of the Eltsin era, and has given more autonomy to the developmental strategy of Russia.

Poland has also experienced a shock-therapy implemented from January 1st, 1990. Prepared by a commission led by the economist and then Prime Minister Leszek Balcerowicz (and with the support of some world famous economists, such as Jeffrey Sachs), the Polish shock-therapy was as well of clear neo-liberalist inspiration, and was approved by the IMF and the World Bank. Its effects are still today controversial; it is generally admitted that in the short term the "Balcerowicz plan" provoked both a sharp rise of inflation and unemployment, and a dramatic fall of the economic growth.[31] However, for the long term, it is generally considered that the shock-therapy has been beneficial to the Polish economy.

Moreover, contrary to the Russian case, Poland and Ukraine have been attracted by the European Union that, as we have already mentioned, has posed some clear conditions for accession. These include the implementation of the features of liberal democracy and market economy, and the introduction in their institutional order of the so-called "acquis communautaire" of which many policies are of a clear neo-liberal character. Moreover, as Olivier Brenninkmeijer has developed in Chapter 3, the EU has taken many initiatives and adopted many regulations in favour of PPPs. There are therefore more prospects for developing PPPs in Poland and Ukraine (especially when it has complied with all the EU requirements for membership). The case of China is at the same time different and similar. Different because China has on its own initiative considered at the end of the 1970s that by opening its economy to the world, it would put some additional pressure on Chinese enterprises (both SOEs, private and semi-private) thus forcing them to improve their efficiency. The idea of introducing competition is perfectly in line with liberal economic theory, but the decision is taken independently of external pressure. The similarity becomes apparent after China's accession to WTO, as now it has to comply with the rule of WTO. Russia will be in a similar situation when it will access to WTO. Nevertheless we know from experience that countries that face difficulties in their economy because of the opening of their national market, can take measures to protect the domestic sectors, be it in accordance of WTO regulations or even in contradiction with them.

The Impact of the Geographical Situation

The geographical situation is another set of factors that can condition the decisions countries may take in favour of PPPs. Although this is not apparent in all our four countries,[32] the case of Ukraine is a good example in this context. As Tatiana Chernyavskaya and Oleg Gurynenko explain in Chapter 7 quoting an assessment by the Economist Intelligence Unit, the situation of Ukraine as a potential gateway between central Europe and other members of the Commonwealth of Independent States (CSI) may be a factor leading its government to develop the transportation infrastructure that is presently underdeveloped. But as the country lacks the capital needed for this endeavour, the option in favour of PPPs (and very likely with foreign investment) becomes a plausible one.

The Impact of Special Events

At the beginning of this concluding chapter we have already mentioned the dramatic events that led to the introduction of market mechanism in our four countries, namely the collapse of the Soviet Union and the Chinese Cultural Revolution. These have been events we may qualify as a dramatic "big bang" without which the changes introduced in these countries would have been very difficult to implement, as Gorbachev's reforms have shown, or as in China before 1978, in spite of opinions expressed in favour of reforms within the Chinese leadership before the Cultural Revolution.

In the following paragraphs we will refer instead to less dramatic events that may occur after the "big bang," but that can (in conjunction with other factors) favour PPPs. During our research we came across two important events that can be placed under this category: the Olympic Games attributed to Beijing for 2008, and the European Football Championship attributed to Poland and Ukraine for 2012. Given the increasing interest and enthusiasm of the population of practically all the countries for events like these, it is expected, on one hand, that a huge amount of people attend these events and on the other hand, that athletes and their federations require modern sport infrastructure. Therefore stadium must be upgraded or built anew, roads, railways, airports, hotels and other facilities must be built or upgraded. There are nevertheless some differences in the capacity of these countries to take advantage of these events for the development of PPPs. For China the Olympic Games of 2008 have represented a good opportunity for developing sport infrastructure: it seems that the construction of the sport facilities has been realized through PPP for at least 30% of the constructions. As for the European Football Championship, there is an important difference between Poland and Ukraine. Whereas in Poland the institutional arrangements set up for favouring the implementation of PPPs (se Chapter 5) seems to be on the right way for providing at least part of the infrastructure by PPPs, in Ukraine some difficulties have arisen recently to the point that some people fear that Ukraine may not be able to organize its part of the event.[33]

The Operational Level

It is not surprising that the operational level as it is presented by our respondents is quite similar to the one described by Olivier Brenninkmeijer in Chapter 3 for Western countries. This is probably due to the fact that institutional arrangements like PPPs, that are very closely linked to the logic of market economy, need everywhere the same technical conditions to produce the expected results, i.e. reduction of cost for a given output (or value for money), improvement of quality, technical and managerial innovation, timely delivery of the service or infrastructure agreed upon in the contract, as well as all the related conditions that will make these outputs possible, such as competition (at least for the market, if not in the market), transparency, accountability, evaluation of performance (or performance management) and monitoring. It is therefore not surprising that the majority of our respondents have mentioned many of, if not all these technical conditions, that should make the implementation of PPPs a success. The general and combined role of these conditions is to create a secure institutional, legal, and political environment favourable to the development of private activities, of which PPPs are a special case. Some of our respondents also mentioned conditions that should protect the public, and more particularly people belonging to vulnerable groups, who may not be in a position to have access to the service provided by PPPs, if access would be conditional upon the payment of a fee these people could not afford to pay.

Differences in the opinions expressed by respondents in our four countries are not very important, especially if we remind that our respondents have not been chosen by a random sampling procedure.[34] Small differences cannot therefore be considered as significative, and we will therefore take in consideration much more the similarities than the differences.[35] Now, it just happens that many of these conditions have in common a very important characteristic: they are closely linked to the concept of the rule of law. Here of course one could conclude that this is the proof of the validity of the convergence thesis. Our research brings an additional argument to this thesis, if we take into consideration Poland, Ukraine and Russia (who are clearly moving towards the Western legal system based upon the rule of law (even if Russia is moving more slowly according to some Western critics), but not so much if we take China. For this country, the thesis is still true if we take this demonstration in a very general sense, by referring more to the objective (security) than to the actual means for realizing security (Western legal systems), but not necessarily if we refer to the means. If we explore this path, we could formulate the hypothesis that there may be alternative legal systems, different to the Western ones, which can also satisfy the objective of security. In fact, research is going on in several academic institutions to determine whether there exist non-liberal variants of the rule of law. Randall Peerenboom adds another dimension which is essential for in-transition countries, i.e. transition is more an historical process than a state as it is defined by Western standards. From this perspective we could say that China is more in transition than for example Poland. But in transition towards what? Peeremboom suggests that if the Chinese transition is certainly leading the country towards a more prosperous society, with an enlargement of human rights, and a better balance between efficiency and equity, we must not forget that "different normative systems and social-political philosophies will lead to different thick conceptions of rule of law"[36] and that "when laws are at odds with the dominant values they are rarely implemented."[37]

Bearing this in mind, what are the main technical conditions mentioned by our respondents? Let us mention them without entering into technical consideration that are in any case outside the scope of our research, and for whom there exist already a vast and serious literature. Moreover, they have been described with a sufficient level of precision in Chapter 3 by Olivier Brenninkmeijer.

Law and Regulations

First of all there should be rules protecting private property, fair compensation in case of nationalization, possibility of repatriation of profits for foreign investors. Second there should be a fair, clear and transparent tendering procedure, assuring competition, and a competent and fair evaluation of the proposals. Moreover there should be measures for avoiding corruption, and this may necessitate the creation of an independent institution either for managing the tendering procedure or at least for supervising it. In any case it is suggested that this task should be performed by a body composed of several persons representing the major stakeholders. And the need for procedures for arbitration and mediation has also been considered by many as a necessity in case problems may occur. Technical competence is in any case a must for managing these different aspects and phases of the adoption and implementation of PPPs: the people representing the public authorities should be capable of mastering all the technical and legal aspects implied in the evaluation of the tendering procedure.

In this context, the most negative aspects at the operational level put forward by our respondents in the four transition countries concern lack of a sufficiently developed administrative and legal framework, the lack of supervision, the lack of competition (related to the complexity of the procedure and/or to the lack of supervision), the confusion of roles between central and local authorities (especially in Russia and China), frequent changes in government (that is of course at the conjunction between politics and administration, and has been put forward in Poland, and is certainly also an important factor in Ukraine after the "Orange revolution"), the impossibility for local government to issue bonds (in China).[38]

To solve theses problems from a technical point of view, the experience accumulated in Western countries could be useful, if it is carefully examined in light of the local conditions of the strategic and contextual levels. The solution of the problems mentioned above is linked to the definition of the formal rules of the game, the other rules are related to the strategic level and can only be determined by constitutional rules (that should pose some general and fundamental principles) those related to the contextual level being largely outside the reach of formal legislation. The generally accepted Western rule of legislative technique is that the rules of the game should be defined with the necessary clarity and precision. Lack of clarity and complexity has been mentioned by many of our respondents. Maybe even more important is the lack of legal instruments subordinate to laws that can bring more precision and legal security to the process, as it has been put forward by Russian respondents. On the contrary, some Polish people have complained about the excessive rigid legal apparatus that makes the process too long and complicated.

In any case there will remain at least the following dilemma, the solution of which could be rather difficult as it points inevitably towards a trade-off. This dilemma concerns the level of precision of the legal rules governing the procedures. If the legislation is composed of general principles and rules, this could lead to dysfunctions and eventually to sub-optimal outcomes, or even to corruption. If the rule is too precise, this could make the process too long and complicated and this could discourage potential private partners. The choice is not an easy one. If corruption practices have been numerous in the past, a more strict legislation would be advisable. Here we can see the importance of the adequacy of formal instruments to the cultural values and habits that prevail in all the countries. Countries like Poland, with a high degree of convergence with the Western way of managing the public sector and the relationship between State and economy, may very well adopt the formal framework of the West. Other countries may be advised to look for functional equivalents better adapted to their culture, without forgetting that the goal is to sustain economic development so that it can improve the attainment of four interdependent values: the economic use of resources for producing goods and services (economic efficiency) in ways that safeguard resources for future generations (sustainability), while assuring a fair distribution of the wealth thus created (equity), and a secure national and international environment without which the other values can not be realized. And this is what we are going to examine in the last part of this conclusion: to what extent can PPPs allow a transition country to realize all or at least one of the four values without simultaneously hampering the others?

THE CONTRIBUTION OF PPPS TO EFFICIENCY, SUSTAINABILITY, EQUITY AND SECURITY

In the preceding paragraphs of this conclusion we have seen that it has been quite easy to identify with precision the varied and many strategic, contextual, and operational conditions favourable to the adoption and implementation of PPPs in our four transition countries. Moreover, these findings are confirmed by what we know in Western countries, especially with regard to the contextual and operational conditions (as discussed in Chapter 3). On the contrary, determining to what extent PPPs in these countries can improve, and in fact have improved efficiency, sustainability, equity and security has been a more difficult task. The main reason is that, as we have noted more than once, experience with PPPs in these countries is rather recent, and therefore empirical evidence is at best scarce and/or balanced, at worse inexistent. Moreover, many of our respondents admitted a low level of knowledge about PPPs in general, i.e. both for their country and abroad.

Consequently, we are left with the opinions of our respondents and with the available empirical evidence from Western and other transition countries. When discussing the four prior decisions in favour or against PPPs, we have already mentioned that the great majority of our respondents have been unable to sustain their faith in the superiority of private provision of services and infrastructures by referring to empirical evidence; and this is true not only as regards economic efficiency (or value for money) but also as regards equity, sustainable development, and security. Of course this does not mean that PPPs cannot in fact realize one or several of these four values, there being empirical evidence (see Chapter 3) that in some cases PPPs have indeed delivered satisfactory results in both Western and transition countries. But, as at the same time there is empirical evidence to the contrary, the only conclusion we can draw from our interviews in these countries is that our respondents' opinions are based upon a theoretical (or even an ideological) bias in favour of PPPs. Moreover, as we have already mentioned, this bias is sustained by the too often poor performance (both in quality and quantity) of public services and infrastructures provided by the State in the framework of the former command economy. Of course, this poor performance has often been counterbalanced by equitable access, and this may have played against PPPs, at least until information about the better performance of public infrastructure and services in the West became widely available in transition countries. As we have already noted, quasi universal access to information in transition countries about the quality of services in the West very likely explains today the desire of people in these countries to have access to services of better quality and quantity based on the Western model, even if quality in the West is in some cases counterbalanced by inequitable access, one of the most striking cases being medical care. But here again, we are dealing with opinions more than with considerations sustained by empirical evidence.

As for the empirical evidence available for Western and transition countries, we will refer the reader to what we have already said in Chapters 2 and 3 and in the first part of this conclusion. We will simply add some considerations developed in the chapters on our four countries and in the last

OECD book on PPPs[39] and we will summarize the main recommendations we can address to the policy-makers of these countries, not forgetting, however, that the suitability of these recommendations should be evaluated in the framework of the domestic conditions prevailing both at the centre and at the periphery. As these conditions are based on the fundamental values and habits prevailing in these countries, deciding in favour of PPPs will therefore necessitate some political arbitration. It would therefore be pretentious on our part to consider our recommendations as having a prescriptive or normative "scientific" character, as this task will of course be performed by the political leadership of the countries concerned.

Opinions About the Impact of PPPs in the Four Countries

Overall, we can say that the majority of our respondents expressed a favourable opinion on the capacity of PPPs to perform better than the State for the provision of infrastructure and services practically on each criterion: economic efficiency, sustainability of economic development, equity and security. This is also true for the more detailed and practical dimensions of PPPs like transparency, accountability, monitoring, and limitation of corruption. But, as we have already mentioned, only a very few of them could sustain their opinion by providing empirical evidence based upon positive experiences gained in the West or in their own country. Of course some doubts and even negative opinions have also been put forward, more often by NGOs and University people having empirical knowledge of both success and failures of PPPs, but also by public officials of our transition countries.[40] The doubts or negative opinions of the latter may be explained by their ideological attachment to the former planned economy, by the persistence of vested interests (as some members of the old nomenklatura still hold today official positions both at the central and local levels) or by a genuine concern about the negative impact PPPs may have upon equitable access to public services in some domains like health and education.

We can conclude that in our four countries there is an overall favourable actors' environment where the ideas of implementing PPPs as a viable alternative for providing infrastructure and social services may gain the support of a majority of stakeholders. Nevertheless, and in spite of the overall positive picture, it is worth noting that even if the doubts and negative opinions have been generally put forward by a minority of respondents, they correspond to important practical difficulties and/or the intrinsic theoretical weaknesses of PPPs dealt with in the scientific literature. Moreover, the last publication by the OECD, that became available at the time we were writing the conclusion to our report, very clearly constitute a powerful caveat to all those who may be tempted to implement PPPs in a variety of domains mainly on ideological grounds, without taking the time, and effort, to consider the difficulties and limits of this way of providing public services and infrastructures.[41] Moreover, OECD warns that "PPPs should not be seen as a mechanism that will largely replace public procurement in the future.[42] This report, that concludes several years of research, international meetings and seminars organised by OECD with members and non-members, is a valuable complement to our research findings; we will try to take advantage of its conclusions and combine it with empirical and theoretical evidence available elsewhere in the scientific literature.[43]

Evidence from Empirical Research

Let us note first of all that the 2008 OECD report concedes that the move of Governments to rely increasingly on the market for the provision of public services "has been made both for ideological reasons and in the pursuit of value for money (...) Public-private partnerships are part of this trend."[44] The aim of OECD is "to provide governments with a toolkit of issues to be explored and resolved from a public governance perspective before engaging in a PPP project."[45] It further concedes that "the mere participation of the private sector in the delivery of the service is not sufficient to ensure improvement in service delivery and efficiency."[46] But OECD remains a strong defender and believer in the superiority of the private sector, as this sentence is preceded by the assertion that the "private sector participation in PPPs frequently contributes to higher levels of efficiency"[47] and in the belief of the superiority of the management skills of the private sector.[48] Moreover, the whole treatment of the conditions under which PPPs will yield the expected results (i.e. basically value for money, that OECD considers as the primary objective of PPP) very clearly places the burden for the viability of PPPs on market or quasi market mechanisms, namely competition for the market during the bidding phase, and contestability after the contract has been signed.

This permanent, and, we must recognize, consistent faith of the OECD in market mechanisms, even when markets very clearly do not exist, presents a remarkable similarity with the position of the International Monetary Fund mentioned by Joseph Stiglitz and associates in their last book about capital market liberalization: even if IMF experts recognize that capital market liberalization has not led to growth and efficiency, they persist in considering that it "should," and qualify as "anomalous" the empirical findings that prove that liberalization does not bring the benefits promised. And Stiglitz and associates conclude that "the basic problem is that their 'theory' (i.e. orthodox neoclassical theory) is predicated on perfect capital markets (...). Yet it has long been recognized that such assumptions are also entirely unrealistic."[49]

Moreover little is said in the 2008 OECD report about the impact of PPPs on equity[50] and security[51], and nothing about the impact of PPPs on sustainable development, nor on the place PPPs may take within the national development strategies. It is true that transaction costs are mentioned at least five times, but without dealing satisfactorily, in our opinion, with the problems of their identification and measurement of their size; in view of the fact that efficiency (value for money) is for the OECD the primary objective of PPP design and transaction cost may be quite large, their calculation should become of paramount importance for deciding whether PPPs are better than traditional procurement.[52] Without a proper and precise methodology for calculating transaction costs, OECD is forced to place great faith in the virtues of market (and more often of quasi market) mechanisms to reduce these costs.[53]

The methodological problems with transaction costs will become even more important when linked to the fact that the market for PPPs is generally very limited both on the supply and the demand side.[54] Let us remind the reader that for OECD "competition remains the main driver of value for money."[55] But OECD is forced to concede that most of the time there is only a limited number of bidders that, moreover, may start exhibiting oligopolistic behaviour, and that, on the buying side, the market for a particular service may be dominated by a monopsonist (the government). In order to escape from this uncomfortable situation in such a setting, OECD proposes to use the Public Sector Comparator (PSC): "whether or not the price established in such a setting will ensure value for money cannot be determined *a priori*, which explains why the existence of a thin market may require the use of a Public Sector Comparator (PSC). The public sector comparator does not replace or simulate the effect of competition in a thin market; competition remains the main driver of value for money. However, the PSC, in effect, is used to establish whether or not the oligopolistic structure of the market does not undermine the pursuit of value for money."[56]

It is therefore clear that OECD considers PSC as a second best, and formulates the hope that "in time, a large number of awarded contracts may yield the details necessary to compile a database that in turn can be used to compile benchmarks of best practice. Thus, with higher levels of competition, the need to have a public sector comparator may be reduced, but only if reliable best practice benchmarks have been created on the basis of past data. Therefore, in countries that are currently still setting up PPP frameworks and in which the number of PPP contracts has not been extensive, such a database and the resulting benchmarks do not exist. In the absence of benchmarks, the PSC may again be a valuable tool to ascertain value for money, at least until such time as the government has collected enough information with which to compile reliable benchmarks."[57] And this may be an interesting alternative for our transition countries.

Unfortunately, OECD recognizes that the implementation of PSC presents such a great number of major difficulties and limits that one can at least express some doubts about the effectiveness of this device to help governments to measure with the necessary precision the comparative value for money of PPP and traditional public procurement.[58] We remind the reader that value for money is, according to OECD, the primary objective of PPPs.[59] Now, in the absence of a robust methodology for evaluating the difference in efficiency between the provision of services by PPP or the traditional method, political and ideological considerations may be the decisive criteria for deciding, especially if the difference is rather small.

In spite of these remarks, our analysis of the 2008 OECD report should not be considered as a total rejection of the OECD approach to PPPs, but it simply stresses the differences between this report and our research, especially in regard to transition countries: the goal of the OECD report is clearly to find means for building viable PPPs and to determine in what environment and sectors this is possible.[60] Our goal is to determine under what conditions PPPs can improve in-transition countries at least one of the following values without damaging the others, i.e. economic efficiency, sustainable development, equity and security.

Having said that, it is a pity that the OECD exclusively focuses its attention and efforts in seeking means for discovering if, when, and how PPPs bring more value for money than the traditional public provision, and moreover does not even mention either the possibility of improving State provision of public services (be it through traditional public procurement or SOEs) or the possibility of using Public-Public Partnership as an alternative to PPPs.[61]

With these limitations in mind, we consider that the 2008 OECD report is a remarkable document that will certainly not only fuel the debate on PPPs and traditional procurement, but also constitute a very useful guideline for governments and private investors, if it will be remembered that many aspects of the methodology of PPPs design and implementation must be further tested and improved, and that, as the OECD report concedes, the questions whether there should be public or private provision of services that are traditionally provided by the public sector "involve economic and political choices that depend on the relative efficiency of public services in a given country, on the potential availability of capital, and on the social consensus about acceptable ways of delivering certain services. The public and social acceptability of such partnerships is often a key factor."[62]

Moreover, and more interesting for us, the OECD report confirms many of the conclusions of our research and puts forward an idea that complements very well our "four prior decisions approach" (to be discussed hereafter), by introducing the concept of affordability, that constitute together with value for money the two "benchmarks for PPP viability. In principle, affordability is about whether or not a project falls within the intertemporal budget constraint of the government. If it does not, then the project is unaffordable."[63]

Apart from the central place that market mechanisms take within the OECD approach and their consequences we have commented above, there are some remarkable similarities with our own approach (presented in Chapter 2) and our own findings (Chapters 3 to 8) especially at the operational level (see Figure 9.1 and comments above). In order to best appreciate these similarities, we will briefly comment upon the OECD approach on the basis of Figure 9.2, we have especially constructed for this purpose. Understandably, is not possible, nor necessary, to present in detail the OECD approach in this conclusion, but we will briefly comment upon some of its features that are controversial or that add something new and valuable to our own approach.

First of all, there should be a strong political leadership (point 1 in Figure 9.2) showing a high political commitment (point 2) in favour of finding the best way of providing public services and infrastructures. This political will must be complemented by a high degree of expertise (point 3), necessary for establishing a suitable governance framework (point 4). For deciding between traditional procurement and PPP it is necessary to take into consideration a certain number of criteria (point 5), and first of all the two benchmarks for PPP viability, i.e. value for money (or efficiency) and affordability. Value for money is further linked to the concepts of competition and risk transfer. Given the "market approach" of the OECD, it is not surprising, as we have already noted, that competition is considered as a necessary condition both during the bidding phase and after the contract is signed (here competition is designated by the concept of contestability).

For risk sharing OECD "argues that sufficient transfer of risk to the private partner is necessary to ensure efficiency and value for money.[64] For the transfer of risk to be the most effective, risk must also be transferred to the party best able to carry it. By defining risk as the probability that the actual outcome (i.e. sales, costs and profits) will deviate from the expected outcome (...) the book argues that efficiency depends on a sufficient transfer of endogenous risk to the private partner. The book also refines the principle that risk should be transferred to the party best able to carry it, by clarifying that 'best able to carry it' means the party who can carry the risk at least cost, be it the government or the private partner."[65]

As said before, affordability is about whether or not a project falls within the intertemporal budget constraint of the government. If it does not, then the project is unaffordable. The great advantage of this concept is that it definitely discredits the fallacious belief of some governments that "if a project is off the government books, it becomes more affordable."[66] This concept is an excellent complement to our "four prior decisions approach" presented in Chapter 2. The four prior decisions concerned the necessity to evaluate first the urgency of providing or of upgrading a service, taking into consideration the strength of the demand from the population; second, the

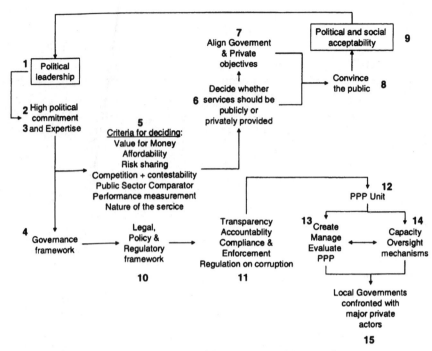

Figure 9.2.   A Simplified Presentation of the 2008 OECD Approach to PPPs*

*Our interpretation of the approach presented in OECD, *Public-Private Partnerships. In Pursuit of Risk Sharing and Value for Money*, Paris, 2008.

efficiency of PPP compared to State provision; third, and related to the second decision, whether the private sector is able to provide a more effective and efficient managerial capacity; and fourth who will in the end pay for the service. In relation to this fourth decision our discussion commenced by putting forward a truism, i.e. that money must come from somewhere, meaning by this that no cheap a solution can come out of a poor or inexistent service. It must be built or refurbished and someone has to pay for it. We went on to say that if private companies are the only investor in a PPP, money will have to come from consumers, and as this will have to cover production costs (including profits) this may pose some problems for equitable access. If on the contrary, the money comes from the government (either for PPPs totally or partially funded by public money)[67] this may pose problems of high taxation (that may be supported by companies and/or tax-payers), increasing public debt, reduced efficiency and quality of the service provided. But this discussion did not make it clear that even if a positive answer could be given to the four questions, there could still be a major problem: the service could not be affordable because neither a single actor nor a combination of actors could sustain its cost.

The concept of affordability further completes and clarifies this discussion, at least inasmuch as it concerns the financial capacity of the government. Moreover, the OECD report warns against the use of PPP as a means to escape from the obligation of introducing expenses into the annual budget. With very good reasons OECD considers that this solution is not acceptable as it does not comply with the idea that expenses for the project should fall within the intertemporal budget constraint of the government. Finally, the concept of affordability is quite useful for another reason: we remember that the main reasons given by our respondents in favour of PPPs was the urgency of providing or upgrading services and infrastructures in the absence of sufficient governmental financial means. Little attention was given to the "who will pay in the end" questions, nor to the related questions of fiscal policy. Now the concept of affordability shows that this motivation is not valid on all occasions: it is valid only if the expenses of PPPs fall into the intertemporal budget constraints of the government.

These considerations put an additional burden on the political leadership: i.e. it has to explain to the citizens that the desirability of better services and infrastructures is closely linked to the financial capacity of the State, and this in turn depends on the country's economic development. So we are driven back to one of the ideas presented in Chapter 2: in case of insufficient financial means for rapidly providing new or upgraded infrastructures (i.e., in the language of OECD, in case of lack of affordability), the government should instead set up the public policies aimed at boosting economic development instead of embarking itself and the country on the dangerous road of persistent public deficits and public debt. In these circumstances, only this strategy can favour the development of a robust economy in which the governmental fiscal policy can obtain the financial means necessary for co-financing PPPs and/or for providing sufficient guaranties to the potential private partners. As we have already said, the other guaranties are to be assured by the establishment of a robust legal system. This discussion about affordability also shows that it would be foolish to expect that potential private partners would be willing to support alone the financial risk. In the domain of economic development and the development of public services there is clearly no free lunch.[68]

Two other factors are considered by OECD as criteria for evaluating PPPs: performance measurements and the so-called Public Sector Comparator, two criteria closely linked together, that cover a number of sub-criteria to be used for evaluating, both *ex-ante* and *ex-post*, the superiority of PPP compared to the traditional State procurement.[69]

In the process of deciding, on the basis of the above-mentioned criteria, whether services should be publicly or privately provided (point 6 in Figure 9.2), the Government should also find the means of aligning public and private objectives (point 7) and this will enable it to convince the public that it has made a "good" decision (point 8); if it succeeds in doing so, then it will have obtained political and social acceptability (point 9), and will be able to count on public support during the implementation phase, provided of course, may we add, that it delivers satisfactory results.

Going back now to point 4 of Figure 9.2 (Governance framework) the OECD 2008 report further specifies that a sound political, legal, and regulatory framework should be established (point 10) based upon the principles (point 11) of transparency, accountability, compliance and enforcement, and capable of limiting (and possibly eradicating) corruption. In order to better implement the governance framework for PPPs it is further strongly suggested to set up a PPPs Unit (point 12) whose role is on one side to help the government to create, manage, evaluate PPPs (point 13) and on the other side to increase the overall capacity of the Government, and more particularly its oversight mechanisms (point 14). The latter are more especially needed to help the local governments that are confronted with major private actors (point 15).

Combining the results of our research and the conclusions of the OECD 2008 report, we may conclude by formulating some general recommendations and caveats. But first of all let us concede that it is impossible to provide a fully rational methodology for making decisions about the provision of infrastructures and services in transition countries that simultaneously improve efficiency, sustainability, equity and security, or that just improve one of these values without damaging the others. As Nobel Prize winner Herbert Simon has demonstrated years ago, only limited rational decisions are possible in situations of incomplete information.[70] Decisions are in fact a bet on the future. As it would be foolish not to take advantage of the information and robust methodologies available at the time of decision (provided of course that their cost does not exceed a reasonable proportion of the expected benefits) it would equally be foolish (and perhaps also immoral) to pretend that we possess the methodology for making totally rational decisions. The case of infrastructure and services in transition countries (but the same is true for any country) is a good case in point. In our opinion the major determinant of decisions for arriving at outcomes satisfying (even if not optimising) the four values, is the vision and will of the leadership of the countries concerned. All the four values are necessary for the sound development of a society: efficiency in order not to waste precious resources (both natural and human), sustainability so as not to damage the living conditions of future generations (and again, both for the human and the natural environment), security for assuring the peaceful and secure environment necessary for the development of all societal activities, and finally equity is necessary not only to avoid injustice (which is necessarily based upon moral norms that not everybody may share) but also to assure the national cohesion without which the peaceful development of society would most likely be in danger. Any type of infrastructure and service (be it a PPP or any other form of organization), if not well conceived and managed, may very well contribute to damaging one value while contributing to improving one or several of the other four. A well-known case in point is an infrastructure contributing to economic efficiency but damaging the environment. It is up to the political authorities to set up infrastructures (either through PPPs or the traditional method) so that the four values are safeguarded at least in the long term. On the basis of scientific evidence (drawn from both the natural and the social sciences) this is certainly possible today even in a situation of incomplete information. Only policies based upon blind ideology can favour solutions that damage efficiency, sustainability, security and equity. It is up to the political leadership of these countries to develop public services and infrastructures in such a way as to realize the four values to a reasonable level. And this will need much more than technical expertise. What is needed is a political philosophy of man and society based upon the respect of the four values.

In this (may we say: more reasonable) perspective, our research provides a checklist of conditions that the leadership of transition countries may consider when deciding how to provide services, knowing that both traditional procurement and PPPs may satisfy or not the four values. The main hypothesis put forward by our research that PPPs can provide citizens with costly infrastructure and public services that they might not otherwise have been able to afford, *under certain conditions* has been largely confirmed. These conditions have been presented in the chapters analysing the situation in our four countries, and have been summarized above in our comments of Figure 9.1 and complemented by available evidence from Western countries (Chapter 3). Without entering into too much detail:

1. *At the contextual level*:
   Conditions favouring the development of market economy (or at least some market mechanisms); these may be largely independent from the will of the political leadership of the countries concerned, but as noted hereafter in point 2.1 the leadership may take advantage of these contextual conditions.
2. *At the strategic level*:
   2.1. A strong political leadership at the top of the political system able to take advantage of favourable contextual conditions
   2.2. A strong political will at the top favourable to market economy (or at least to market mechanisms), able to maintain a stable social and political environment in which the economy can develop at a steady pace
   2.3. High expertise at the political and administrative level
   2.4. High political capacity to interpret the needs of the people

2.5. A strong leadership willing to associate people (civil society) to the design, implementation and evaluation (*ex ante* and *ex post)* of PPPs

2.6. High capacity of the political leadership to assure compliance and enforcement of policies, laws and regulations, especially at the local level (in general and with regard to PPPs)

2.7. High capacity of political leadership and its administration for evaluating the contribution of PPPs to economic efficiency, sustainability, security and equity

2.8. High expertise in the private sector (if private domestic money is not available for PPPs, foreign private money may be used; nevertheless care should be taken to develop in the meantime the capacity and expertise of domestic private actors)

2.9. A robust financial system (and for this it is also necessary to develop expertise) both in the public and private sectors, given the inter-dependence between private and public finance.

3. *At the operational level*:

3.1. Develop the legal system in order to achieve legal security, capable of sustaining the development of the economy, especially property and contract law. If necessary, establish special laws and regulations for PPPs (including a fair, transparent and clear bidding procedure)

3.2. Develop a culture of "rule of law," even if it does not necessarily correspond to the "rule of law" of liberal democracies

3.3. As a consequence introduce formal means to assure accountability and transparency in both the public and private sectors and limit or eradicate corruption

3.4. Set up a PPP Unit, eventually also an Investment Fund

3.5. Set up training programmes for politicians and civil servants in all the methodologies related to the mastering of PPPs; these should cover all the range of expertise needed (as mentioned or suggested in this research) and not only expertise based upon economic and managerial theories and models

3.6. Take decisions about the way of providing infrastructure and services on the basis of empirical evidence as far as possible

3.7 Take decisions that improve infrastructure and services in such a way as to obtain a reasonable balance between efficiency, sustainability, equitable access, and security, especially in the medium and long terms.

Finally, we would like to remind the reader that PPPs should be placed within the development strategy of transition countries. This has been recognized by the scientific literature[71] and by many of our respondents that favoured the creation of a PPP unit able to help the political leadership in creating, managing and evaluating PPPs.[72] Evaluation is essential of course, especially periodical monitoring, that will make it possible to eventually correct mistakes. It should nevertheless be noted that mistakes in the setting up of heavy infrastructures may be difficult to correct in the short run and may entail important costs. Hence the importance of *ex ante* evaluation, bearing in mind the difficulties we have discussed above. Moreover, the possibility to experiment before taking decisions for the entire country should not be neglected. This is maybe one of the greatest advantages of the strategy of the Chinese leadership that experiments locally different alternative means before deciding which one is the best for the entire country. Of course this is facilitated by the vast territory and the huge size of its population. But are the European Union and the USA such small entities? But this may be the beginning of another research suggested years ago by Randall Peeremboom and other academics and practitioners who try to discover and propose alternative modes of managing our societies.[73]

NOTES

1. Ivan Szelenyi, "A Theory of Transitions," *Modern China*, Vo. 34, N. 1, January 2008, pp. 165–175. For a critique see Sun Liping, "New Issues in the Field of the Sociology of Development," ibidem, pp. 88–113.

2. Szelanyi uses the following categorization: Eastern Europe includes Russia, Byelorussia and Ukraine; Central Europe refers to the former Czechoslovakia, Poland and Hungary. For the other countries he remarks that "Arguably, as they join the European Union they are shifting from Eastern to Central Europe," ibidem, p. 174, note 1.

3. Szelenyi founds this assertion on Lawrence King, "Foreign direct investment and transition", *European Journal of Sociology*, 41, 2, pp. 189–224.

4. Ibidem, p. 174.

5. Nevertheless it seems that the Chinese leadership is "coming back" to agriculture, as the last Party Congress of November 2007, has decided, among other things, to reinforce public policies (both in hard and soft infrastructures) aimed at reducing the gap between urban and rural areas.

6. Ibidem, pp. 170–171.

7. The cases of similar opinions between Poland and Western experts are the following: (1) corruption considered as an obstacle to PPPs (Western countries 45%, Poland 23%, whereas Russia 77%, Ukraine 80%, China 54%); (2) evaluation of public opinion towards PPPs (59,1% of people from both Western countries and 64% for Poland express a negative opinion, but only between 11,5% and 30% for the other countries that present moreover a higher percentage of neutral opinions, for more details see table 8 of Chapter 4); and (3) the existence of conflict resolution procedures for mediation: Western countries and Poland answered YES (73.3% and 63% respectively, only 4% for Russia, 28.6% for Ukraine and 33.3% for China).

This last result for China is interesting as it shows that in spite of the fact that the Chinese legal system is not (yet) similar to the Western one, a third nevertheless, at least in the opinion of the Chinese respondents, considers that it possesses conflict resolution procedures. We will come back later to the legal system of China.

8. This will be the case if the government plans to finance the repayment by taxation. If on the contrary it is willing to allow the private partner to make the users pay a fee (e.g. for a toll highway) then the present, and very likely also the future users, will have to pay a higher price than if the government would finance the service by borrowing on the market.

9. We have introduced and explained the importance of the distinction between hard and soft infrastructure in Chapter 2.

10. May we add that this is the case for example for China, if we pay credit to John Adams, Alistair Young, and Zhihong Wu, "Public private partnership in China, system, constraints and future perspectives," *International Journal of Public Sector Management*, Vol. 19, N. 4, 2006, p. 384–396. Although these authors admit that among the different types of Chinese PPPs "very few of these have been applied in the areas of health, education, social care or housing" (p. 390), they consider as valid the use of PPPs with arguments that we have already presented in Chapters 2 and 3: "the key argument for the use of PPP is that it will reduce the burden on taxpayers in the delivery of both capital and long-term service contract by the introduction of private capital, private expertise and competitive business practices to the provision of public services. These include education, housing, health care, transportation, social care and many other areas commonly associated with the public sector." (p. 385). On the other hand, they concede that "A more fundamental (and debatable) argument is that the private sector is better able to provide services at a higher level of efficiency and effectiveness than the public sector which is typically hindered by its bureaucratic, mechanistic and politicized methods of operation." (ibidem). See also note n. 70, Chapter 2.

11. For the domain of health see David Blumenthal and William Hsiao, "Privatization and its Discontents: The Evolving Chinese Health Care System," *New England Journal of Medicine*," September 2005, pp. 1165–1170. According to Jens Leth Hougaard, Lars Peter and Yi Yu, "The Chinese Health Care System. Structure, problems and Challenges," Department of Economics, Univ. of Copenhagen, *Discussion Papers*, January 2008, p. 31: "according to the survey of Chinese hospitals Holding Ltd, there are approximately 60 billion US dollars of funds in attention to China's medical market."

12. As I have pointed in Chapter 2, best Western practices cannot be transposed as they are in in-transition countries, without taking into consideration the characteristics of the local environment that may not be suitable for the transposition of Western practices.

13. It is perhaps now necessary to recall the famous criterion attributed to Deng Xiaoping: no matter that the cat is black or white, provided it catches the mice: *Selected Works of Deng Xiaoping* (Volume 1, p. 323), Beijing, People's Publishing House, 1994. We will not discuss here if the changes introduced into China after 1978 are based upon a change in the official ideology or not, as it is not a central point for this research. We deal with these aspects in the first chapter of "Reconciling State, Market, and Civil Society in China," op. cit.

14. We recall the results presented in Chapter 4: 73% of people from the public sector, 90% from the private sector, and 88% from NGOs consider that the lack of political will is a barrier for the implementation of PPPs.

15. This is due to the substantial differences amongst the various Chinese regions (3 or 4 according to the authors) which make it difficult to adopt a single model for the entire country. This is presently the case for the establishment of the new health and safety net system, for which China is considering two different systems for the rural and the urban areas.

16. For the differences amongst countries and sectors see Chapter 4.

17. David Chapman and Theo Cowdell, *New Public Sector Marketing*, London, Pitman Publishing (for Financial Times), 1998, Jennifer Lees-Marshment, *The Political Marketing Revolution. Transforming the Government of the UK*, Manchester, Manchester Univ. Press, 2004, Jennifer Bean and Lascelles Hussey, *Marketing Public Sector Services*, London, HB Publications, 1997.

18. Amongst people who answered our standardized questionnaire: 76% considers that PPPs can improve value for money (measured by the price-quality relation), 77% that they can keep cost, 83% that they can deliver in time, and 80% that they can improve the modernization of infrastructures.

19. We recall that a majority of people who answered our standardized questionnaire considered that corruption is an obstacle to PPPs in their country: 77% in Russia, 80% in Ukraine, 54% in China; if only 45% in Western countries and 23% in Poland consider that corruption is an obstacle to PPPs, this is very likely because they believe that corruption does not exist and/or has a very low impact in their country.

20. This is the case of Yi-min Lin, *Between Politics and Markets*, Cambridge, Cambridge Univ. Press, 2002, who nevertheless admits that these behaviours could result in inefficiencies, like over-production, and the artificial (i.e. non economic) survival of inefficient firms.

21. Angang Hu, *Economic and Social Transformation in China*, New York, Routledge, 2007, Ch. 11: "Corruption: an enormous black hole: public exposure of the economic cost of corruption," pp. 217-223. Corruption is also taken very seriously by the Chinese leadership that has taken several measures in order to fight against it, and can count on research conducted by official think tanks and academic institutions like the Centre for research on corruption of the Tsinghua University.

22. Ibidem, p. 217.

23. In the case of China (but the same is very likely true for Russia and other former Eastern European Communist countries) the introduction of market mechanisms too abruptly (as it was case in Russia after the collapse of the Soviet Union and to a certain extent also in China during the 90's) resulted in the transfer of public property to the private sector. This occurred in too many cases via corruption and other methods of a mafia character, especially by people belonging to the political-administrative elite. But as has been born witness to in the public domain, the regrettable effect was the spreading of this type of behaviour to larger segments of the population, where the major, if not the only, goal became the enriching of oneself without any moral restraint, this being of course reinforced by the limited access to consumer goods during the preceding period. For China see: Xiaoying Wang, "The Post-Communist Personality: The Spectre of China's Capitalist Market," *The China Journal*, n. 47, January 2002, pp. 1-17.

24. This is confirmed by the analysis of the standardized questionnaires presented in Chapter 4: the majority of our respondents think that there is a lack of experience (70%) and a lack of knowledge (90%).

25. This is true for both the face-to-face interviews and for the answers to the standardized questionnaires (for a detailed analysis see Chapter 4).

26. According to the website of the official Chinese Xinhua Agency (accessed 2006-12-18 21:00): in December 2006 the State Assets Supervision and Administration Commission (SASAC) published a list of seven sectors critical to the national economy and in which public ownership is considered essential: armaments, electrical power and distribution, oil and chemicals, telecommunications, coal, aviation, shipping. The situation is more complicated in Russia, at least as far as formal rules are concerned, where a new law was approved by the Parliament on April 2, 2008, approved by the Federation Council on 16 April and 29 April signed by the President of Russia on 29 April. The law recognizes 42 strategic activities in the nuclear, space and aviation industries, in the areas of production and trafficking of arms, military and special technology in the field of subsurface geological study, exploration and mining in areas of federal significance. Strategic status was also attributed to television and radio broadcasting in the territory, where the population was of half or more than half the size of the Federation entity, as well as the issue of periodical publications, products which are issued in separate circulation numbering at least 1 million copies each, such as "Rossiyskaya Gazeta."

27. We will come back to this important point when examining the conditions of the operational level.

28. This is generally recognized in the literature as being an important element because at the local levels some small or medium size services can be better organized and managed by relatively small PPPs. Moreover, large international multinationals may not be the best partners, especially in view of satisfying the criterion on equity. See for example for water supply the UNDP Human development report 2006; Emanuele Lobina and David Hall, "Problems with private water concessions: a review of experience," PSIRU, Business School, University of Greenwich June 2003, available at www.psiru.org; Emanuele Lobina and David Hall, "Water privatisation and restructuring in Latin America," September 2007, PSIRU, Business School, University of Greenwich, available at www.psiru.org.

29. On the difference between the XIX century and the present globalization see Daniel Cohen, *La mondialisation et ses ennemis* Paris, Hachette, 2004, especially pp. 41–126.

30. For transition countries the most recent references are: Ha-Joon Chang, *Bad Samaritans. The Myth of Free Trade and the Secret History of Capitalism*, New York, Bloomsbury, 2008, and José Antonio Ocampo, and Joseph Stiglitz, Joseph E. (eds.), *Capital Market Liberalization and Development*, Oxford, Oxford Univ. Press, 2008. Although this book deals mainly with capital market liberalization, several contributions deal more generally with neo-liberal orthodoxy. See also: Joseph E. Stiglitz, *Globalization and its Discontent*, New York, W.W. Norton, 2002, *The Roaring Nineties. Why We are Paying the Price for the Greediest Decade in History*, London, Penguin Books, 2003, and *Making Globalization Work. The Next Steps to Global Justice*, London, Penguin, 2006; see also Joseph E. Stiglitz, Joseph E. and Amdrew Charlton, *Fair Trade for All. How Trade Can Promote Development*, Oxford, Oxford Univ. Press,

2005, and Ha-Joon Chang (ed.), *Institutional Change and Economic Development*, Tokyo, United National University Press, 200. For developed countries see Ezra Suleiman, *Dismantling Democratic States*, Princeton, Princeton Univ. Press, 2003. May we add that some scholars, who have been making research on the New Public Management during the last 20 years or so, are now taking stock of the flaws of this movement and are returning to Max Weber for the purpose on (re)constructing a New Weberian Bureaucracy: Geert Bouckaert, "La réforme de la gestion publique chang-t-elle les systèmes administratifs?, *Revue française d'administration publique*, N. 105–106, 2003, pp. 39–54, and Laurence E. Lynn, Jr, "What is a Neo-Weberian State? Reflections on a Concept and its Implementions," Draft, 24 January 2008 (I am grateful to Fredéric Varone—University of Geneva—who has given me a copy of this paper).

31. We should remember that it is difficult to determine with precision its influence on these phenomena, since the simple transformation from a planned to a market economy inevitably implies an economic crisis. Nevertheless it is interesting to note that contrary to the Russian and Polish examples, the Chinese case shows that it is possible to move towards a market economy without a major economic crisis, provided that the transition is incremental and governed by a strong political leadership.

32. This is true if we take into account only the geographical situation, and not the other factors linked to the territory, like the natural resources, like forest, agriculture, water, gold, coal, natural gas, petrol, etc. It is clear that in case domestic capital and expertise for developing economic activities in these sectors were not available, the use of PPPs could be a choice the government could seriously consider.

33. We recall here the information already given in note 14 of Chapter 1: The President of the Ukrainian Football Federation, Grigori Sourkis, has recently declared that for the moment no Ukrainian airport satisfies the requirements of the European Football Union (UEFA) and he expressed fears that Ukraine could lose the organization of this event. As reported by the Geneva newspaper *Le Temps*, Geneva, April 23, 2008.

34. Let us note that considerable differences appeared in the answers to the standardized questionnaire between Western countries and all the four transition countries: only 8% of Western respondents consider that the legal framework is not sufficiently developed in their countries, whereas the percentage is more than 60% for Poland and Russia.

35. However it should be noted that contrary the thesis of the convergence we have already mentioned in the first chapter, this does not mean that every county will use the same technical device for realizing the general objective of creating a secure environment for private activities.

36. Peerenboom gives the following definition of thick and thin conceptions of rule of law: "Briefly put, a thin theory stresses the formal or instrumental aspects of law—those features that any legal system allegedly must possess to function effectively as a system of laws, regardless of whether the legal system is part of a democratic or non-democratic society, capitalist or socialist, liberal or theocratic. Although proponents of thin interpretations of rule of law define it in slightly different ways, there is considerable common ground (...) In contrast to thin versions, thick or substantive conceptions begin with the basic elements of a thin conception,

but then incorporate elements of political morality, such as particular economic arrangements (free-market capitalism, central planning, etc.), forms of government (democratic, single party socialism, etc.), or conceptions of human rights (liberal, communitarian, collectivist, 'Asian values', etc.)": Randall Peerenboom, *China Modernizes, Threat to the West or Model for the Rest?*, Oxford, Oxford University Press, 2007, pp. 306-307. Then referring to the case of China, Peerenboom goes on to say that there is relative little controversy over the merits or elements of a thin rule of law; on the contrary, "there are competing thick conceptions of rule of law, and considerable disagreement over particular aspects of particular thick conceptions in China, Asia, and elsewhere.", ibidem, p. 307.

37. Ibidem, p. 288. Peeremboom continues to say: "China's socialist rule of law, Singapore's soft-authoritarian or communitarian rule of law, Islamic rule of law, and liberal democratic rule of law will produce different outcomes in particular cases because the laws and practices reflect different values. (...) laws must reflect social norms and conditions. Liberal laws are not always appropriate. When laws are radically at odds with the deeply held views of the dominant majority, they are rarely implemented. This creates a gap between law on the books and the actual practice that undermines respect for the legal system and rule of law, and fuels resentful nationalism in Asia and other developing countries over the neo-imperialistic imposition of contested values."

38. Although Chinese local governments are not allowed to issue bonds, they find alternative ways, like borrowing from banks, to raise the fund for development. In China, Local Government Debt has become a big problem and risk in China's financial reform. The amount of local government debts is extraordinarily huge.

39. OECD, *Public-Private Partnerships. In Pursuit of Risk Sharing and value for Money*, Paris, 2008.

40. We remind the reader that we also sent a standardized questionnaire to Western people representing the public and the private sectors, as well as University and NGOs representatives, and that doubts and negative opinions have been more numerous amongst Western countries than in transition countries (see Chapter 4). We have explained this difference by the better knowledge Western people have acquired about PPPs.

41. OECD, *Public-Private Partnerships*, op. cit.. The Foreword informs us that: "This book discusses important issues for countries that use PPPs or are considering their use. It also discusses the extent to which countries are now using public-private partnerships in service delivery. Issues include affordability and value for money, how PPPs are accounted for and treated in national budgets, and the institutional framework for a PPP process. The book also highlights ten good practices, summarising what countries should consider before entering into long-term contracts such as public-private partnerships."

42. Ibidem, p. 28, and OECD also remind us that "for a number of years in the United Kingdom, private finance initiative deals (PFI) have made up a mere 10-15% of the total annual public investment expenditure, thus a small proportion in the country probably best known for its relatively extensive use of public-private partnerships."

43. Let us remark that OECD defines PPP in a more restrictive way by considering only private investors on the side of the private partners, thus excluding NGOs

(ibidem pp. 12 and 132). Also OECD considers that PPPs are different from concessions (although it admits some important overlappings): see pages 12, 18-24, 95 (Box 4.2.) and 132. We remind the reader that David Hall includes concessions in the vast category of PPPs along with out-sourcing, the British Private Finance Initiative, Lease, and BOT (David Hall, "PPPs: a critique of the Green Paper," available on the website of the Public Services International Research Unit (PSIRU), Univ. of Greenwich, London, 2006.

44. OECD, op. cit., p. 3.

45. Ibidem, p. 12.

46. Ibidem, p. 18.

47. The link between the two sentences is given in ibidem: "the discussion below will show that, although private sector participation in PPPs frequently contributes to higher levels of efficiency, the mere participation of the private sector in the delivery of the service is not sufficient to ensure improvement in service delivery and efficiency." And the decision between PPP and Government procurement will be taken as follows: "the distinguishing feature that determines whether a project is defined as traditional public procurement or as a public-private partnership should be whether or not a sufficient amount of risk has been transferred.," ibidem.

48. Ibidem, p. 133. Box 1, point 2.

49. José Antonio Ocampo, Shari Spiegel, and Joseph E. Stiglitz, "Capital Market Liberalization and Development," in Ocampo and Stiglitz, op. cit., pp. 3-4. Moreover, they inform us that: "Theoretical and empirical research over the past quarter century have helped explain why the market economy often does not function as well as free market advocates had hoped."

50. Equity is mentioned only twice in the text of the book (pp. 61 and 67) and once in footnote 12 of page 47. True, these are very important aspects, but one could have expected a more profound treatment of such an important dimension as equity.

On page 61: "Nevertheless, efficiency is not necessarily the only reason for using a public-private partnership. Even if the service is not a general interest good but a private good (meaning it has no externality), a PPP can be preferred to both traditional procurement and full-blown privatisation. This preference occurs when effectiveness, in addition to efficiency, is also an aim of government policy. Effectiveness becomes important with issues such as equity where poverty levels prevent the poor or financially less well-off from making an effective demand for a service even when their need is large (e.g. electricity supply to poor and remote areas in developing countries, or the provision of expensive medical procedures in any country)."

On page 67: "If renegotiations fail, or if the private operator fails, the PPP contract is in danger of terminal failure. Failed renegotiation that results in the termination of the contract can often be ascribed to tensions that occur in the contractual relationship. Examining these tensions for least developed countries, Estache (Estache, A., "PPI Partnerships vs. PPI Divorces in LDCs," Review of Industrial Organization, 29, pp. 3-26, 2006, p. 18) found that, although PPPs resulted in higher levels of efficiency, quality and access rates, their fiscal and distributional (as in social equity) costs were higher than expected. This combination of efficiency, quality, access and costs leads to tension between a government and its private partners and, according to Estache (ibidem), explains the higher degree of partnership divorces."

In note 12 of page 47 (dealing with the role and nature of risk by taking into consideration three types of efficiency): "Note that allocative efficiency is only one of the grounds on which a government can decide to deliver goods. The government might also decide to deliver goods on the basis of their distributional effects, e.g. free education or health care to all, including the less well-off who would not otherwise be able to afford it. As is the case with allocative efficiency, once the decision to deliver the goods has been taken, the next decision is about the mode of delivery, i.e. deliver the goods through traditional procurement or a public-private partnership. If a PPP is selected, the distributional element might impact on the decision whether the private partner will receive a fee from the government, thereby obviating the need to charge a user charge on the relatively less well-off consumers of the goods, or whether to allow the private partner to charge a user charge, but with the government then subsidising the relatively less well-off."

51. Security is mentioned only once on p. 128 (OECD, *Public-Private Partnerships*, op. cit.) by reference to the United Kingdom case: "… the legal framework must confer on the public authorities the right to take over service operations under extreme cases or in the case of default. In extreme cases, the United Kingdom government retains the right to take over services when there is a serious risk to public health and safety; there is a serious risk to the environment; the government is required to exercise its statutory responsibilities; there are national security implications."

52. Ibidem, pages 63-64, 78, 79, 110, and 134:

Pages 62-63: "The complexity of negotiating a public-private partnership may generate substantial transaction time and costs that could cancel out the purported benefits of a PPP and that might be much higher than in other forms of delivery. For instance, in a review of 42 United Kingdom projects in health, education and civil engineering, Ahadzi and Bowles ("Public-private Partnerships and Contract Negotiations: An Empirical Study," Construction Management and Economics, 22, November 2004, pp. 967-978) noted that there were excessive time overruns in the pre-contract stages which in turn resulted in large advisory cost overruns. (…) In addition to pre-contract time overruns, there were also substantial precontract cost overruns which ranged between 25-200% and were due to the continued retention of advisors by the government and the private parties during negotiations."

Page 78: "When putting together project designs and contract details in the case of only one buyer and only a few projects, there is not much scope to exploit economies of scale if the scale depends on the number of projects. The relative transaction cost per contract will be increased; and the higher the transaction cost, the fewer bidders there will be.

Page 79: "At lower levels of government, there is the possibility of deeper markets— in particular, for instance, if there is a large group of local authorities that all use public-private partnerships. This group of local authorities constitutes a larger group of buyers, thereby approximating more closely a true competitive market ideal. The larger group of buyers also gives sellers the opportunity to participate in more bids. If contracts for projects and the procedures are standardised from the buyers' side, the positive effects can be improved even further. Sellers know that if they fail in their bid for one contract, they can merely bid on the next. If the service and the design of the assets with which the seller must deliver the service have a significant level of homogeneity, economies of scale might exist in contractual design and bidding, with the scale to be found in the number of contracts. Transaction costs will be reduced, which in turn might cause the number of sellers that bid for a contract to increase. This increase in the level of competition may increase the potential for value for money. (However, care should be taken that the same group of companies does not dominate bidding, which again raises the danger of oligopolistic behaviour.)"

Page 110: "The main task of the PPP unit is not to advocate PPP projects, but to ensure that transaction costs are as low as possible and that value for money is the main criterion. "

Page 134: "Where possible, contracts can be standardised to improve clarity and to reduce transaction costs."

53. See the quotation on page 79 in note 52 above.

54. In these circumstances one can hardly speak of a "real" market. There is even a rather funny sentence on page 78: "PSCs are also useful instruments for governments to use in *markets that may lack competition*." (underlined by us).

55. Ibidem, p. 79.

56. Ibidem, pp. 78–79.

57. Ibidem, p. 79.

58. Ibidem, pp. 78–88. The next paragraph is sufficient to explain our doubts: "When using a public sector comparator, a government should not just mechanistically compare the PSC and the public-private partnership, but should take note of the "dangers of putting disproportionate emphasis on a single figure comparison" (...). In essence, the PSC is used to generate a net present value (NPV) of what traditional procurement would cost. This NPV must then be compared to the NPV of either a reference PPP or the actual PPP bids (or both). Because a PPP and a PSC both involve assumptions about the future and projections that include risk assessments, one danger of using a public sector comparator is that of spurious precision (...). In such a case, the NPV calculations in the PSC and the PPP proposal might be very close. A slight change in assumptions or in the assessment of risk may change the NPV calculations and cause the preference for a PPP to shift in its favour or against it." (ibidem, p. 75).

59. Ibidem, p. 133, Box 1, point 2.

60. We remind the reader that the OECD book is meant for any country using or envisaging using PPPs, and, in spite of some caveat about some sectors like health and education, the report gives the impression that PPPs may produce good results in a great variety of sectors including health and education. In Chapter 2 (note 70) we have drawn to the attention of the reader that some proponents of PPPs envisage their implementation in a great variety of sectors, including schools, hospitals, water, energy, and social services.

61. See for example Emanuele Lobina and David Hall, "Public-Public Partnerships as a catalyst for capacity building and institutional development: Lessons from Stockholm Vatten's experience in the Baltic region," PSIRU, Business School, University of Greenwich, Old Royal Naval College, London, 15th August 2006.

62. OECDE, *Public-Private Partnerships*, ibidem, pp. 11–12.

63. OECD, *Public-Private Partnerships*, ibidem, p. 133.

64. The reason for this given by the OECD report this that "risk is an important part of the incentive mechanism for the private partner to be as efficient as possible," ibidem, p. 133.

65. Ibidem, p. 13. The difference between exogenous and endogenous risks is explained in this way: "Unlike exogenous risk, endogenous risk represents the case where the private partner can do something to ensure that the actual outcome approximates the expected outcome," ibidem, p. 14. note 2.

66. Ibidem, p. 36. OECD further notes that "affordability is not only related to PPPs, but to government expenditures items in general."

67. This is because we cannot exclude intermediate situations where the government subsidizes a service (that could be provided either by a SOE or by a private company) in order to reduce its selling price.

68. The strategy to be followed in this case is discussed by specialists of economic development for transition countries. See for example: Stiglitz, Joseph E., *Making Globalization Work. The Next Steps to Global Justice*, London, Penguin, 2006; Stiglitz and Charlton, op. cit.; Sen, Amartya, *Development as Freedom*, Oxford, Oxford Univ. Press, 1999; Chang, Ha-Joon (ed.), *Rethinking Development Economics*, London, Anthem Press, 2003; Ha-Joon Chang, *Globalization, Economic Development and the Role of the State*, New York, Zed Books, 2003; *Kicking Away the Ladder. Development Strategy in Historical Perspective*, London, Anthem Press, 2003; and his last book: *Bad Samaritans. The Myth of Free Trade and the Secret History of Capitalism*, New York, Bloomsbury, 2008; Ha-Joon Chang and Ilene Grabel, *Reclaiming Development. An Alternative Economic Policy Manual*, New York, Zed Books, 2004; Ha-Joon Chang (ed.), *Institutional Change and Economic Development*, Tokyo, United National University Press, 2007; Jorge Braga de Macedo and Tadao Chino, *Sustainable Recovery in Asia, Mobilizing Resources for development*, Paris, OECD, 2000; World Bank, *World Development Report 2006: Equity and Development*, New York,The World Bank, 2005.

69. In the framework of the criteria for deciding (5 in Figure 9.2) OECD also proposes to consider the nature of the service. But, as we have already said above in note 60, the report gives the impression that PPPs may produce good results in a great variety of sectors including health and education.

70. Herbert Simon, *Administrative Behavior. A Study of Decision-Making Processes in Administrative Organization*, New York, The Free Press, 1997, fourth edition (first edition 1945).

71. See for example the references given in note 30 of this conclusion, and in notes 19, 26, 56 and 64 of Chapter 2.

72. This has also been confirmed by the OECD 2008 report that proposes the creation of a PPP unit, even if it does not consider PPPs within an overall strategy of economic development.

73. This is the case of Randall Peerenboom who has served as an experts witness on PRC legal issues and a consultant to the Ford Foundation and the Asian Development bank on legal reforms and rule of law in China; he is presently Professor of Law at UCLA Law School: *China Modernizes. Threat to the West or Model for the Rest?*, Oxford, Oxford Univ. Press, 2007, and "A Government of Laws. Democracy, Rule of Law, and Administrative Law Reform in China," in Suisheng Zhao (ed.), *Debating Political Reform in China. Rule of Law vs. Democratization*, Armonk, New York, M.E. Sharpe, 2006, pp. 58–78. For a more general, more critical and theoretical approach: Roberto Mangabeira Unger, *Politics. The Central Texts*, London, Verso, 1997 (edited and introduced by Zhiyuan Cui).

Index

About the Editor and Authors

Olivier Brenninkmeijer holds a PhD from the Graduate Institute of International and Development Studies in Geneva and has published on multilateral dispute resolution, European security, public safety, and peace-building in post-conflict countries. His interests are in innovative approaches to education, public-private partnerships, conflict prevention, human security and sustainable development. He has worked in academia, in international organisations and the private sector in Canada and Switzerland and is currently the Associate Dean at the University of Business and International Studies, Geneva.

Tatiana Chernyavskaya holds a university degree (M.A. level) in international economics and certificate on professional language training from Baikal State University of Economics and Law (Irkutsk, Russia, 2003). She has attended mandatory courses of the DAS Programme on International Economics at the Graduate Institute of Economics and Law (Geneva, Switzerland, 2003–2005). She comes from Russia, but has deep family roots in Ukraine. Her interests include research on public-private partnerships, economic development, foresight, S&T and innovation systems. She has worked on these topics with the UNECE (Geneva, Switzerland) and UNIDO HQ (Vienna, Austria).

Paolo Urio is a political scientist with a first degree in international relations and a PhD in economics and social sciences. Until 2005 he has been full professor of political science and public management, and director of the Master in Public Management at the University of Geneva. He is presently professor at the University of Lugano (Switzerland). He has published in the domains of political decision-making and implementation, public administration and public management. His present research interests are in the domains of New Public Management and privatizations, Public-Private Partnerships, and the reform process in China.

Vladimir Varnavsky is doctor of sciences (econ.), leading research fellow at the Institute of World Economy and International Relations, Russian Academy of Sciences (Moscow). Fields of his research are natural monopolies, transport infrastructure, Public-Private Partnerships (PPPs). He has published a few monographs and many articles on PPPs and concessions. He is member of the Council of Experts on Concession Legislation of the State Duma of the Russian Federation and Expert on PPPs of the Council for Competitiveness and Entrepreneurship of the Russian Government.

Yongheng Yang is an Associate Professor in the School of Public Policy & Management at Tsinghua University. He received his PhD degree in Service Operation Management at City University of Hong Kong. His present research focuses on public service management, government performance evaluation, government capacity building, and public decision making.

Thomas Zacharewicz is a political scientist with a first degree in European studies obtained at the Strasbourg Institute of Political Studies (2005) and a M.A. degree in Central and Eastern European Studies obtained at the Jagiellonian University Centre for European Studies (Cracow, Poland, 2006). His research interests include studies on the New Public Management, economic and political transition in Central and Eastern Europe, and literature theory in post-communist Poland.

Zhang Wankuan is a doctor candidate at the school of public policy and management at Tsinghua University. He has a Master degree of chemistry and worked for 6 years in the pharmaceutical industry before entering Tsinghua University in 2005. His research direction is government management and innovation, and his current research is concentrated on public governance and public-private partnerships. His dissertation topic is about the institutional arrangements and governance mechanism of public-private partnerships in transition countries.

* * *

Made in the USA
Middletown, DE
20 May 2016